LITERACY PORTFOLIOS

Improving Assessment, Teaching, and Learning

Second Edition

Judith H. Cohen
Adelphi University

Roberta B. Wiener
Indiana–Purdue University, Ft. Wayne

Merrill
Prentice Hall

Upper Saddle River, New Jersey
Columbus, Ohio

Library of Congress Cataloging-in-Publication Data

Cohen, Judith H.
 Literacy portfolios : improving assessment, teaching, and learning / Judith H. Cohen,
Roberta B. Wiener.--2nd ed.
  p. cm.
 Wiener's name appears first on the earlier edition.
 Includes bibliographical references and index.
 ISBN 0-13-045324-2
  1. Reading--Ability testing--United States. 2. Literacy--United States--Evaluation. 3.
Portfolios in education--United States. 4. Language arts (Elementary)--United States. 5.
Language arts--Remedial teaching--United States. I. Wiener, Roberta B. II. Title.

LB1050.46.W547 2003
372.41--dc21   2002025088

Vice President and Publisher: Jeffery W. Johnston
Editor: Linda Ashe Montgomery
Production Editor: Mary M. Irvin
Design Coordinator: Diane C. Lorenzo
Text Design and Production Coordination: Clarinda Publication Services
Cover Designer: Ali Mohrman
Cover Art: Laura Velasco, age 5
Production Manager: Pamela D. Bennett
Director of Marketing: Ann Castel Davis
Marketing Manager: Krista Groshong
Marketing Coordinator: Tyra Cooper

This book was set in Usherwood and Frutiger by The Clarinda Company, and was printed and bound by Banta Book Group.
The cover was printed by Phoenix Color Corp.

Q
372.41
C 678

Pearson Education Ltd.
Pearson Education Australia Pty. Limited.
Pearson Education Singapore Pte. Ltd.
Pearson Education North Asia Ltd.
Pearson Education Canada, Ltd.
Pearson Educación de Mexido, S.A. de C.V.
Pearson Education—Japan
Pearson Education Malaysia Pte. Ltd.
Pearson Education, *Upper Saddle River, New Jersey*

10 9 8 7 6 5 4 3 2 1

ISBN 0-13-045324-2

Foreword: The Politics of Assessment

Many concerns are being raised about basing educational reform primarily on the results of standardized tests. As the nation's education agenda has shifted to one of greater school accountability, the need for outcome measures has renewed the debate over the few strengths and many weaknesses of high-stakes standardized tests. In particular, there is concern about potential negative consequences when these tests are used as the basis for school reform. We are very pleased that Richard Rothstein, Education columnist for *The New York Times*, who has written with eloquence and insight on this topic, has given us permission to reprint a recent column, presented below.

WHAT'S WRONG WITH A SINGLE TEST SCORE DETERMINING SUCCESS?

"How Tests Can Drop the Ball" September 13, 2000, *The New York Times*

Mike Piazza, batting .332, could win this year's Most Valuable Player award. He has been good every year, with a .330 career average, twice a runner-up for m.v.p., and a member of each All-Star team since his rookie season. The Mets reward Piazza for this high achievement, at the rate of $13 million a year. But what if the team decided to pay him based not on overall performance but on how he hit during one arbitrarily chosen week? How well do one week's at-bats describe the ability of a true .330 hitter? Not very. Last week Piazza batted only .200. But in the second week of August he batted .538. If you picked a random week this season, you would have only a 7-in-10 chance of choosing one in which he hit .250 or higher.

Are standardized-test scores, on which many schools rely heavily to make promotion or graduation decisions, more indicative of true ability than a ballplayer's weekly average? Not really. A professor of educational statistics at Stanford University has calculated the "accuracy" of tests used in California to abolish social promotion. (New York uses similar tests.) Consider a fourth-grade student whose "true" reading score is exactly at grade level (the 50th percentile). The chances are better than even (58 percent) that this student will score either above the 55th percentile or below the 45th on any one test.

Results for students at other levels of true performance are also surprisingly inconsistent. So if students are held back, required to attend summer school or denied diplomas largely because of a single test, many will be punished unfairly. About half of fourth-grade students held back for scores below the 30th percentile on a typical reading test will actually have "true" scores above that point. On any particular test, nearly 7 percent of students with true scores at the 40th percentile will likely fail, scoring below the 30th percentile.

Are Americans prepared to require large numbers of students to repeat a grade when they deserve promotion? Test publishers calculate reliability by analyzing thousands of student tests, to estimate chances that students who answer some questions correctly will also answer others correctly. Because some students at any performance level will miss questions that most students at that level get right, test makers can estimate the reliability of each question and of an entire test.

Typically, districts and states use tests marketed as having high reliability. Yet few policy makers understand that seemingly high reliability assures only rough accuracy. But when test results are used for high-stakes purposes like promotion or graduation decisions, there should be a different concern: How well do they identify students who are truly below a cutoff point like the 30th percentile?

Surprisingly, there has not yet been a wave of lawsuits by parents of children penalized largely because of a single test score. As more parents learn about tests' actual accuracy, litigation regarding high-stakes decisions is bound to follow. Districts and states will then have to abandon an unfair reliance on single tests to evaluate students.

When Mike Piazza comes to bat, he may face a pitcher who fools him more easily than most pitchers do, or fools him more easily on that day. Piazza may not have slept well the night before, the lights may bother him, or he may be preoccupied by a problem at home. On average, over a full season, the distractions do not matter much, and the Mets benefit from his overall ability. Likewise, when a student takes a test, performance is affected by random events. He may have fought with his sister that morning. A test item may stimulate daydreams not suggested by items in similar tests, or by the same test on a different day. Despite a teacher's warning to eat a good breakfast, he may not have done so.

If students took tests over and over, average accuracy would improve, just as Mike Piazza's full-season batting average more accurately reflects his hitting prowess. But school is not baseball; if students took tests every day, there would be no time left for learning. So to make high-stakes decisions, like whether students should be promoted or attend summer school, giving great importance to a single test is not only bad policy but extraordinarily unfair. Courts are unlikely to permit it much longer.

To our husbands, Stuart and Len
who have shown love, patience, and support
throughout this project.

Preface

Since the publication of the first edition of this book, there have been remarkable changes in education. Never before has there been such concern about raising performance standards of children in elementary and secondary schools; and never before has there been such an increased call for more assessment. Although assessment had always been a concern of educators, it was seen as an important and necessary aspect of the cycle of effective teaching to both monitor the effectiveness of teaching practices and determine if students were making appropriate progress. Currently, assessment has an extraordinary political dimension, with the call for more testing, more rigorous testing, and more high-stakes testing, thus making testing the centerpiece of school reform. A recent political cartoon depicted the President in front of a microphone saying "Testing, testing, testing," seemingly to determine whether the sound equipment was working. Actually his response was an answer to the question: what's your educational agenda?

We have always believed that assessment is important and that there are various forms of assessment that contribute to quality education. Standardized testing has very legitimate purposes, and we are certainly and clearly not calling for their elimination. Especially since "Standard-based reform has become the central thrust of federal education policy, as it already was in most states" (Traub, p. 2). However, we are calling for the judicious use of these tests to be balanced with informal assessment measures that have significant usefulness for teachers, students, administrators, and families. To base educational decisions and to make high-stakes decisions regarding a child's placement, promotion, graduation, or future on the basis of a standardized test is counterproductive and frankly destructive to the educational process and the welfare of children. How can we justify mandated testing when rankings on these tests were "almost indistinguishable from the socioeconomic scale, with wealthy suburbs on top and the big cities on the bottom" (Traub, p. 3).

Since the publication of the first edition, we feel that it is even more important for literacy educators and those who have a stake in literacy learning to know about portfolios as an important assessment tool that is integral to literacy improvement. Literacy portfolios, when used thoughtfully and insightfully, will assist teachers in using multiple assessment measures to indicate the richness of the curriculum and children's involvement in the learning process (hence the new title of the current edition).

TEXT ORGANIZATION

In reviewing the comments from readers of the first edition, some felt that the opening of the book should quickly immerse the reader into the application of portfolios in actual classrooms before delving into theory. Consequently, Chapter 1, "Welcome to Our Classrooms," provides readers with the application of literacy portfolios at three levels of education—primary, intermediate, and middle school—written by educators who have used portfolios in places as diverse as Colorado, urban and suburban New York, and

Texas. As different as these locales are, readers will note that there are similar overriding concerns of all these teachers: documenting accountability, student progress and performance, enhancing literacy education, and meeting the needs of diverse and often underprepared learners. We are pleased to have the contributions and experience of Linda Vizyak, Robyn Lane, Glenda Moss, and Carole Rhodes.

In Part One, Chapters 2, 3, and 4 discuss the theory of literacy portfolios as well as provide ideas for exemplary portfolio practice. Note that Chapter 3 is followed by a brief Appendix in which Mark Quigley, Carole Rhodes, and Jeff Nowak discuss the use of technology in creating electronic portfolios—a tool that holds much promise. In Part Two, Chapters 5 through 8 offer guidelines for using portfolios as part of literacy programs. Dr. Giselle Martin-Kniep, in Chapter 7, demonstrates how literacy portfolios clearly help teachers in reaching curriculum goals, especially with increased pressure to raise standards while documenting both process and product.

Finally, Part Three contains two new chapters, written by three educators: Professor Leslie Soodak, Beverly Parke, and Brett Blake that answer the challenge of how portfolios can be used to assess and monitor the growing population of diverse learners—students with special needs and those for whom English is a second language. Students with limited English knowledge and students with various learning disabilities are often in mainstreamed classes and all teachers need to fairly and effectively evaluate their learning. Portfolios are used with notable success with diverse student populations, reflecting students' authentic growth, classroom performances, and literacy learning.

ACKNOWLEDGMENTS

We hope that the insightful comments in the Foreword, shared by Richard Rothstein, Education Columnist for *The New York Times,* will help place our concerns about assessment within the broad context of what we are calling the "politics of assessment." We appreciate his national views on the topic and thank him for his perspective and contribution to this new edition.

We gratefully acknowledge and appreciate the contributions to this book by our undergraduate and graduate students at Adelphi University, New York, and colleagues at Indiana-Purdue University-Fort Wayne, as well as classroom teachers from all across the country. We thank them for sharing their time, insights, and student work to assist this project's development. The experiences they share with us transform theory into reality.

In addition, we would like to thank Linda Montgomery, Acquisitions Editor, who has supported this project through its many phases from a kernel of an idea into the first and second editions. Her patience, insights, and personal warmth have made her instrumental to our ability to write both editions.

We thank the reviewers of our manuscript for their comments and insight: Dennise, Bartelo, Plymouth State College; Donna Camp, University of Central Florida; Martha Combs, University of Nebraska; Laurie Elish-Piper, Northern Illinois University; Mary-Margaret Harrington, Southern Illinois University—Carbondale; Patricia P. Kelly, Virginia Technical University; Jill P. May, Purdue University; Beverly Otto, Northeastern Illinois University; Timothy Rasinski, Kent State University; Kathy Roskos, John Carroll University; Terry Salinger, International Reading Association; and Sam L. Sebesta, University of Washington.

We share with you our thoughts and experiences from places as seemingly diverse as suburban and urban New York and urban and rural Indiana, and ask that you correspond with us about your reaction to this new edition and your ideas about literacy portfolios.

Judith H. Cohen, Ph.D., J.D., Professor of Education,
Adelphi University, Garden City, New York

Roberta B. Wiener, Ed.D., Dean, School of Education,
Indiana-Purdue University, Ft. Wayne, Indiana

Discover the Companion Website Accompanying This Book

The Prentice Hall Companion Website: A Virtual Learning Environment

Technology is a constantly growing and changing aspect of our field that is creating a need for content and resources. To address this emerging need, Prentice Hall has developed an online learning environment for students and professors alike—Companion Websites—to support our textbooks.

In creating a Companion Website, our goal is to build on and enhance what the textbook already offers. For this reason, the content for each user-friendly website is organized by topic and provides the professor and student with a variety of meaningful resources. Common features of a Companion Website include:

For the Professor—

Every Companion Website integrates **Syllabus Manager™**, an online syllabus creation and management utility.

- **Syllabus Manager™** provides you, the instructor, with an easy, step-by-step process to create and revise syllabi, with direct links into Companion Website and other online content without having to learn HTML.

- Students may logon to your syllabus during any study session. All they need to know is the web address for the Companion Website and the password you've assigned to your syllabus.

- After you have created a syllabus using **Syllabus Manager™,** students may enter the syllabus for their course section from any point in the Companion Website.

- Clicking on a date, the student is shown the list of activities for the assignment. The activities for each assignment are linked directly to actual content, saving time for students.

- Adding assignments consists of clicking on the desired due date, then filling in the details of the assignment—name of the assignment, instructions, and whether or not it is a one-time or repeating assignment.

- In addition, links to other activities can be created easily. If the activity is online, a URL can be entered in the space provided, and it will be linked automatically in the final syllabus.

- Your completed syllabus is hosted on our servers, allowing convenient updates from any computer on the Internet. Changes you make to your syllabus are immediately available to your students at their next logon.

For the Student—

Topic Overviews—outline key concepts in topic areas

Strategies—These websites provide suggestions and information on how to implement instructional strategies and activities for each topic.

Web Links—A wide range of websites that allow the students to access current information on everything from rationales for specific types of instruction, to research on related topics, to compilations of useful articles and more.

Electronic Bluebook—send homework or essays directly to your instructor's email with this paperless form

Message Board—serves as a virtual bulletin board to post—or respond to—questions or comments to/from a national audience

Chat—real-time chat with anyone who is using the text anywhere in the country—ideal for discussion and study groups, class projects, etc.

To take advantage of these and other resources, please visit the *Literacy Portfolios: Improving Assessment, Teaching, and Learning* Companion Website at

www.prenhall.com/Cohen/Wiener

Contents

Part One

Integrating Portfolios Into Literacy Classrooms

CHAPTER

1

Welcome to Our Classrooms

Essays

A. *Using a Literacy Portfolio in First Grade—L. Vizyak*

B. *Anatomy of a Year: One Teacher's Experience With Long-Term Portfolios in Grades 4–5—R. Lane*

C. *Students in the Middle: Reflections on Literacy Portfolios for Sixth, Seventh, and Eighth Graders—C. Rhodes, G. Moss*

<hr>

ESSAY A

Using a Literacy Portfolio in First Grade

by
Lindy Vizyak

First-grade teacher, Cotton Creek Elementary School,
Adams County Five Star Schools, Westminster, Colorado

Let me provide you with some background. I have been a first-grade teacher for 23 years. I teach in a large school district, enrolling approximately 30,000 students, located 18 miles northwest of Denver. This school district covers five different cities. We are organized into 26 elementary, 6 middle, and 3 high schools. The district is composed of families from all economic groups, but there is diversity and we have teaching English as a second language (TESL) and Chapter One classes. Cotton Creek Elementary School enrolls about 600 students, predominantly from middle-class families, but about 15% of the students come from poor families. Most of the students are White and the typical class size is about 22 to 26 students. Twelve years ago I began searching for alternative methods of documenting the learning in my classroom. I had adopted a holistic philosophy of teaching, and as my teaching had changed, so did my needs for assessment. Consequently, I began using portfolios. I think that they are critical for documenting students' progress toward meeting standards and are a good place to collect the kind of assessment information I feel is helpful for teaching first graders effectively.

Colorado has clearly defined standards for literacy and at the district level, a Curriculum Framework is used to translate the statewide goals into specific expectations for each grade level. Figure 1–1 shows the reading expectations for first graders in our school district. There are no requirements for standardized testing with first graders in Colorado. The state requires standardized literacy assessments for grades 4, 8, and 10 and the teachers from grade 3 and above are feeling much more pressure than I am to prepare students for the state-required tests. These teachers have modified their curriculum to provide more time for teaching test format and content. I personally don't give these state tests, but am required to do assessment by the district in reading, writing, and math. It's very important to me that all of my first graders develop good reading and writing skills in my classroom. I know that, too often, when students fall behind even in first grade, this trend is hard to alter in future years. I am most fortunate to be in a school where my principal is both a friend and former teacher, and she sets the tone for a building where true collaboration and joint decision making create an atmosphere for teachers that is both supportive and professional.

My classroom is child-centered, and students are involved in many decisions that affect their learning, such as classroom rules, course of study, and projects. Students know what is expected in terms of learning and behavior, and they take responsibility for both. In this class, there is a strong sense of community that values the strengths and abilities of each child. My role is that of teacher, facilitator, collaborator, and co-learner.

MY APPROACH TO LITERACY INSTRUCTION ASSESSMENT

Our reading and writing programs are literature-based. A large block of 2 hours and 45 minutes each morning provides the necessary time for students to read, write, illustrate, research, and share information. In my class, students are immersed in the rich language of a wide variety of genres, such as environmental print, fiction, nonfiction,

Grade 1—Reading Proficiency Checklist

Student _____

Teacher _____

School _____

DRA _____ RRL _____ DRA _____

DRA Level—90–94% accuracy on unseen text. (See Pacing Chart for desirable levels.)

The student . . .	Initial			Mid-Year			Final		
	Date _____		On GL	Date _____		On GL	Date _____		On GL
	No	Sometimes	Yes	No	Sometimes	Yes	No	Sometimes	Yes
Concepts About Print									
uses concepts about print (Refer to Kindergarten Checklist if student is marked "No".)									
Reading Comprehension									
makes and confirms predictions									
reads and comprehends both fiction and nonfiction									
retells stories including character(s), setting, beginning, middle, end									
identifies main idea and some details from nonfiction									
shows understanding of story or passage in writing									
correctly answers questions about text									
Reading Strategies									
uses voice/print match									
uses pictures as a source of information									
uses sentence structure/word order to construct meaning									
uses visual cues (word structure, chunks, and letter sounds) to figure out unknown words									
knows when meaning is lost and attempts to self-correct									
integrates cueing systems (meaning, structure, visual)									
demonstrates phonemic awareness (rhyming, blending sounds, isolating sounds, and segmenting sounds)									
rereads									
Skills; Phonemic and Phonological									
identifies all uppercase and lowercase letters	/52			/52			/52		
identifies letter sounds (consonants and short vowels)	/26			/26			/26		
identifies consonant blends and digraphs (90–100% expected)	/30			/30			/30		
reads high-frequency Grade 1 Fry words (90–100% expected)	/100			/100			/100		
Fluency (on familiar text)									
reads in phrases									
uses punctuation while reading									
adjusts voice for print variation									
Reading Behavior									
chooses to read independently (5–10 minutes)									
Other:									

Form 10-15 (June 00)

FIGURE 1–1 A sample checklist. *Source:* Courtesy of Adams Twelve Five Star Schools.

poetry, songs, fairy tales, and nursery rhymes. Reading material is readily accessible for students of all reading levels, whether emergent, early, or fluent readers. Our classroom has over 1000 books with a core collection of 500 books always available for independent reading. The other 500 books are single copies and multiple-copy sets that regularly change to support unit studies, cultural studies, holidays, and other thematic projects. Shared reading, guided reading, reading aloud, and independent reading are all components of the reading program. Each format provides opportunities for involving students as they develop skills and strategies to become independent problem solvers.

Guided reading is the heart of my reading program, using quality literature and a variety of fiction and nonfiction books. After gathering information from running records taken on leveled texts, I group students by ability. The groups are flexible and change frequently during the year, as students' needs change. I focus on teaching strategies (e.g., picture clues, letter sounds, vocabulary building) that students need. The whole class may read from many different kinds of books to support units of study, but students are also encouraged to work independently by reading and responding to different texts. A key component of my literacy program is daily book checkout. Parents are expected to read at home with their children and the procedure is explained during the first parent conference in September. Parents sign and return slips with the titles of books read "to child," "with child," or "by child." This information is transferred at the end of each month to a form that is kept in each child's portfolio and indicates the number of books read independently as well as the class average. Parents are also provided with a written explanation of the decoding strategies that are taught at school and, therefore, I expect that they will support their child's reading development with more options than just telling the child to "sound it out." Daily parental involvement has had a major, positive impact on student reading progress.

Many different reading assessments are used during the year. My district mandates the use of running records as our first grade assessment. Running records help me to obtain baseline data for each student and to identify instructional needs. I have been giving running records on unseen text for all students at least five times per year for the past 5 years. More frequent running records on seen text are also done using the leveled texts. I analyze the running records for accuracy rate, self-corrections, strategies used, and reading behaviors and find that this information is invaluable (see Figure 1–2). Ongoing assessments that inform my instructional decisions also include observation, conferences, and oral and written comprehension activities. Copies of these individual assessment are included in each student's portfolio (see Figure 1–3).

The writing program is based on a Writer's Workshop approach. Each student has a colored file folder for keeping completed writing as well as works in progress. Folders are kept in the students' desks to encourage them to write during free time as well as during our daily writing time. Students also write in spiral-bound journals. Sometimes the journals are used as diaries to record personal thoughts and events, whereas at other times they serve as learning logs in which students reflect on daily activities by responding to sentence starters such as, "I learned that Martin Luther King, Jr. . . ." Writing instruction is delivered through minilessons that address specific needs identified through each student's writing samples taken from their journals, writing folders, or responses to literature. The lessons often focus on author's craft, mechanics, legibility (still a concern for emergent writers), or message quality.

I meet with students individually at least once every 6 weeks to assess writing progress. During these conferences, as students individually read their piece to me, I note spelling development, skills exhibited (e.g., capitalization, punctuation, dialogue, editing strategies), and message quality. I then identify one or two instructional goals, which I immediately address with the student. These conference notes are recorded on a form that goes in the student's portfolio. As with reading, writing evaluation is based on district standards developed for the first grade. If a student is writing at an advanced level, then the writing can be evaluated with a second-grade or above writing rubric developed by the school district. Figure 1–4 is a summary of my notes about one child after four writing conferences held in September through December. These conferences

Name _René_

Date	Title	Level	Accuracy Rate	Self-Correction Ratio	Retell	Comments
1/14	Cookies unseen text	1	75%	0	ok—some detail	• level is too hard • lacked some knowledge of cooking items • knows letters/sounds but doesn't apply knowledge Need—look at beginning sound
1/21	I Can Jump seen text	4	100%	0	Complete	• good expression • more confident • Said, "There is the little word fly in butterfly."
2/3	Little Pig seen text	4	94%	1:2	Complete	• much improvement! • increasing sight vocab. • usually uses letters/sounds (phonics) to figure out new words
2/26	A Monster Sandwich unseen text	3	89%	0	Limited—few details	• beginning to cross check • mostly uses visual—letters/sounds to figure out new words
4/5	Time for Sleep seen text	5	96%	0	Good—more details than last retell	—Good expression—used meaning and structure to figure out an animal noise.

FIGURE 1–2 Sample running record summary. *Source:* Courtesy of L. Vizyak.

provide an excellent opportunity for individual evaluation of the student's literacy development and also for setting instructional goals appropriate for individual needs. Even in first grade, students show a remarkable range in literacy development. Figure 1–5 is a writing rubric designed by our district to assess first grade personal narratives.

The Curriculum Framework used in my district is helpful for providing information to each child's parents about the child's literacy progress throughout the year. Curriculum Framework reports that describe the first grade standards are shared with parents and students at the first conference in November and are updated at period conferences. A completed copy of the report is included with the student's final report card in June. All partners in a child's education are kept informed about the child's progress, and my use

FIGURE 1–3 Demonstrations of student learning. *Source:* Courtesy of L. Vizyak.

Student Presentations	Writing Sample	District Assessment	Standardized Tests
Journal Writing	Performance Tests	State Assessment	Student Self-Assessment
Interviews/Surveys	Teacher-Made Tests	Student Projects	Teacher Observations

Name _Brian_____

Writing Progress

Date		
9/3	Topic: My Stuffed Animal —prompted writing— district writing sample	Comments: —many random capital letters —wrote 2 sentences —some detail
	Spelling: Purl = is purple tes = this Bear my Favrt = favorite Baby suft = stuffed	Instructional needs: —handwriting —end punctuation
10/21	Topic: Halloween —personal narrative	Comments: —good handwriting and spacing —capitalizes: I —end punctuation: (.)

	Spelling:
	am be anakin
	      gouing = going
		Instructional needs: Add detail
		—spelling: look for correct
		      spelling from books, charts, wkbk
		—capitalize a title
		—correct spelling of: going

11/8	Topic: Journal Writing	Comments: —b/d confusion —3 sentences/good detail —no random capital letters

	Spelling: nit = night
	haoos = house fend = friend
	sad = stayed me at my
	las = last
	      and playd = played
		Instructional needs:
		—blends—fr/st
		—vowel—gāme/dāy
		—capitalize the first word in
		   a sentence

1/7	Topic: My Winter Vacation prompted narrative writing	Comments: —imaginative writing —detail —reversal (b/d) —consistent end punctuation —capitalizes: names

	Spelling: I ^up stad = stayed
	went until the day
	   and muorning = morning
	frened = friend
	            druther = brother
	Stor Wurs = Star Wars
		Instructional needs:
		
		—capitalize I and the first word
		   in a sentence

Lindy (Plus)/Portfolio Book/Illustrator/Writing Progress.eps

FIGURE 1–4
Source: Courtesy L. Vizyak.

of portfolios helps me to share with the child and family by providing true evidence of the child's developing literacy ability. Figure 1–6 is a sample of a student evaluation that is given to the parent with report cards distributed each quarter. It can also serve a larger purpose of guiding instruction and evaluating teaching strategies.

	1 - Unsatisfactory	2 - Partially Proficient	3 - Proficient	4 - Advanced
Content	■ does not address prompt or generated topic is not clear ■ lacks main idea ■ unrelated thoughts or insufficient thoughts to evaluate	■ partially addresses prompt or generated topic is somewhat clear ■ main idea is not clear ■ 3–5 nonrepetitive thoughts related to topic	■ addresses prompt or generated topic is clear ■ one main idea ■ 6 or more nonrepetitive thoughts related to topic	Paper meets all standards for the proficient level, but does so: —in an insightful and/or creative manner OR —by providing exceptional idea development
Organization	■ lacks logical/sequential organization of ideas ■ lacks title	■ logical/sequential organization is not maintained ■ title does not relate to anything in the story	■ logical/sequential organization of ideas ■ title relates to story	Paper meets all standards for the proficient level, but moves beyond the formula in an innovative manner.
Style	■ lacks descriptive language ■ lacks variation in sentence beginnings	■ little descriptive language ■ few sentence beginnings are varied	■ some descriptive language ■ some sentence beginnings are varied	The paper meets all standards for proficient level, but stands out from others through: —strong word choice —language that invites expressive oral reading —a voice that is compelling and engaging
Conventions	■ many fragments/run-ons ■ many errors in mechanics —capitalization —punctuation —spelling —grammar ■ many errors in format (spacing, margins, handwriting)	■ some fragments/run-ons ■ some errors in mechanics —capitalization —punctuation —spelling —grammar ■ some errors in format (spacing, margins, handwriting)	■ few fragments/run-ons ■ few errors in mechanics —capitalization —punctuation —spelling —grammar ■ few errors in format (spacing, margins, handwriting)	The paper is virtually error free

FIGURE 1–5 Grade 1 personal narrative writing rubric. *Source:* Courtesy of Adams Five Star Schools.

First Grade Progress Report
Third Quarter

Name _René_   Date _April 2, 1999_

Reading:

~~Level in September~~ _NA_   Level in January _0_   Level in March _3_

René arrived in January

                                                             (District expectations: minimal level of 10)

below grade level
René needs to read on Level 14 by the middle of May. Your daily help at home could make a difference for her.

Blends/digraphs _26/30_

Percentage of 100 first-grade words known _47%_

Writing:

- ⋇ Writes legibly
- ⋇ Writes daily in journal and/or writing folder
- ⋇ Spells most first-grade words correctly (and, the, in, like, etc.)
- ⋇ Uses "temporary" spelling when writing more difficult words
- ⋇ Willingly shares writing
- ____ Uses correct end punctuation (. ?) _— working on_   _working on_
- ____ Uses correct capitalization (I, own name, first word in a sentence)

Math Tasks completed this grading period:

- ✓ Identifies and names coins (penny, nickel, dime, quarter)
- ✓ Knows values of coins (penny, nickel, dime, quarter)   _6/16_
- ✓ Adds groups of like coins (pennies, nickels, dimes) _60%_
- ⋇ Solves subtraction problems _100%_
- ⋇ Writes addition problems _100%_
- ⋇ Writes subtraction problems _100%_
- ⋇ Reads and writes time to the hour _100%_

Science and Social Studies Unit tests this quarter:

_____

FIGURE 1–6 Sample progress report. *Source:* Courtesy of L. Vizyak.

9

This year my class of 24 first graders includes a wide range of ability levels. Three students have special educational needs, and one student receives daily pull-out services from our school's learning disabilities teacher. Two students are enrolled in a class for severe/profound cognitive and educable mentally retarded (EMR) students. These students are fully included in our class and share a specially trained paraprofessional aide. Each of these students has a portfolio that documents growth toward their Individual Educational Plan (IEP). The special circumstances of each sample of work in these students' portfolios is described; for example, "Writing was done hand-over-hand with a paraprofessional," or "When given a choice between 'happy' and 'sad' pictures, Amy chose the one that best described how she felt today and pasted it in her journal." I have more anecdotal notes about these special students than others because they have limited speech and writing skills. For example, an entry in one of these students' portfolios reads, "Raymond has memorized his *What's for Lunch* book. He points to the word that names the food pictured on each page. He holds the book and turns the pages correctly. He eagerly shares the book with the class in the author's chair." As with other students, I use observational data recorded in portfolios to plan learning experiences and to note progress toward specific goals. All students in my class show growth over time, regardless of ability, race, culture, or gender. Portfolios clearly are for everyone.

USING A PORTFOLIO PROCESS

I employ a portfolio system that complements my philosophy of literacy teaching and facilitates individual assessment. The first year of using a portfolio approach to evaluation, I began very slowly. I attended workshops and read current research on portfolio assessment. Working with our school's reading resource teacher, my initial focus was on reading and writing progress. I collected handwriting samples, reading conference observations, and independent reading logs. I also developed forms, checklists, and tests to provide a means for recording data. I now include mathematics, social studies, and science samples in the portfolios. My specific suggestions for implementing a portfolio process in primary grades are fully described in a handbook I've written, which also includes many reproducible forms, surveys, and checklists (Vizyak, 1996).

The portfolio model I have developed is comprehensive and shows a student's educational experiences and growth during the school year in many different areas (see Figure 1–7.) In addition to using portfolios to document students' progress towards meeting grade level standards, I find them especially helpful at parent conferences. Students lead these conferences in March at all grade levels, and in my class they use samples from their portfolios as the focus of the conference. Portfolios, to me, are a carefully selected collection of student work that provides clear evidence to the student and others of the student's knowledge, skills, strategies, concepts, attitudes, and achievement in a given area or areas. My portfolio system has two major components: Student-Managed Portfolios and Teacher-Managed Assessment Portfolios. This Teacher/Student Assessment Model contains self-selected works, surveys, projects, tests, conference and anecdotal notes, evaluation data, self-assessment, and works in progress. (The Student-Managed Portfolio process is described more fully in the next section about how the system has changed.) It's interesting to me that my original portfolio model was much more teacher-controlled. As I became more comfortable with portfolios, I developed a system where the student and I collaboratively created the teacher-managed portfolio. During periodic conferences, the student and I select work samples from the student portfolio for inclusion in the teacher portfolio. It's very important that guidelines be developed to aid in the portfolio assembly. The following guidelines are helpful to both me and the students when we review their work for inclusion in the portfolio:

Items are selected for the students' portfolios to document growth in these areas:

1. Samples that show evidence of self-reflection and self-evaluation (demonstrated through samples of published writing, surveys, or reading and writing conference notes)

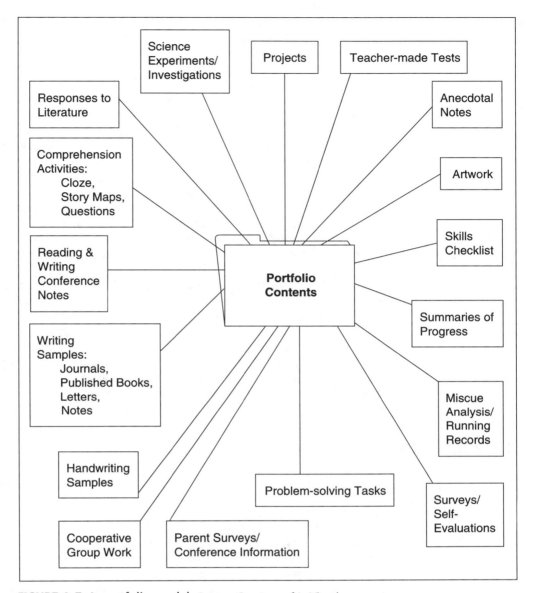

FIGURE 1–7 A portfolio model. *Source:* Courtesy of L. Vizyak.

2. Samples that show progress toward clearly defined learning goals (based on district, building, and classroom assessments)

3. Samples that are collected at regular intervals during the year to show growth over time (running records, writing samples evaluated with rubrics, and responses to literature)

I collect data and work samples in a manila folder. On the front cover, I create three vertical columns: Reading, Writing, and Math. On the back cover, Science and Social Studies are recorded. Under each heading, I keep a record in chronological order of observations and testing information. Products and notes inside support all comments on the cover. The information is used for parent conferences and report cards.

Our school district fully supports the development of portfolios as an authentic form of assessment. Classes have been provided through the staff development department. The principal of my building, Mrs. Carol Kiernan, has consistently supported efforts at the building level by providing staff development, encouraging teachers to attend workshops/conferences, sharing current research articles, and purchasing books for our professional library. Many teachers in our district use classroom portfolios and we also have "pass-on" portfolios to document K–5 literacy. It's apparent that when teachers use classroom portfolios, different models are being used depending on the purpose(s) being served. Some are using Showcase Portfolios that contain examples of only "best work." Other models are being used to document achievement and contain a wider range of process and product work as well as assessment data. Regarding the "pass-on" portfolios, the cover of this blue folder contains required assessment data in reading and writing. Running record and writing rubric scores from kindergarten through fifth grade are required by the district and data are collected in September and May of each year. Students' writing samples are also contained in these portfolios and each year's teacher can benefit from noting the student's progress in previous years. My classroom Student/Teacher Assessment portfolio (described above) serves a different purpose and belongs to the student, and therefore is taken home at the end of the school year.

Parent support is an important component of this evaluation process. At the first conference in November, I tell parents about the portfolios kept for each student. I show a completed portfolio from the previous year. During the year, I share portfolios with parents at conferences and at student-led conferences in March. For the past 8 years, surveys have indicated that parents value having samples of their child's work, understand information contained in a portfolio, and can easiliy see growth over time. Parent comments on the surveys include, "I know more about Jeff than I have ever known about any of my children," and "It was wonderful to see Jennelle's work. What a great opportunity for building self-esteem!"

My student portfolios are not translated into letter grades. However, the contents are used to evaluate student understanding and application of reading and writing skills and strategies. Data provide report card and conference information. It can also serve a larger purpose of guiding instruction and evaluating my teaching strategies for effectiveness.

THE PORTFOLIO MODEL CHANGES

Over the past years, I have made changes in my portfolio model. As I continued my research about alternative methods of assessment, I became increasingly uncomfortable with my teacher-controlled model of portfolio entries in which student participation and access were limited. This practice did not align with current research, which stresses the importance of students' applying the processes of self-reflection and self-evaluation to set personal learning goals. Six years ago, I put my research-based knowledge into practice and changed my portfolio process at the beginning of the year. I provided blank file folders for the children to collect their work. Some students collected work samples, but most did not. At the end of the year, I reflected back on this less-than-successful experience and made several discoveries. I had not properly modeled the process, nor had I discussed possible contents of a portfolio or reasons for selecting the contents with my students. No wonder these very young children had difficulty. This realization prompted my decision to provide a structure the following year that would support my goal of developing a collaborative assessment model.

I implemented my new plan by introducing the term portfolio during the first week of school. To provide a clear model, I shared my own portfolio with the class. I had decorated the cover of an 8-by-12-inch manila folder with a drawing of the cover of *The True Story of the Three Little Pigs* (Scieszka, 1989), which is a favorite children's book, a drawing of my family, a University of Colorado logo (my son's college) and, especially, a photo of my new granddaughter. I also shared the contents of my portfolio with the students and explained why each entry was included, based on the significance of each piece. Then I gave my students blank folders to decorate and share with the class. This first step created instant ownership and certainly enhanced the students' personal commitment to a portfolio collection.

Several times per month, students shared pieces from their portfolios and explained the reasons for their selections. At the beginning of the year, students had no previous experience with this process and most found it difficult to explain their choices. Ryan shared a story he had written about his dog and said, "I put this in my portfolio because it is about my dog and I like my dog." I wanted to model other possible reasons for Ryan including the story in his portfolio, so I said, "I know that Ryan loves to write and often writes at home and during his free time; I also see that he has a title for his story." Ryan promptly added, "Oh, yeah. I also have a summary on the back of my story." I asked him where he got the idea of including a story summary, and he said that he noticed that many of the books I read to the class had a summary on the back. Ryan had clearly made a connection between reading and writing!

The students clearly needed more direction about the portfolio process. Drawing on my experience with writer's workshop mini-lessons, I structured portfolio mini-lessons. These lessons focused on the content of student-managed portfolios and reasons for selections. Most important, these lessons provided the language needed for self-reflection. The majority of the first student selections were examples of best work. As the year progressed, mini-lessons explored other reasons for selecting portfolio pieces, including the following:

- Something new you have learned (growth)
- Something that took a long time (effort)
- Something that was challenging (risk taking)
- Something that shows interests outside of school (holistic learning)

The students also generated a chart listing "Things That Can Go in a Portfolio." It included a story or book, science projects, letters, notes, cards, best work, math papers, artwork, photographs, things from home, challenging things, things that show improvement, and work from the student's favorite subject. The list is ongoing and expands as students discover new categories of possible portfolio inclusions. As a result of these efforts, the students' portfolios are becoming much more expansive. My students are also learning self-selection and seem to take great pride in their large collections. Each Friday, anyone who has a new portfolio entry (including me) is invited to share it with the class. These regular sharing sessions have resulted in improved metacognition and opportunities for building self-esteem and confidence as students develop a voice in the assessment process.

Once every trimester grading period, students meet with me individually to choose two or three pieces from their student-managed portfolios to include in our teacher-student assessment portfolio. An entry form explains the student's reason(s) for each choice and the student attaches it to the appropriate piece. Students may select anything they have collected in their own portfolios. For example, one student included a computer-generated text and illustrations in his portfolio because it was his first composition on the computer and he was very proud of his accomplishment. This process provides valuable information about each student's ability to self-reflect. I feel confident that this new teacher-student portfolio is a successful marriage of student self-reflection and self-evaluation as well as helpful for teacher accountability. Of great importance to me is that this portfolio process facilitates my ability to truly know each student far better, so that I can be a better teacher and meet each student's academic and personal needs.

BENEFITS OF LITERACY PORTFOLIOS

A portfolio approach to evaluation enables me to provide authentic assessment that serves as a record of a student's learning, development, behaviors, and attitudes over time. It provides a collaborative, developmentally appropriate model that reflects my program and philosophy of teaching because it focuses on the students' many unique talents, strengths, and abilities, not their shortcomings, which had often been the focus of classroom assessment. For a portfolio process to work, it should be a natural extension of teaching and should be individualized to meet each teacher's needs and goals.

Before starting a portfolio process, here are a few last tips. Be sure to start slowly and to gradually integrate portfolios into your class. Set realistic goals by reflecting on your philosophy of teaching, your school's curriculum requirements, and your teaching needs. I've found that establishing a 4- to 5-year time line (Vizyak, 1995) may be helpful to develop a good system. Be consistent, and set aside time each day for assessment and record keeping. Make sure to commit sufficient time to working with individual students as well as small groups each day, and be sure to distribute your time equitably with all students. Involve parents at every phase by having them complete surveys, attend portfolio conferences (which can be run by the students after training), and attend portfolio night celebrations. Parent involvement can also be stimulated through newsletters. My experience has shown that a portfolio process can certainly be done with students as young and diverse as my first-grade class. I truly believe that a portfolio process enhances both literacy instruction and student growth.

REFERENCES

Vizyak, L. (1995). Student portfolios: Building self-reflection in a first-grade classroom. *Reading Teacher, 48,* 362–364.

Vizyak, L. (1996). *Student portfolios: A practical guide to evaluation.* Bothell, WA: Wright Group.

ESSAY B

Anatomy of a Year: One Teacher's Experience With Long-Term Portfolios in Grades 4–5

by

Robyn S. Lane
West Patent Elementary School,
Bedford Hills, New York

My initial interest in portfolio assessment had less to do with my professional curiosity than with my maternal awareness. My daughters, who were then in elementary and middle school, would bring home evidence of great learning. Test papers, graded reports, homework assignments—all the traditional indicators parents crave—were neatly presented and commented upon by wonderful teachers. Yet, why were these papers being tossed in the trash so quickly? Why didn't my own kids seem to value what I as a professional wanted them to value? After all, hadn't they worked hard for all this feedback? What was the missing link that connected what they *did* with care to what they *cared* to do? What implications did this have for me as a teacher of 9- and 10-year-olds? Were all of my students' hard work and my belabored comments also quickly going into the trash at home? Were students, even the most motivated ones, interested only in short-term gratification? Could it be that I wasn't doing the job I wanted to believe I was doing?

I teach in Bedford Hills, New York, a community approximately 1 hour's drive north of New York City. The district contains diverse economic groups, including blue collar to upper-class families. Our district has five elementary schools and my school was designed as an "open space" environment in the 1970s to accommodate an open-education program. My teaching situation is rather unique because our school is divided into four different teams, with approximately 100 students and 4 teachers assigned to each team. I teach an interage combination of fourth and fifth graders, whose skills range from barely reading to advanced middle school level. Most of the curriculum is team taught and both teachers and students seem to profit from this approach, which I characterize as very cooperative and supportive. I especially enjoy the interage arrangement, because I can spend 2 years with my students and during that time I see great growth and change. I have been using portfolios for approximately 5 years and find that each year I need to modify what I did the year before. The reuse of portfolios has changed the way that I view teaching and assessment and certainly has changed the way that my students come to value their work.

ESTABLISHING A PURPOSE

As Donald Graves has been known to say, "Good questions don't go away." I knew from the start of my involvement in creating and maintaining portfolios in my classroom that I was searching for a way to make my students' products and efforts more meaningful to *them*. I was deriving a great deal of both pleasure and frustration from their accomplishments, but there was a definite disparity in the degree of investment by me, my students, and their parents. That nagging feeling was what led me to define the three-fold purpose of using portfolios in my classroom: (1) to demonstrate growth in my students' ability to use their literacy skills and communicate for a variety of purposes, (2) to make this growth more apparent to all invested parties, (3) and to engage students in the process of reflection.

In my opinion, the most critical part of the entire process lies in answering that question of purpose for yourself. What is it you want to document or achieve with a portfolio? For many of us, answering this question means making choices. There are many different kinds of portfolios: some serve as a "showcase" of students' best work (possibly from a unit of study or from a year's worth of work); some document growth within a specific content area; some are used to evaluate students' progress and to show their growth developmentally, as with a year-long reading and writing portfolio; and some are designed to reveal additional information about students to learn more about them, but not for evaluative purposes. Through the years I have tried various portfolios to accomplish a variety of purposes. However, last year as I reflected on my own instructional goals and the goals I had set for my students, I decided it would be best for me to implement a *communications portfolio*, designed to document growth over time in the language arts by representing students' writing activities that occurred in the classroom throughout the year.

THE PROCESS OF IMPLEMENTING A LONG-TERM COMMUNICATIONS PORTFOLIO

To begin this huge undertaking, I looked at the "blueprint" or scope of my school year and recorded student experiences that provided writing opportunities and enabled data collection. I planned to use the learning experiences so that the portfolios mirrored the year instead of "driving" it. The language-arts activities I planned included experiences that spanned many curriculum areas and focused on student writing using these forms: personal narratives, descriptive paragraphs, persuasive essays, point-of-view pieces, business letters and letters to friends, personal journals, content-response journals, literature-response activities, news summaries, book reports, projects in different curriculum areas, and research reports. All of these experiences provided opportunities for students to write and produce work that they could consider for inclusion in their portfolios.

Once I felt comfortable with the focus for the portfolio, the process began. I was still faced with both philosophical and pragmatic questions: What would these portfolios look like at the end of the year? Was there a right or wrong way to do this? How would I handle a year's worth of paper? How would I guide students through the process? Could children at this age be reflective enough to make the portfolio a useful tool? This stage of teacher insecurity is to be anticipated, and I learned that students will benefit from the portfolio experience even if there are some logistical errors. The process is similar to taking a journey together. Sharing errors with students along the way created an atmosphere of trust. I had to be prepared to change what wasn't working, as teachers routinely do for class lessons. The main advantage of this long-term portfolio, compared with a short-term content portfolio (which I have used successfully to culminate a unit of study), was that I was *not* using the portfolio to evaluate or grade students but to document their growth and provide the opportunity to establish learning goals. The real challenge of this long-term portfolio, however, was to keep it from becoming overwhelming to me and my students. Even after using this long-term portfolio for several years, I am still looking for ways to refine it by reducing paperwork and increasing authenticity.

There were a number of logistical issues to tackle in implementing portfolios in my classroom. First, I decided that work could not go home without being returned to school. I created a file of manila folders and placed them in hanging files to store daily work. The students and I referred to these as *holding folders*. Their purpose was to contain everything for us to consider until we made decisions about portfolio contents. Students also maintained individual writing folders that held works in progress. This system worked well for me as long as I took the time early in the year to create a "think portfolio" mindset. Students needed reminding to date and store their work in the folders, especially when they worked with specialty-area teachers in subjects other than language arts. The work from these subject classes also "counted" as part of portfolio contents. As the year progressed, students generally began to internalize the system and the holding folders became delightfully full and never dusty.

The "think portfolio" environment was most important. I found that students may not initially understand the portfolio concept, and I needed to introduce it to them in a tangible way. One way is to share an actual artist's portfolio or one that you have created yourself. In our school, we have been fortunate to have a few grade levels involved in portfolios, and our fifth graders share their work with younger students. In the beginning of the year, I find that students collect work without truly understanding the purpose of portfolio collection, but this soon changes. In addition to setting the stage at the beginning of the year, I discovered that other activities can be completed to create the foundation of a portfolio. Our students were asked to complete a writing sample for their permanent writing folders, a district requirement. I made copies of each student's piece and used these as a baseline for individual portfolios, because I wanted to demonstrate growth in writing throughout the year. Fortunately, the writing sample the district required was a friendly letter to the teacher in which the students were asked to describe themselves and tell of their expectations for the year. Not only did this give me a baseline of the students' writing ability, it provided me with information about the students' backgrounds and put me in touch with their personal goals.

Portfolios also provided a golden opportunity to enhance the school-home connection. Periodic parent feedback is invaluable. It provides students with the realization that teachers do not work in isolation and that each child's success is orchestrated and celebrated by all who care about him or her. Of course, not all parents participate as much as we would want them to, but we need to consistently provide opportunities for them to do so. I send home a portfolio questionnaire at the beginning of the year, focusing on the parents' view of how each child learns. A similar questionnaire is sent home in June, and it's quite interesting to compare the two. Figures 1–8a and 1–8b are samples of parent questionnaires at the beginning and end of the school year. Students also complete a questionnaire at the beginning of the year, shown in Figure 1–9. It is also interesting to compare the parents' responses with those of their children.

Once we collected initial information, the students and I needed to start making portfolio selections. After my first year's experience, I established a goal of making portfolio selections more frequently. This is easier said than done, because the process takes time, and we all know how little extra time we have in the classroom. I was able to plan 3 selection days, even though I had wanted to have students make selections every 6 weeks. The first round of making selections was the most difficult. It was important to first model the selection process with my class and discuss the purpose for making selections early in the school year. I acted as if I were a student, sorting my work into piles and then narrowing down the choices to what I felt very strongly about keeping based on selection guidelines.

During my first year of using the portfolio process several issues arose:

- Would students always select pieces of work to which I, their teacher, responded favorably? If so, how could I avoid my evaluation being substituted for theirs?
- What if the students chose selections from their ongoing journals or the selections were otherwise not easily accessible on selection day?
- What should I do with the work the students did (or didn't) select?
- How should I guide the students, but not direct them, through this process?
- How many selections should be made? Must they be in final form?
- Is all work potentially portfolio material, or are there limits?
- What about the child who doesn't want to participate?

A general answer to each of these questions is, "It's entirely up to you!" There is no simple right or wrong answer, although the risks for wrong answers are low if you are not using portfolios to evaluate your students. Teachers should refer back to their purpose for doing a portfolio and try to answer each question in relation to it. I learned that there is no single exemplary portfolio design, although I spent much time looking for one. I also learned a few other things that may be helpful for other teachers who are considering using portfolios in their classrooms.

Student's name _Jessica_   Date _Sept. 16_

1. What would you identify as a strength of your child's writing?

   Creative expression,—that she enjoys writing

   and research for writing

   _____

2. What would you identify as an area for most improvement in your child's writing?

   To take time—the process is as important

   as the final product

   _____

3. If you could improve something about the way your child reads, what would it be?

   That she takes challenges to read different

   types of books.

   _____

4. My child does his/her best when _She can work by_

   herself or small group. Large group is very

   risky for her.

   Please feel free to provide additional information on the back of this form. THANK YOU!!!

   R. Lane 94-95

FIGURE 1–8A Parent response form (pre-portfolio). *Source:* Courtesy of R. Lane.

SOME RECOMMENDATIONS BASED ON EXPERIENCE

After reflecting on the process based on my experience, here are some recommendations for making successful portfolios. First, try to live with life's imperfections. Students are insecure when they make their first selections, and they want indicators of success. For many, this may mean selecting a piece for which they received a good grade or one that looked neat. The students' ability to make choices develops over time based on their use of specific and clear criteria. As teachers, we can provide students with helpful information, such as the realization that not everything in a portfolio has to be in final form.

Second, students choose different pieces for a variety of reasons. If students chose a test to keep in the portfolio, it might mean that they studied especially hard for the test and the success meant a great deal to them. The important issue here is to inform the students that they are the decision makers about selections, but they must be able to explain why

Student's name: _____   **Date:** _____

Dear Parent,

Enclosed is your child's final portfolio representing student and teacher selected samples of his/her growth as an effective communicator this year. As we discussed earlier in the year, the purpose of this portfolio is to document how your child's ability to communicate for a variety of purposes has developed over the past 10 months. The portfolio also gives your child an opportunity to select, evaluate, and reflect on his/her own progress as a communicator. This will hopefully enable him/her to set goals for improving skills and see more clearly how much has been accomplished.

Your child has practiced the way in which he/she will present the portfolio to you. I encourage you to spend some time with him/her as he/she shares this new adventure with you. I am sure that you will enjoy every moment of the trip!

I would greatly appreciate feedback from you and would find your responses to the following questions extremely helpful. Thank you for your continued enthusiasm and support.

Sincerely,
Robyn Lane

1. After viewing the portfolio, I found evidence of growth in the following areas:

    A. Expression of ideas   _____
    B. Focus (staying on topic)   _____
    C. Vocabulary/language   _____
    D. Spelling   _____
    E. Punctuation (commas, capitals, periods, etc.) _____
    F. Ability to revise from first to final draft   _____
    G. Organization   _____

2. I feel my child has shown the greatest growth in the following area:

    _____

    _____

3. I would like to see my child further improve in:

    _____

    _____

4. Please explain if, and in what ways, you have seen growth in your child's reading ability and/or interests:

    _____

    _____

5. Additional comments:

    _____

    _____

Parent/Guardian signature: _____

FIGURE 1–8B Parent response form. *Source:* Courtesy of R. Lane.

Name: *Abby* Date: *9/21/*

Pre-portfolio Questionnaire

1. Do you like to write: (Check one answer)

   _✓_ I enjoy writing

   _____ I sometimes enjoy writing

   _____ I write only when I have to

2. On the following list, place a check next to the writing skills you most want to improve this year: (Choose no more than 5)

   A. Spelling _____✓_____

   B. Making paragraphs _____

   C. Punctuation (commas, periods, question marks, quotation marks) _____

   D. Having an interesting introduction _____

   E. Having a strong concluding paragraph _____

   F. Putting events in the correct order _____

   G. Keeping to the topic _____

   H. Using more interesting words _____✓_____

   I. Starting sentences in a variety of ways _____

   J. Thinking about what to write/starting _____

   K. The revising stage of the writing process _____✓_____

   L. Other: *Picking the title* _____✓_____

3. Please explain the kinds of things that help you when you're writing.

   Quiet.

   Time.

4. What kinds of problems do you have when you write?

   Remembering what I was going to do, like when we shop and I get my mind on something else.

FIGURE 1–9 Pre-portfolio questionnaire. *Source:* Courtesy of R. Lane.

20

5. Check your 2 favorite kinds of writing:

1. personal narrative (about yourself) _____   4. letters _____

2. make-believe stories ✓_____   5. poetry _____

3. factual reports ✓_____   6. journals ____

6. What do you read in your free time? (Check one or more)

_____ short stories   _____ poems

_____ magazines   _____ comics

✓ fiction books   _____ biographies about famous people

✓ non-fiction books   _____ I don't read in my free time

7. I like to read books and stories about _people for instance,_
the Babysitter club (is my favorite).

8. When I read by myself, I feel _indipendant and I am doing_
Something good.

9. When I read with a group of other students, I feel _like I'm_
doing something fun. Can't wait to hear what will happen

10. When I come to a word I do not know, I _try to ~~spell~~ sound it out_
or ask a teacher

11. When I don't understand something I've read, I _read it over_
again a try to understand it.

12. The time of day when I most enjoy reading is _at nigh befor bed and in school_

13. How do you think I might help you become a better reader or writer?
~~I don't know~~ Mabey you could let
us read any Kind of book we want?

FIGURE 1–9 Continued.

they made their choices. One tip I can never stress enough is to make sure that the students put the date on all their work, because this saves time and aggravation later in the year.

Third, work that is contained outside of the holding folders (in journals, for instance) needs to be managed. I gave students a worksheet that listed suggestions for choices and had the students write down some information about each of their choices. If an entry came from a journal, the students listed the selection on the worksheet and put a sticky note on their journal. They turned the journal in with their other selections, and I

Student Reflection Form
(To be filled out by student after making a selection for the
Portfolio and then discussed during student/teacher conference)

Name: _____   **Date Piece Was Written:** _____

1. I think this is my best sample of a _____

   because _____

   _____

2. Some of the things I learned from completing this writing sample are:

   _____

   _____

3. One way I think I have improved is: _____

   _____

4. Some things I still have to improve on are: _____

   _____

FIGURE 1–10 Sample student reflection form.

copied or extracted the work for them. The selection worksheet also provided a framework for students to use to help them make selections. I reinforced the concept that the final decision is always theirs. I reminded the students that the purpose of the portfolio was to show their ability to write for a variety of purposes and, therefore, I advised them to include different forms of writing when they made their selections. I urged them not to choose too many pieces and to be selective. Some teachers may want to be more direct about the type and number of selections for a portfolio. Again, the decision should be made based on the portfolio's purpose and intended audiences.

It's also important to discuss "ownership" with the students. In my class, it's quite clear that the students own their portfolios, and the audience consists of their parents and me. The students are aware of this, and they end the school year by taking their portfolio treasures home. I don't grade their work and the portfolios are not given to the next year's teacher, because I want the students to enjoy them without being concerned about evaluation. However, a number of school districts now require portfolio assessment for student evaluation throughout elementary school.

REFLECTIONS ON SELF-REFLECTION

It's important to think about ways to help students reflect about themselves and learn to set goals. I know how difficult this can be for my students. Learning to be self-analytic is a developmental process and, as with other skills, guidance and practice leads to improvement. It's important to provide lots of opportunities for self-reflection and to model the behavior. Teachers should also be reminded to listen to their students, because there may be more reflection occurring than they think. I found this out the first year I attempted to document self-reflection. I had asked students to complete a reflection form for each piece they selected for their portfolios (see Figure 1–10). However, I was disappointed in the quality of their responses: for example, "I chose this piece because it was good" and "I liked my handwriting that day." I was almost convinced that students of this age were limited in their ability to be reflective about their work. I discussed the problem with the project facilitator, who advised me to change the way I was looking at reflection. Consequently, I decided to videotape my class on the next selection day. When I viewed the tape, I wrote down words and phrases that my students said as they made their selections, and what a difference I found. Typical comments were: "Wow! I can't believe I used so many descriptive words in this" and "This is interesting to read." Wasn't this reflection? The students may not have written insightfully on their forms, but their oral comments showed me that they were invested in the process.

Because of these comments, I decided to document reflection in a less restrictive fashion. Although I still required students to complete a reflection form for at least one piece of work, I also asked them to assess any final piece of writing with a rubric that we devised together in class (see Figure 1–11). To develop this rubric, we talked a great deal about what constitutes good writing. By applying the rubric in this concrete fashion, students clearly understood how they were to apply the criteria to their work.

In addition to these reflective activities, students were required to complete a mid-year reflection sheet once they had the experience with two separate portfolio selection sessions. I tried to have this coincide with mid-year because I have found that the second selection day is best done after the December vacation. I also find that these forms are valuable when I meet with parents during conferences. Figure 1–12 shows a sample

---

Writing Rubric

3. My writing . . .
   - stays on the topic (is focused) from beginning to end
   - has a strong introduction that interests the reader
   - is developed enough to cover the topic
   - has a strong concluding paragraph
   - uses descriptive language in a way that makes the piece more interesting
   - has sentences that start in a variety of ways
   - has few mechanical or grammatical errors (spelling, punctuation, paragraphs, capital letters)
   - is neatly presented/legible handwriting

2. My writing . . .
   - stays on the topic (is focused) for most of the piece but parts could be taken out or changed
   - has an introduction
   - covers the topic but could be more developed to include more details or information
   - has a concluding paragraph
   - uses some descriptive language
   - has a few sentences that start in an interesting way
   - has some mechanical and grammatical errors (spelling, punctuation, paragraphs, capital letters)
   - is mostly neat and easy to read

1. My writing . . .
   - gets off the topic or includes details that are not related to the topic
   - does not have a clear introduction
   - does not give the reader enough details or information
   - does not have a clearly written conclusion
   - does not use descriptive language
   - has most sentences that start in the same way

FIGURE 1–11 Sample writing rubric.

R. Lane
Name: _____   Date: __2/8/__

Mid-year Reflection

1. As I look at my portfolio selections, the piece I like best is

   <u>Cheese Cake and my Crave for it.</u> I like this piece because

   it is discriptive, funny, and had no errores.

2. The hardest piece for me to write was __My dsebel piece__

   because it took alot of time to

   write what would happen to Isebel
   when she got to the whitches bee.

3. After reviewing my mid-year portfolio, I feel __that I have__

   grown better at spelling and breaking

   my story up into paragraphs

4. I was pleased with the way I __have became more__

   discriptive in my pieces, like in Cheese
   Cake and my crave for it.

5. I was not pleased with the way I __made some spelling__

   errores in some pieces.

6. My goal for the next part of the school year is __to write__

   a really adventures story and alot

   more poems.

7. I think I can achieve this goal by __putting time every__
   day to write my story, and make
   one of the best stories I have
   ever writen.

FIGURE 1–12 Sample mid-year reflection sheet. *Source:* Courtesy of R. Lane.

of a completed mid-year reflection sheet that reveals good insights not only about the work but about the learning process as well.

I find that the most valuable form of reflection is the "Dear Reader" letter. This letter introduces the student to the reader and provides a forum for sharing information about themselves and their accomplishments. Figure 1–13 is a letter done by a fifth-grade student, and Figure 1–14 was written by a fourth-grade student. Although there is clearly a wide difference in these students' abilities, both pieces provide evidence of self-reflection, which was one of my goals for them.

May 31,

Dear Reader,

You are now looking at my [name deleted]
(   ) portfolio, throughout the
year I have written many writing pieces,
such as descriptive, short stories, and
point of view, ect. Now I would like to
share this work with you. A portfolio,
though, does not just contain all your
work, it is made up of special writing
pieces and shows growth throughout
the year.

You will read everything I'm
sure, yet I would like you to notice
my growth and how much more descriptive
I have become. Not to mention how much
longer my writing has become!

I am very proud of this accomplishment
and I feel special to be able to say
"I have a portfolio!" I hope you will
feel the same way and maybe start a
portfolio of your own ounce you
look over the contents in it!!!

Sincerely,

[name deleted]

FIGURE 1–13

Dear Reader,

This portfolio show the work I have been working on in this school, year, It reresents some of my best, work.

You will find a lot of my work from this school year, You can tell which was writen in Setember and which was writin in May. You will find a lot of personal martive becase I feel I put a lot of effart into them.

I want you to notice the learahs of my work and look at the effort I put into them.

ginaerely

FINAL THOUGHTS ON USING PORTFOLIOS IN THE CLASSROOM

Once the students reflected on the year's efforts, it was time for a response from both me and the parents. The students and I planned a portfolio party. In preparation, they practiced ways in which they could present their portfolios to their families. Parents were also asked to complete an end-of-term questionnaire. I personally responded in each student's portfolio and related how I'd seen him or her grow in communication ability, and I identified areas in which I thought the student could improve. I also included a statement about how I enjoyed a specific experience working with the student. This collection, which contained a blend of student and teacher selections, was then turned over to the rightful owners: the students.

The true worth of keeping portfolios comes during the final hours of the school year. I will never forget the silence when my students opened their final portfolios that were complete with their selections, my reflections, and responses from other teachers and their family. I now realize that, without my ever intending it, these folders became a great equalizer in my classroom, which was made up of students from a diverse array of backgrounds, some of whom were advanced readers and some of whom could barely get by. There was a smile on each student's face, whether the student was a high achiever or always seemed to be struggling. For some, this smile represented validation of ability, and for others it meant recognition that they too had come far during the year. All held tangible examples of success in their hands.

I join with many other educators who continue to experiment with more effective ways of educating students, and I offer this encouragement to those who are interested in beginning a portfolio process. Keep it simple and follow your instincts; they're probably correct. Share with others; it really helps a lot. When you have questions or problems, discuss the issues with your students; their answers may surprise you. My students and I learned a great deal from our use of portfolios. I end with this quotation from one of my fifth-grade students: "Keeping a portfolio is like having a reminder to not be too hard on yourself. You can see the whole picture better."

Students in the Middle: Reflections on Literacy Portfolios for Sixth, Seventh, and Eighth Grades

Note: The following reflections are from two very different middle school environments—one from a Texas school district and one from a school district in the Bronx, New York City. As different as these locations might seem to be, there are striking similarities. In both places teachers are faced with many similar challenges: underprepared students, students of low socioeconomic status, and many students who have ceased to care about reading and writing. Both school systems also require that teachers prepare students to pass state mandated literacy assessments, and there is increased pressure on teacher accountability. Both systems tend to measure success by students' scores on high stakes literacy tests.

Anyone who has worked with young adolescents is well aware of the unique challenges that this population presents. It's especially interesting that the teachers in both of the teaching situations cited here reflect that beyond using portfolios as means to improve literacy, the use of a writing portfolio gave them greater insights into the emotional life of children in their classrooms at a time when their psychological and social needs are so important.

Reflections From Tyler, Texas

by
Glenda Moss, Ed.D.
Assistant Professor, School of Education, Indiana-Purdue,
Ft. Wayne, Indiana

Before I entered my current profession as a teacher educator, I taught middle school students in Tyler, Texas. For those of you unfamiliar with Texas, this is the largest school district in northeast Texas, serving approximately 16,000 students. Located midway between Dallas and Shreveport, Louisiana, Tyler's population is about 85,000. Tyler Independent School District has about 1153 classroom teachers; 35% of the staff members are minority and 43% of the students are economically disadvantaged.

Educators all over the country are struggling to align curriculum and teaching practices with the forms of outcome assessment required by their state education departments. In Texas, the Texas Education System shaped the frame within which my local school district designed a comprehensive writing portfolio process to span the children's schooling from grades 1–12. Critical to understanding my experience is familiarity with the Texas Education System, which has two parts: the Texas Essential Knowledge and Skills (TEKS) and the Texas Assessment of Academic Skills (TAAS). TEKS consists of the state-mandated curriculum guidelines, which established what every student, from elementary school through high school, should know and be able to do. TEKS was designed to align the new curriculum with TAAS, the state's student performance test. The testing system has been used as an accountability system through which teacher effectiveness is measured by student success on the test. It was within this context that my district chose to implement writing portfolios across the district.

ORIGINS OF PORTFOLIO USE

Reflectivity, creativity, and sound teaching practices were my base principles and response to the district mandate that all middle school language arts teachers participate in the district-level writing portfolio project. The idea was to begin in first grade. Each year teachers would choose writing samples of their students' work and put them in a cumulative writing portfolio, which would accompany the students through graduation. The portfolios were collected by the instructional consultants at the end of each school year and passed on the next grade level teachers at the beginning of the new school year.

I realized the value of writing portfolios in helping middle school students shift their perspective from writing as an assignment or task to be completed in less than a 45-minute time period to a perspective of writing as an ongoing, evolutionary process. I wanted my students to move away from the idea that writing could be reduced merely to a formula with sequential steps needed for demonstrating mastery on the TAAS. TAAS assessment of writing required students to "describe" a picture, to list the steps in a "how-to" paper, to discuss the pros and cons in a "classificatory" paper, or to present the reasons for or against in a "persuasive" paper. I had noticed that many Texas teachers were teaching students to memorize writing formulas that resulted in five-paragraph themes. My district required language arts teachers to have their students choose one writing product from their work during the first 3 months of school, one from the second 3 months, and one from the final 3 months to be placed in their writing portfolios for their teachers the following year. My response to this developmental evaluation process was to use portfolios as an ongoing and integral part of the writing process in my classroom. There were three parts to my use of writing portfolios with seventh and eighth-grade students—journals, works in progress, and finished projects. I purchased 150 three-ring binders to be used as writing portfolios, plastic file crates, and boxes of hanging files. Organizationally, four students were assigned to work at each table in the classroom. (If desks are the norm in your classroom, they can be clustered for students to a group for cooperative learning.) Five crates, one for each class period, were stacked on the floor next to each table. In the crates were four different-colored hanging files, four blue binders, and four spiral notebooks for journal writing. Each binder contained 200 sheets of lined paper and a plastic supply bag with pens and pencils. The students were required to bring the paper, pens, and pencils at the beginning of each semester or contribute $3.00 for me to purchase their supplies. All supplies remained in the classroom.

I also provided a set of resources for each group of four students. These writing aids, including several different English grammar textbooks, thesauruses, dictionaries, and computerized spell-checks, never left the room. Also, a plastic box at each table supplied the students with rulers, colored pencils, colored markers, scissors, glue, stapler, and staples. We referred to the tables as the students' offices. I'm a very organized person, and I feel that organization is essential to success in any classroom, especially when working with a large number of students who come and go in limited time periods! Every minute counts in this learning situation, and I wanted my students to get the most out of every classroom session.

CLASSROOM PROCEDURES

The procedures in my classroom were centered around students' use of writing portfolios as a tool for developing literacy skills. When the students entered the classroom each day, they secured their journal and writing tools and proceeded to respond to the prompt on the board. Prompts were related to something we were reading, a news event, or a school issue and motivated the students to think creatively or critically. Some prompts required self-critical reflection, whereas others provided critical feedback to my teaching. Some examples of topics that really worked for me were:

- What did you learn in my class yesterday?
- What did you learn at home last night?
- What did you learn over the weekend?
- What do you like about the classroom environment in my room?
- If you could change something about this class, what would it be?
- If you could choose to be any animal in the world, what would you choose? Why?
- What is your goal for today?
- Evaluate how you have done the past 6 weeks.

While reading *The Lilies of the Field*, journal topics included the following:

- Describe Homer Smith.
- Think about Homer as representative of man. What did you learn from the story about how man versus man, man versus society, and man versus the environment?
- If you had been in Homer's place, what would you have done?
- How have you had to come up against other people, society, or the environment?

On more than one occasion, a student from my school was killed violently—two by gunshot and another by an automobile crash. Each time, I let the students write about what they were thinking and feeling about the event.

As students completed their journal entries, they returned their journals to their assigned crates and secured their work-in-progress from their hanging files. Writing projects generally took 3 days to complete. Research reports in preparation for science projects and history projects took 2 weeks, as did interdisciplinary projects. Students were responsible for utilizing class time to learn, to contribute to others' learning, and to produce finished products. Depending on where students were in the writing process, on any given day some would be writing alone and others would be engaged in dialogical critique. Students were expected to give critical feedback to peers and discuss writing during the process. Artifacts to show the planning process—mapping, Venn diagrams, T-bars, or outlines—accompanied all writing products. Rough drafts evidenced the stages of reading, responding, and editing that preceded the writing of the "published" product presented to the teacher for evaluation and grade based on a rubric:

1. (unacceptable): off topic, wrong mode, too short (less than six sentences).
2. (minimal passing, below-level standard): on topic, correct mode, at least six sentences, topic sentence, evidence of some organization, serious mechanical problems, serious grammar errors.
3. (passing, acceptable work): clearly focused topic sentence, on topic, correct mode, well-organized, three to five paragraphs, evidence of elaboration, effective use of vocabulary, limited mechanical problems, limited grammar errors.
4. (mastery): clearly focused topic sentence, on topic, correct mode, well-organized, three to five paragraphs, well-developed sentences, evidence of rich elaboration, effective use of advanced vocabulary, free of run-on sentences and sentence fragments, evidence of standard English syntax.

Following teacher evaluation based on the above rubric, students filed the work in their portfolio of finished products or they continued to revise the paper for a higher quality product and a higher grade. Once a paper was filed in a portfolio of finished products, the student could still go back to the paper at a later time and advance the paper to a new level by adding details or reconstructing sentences on a more complex level. These products became the source for choosing samples for the district-wide portfolio.

TRANSCENDING PROCEDURAL USE OF WRITING PORTFOLIOS

Writing portfolios in my classroom transcended the district's minimum standard that students choose three writing samples during the academic year to place in a writing portfolio for their next-year teacher. For each student, the writing portfolio became the central tool through which they developed their literacy skills, reading and writing, and learned to both communicate and critically examine their communication skills. Whether they were working on creative writing, a technical writing pattern for TAAS mastery, a research report, on analysis of literature; sharing personal experience; or critically reflecting on personal development, students were contributing to their portfolio. For me as teacher, the portfolios became the data from which to evaluate my students' explicit writing patterns and, more important, to gauge their implicit critical thinking patterns and often their emotional patterns.

TAAS Portfolio

Two other uses of portfolios became an integral part of my teaching and classroom management. First, I maintained a TAAS portfolio for each of my students. I designed a recording form to aid me in examining each student's progress toward demonstrating academic mastery as defined by the Texas Education System. This form provided space to record scores on pretests and post-tests aligned with TAAS. It also provided space for recording intermittent progress for each 6-week period. This portfolio, aligned with TAAS testing, served two purposes. On the one hand, it served as a diagnostic tool through which I could determine the language mechanics that the students continued to have difficulty mastering. On the other hand, this portfolio served as an authentic accountability measurement for me as teacher.

It's not easy for teachers to work within the tension created by an accountability system that does not take into consideration individual growth or rate of progress and uses a standardized test as the one-time, single measurement of growth. Because of the constant threat of having my effectiveness and professionalism judged by the TAAS results, I created a form to profile each student's starting point in my class, record students' intermittent progress, and profile students' ending point in my class. I used this data to personally evaluate my teaching effectiveness, knowing that the picture presented by looking only at the number of my students who passed the TAAS often was very incomplete in terms of the gains they had made in response to my effective teaching practices. I felt confident in being able to see the students' actual progress, rather than relying on the standard of measurement used in Texas. Although I keenly focused on the standard of measurement for success, I also focused on the portfolio of each student's development as a whole person.

Interdisciplinary Team Portfolio

A final way that I implemented portfolios was within the interdisciplinary team of which I was a member. The teams were composed of one teacher from each of the core content areas: math, science, language arts, reading, and social studies. Using two filing crates to hold 125 hanging files, my team members and I maintained an interdisciplinary team portfolio. The hanging files were labeled by students' names in alphabetical order. These files contained progress reports, 6-week report forms, disciplinary reports, conference forms, records of phone conferences, and any other artifacts deemed important by a member of the team. These interdisciplinary team portfolios were instrumental when conferencing with students or their parents. Noting any significant behavior problems was part of the data for the files, because poor performance in adolescents is sometimes caused by poor behavior, and changes in behavior often result from poor academic progress. Conferencing, both with the team and with the students and families, was necessary to determine what kind of assistance the students needed. As a language arts teacher, I utilized all the portfolios when conferencing with parents. I would pull the student's team file, work-in-progress file, finished products binder, and journal. This comprehensive portfolio system made it possible for me to address the Texas accountability system, provide for rich literacy development, and monitor my students' social and emotional development.

REFLECTION ON KNOWING ONE CHILD

In teaching, there are always children you never forget. I will never forget Waylen and the way in which my use of portfolios helped me to know about his struggles and how I could become a better teacher. I ran into him a few years ago in a store, where he and his wife had come to have a picture taken of their baby. Waylen was only 19 years old. I felt sad that he was not in college as I remembered how smart he was and his dreams of becoming a marine biologist. He had the intellectual potential but was lacking in the resources and family support that would have helped him fulfill his goal and dreams.

Meeting Waylen reminded me of the day that he turned in a creative writing piece about the animal he would choose to be if he could be any animal in the world, as a response to a prompt I had on the board one day for my seventh grade class. This is a good example of how a writing portfolio has the potential of facilitating understanding of adolescents through writing. When I reviewed Waylen's work, I saw that, in terms of mechanics and standards, Waylen demonstrated average writing abilities: correct indention, complete sentences, and correct usage and capitalization. Waylen's writing sample also revealed that he had not mastered other standard punctuation rules. His weaknesses interfered with his meaning. Although Waylen's writing lent itself to a punctuation lesson from me, I never got to address Waylen's mechanical mistakes. Instead, I heard Waylen's implicit message in his piece. Waylen was smart and creative and he communicated on a deep and insightful level. After reading this piece and having noticed other aspects of Waylen's behavior all year, it appeared that he was living with an abusive parent. I spoke to Waylen's teacher from the previous year and she reminded me of another of Waylen's journal entries that she had shared with me. In that entry Waylen described his father's pattern of outrageously brutal physical discipline with Waylen and his three brothers. He did not consider this pattern of behavior as abuse, but accepted it as the norm.

Waylen felt trapped in his home and I understood his sense of worthlessness along with his self-awareness of his intelligence: Waylen was smart enough to protect his dad in the guise of writing a "fictional" piece about a hunted animal. I know that teachers have both a legal and moral duty to report suspected child abuse and I followed appropriate reporting procedures, although Waylen, when confronted, said, "It's just a creative story that I made up."

Waylen was using his writing abilities as a way to cope with his life situation while trying to grow and learn. He often brought me imaginative stories, not for extra credit but to communicate as a writer and as a person. I know that teachers aren't therapists and that our primary role is supposed to be to educate children. However, English teachers often learn a great deal of personal information about the children in their classes and they respond to the important themes in what they read. True engagement in learning comes when children relate their own personal histories to the work in class. The writing portfolio for Waylen was an outlet for important events in his life and gave me, his teacher, an opportunity to promote his well-being in more ways than merely creating a composition based on what would later be on the standards exam. Writing gives children, particularly those who seem to be powerless, a real voice. Children's writing also gives the teacher an opportunity to provide for their developmental needs on many different levels. Of course, whenever abuse is revealed, the authorities must be informed.

CONCLUSION

The information in this chapter is not a manual that will guide you to a guaranteed successful experience in implementing portfolios in your classroom. You must examine my story of experience through a critical lens and realize that it was unique to my situation, embedded in my district's policy on portfolio use and responsive to the accountability system of the Texas Education System. After examining my experience, you must critically reflect on your personal situation as it is embedded in your school's curriculum, your district's policies, and your state's education system. Only then will you be in a position to exercise your professional responsibility to implement the best teaching practices and portfolio design for the optimal literacy development of your middle school students.

Reflections From the Bronx, New York

Carole Rhodes, Ph.D.
Associate Professor of Education, Adelphi University,
Garden City, New York

Many years ago, as a literacy consultant to District 10 in the Bronx, I walked into Bonnie Roberts' class and was amazed at her sixth-grade students as they engaged in thoughtful conversations about books they were reading and discussions about how their writing was improving and might improve further. It was clear that Bonnie allowed her students to take charge of their own learning. They shared their work with each other and they reflected on their growth and development as readers and writers. They were able to see concrete evidence of their progress as they leafed through the compilations of work each student gathered. The students were engaged in meaningful, thoughtful, and purposeful discussions about their literacy practices. Bonnie was an integral part of the process and the conversations as she directed the students to look at their work, reflect on their progress, and plan for their continued growth. Her expectations were high and so were those of her students. These middle school students clearly evidenced confidence, drive and a desire to become literate adults. The level of discussion, the accountable talk, the continual striving for excellence, and the reflective nature of the conversations might lead an observer to conclude that these were among the very able students. However, that was not the case. Bonnie's students lived in an area of New York City known for poverty, broken homes, violence, and a high level of illiteracy. They were labeled at-risk for failure, and many of their peers had failed. However, it was clear that many of Bonnie's students would break that pattern—and they did. [Note: Bonnie Roberts, formerly a reading teacher in Middle School 141, Bronx, New York, is now the Assistant Superintendent of District 10, where this middle school is located.]

LITERACY TEACHING IN A MIDDLE SCHOOL

An effective middle school literacy program must be built on an understanding of the developmental needs of young adolescents. Bonnie's literacy program did just that. It was student-centered, flexible, and responsive to students' needs (Davidson & Koppenhaver, 1993; Strauss, 2000). The students' interactions with their peers and their teacher helped form the framework within which they developed as effective and efficient literacy learners. For them, literacy learning was encased and negotiated within a social context (Bloome, 1989; Cazden, 1988; Heath, 1996; Hynds, 1997). Bonnie's literacy program was built on the notion that learning occurs over time, with each learner growing at a different pace. These students and their teacher documented and evaluated their progress through an archaeological dig of literacy artifacts compiled in each student's literacy portfolio.

Middle schools house students at a precarious time in their lives; their minds and bodies often are in disharmony with the world around them. Adolescence is a time when these students undergo more physical, social, emotional, and intellectual changes than at any other time in their lives. The physical changes are obvious and we can often see tremendous growth spurts, resulting in our students bumping into things, knocking things over, or tripping. Some young adolescents appear to be physically mature, yet their outward appearance masks what's going on inside. And how sad it is for those whose appearance doesn't keep pace with the rapid changes occurring with their peers. Physical changes often impact on the way young adults view themselves. Whereas intellectual changes may be less obvious, emotional changes often are revealed through behavior, such as mood swings, anger, depression, disappointment, and bouts of alternately caring about school, grades, and performance followed by a total lack of interest in being in school except for time spent with friends.

Educators who truly understand the special needs of young adolescents find that they must address their psychological and social needs to be effective teachers. Their students can be painfully self-conscious and require varied opportunities to be successful, recognize their own accomplishments, and have their accomplishments recognized by others. There are many educators who prefer the challenge of teaching middle school students who are at an extremely formative time in their lives. They see the emergence of abstract thought, self-reflection, and the struggle for independence. Using the students' curiosity, their need for social connections, and often argumentative nature, the successful middle school teacher can encourage students to take control of their own learning. They recognize that they must have classrooms that are, as Banks (1992) notes, learner-centered and which focus on the needs, interest and talents of the learners. Implicit in effective teaching is setting high standards as well as providing multiple opportunities for student success, and the documentation of that success. Building on the notion of learner-centered literacy classrooms, Powell, Skoog, and Troutman (1996) call for middle school students to be allowed "credible and autonomous voices." An effective portfolio process can certainly facilitate these goals and create a learning environment where middle school students have concrete evidence of their success and their teachers have better knowledge of their students.

LITERACY ASSESSMENT

Assessment is used primarily to educate and to improve student performance, not merely to audit it, and should be linked to instruction in ways that enrich learning. Effective assessment is authentic and should be used to improve teaching by revealing to students what quality work looks like. By reviewing models and exemplars, middle school students gain a clear understanding of the expectations, goals, and standards to which they are being held. Educators are fully aware that the public wants the schools to demonstrate that all students are learning and reaching appropriate standards. The standards movement has become a forceful way to articulate common goals regarding content and performance, which delineate specific expectations for teaching and learning, but more than ever before teachers are being held accountable for their students' performance.

Content standards often result in measuring learning through tests. Embedded in the notion of testing is an assumption that tests are credible and that they accurately measure student achievement, providing a yardstick to determine whether or not standards are being met. In far too many instances, reliance on tests has resulted in teaching to the test, and curriculum reform being driven by what's measured on tests. Unfortunately, standardized tests often measure only details and discrete tasks that have little relevance to real-life performance. What is more frustrating to middle school students than not measuring up to an external source of validation, the state test, that has no relevance to their interests, abilities, and life? We also need to question the wisdom of any assessment system that measures student performance by a "snapshot" approach when dynamic changes take place every day and true mastery requires time.

Another approach in assessment is the use of performance standards as better indicators of whether change has taken place. Performance standards ask the student to "do" the subject as they require a student to use a repertoire of knowledge and skill to negotiate a complex task. Portfolios provide a record of performance over time and are particularly useful with middle school students, who continually seek relevance and meaningfulness in their educational experiences. Middle school students measure success by real-world standards. Portfolios can be responsive to the developmental, social, and cognitive needs of these students because they are student-centered, flexible forms of documenting learning that show performance on day-to-day work in the classroom. They also give students real choices in what is representative of who they are and the quality of their work. Adolescents' strong need to engage in authentic learning tasks parallels the call among curriculum and assessment experts for the development of authentic performance measures (Krest, 1990; Valenica et al., 1990; Wiggins, 1989).

LITERACY PORTFOLIOS ARE PERFECT FOR MIDDLE SCHOOL LEARNERS

The opportunity to be given choices about what they are doing is vitally important to middle school students' educational and emotional needs. Literacy portfolios are created by choosing artifacts representative of the students' engagement in meaningful learning reading, writing, listening, and speaking curricula and provides the basis for real evidence of a student's profile of reading and writing ability. Literacy portfolios enable students to feel a sense of control and ownership in an assessment process that matters to them. Students also should have a clear understanding of what is being expected of them and be aware that portfolios show growth over time. Students should also view the portfolio as an opportunity to stretch their literacy boundaries and demonstrate that at this point in their lives they can integrate and apply what they have learned.

When I work with middle school teachers and their students on the concept of portfolios as representations of experiences, I often talk about my attic. In essence, my attic is my portfolio. If anyone were to walk up to my attic, they would see a compendium of artifacts which represent where I've been, what I've done and, in some cases, where I wanted to go. They might see artifacts that represent how I define my professional success (scrapbooks of published works, thank you letters from students, memos from colleagues) and they would see things that represent goals that were unsuccessfully completed (an unpublished novel, a discarded attempt at a literacy project). As I share why I kept some of these artifacts, the notion of selection and reflection becomes clear. Students often begin the portfolio process incorrectly by haphazardly gathering too many disorganized samples, thinking that a good portfolio contains a great deal of "stuff." As they learn more about the process, they begin to see that it needs to evolve into a more discrete, selective, and reflective process.

I've had ongoing conversations and worked collaboratively with groups of teachers and students in one urban middle school in the Bronx, New York. This group includes Phyliss Shulman, an Assistant Principal, and Alan Baer, an English teacher. Together we have spent a great deal of time talking about portfolios, standards, and their middle school students. We have all been in agreement that the students are fully capable of critical thinking and engaging in reflective thinking about their literacy. Crucial to the success of our work with the students is giving them opportunities to rehearse, practice, consult, obtain feedback, and refine their performance while building their portfolios.

Phyliss and Alan work well together. The school had not yet begun to implement portfolios, but both teachers began to recognize that their students were not actively engaged in the literacy process and felt that portfolios would be very helpful to them. Phyliss, Alan, and I explored the dynamics of one of Alan's classes. This class consisted of students from grades grade six though nine. At the beginning of the year, Alan shared his concerns about one of his students.

> Anthony was an accelerated student and came into the school with all the writing techniques one would expect from an intelligent, young teenager. For example, he *knew* that poetry rhymes, that a poem must talk about an important event, and that each line must begin with a capital letter. In short, Anthony knew very little about the important part of poetry—content—but he'd been getting very high grades for his efforts for many years. His first piece in class was a poem about his lost parrot, Captain. The class was in its second day when Anthony fired off his poem. He was looking to please by having his work ready in 1 day, thereby demonstrating that he was an excellent student because his product was quick, efficient, and orderly. I hadn't taken a sip of my coffee when his little arm shot a piece of paper across the bridge of my nose. His poem. Done. Finished. In neat handwriting (see Figure 1–15).
>
> It was clear that Captain meant a great deal to Anthony, but the words weren't expressing his feelings or the depth of the bond. The words were following a formula of what someone had told Anthony a poem was to look like. He asked me what I thought of his work. I didn't answer directly, I simply asked him a few questions about his affection for Captain. Then, I asked Anthony to look over his poem and ask himself if any of the things he said about Captain were in there. He said no, except for the last line. I told him that he should keep that last line because it told the truth. Also, I asked Anthony to write a few memories of Captain, not rhymes, not sentences, not paragraphs, just a few lines. Simple lines, and memories. I asked Anthony not to think about writing a poem, just think of Captain, and memories, and a few lines. I offered no practical advice, and offered nothing one would consider useful, unless like Anthony, one is already on the road to "getting it."

Phyliss shared her concerns:

> Writing wasn't taken seriously. An assignment was handed out, a paper was handed in, and a grade was given to the student. What were the criteria for that grade? Was there a model for the student to follow? Did the student discover anything in the writing of that paper? The more important question: Did our students enjoy writing? What did they want to write about, and was there any opportunity for them to explore the kinds of things they wanted to write about? How many assignments were given that had to be handed in the next day, regardless of whether it was finished? And what constituted a finished product?

Alan had distinct ideas about how he was going to initiate a portfolio process. The writing class was one opportunity for me to take some of the ideas we all had discussed and put them into practice. I wanted to create a place for students to write freely and really think about their goals as writers. Also, I had hoped that the class would bear out some of the truths about the middle school student: They are absolutely able to run their world if given the chance. They "get it" far more quickly than we would like to admit, and when they don't "get it" and really want to "get it", they ask questions.

We talked a great deal about students taking ownership of their work. We ask them to select pieces that they wish to include in their portfolios, but the pieces they choose are not often genuine choices because they are often work assigned to them by a teacher that received good grades. When the teacher acknowledges the student's work with a high grade, the student feels proud of the work, but unfortunately the work shows that the student has succeeded in fulfilling a teacher's criteria for success. How often do students get the opportunity to take a project of their choice, work it from beginning to end, analyze the problems encountered along the way, reflect on their work, and ultimately present it to a willing, enthusiastic audience? We have begun to try to turn things around on a small scale. Our writing class is a model of how we would like all students to learn in each of the subject areas.

Anthony now had some criteria for which to judge his work. He browsed through his portfolio and decided that the poem about his pet did not truly reflect his true feeling

Prewriting

Writing Class   12/13/00

A Great Pet
a poem by Anthony

rating: 8.9
rating: 9.6
rating: 8.5
rating: 8.9

I once had a pet.
an amazon parrot to be exact.
He was very green,
and very clean.
I enjoyed playing
and talking with him,
although all he would say
was hello.
I remember that day,
when he flew away.
I knew that I would
miss him,
for the rest of my life.
Forever.

FIGURE 1–15

nor did it represent work that met the standards. He worked diligently to revise the poem and included it in his portfolio only when he felt it met the standards and criteria with which he was now familiar (see Figure 1–16).

Anthony and his classmates were engaged in thoughtful conversations about their reading and writing. The focus in their reading encounters was on the transactions they had with text. They became far less concerned with remembering facts about a book and far more concerned with what the book meant to them and ways in which they could make the literary experience a building block for others. When looking at writing, there was less emphasis on writing mechanics as the most important measure of success. The students in this class began to think more about good writing and created these charts to list what they felt to be most important (see Figure 1–17). The students began to look at their writing as something important to them, not just work to be graded by the teacher.

The middle school team of teachers worked to develop portfolio guidelines for the students. As Figure 1–18 shows, the guidelines were clear indicators of what was expected. Guidelines were also given to the teachers to help their students with the development of portfolios. Phyliss sent them the letter shown in Figure 1–19.

The implementation of literacy portfolios took time. As teachers embraced the process, so too did their students. Pedro, an eighth-grade student, chose to place in his portfolio a memoir, written about a time that was particularly painful for him. Annie, a seventh-grade student, chose a poem that also reflected some painful emotions. These types of selection are common with middle school youngsters. They often use their writing to try to make sense of their world, to vent feelings, or to express emotions that they too often cannot voice in any other way. Pedro's essay in Figure 1–20 is an example of this. Students were asked to reflect on why a piece should be put into the portfolio. Pedro reflected on his submission:

> My memoir of my parents' divorce was very important because it was the single most emotional point in my life thus far. I felt sadness too powerful for tears. I had lots of emotions bottled up with no form of release. So I wrote about it. Writing relieved me of all the stress, stress that held an emotional barrier, but was knocked down. This writing piece was probably my most emotional yet it also showed that I had come a long way from 6th grade in my writing. It was also the best that I had, and showed my kind of writing. That made it perfect for my portfolio.

Annie, a seventh-grade student wrote the following poem (shown in Figure 1–21). As in Pedro's piece, Annie's reflection revealed her thoughts and turmoil:

> During the summer before the 7th grade I was extremely insecure with displaying my true emotions and my appearance. I had put all of these near impossible goals on my shoulders and felt as if I had to always look happy. It was as if I was wearing a mask. In the poem, all of the people I love are trying to find out who I am: my true self, as sappy as it may sound. I chose to put this poem into my portfolio because it caught a snapshot of how I was feeling at a certain time. I also think that other people can apply their lives to this poem, because insecurity is a universal theme.

The teachers in this school have seen the success of this approach with their students. They report that there is far less "paper work" and more conversation about content. Teachers need to really understand the purpose of a portfolio to share this with their students and to help their students. Because there are many options, a dilemma that these teachers still face is how they want the portfolio to be used. Is it to be a showcase portfolio, highlighting the student's best work? Should it be a work in progress, containing all drafts and the process the student went through to get to a final piece? To be successful, a portfolio must become part of the everyday life of the students and the teachers. It should be an integral part of the classroom, as important as the notebook, pen, and paper. It should be a place of self-reflection, self-evaluation, and self-review. And most important, the literacy artifacts that go into the portfolio should be genuine, purposeful, and meaningful.

My Noble Parrot

When I come to him he hides,
When I find him he flies.
In his cage he is so noble and strong,
In the rain he squeaks so loud.
In the night he used to stalk me
like a spy
or someone that
does not want to be seen.
He used to fly around the house
and bump into everything in sight.
I would put out my arm,
and he would fly to me
like a faithful eagle.

I remember that day,
when he flew away
I knew that I would miss him
for the rest of my life...

Forever...

FIGURE 1–16

	Well Done	Almost	Getting There	Needs Help	Go Back and Try Again
Content	Story should have vivid description. The story should give the reader a strong visual sense. The individuality of the author should be jumping off the page. The topic should be interesting, and the writing should be focused. Author handles the use of higher vocabulary well, and it works in the piece. The piece should be detailed and the details should be relevant and interesting. Emotion and feeling should drip off the page. Author reflection is evident instead of cold analysis. The piece should grab the reader's attention from the very first line.	Story has some vivid description. Story gives reader some visual sense. The individuality of the author is present. The topic is interesting, and mostly focused. There is evidence of an attempt at proper use of higher vocabulary. The piece is mostly detailed and is mostly relevant and interesting. There is emotion and feeling for the most part. The piece grabs the reader early in the piece, but not from the start.	Story has limited vivid language. There is only limited evidence of visualization. Vocabulary is limited. There is little evidence of details, and they are not completely relevant. There is some emotion, but it is not well conveyed. The piece doesn't get the reader's attention right away.	Story has weak description. Little visualization evident. Vocabulary is weak. Details are sketchy at best. The piece doesn't grab the reader's attention except in a few places.	Opening is unrelated and irrelevant. No feeling or emotion. Topic doesn't capture the reader's attention. Constant digression. No descriptive details. Story doesn't flow. Choppy. The piece lacks individuality. Author's voice is not present at all. Vocabulary poor. Same words used over and over. Looks like it took 5 minutes to write. The reader's imagination is not challenged.
Mechanics	Grammar, spelling, punctuation should be edited, and written correctly. Paper should be legible. Verb tenses should agree when appropriate.	Grammar, punctuation, spelling are mostly correct. Paper is mostly legible. Most verb tenses agree.	Grammar, etc. are not properly edited. Paper is not legible.	Sketchy and spotty use of grammar, punctuation, spelling. Paper is illegible.	Nothing close to correct.

FIGURE 1–17 Personal Narrative Criteria Chart.

The David A. Stein Riverdale MS 141

Portfolio Guidelines for Students

A portfolio is a compilation of your work selected from each subject area. It will include work that is meaningful, work that makes you proud, and shows both progress and achievement.

In each of your classes you will have a folder that will be used to gather all your assigned work. You will choose specific pieces of work from the class folder to add to your portfolio.

You will be given a checklist of the types of items you might wish to put in your portfolio. Your portfolio should include a variety of the following items:

- essays, research papers, narratives, verse
- brainstorming sheets, planning sheets, outlines, webs, notes
- journals or journal pages, notebooks, learning logs
- graphs, charts
- drawings, collages, paintings
- tests, quizzes, exams
- photographs of items too large to fit into your portfolio
- evidence of group projects, planning sheets, daily logs, notes
- audiotapes, videotapes
- computer disks

Any work you choose to include in your portfolio should demonstrate:

- thoughtful and insightful work
- improvement
- effort
- achievement

Finally, you will write your thoughts about each piece of work you select. At the end of the year, you will write your thoughts about your portfolio as a whole. These self-reflections will help you evaluate your progress and growth throughout the year.

Good luck!

FIGURE 1–18 Sample portfolio guidelines for students.

CONCLUSION

It would be naive to think that simply adding a portfolio process to a literacy program will make it an excellent program. However, based on the experiences of these teachers in a demanding, urban setting thinking about portfolios is an enhancement for both teachers and their students. Middle school students want their education to be meaningful and they want choices. They also want to feel good about themselves, and certainly this is a time in their life when they have the ability to use higher-level thinking skills and apply reading and writing to everyday life situations. These teachers have found that giving students reading materials that interest them and creating a "safe" place to collect their thoughts are key to success. As these teachers and students demonstrate that they are capable of reaching high standards, portfolio practice is a meaningful aspect of good teaching and helpful assessment. Undoubtedly, their use of portfolios will change each year and be different in various classes, but the portfolio process is flexible enough to accommodate all students. The portfolio also gives these teachers greater insight into the "inner" life of their complicated, adolescent students and provides the kind of information that they need to make them more effective with each student.

Riverdale Kingsbridge Academy

January 2001

Dear Teachers,

All students are required to choose at least one piece of work from each subject area to include in their student portfolio. Portfolio contents must represent what the students are doing in their classes and reflect their progress toward instructional goals.

Unlike single test scores and multiple-choice tests, portfolios provide a multidimensional perspective on student growth over time. The use of portfolios encourages students to reflect on their work, to analyze their progress, and to set improvement goals.

Along with samples of student work, portfolios should include student self-assessment and clearly stated criteria on which their work was graded. The sample should include all drafts and a final product.

The self-assessment can be one of the following: documentation, comparison, and integration.

Documentation: The student provides a justification for the item selected for the portfolio. Why did he/she pick this piece? The student can indicate that the piece was chosen because he/she liked the topic or liked what he/she said.

Comparison: Students compare a recent piece of work with an earlier one by looking for ways that they have improved.

Integration: Students use the portfolio to provide examples of their growing strengths in oral or written language, or their independence as learners.

Finally, students need to know how their work will be evaluated and by what standard their work will be judged. Criteria charts outlining the specific standards and specific goals must be included in the portfolio.

The portfolios will be reviewed by the supervisors on your floor and may be viewed by parents, the Instructional Support Team, guidance counselors, and other staff members. These portfolios serve as vehicles for observing gradual change and for helping teachers make professional judgments about individual students.

Phyliss Shulman
Assistant Principal

FIGURE 1–19 Phyliss' Letter. *Source:* Courtesy of P. Shulman.

I am writing about an event in my life that I know every child fears in the backs of their minds. For me it was a reality, as it probably has been for some of you. It happened two years ago—it is the memory of my parent's divorce.

My parents had already been separated for a few months. It was routine not to see my dad around the house anymore. We still saw him on weekends, but it felt hollow somehow. That night, the night it happened, my father came to us while we were watching TV, and told us to turn it off.

"Guys," he said, " you know I love you and your mother very much, but I think," he started to sniffle, "I may never be coming back." My little brother and he began to sob. I wasn't crying, though; I don't cry during the saddest moments, I just sat and felt empty. As I sat, I thought; I thought of what it will be like without him, and what will he do? I went to sleep thinking, and still feeling badly, as though it as my fault.

In the year that followed, I saw my dad more often than I had when he was living at home. Every Friday after school we would go to his apartment, and sleep over. We took a couple of trips together; once to Disney World, and once to Hershey Park.

Then, one summer night, my whole family went out for dinner to Park Place. Out of nowhere, my dad tells me to hold onto some rings, I think it was their engagement rings. I was nervous that I might lose them, like in one of those wedding movies. This didn't happen, though. I was elated to see my dad again, the two-year emptiness was filling up, again. The only downside was that the food took an hour to arrive.

FIGURE 1–20 Pedro's Essay. *Source:* Courtesy of P. Shulman.

FIGURE 1–21 Annie's Poem.

Hide and Seek by Annie (8th grade)

She quickly runs to a hiding spot
As they count,
1 . . . 2 . . . 3 . . .
looking for her.

They search far and wide,
over vast valleys and
seas,
seeking traces of her,
but
she is hidden so profoundly
under a great shell that is thick
and unbreakable.
No one will ever find her

REFERENCES

Banks, J., Darling-Hammond, L. & Greene, M. (1992). *Building learner-centered schools: Three perspectives*. New York: NCREST, Teachers College Press.

Bloome, D. (1989). Beyond access: An ethnographic study of reading and writing in a seventh grade classroom. In D. Bloome (Ed.), *Classrooms and literacy* (pp. 53–106). Norwood, NJ: Ablex.

Cazden, C. B. (1988). *Classroom discourse: The language of teaching and learning*. Portsmouth, NH: Heinemann.

Davidson, J., & Koppenhaver, D. (1993). *Adolescent literacy: What works and why*. New York: Garland.

Heath, S. B. (1996). A lot of talk about nothing. In B. M. Power & R. S. Hubbard (Eds.), *Language development: A reader for teachers* (pp. 55–60). Englewood Cliffs, NJ: Merrill.

Hynds, S. (1997). *On the brink: Negotiating literature and life with adolescents*. New York: Teachers College Press.

Krest, M. (1990). Adapting the portfolio to meet student needs. *English Journal, 79*(2), 29–34.

Powell, R., Skoog, G., & Troutman, P. (1996). On streams and odysseys: Reflections on reform and research in middle level integrative learning environments. *Research in Middle Level Education Quarterly, 19*(4), 1–30.

Strauss, S. E. (2000). Literacy learning in the middle grades: An investigation of academically effective middle grades schools. Unpublished doctoral dissertation. Florida State University, Tallahassee.

Valencia, S., McGinnley, W., & Pearson, P. D. (1990). Assessing reading and writing. In G. Duffy (Ed.), *Reading in the Middle School* (2nd ed, pp. 124–153). Newark, DE: International Reading Association, 124–53.

Wiggins, G. (1989). A true test: Toward more authentic and equitable assessment. *Phi Delta Kappan, 70*(9), 703–13.

CHAPTER

2

Introducing Portfolio Practices

KEY WORDS AND CONCEPTS

portfolio writing folder
literacy portfolio

portfolio process
standards movement

As an old song laments, "The times they are a-changing," and these are certainly changing times in schools all across the country. School reform is a dramatic part of national headlines. Locally and nationally there are strong statements about the need for revised policies, and many voices complain about what's wrong with American education and propose how schools should be changed. New curricula have resulted from directives issued by state education departments, local school boards, curriculum coordinators, and school administrators, who now provide the expected and specific educational outcomes for students of all ages. Incorporating learning opportunities that promote the acquisition of skills, strategies, and knowledge needed to demonstrate the attainment of these standards has required teachers to modify their educational goals and certainly to change what is being taught and how it is being presented. The public demands that educators be accountable for what goes on in the classroom and they need to be assured that students are reaching new and higher standards for learning. The pressure on teachers is tremendous—pressure to teach to the standards and pressure to demonstrate that all students can reach these new and higher standards of educational attainment. Consequently, evaluating performance is an integral part of the current direction in educational reform from kindergarten classrooms through twelfth grade and even at the university level. Concern with testing seems to override quality instruction in many classrooms, and it certainly takes up a great amount of instructional time!

Literacy acquisition is the cornerstone of all educational accomplishment and without proficient reading and writing skills, an individual's prospects for life success and personal gratification are diminished. Assessing and documenting students' literacy learning has always been a concern of the classroom teacher. Whereas standardized tests are mandated by school districts and state education departments, portfolio use can enrich the assessment model by supplementing information from tests and providing more meaningful information for classroom teachers. Portfolios used in literacy programs not only document and assess what children learn but also promote literacy attainment. A growing number of teachers are using portfolios not only to showcase children's literacy learning by collecting and reflecting with their students on their actual work but also to foster the development of literacy. Observing students during learning, collecting their work, and collaborating and developing goals with them are essential components of performance based assessment through the use of a portfolio process. Portfolios provide the materials that encourage students to reflect on what they learn each day and provide a convenient means by which to demonstrate how students construct knowledge and apply strategies as they grow and learn.

Portfolios are the ideal structure for the assessment of what children actually learn because they fully capture the accomplishments of the learner and document children's growth. Teachers and learners can provide clear evidence that specific standards have been incorporated into the students' knowledge base through their work as shown in their portfolio. It is no longer a dilemma to fully capture children's literacy and learning growth. Test scores, report card grades, narrative teacher comments, cumulative record folders, completed assignments, and filled workbooks have traditionally been used to document children's academic accomplishments, but they never provided as full a picture of what children actually do during a school year as does a highly descriptive portfolio.

DEVELOPMENT OF PORTFOLIOS WITH PRESSURE FOR ACCOUNTABILITY

Because of continued criticism about the quality of education and a general concern that schools have been failing the need to document learning outcomes has increased. Many experts have called for the use of new forms of educational assessment, because traditional forms of assessment were being rethought as literacy instruction was transformed. Critics called for assessment methods that were both congruent with newer classroom practices and fairer to all students, allowing for greater sensitivity to differences in gender, ethnicity, and race. With the call to restructure schools, create site-based management, and provide for teacher empowerment, dramatic changes were required not only in curriculum and instruction but also in assessment practices (Gomez & Schenk, 1992).

The concerns about documenting student learning outcomes is now even more evident as part of the "Standards Movement." The increasingly important role of oversight in education is dramatically evident when almost all states have adopted standards-based reform, which translates into specific learning outcomes for students of all ages. Some, however, question whether such reform makes sense as a strategy to ensure that all students have opportunity for learning (Claycomb & Kysilko, 2000). Essentially, standards specify learning outcomes, uniform goals and, unfortunately, uniform measurement. Many school districts are now busy not only aligning curricula with the new learning standards, but attempting to determine how a given assessment can be coordinated with new learning outcomes. For example, New York has recently developed exams in the English language arts that are noticeably process oriented and incorporate writing to determine if students are able to read and write with appropriate proficiency in response to reading literature and text material. These tests measure what students have learned by requiring written responses. Unfortunately, once states adopt new tests, these tests dominate teaching practices and often take up valuable instructional time. It's no longer a cliché to lament the problem of teaching for the test—it's common practice and required in many places! A Colorado educator recently reported that she had been very proud of her school's writing program and was shocked when the students did not perform at the outstanding level of her state's exam. Lack of preparation for this particular test format was found to be the underlying cause and she, as well as all teachers in her school, will have to devote more instructional time to simple test preparation. Figure 2–1 is a humorous look at an alarming trend.

FIGURE 2–1 *Source: Flying by the Seat of Your Pants: More Absurdities and Realities of Special Education* © by Michael F. Giangreco 1999, Peytral Publications, Inc. Minnetonka, MN.

As part of the accountability movement, reading and writing are targeted as essential curriculum areas and scrutinized to determine if teaching and learning in these areas are effective. A major shift in the theory of language arts teaching called for integrative literacy methodology, as well as more direct application of language skills across curriculum areas. Combining portfolios with assessment, however, is relatively new and might have first reached national attention at a 1990 conference of the National Conference of Teachers of English, when the term "portfolio" became "portfolio assessment" because the national climate called for a more dynamic kind of assessment approach in the language arts (Murphy & Underwood, 2001). The portfolio process was quickly adopted by many as a new form of what came to be called authentic assessment. Now it is more commonly referred to as performance based assessment, which demonstrates what students are actually doing in the classroom.

DEFINING THE PORTFOLIO

The term "portfolio," and certainly the concept of portfolio assessment, is a recent addition in education, but the use of portfolios in the workplace is familiar. Artists, models, photographers, and others collect their work in a binder or large portfolio to demonstrate their skills and accomplishments by showing samples of their work. In a competitive marketplace, many job seekers, including prospective teaching candidates, are using portfolios to seek employment. Encouraged to collect and save their projects, papers, and work samples, job applicants approach an interview with a large portfolio that clearly and concretely represents their capabilities.

The term "portfolio" has also been widely used in finance. As early as the 1950s, an investment portfolio described a collection of investments specifically chosen according to certain criteria to maximize return (Seger, 1992). Investors were encouraged to periodically review and reflect on their portfolio to determine if goals were being met. The use of portfolios in education is fairly recent and can be traced to the mid-1980s, when several trends fostered their use in classrooms. However, many educators acknowledge that while the term "portfolio" is relatively modern in education, and some even consider it part of "postmodern" thinking, aspects of portfolio practice have been a traditional aspect of elementary school classrooms (Murphy & Underwood, 2001). Portfolios can be connected to writing folders, which have been an integral part of the writing process approach. Using professional writers as a model, classroom teachers encouraged their students to maintain a collection of their writing in a folder to work on and periodically review. It was important to accumulate students' ongoing work and provide a safe place to store and collect their writing. Ultimately, when these works were edited, polished, and ready to publish (i.e., share with others), they were often displayed in another folder that showed the students' finished pieces. These writing folders showcased the students' writing accomplishments. As teachers began to incorporate the use of reading logs, self-reflective journals, and other written responses to literature as part of daily classroom practice, they saw the need to save these collections as well; hence the emergence of literacy portfolios. This practice was a natural outgrowth of changing methodologies for teaching reading and writing and incorporated new thinking about assessment using a performance-based model, especially with the call to demonstrate students' actual writing ability.

Early childhood teachers also used a portfolio process when they saved students' work in large folders that contain artwork, dictated stories and pictures, or stories using invented spelling. These work folders have been an important aspect of tracing a child's development from a nonreader and nonwriter into an individual whose emergent literacy was evolving. An accumulation of a student's work can easily be reviewed and reflected on to document accomplishment, to identify instructional needs, and to show growth over time.

Although portfolios are becoming widely used and discussed, their definition is confounded by different notions of purpose, type, and format. Murphy and Underwood (2001) make an important point: "When portfolios move beyond classroom walls, they often serve multiple agendas . . . [and] portfolio purposes range along a continuum—

from those of individual students using portfolios to learn in the classroom and to represent themselves to others at one end, to government agencies using the information from portfolios to make decisions about policy and the distribution of resources at the other" (p. ix). Consequently the description and definition of a portfolio has been flexible enough to accommodate its use in many different contexts, with very different purposes. Seger (1992) used an excellent metaphor to describe the evolution of the portfolio phenomenon and the confusion over its definition: "Defining portfolio from such multiple notions would be like an early biologist trying to define mammal when presented with a whale, a human being, and a bat" (pp. 115–116). Ambiguities about portfolios exist, but an often cited and widely accepted definition was developed by the Northwest Evaluation Association and refined by Arter and Spandel (1992), who define a student portfolio as:

> a purposeful collection of student work that tells the story of the student's efforts, progress, or achievement in [a] given area[s]. This collection must include student participation in selection of portfolio content; the guidelines for selection; the criteria for judging merit; and evidence of student reflection. (p. 36)

A review of the literature about portfolios reveals several *essential and commonly cited features*:

- Entries for the portfolio are collected in a *semipermanent holder*, where they should be kept safe but must be readily available for the students' and teacher's use. Reading and writing folders are often used to provide materials from which students and teachers select entries for the portfolio.

- Products chosen for a portfolio are the result of *collaboration* between student and teacher, but the contents must reflect the student's ownership and reflection. Criteria for a portfolio collection *should be jointly established* by the students and the teacher to shape the contents of the collection.

- Works chosen for the collection reflect established *criteria*. A portfolio collection is not a random accumulation of items but results from a purposeful review of potential entries chosen to demonstrate various criteria. Works chosen can reflect the range of the student's abilities, growth in the student's accomplishments, or demonstration of student's special pride in a particular outcome. A table of contents or letter of introduction demonstrates how the collection reflects a meaningful system of organization.

- Significant to the portfolio collection are the *student's thoughts*, often shared with the teacher, that reflect on such concerns as the student's interests, the student's perceptions of the literacy process, evaluation of the literacy products in the collection, literacy goals, and how the student's literacy behaviors have changed. Ultimately, self-reflection leads to a sense of ownership and pride in one's own unique accomplishments.

- Works chosen for the collection present a *chronological development* over time to document the student's progress with literacy. It is therefore essential that all portfolio entries be dated.

- Works chosen *document* the student's ability to use reading and writing for learning in a variety of meaningful ways. Crucial to this concept, the materials chosen reflect authentic, or real, classroom activities and have not been constructed just for the portfolio.

- Entries demonstrate a *variety* of tasks showing the ability to purposefully use reading and writing in various contexts.

- Portfolios also contain *communications* between students, between students and teachers, as well as between students and their families.

- Portfolios often contain *additional material*, including teacher-completed checklists, anecdotal observation, or informal assessments (e.g., miscue analysis, running records) as well as audiotapes or videotapes of the student's literacy performances.

THE PORTFOLIO PROCESS

In this text we refer to a portfolio process and specifically recommend the use of a particular form of portfolio described in Chapter 4. We feel that the portfolio process is distinguished from the simple collection of work into a portfolio, because it is an ongoing process of observations, assessments, conferences, collaborations, and dialogues, including the following:

- Self-reflection by the student, who thinks about and chooses the portfolio selections. (See Figure 2–2 in which Stephen, a struggling second grader, reflects on his reading and writing skills.)
- Dialogue among students as they collaborate, edit, conference, or select projects for their portfolios. (See Figure 2–3 in which Patricia comments on the work of her fifth-grade classmate, Lisa.)
- Self-reflection of the teacher, who observes, describes, and analyzes the student's literacy strategies.

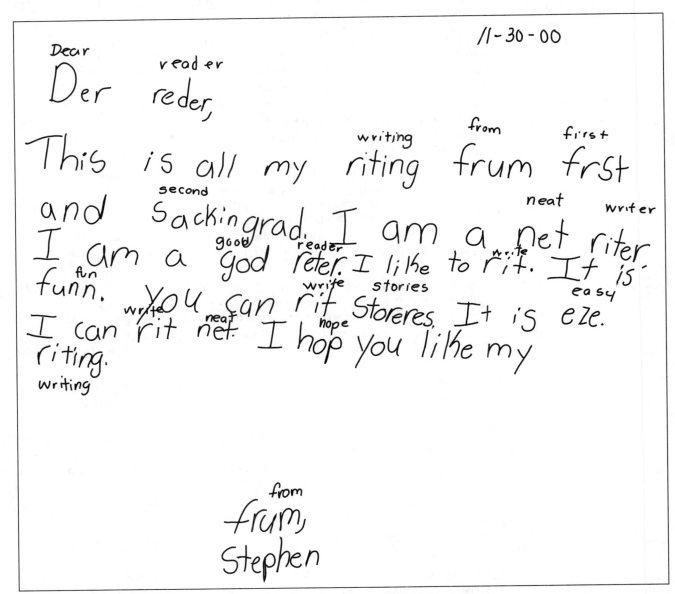

FIGURE 2–2 A second grade student with reading disabilities reflects on his skills.

**Classmate Review Sheet
(intermediate-Grade Level)**

Name of Portfolio Owner ___Lisa___ Grade _5_ Student Teacher _Mrs. A._

Name of Student Who Reviewed This Piece of Writing _Patricia_

Title of Paper _Emma Lazarus_

Date Written _November_

Date Evaluated _November 25_

1. What do you think was especially good about this piece of writing? _I liked that Lisa included many facts, dates and important information about Emma Lazarus and now I know more about her!_

2. Why do you think the writer chose to do this piece of writing? _I think Lisa chose Emma Lazarus because she was an interesting person, she had many things happen to her and Lisa seemed to know alot about her_

3. Suggest one thing for the writer to work on next in his or her writing. _I think maybe Lisa should try poetry because Emma Lazarus was a poet and wrote many famous poems. Lisa seemed to like doing her biography report on her too._

FIGURE 2–3 Classmate Review Sheet (Intermediate-Grade Level). *Source:* From ALTERNATIVE ASSESSMENT TECHNIQUES FOR READING AND WRITING by Wilma Miller Copyright © 1995. Reprinted with permission of Center for Applied Research in Education/Prentice Hall Direct.

- Dialogue between the student and the teacher during portfolio conferences as they reflect on the student's literacy development.
- Dialogue between students and family that demonstrates how literacy skills are evolving.
- Dialogue among the student, the student's family, and the teacher, all of whom use the portfolio as the centerpiece for describing, evaluating, and celebrating the student's literacy development. (See Figure 2–4 in which a parent responds to viewing her son's portfolio.)

Portfolios are also a vehicle for dialogue between members of an instructional team so that they can clearly understand a student's daily performance. This dialogue process can be continued by using the portfolio as means of providing accountability to the stakeholders—the school, families, and other concerned individuals who want clear evidence of student achievement and progress. Obviously, under this scheme a portfolio

FIGURE 2–4 Parents of grade 5 student respond to their son's portfolio.

Thanks for giving us the opportunity to view Matthew's portfolio. During the school year, we only see a portion of Matthew's work as the majority of the writing assignments are done in the classroom. Going through the portfolio enabled us to see how Matt has evolved as a writer and to catch a glimpse of his "creative" side.

Matthew has always enjoyed reading both fiction and non-fiction. While he has always been a strong reader, we feel his willingness to tackle new material is admirable and has enabled him to achieve continued growth in his reading skills. We encourage him by helping him to select books of varied subject matter and difficulty.

As can be seen by his reading choices, Matthew has a wonderful imagination and we feel writing gives him the opportunity to express himself. With the varied assignments that he has been given, Matt has had the chance to practice writing in different styles. We feel that there is always room for improvement particularly in his grammar and vocabulary. Our family has always stressed the importance of reading and writing and this portfolio has given Matthew the opportunity to showcase both skills.

Thanks again,
[signature]

process involves changes in instructional strategies and is more intricate than the simple collection of student work in a new kind of folder.

In summary, by viewing a student's portfolio, the observer should have an excellent picture of the unique features of an individual student's literacy growth and accomplishment. According to Paulson, Paulson, and Meyer (1991), a portfolio becomes a true portfolio

> when it provides a complex and comprehensive view of student performance in context. It is a portfolio when the student is a participant in, rather than the object of, assessment. Above all, a portfolio is a portfolio when it provides a forum that encourages students to develop the abilities needed to become independent, self-directed learners. (p. 63)

The portfolio concept grows and wanes in acceptance, and this trend is likely to continue. Portfolio acceptance reflects the dialogue and tension between those who support standardized forms of assessment and those who call for performance measures, such as portfolios, which are seen as "softer", more time-consuming and, therefore, less useful for demonstrating accountability to state and legislative stakeholders. Conversations with teachers reveal an acceptance of a portfolio process, but they also raise concerns about finding time for portfolios given all the curricular mandates that currently consume classrooms. Graves (1992) also cautioned that portfolios have quickly become popular, sometimes without appropriate reflection: "In a few short years, states and school systems have moved from reading about portfolios to mandating them as evaluation instruments for large school populations [and their] possibilities . . . may be lost . . . in the rush to mandate their use" (p. 1). Graves acknowledged that the portfolio process has multiple applications and can be particularly useful in evaluation and instructional decision making. Learning to use portfolios well takes effort and training and may require shifting priorities, changing instructional practices, and certainly careful time management.

From the time that portfolios became popular in classrooms to the present, portfolio use has varied greatly. It has been widely adopted and supported by many classroom teachers but attempted and discarded by others who have legitimate concerns about time management and balancing competing curricular mandates. Its use has been required by some state education departments and school administrators as part of students' permanent records, and portfolios have even been adopted as part of state-wide assessment systems in such diverse school environments as Kentucky and Vermont. The use of portfolios is not without controversy and it is our opinion that portfolios will never replace standardized tests, because reliance on tests, scores, and numbers is too ingrained in the public's mind and complements the current concern for accountability in the current political climate. However, it is clear that educators recognize that portfolios provide the kind of performance assessment that is needed to evaluate the attainment of standards that policy makers want students to develop and that multiple-choice tests do not and cannot measure more sophisticated and complex aspects of learning (Claycomb & Kysilko, 2001). The richness of a portfolio process must be balanced with time for qualitative involvement and deliberation.

BENEFITS OF A LITERACY PORTFOLIO PROCESS

Why should teachers and schools support the use of portfolios? The following list of benefits gained from the use of portfolios in a literacy program is quite compelling:

Portfolios Increase Teachers' Knowledge About Each Student and Increase Students' Self-Knowledge

The portfolio process gives the teacher a picture of the interests, abilities, goals, learning strategies, and outcomes of individual students. Each portfolio is truly a unique reflection of its creator. From the variety of cover illustrations to the stimulating array of entry types, each portfolio can be used to learn more about even the most introverted students. Because the process requires self-reflection as well as collaboration, thoughtful dialogue between the student and the teacher creates instructional opportunities. The portfolio process is augmented by teacher observation of the student in various instructional settings, so the teacher gains a wide range of insights into how an individual child learns and functions in various educational contexts, including:

- Background knowledge about the student's life outside of school, such as interests, hobbies, preferences, experiences, reactions, and attitudes;
- Insights about the student's ability in reading many different types of materials in multiple contexts and across subject areas;
- Information about the student's ability in writing with various genres in many contexts;
- Knowledge about the student's use of language skills throughout the curriculum;
- Observations of the student's ability to engage in self-reflection and use of metacognitive strategies;
- Documentation of developmental growth in literacy throughout the school year;
- Awareness of the student's goals and priorities;
- Demonstration of the student's ability to engage in collaboration with peers and to use constructive criticism and feedback;
- Opportunities for the student to demonstrate self-initiative as well as self-monitoring strategies; and
- Knowledge of how the student's sense of self can be enhanced.

Teachers who have been using the process with primary students in Juneau, Alaska (Juneau School District, 1993), commented positively on how portfolios have helped them know children better:

It certainly lends itself to analyzing each student's strengths and weaknesses in depth. It's ongoing and process oriented. You learn by doing it.

The process of observing children and their learning has been incredible—most valuable. Language arts, ongoing learning, myself frazzled, but it's been worth it!

Figure 2–5 illustrates how a sixth-grade student reflected on her literacy skills as part of the portfolio process. Recognizing this student's frustration with reading and her motivation to write are important for knowing how to address her literacy needs.

Portfolios Improve the Quality of Teaching

A major benefit of the portfolio process is its ability to merge instruction with assessment and thereby improve teaching. The teacher's ongoing evaluations are central to the relationship between assessment and instruction. As teachers observe children and meet with them to discuss and reflect on their work, they receive valuable information about how each child is progressing. These data are then used to make informed instructional decisions: what needs reinforcement, what skills have been acquired, what the child is ready to attempt, what materials work particularly well, what motivates the child, and what is the best way to proceed and succeed with each individual child.

A key to the success of the portfolio process is the authenticity of the entries that can be collected, because they are the direct outcome of instructional practices and classroom assignments. Because the very product of instruction is the medium by which the teacher assesses the child, there is compatibility between assessment and instruc-

> Myself as a reader and a writer
>
> I think I am not a great reader because of my disabilities. I am not able to say hard words without trying to sound them out of a long period of time. When I read it gets me very frustrated I am not able to say a word and I feel like throwing the book across the room. As a writer I think that I am good because I really like to write long stories. Sometimes I can not even read what I wrote. When I write my stories I like to get straight to the point so that people could understand what I am writing about.

FIGURE 2–5 A sixth-grade student reflects on her literacy skills.

tion. As each child interprets the assignments and produces work that indicates unique capacities and experiences, the evaluation process becomes part of who that child is. Consequently, the diversity between children, given the variability in life experiences, capacities, and language skills, is reflected in the portfolio process; there is complete harmony between how to assess and how to instruct, regardless of the wide range of differences between students.

Gooding (1994) sought to determine if performance-based assessment changes the nature of instructional practices and found that the use of alternative assessment does influence the relationship between teacher and student as well as modify the learning environment and organizational pattern of the classroom. Teachers who use alternative assessment reported they gave students more opportunities to make decisions regarding both assessment and instruction and generally moved away from a teacher-directed to a more student-centered focus using a variety of classroom organizational patterns. This study was conducted with a limited sample; however, it documents the changes that teachers informally report when they reflect on how authentic assessment and portfolio use have helped them rethink and modify many of their practices.

The teacher plays a pivotal role in authentic assessment. Teachers are asked to suggest the tasks that are to be used for assessment; teachers decide collaboratively with students on the criteria for successful performance through the creation of rubrics and other rating systems; and teachers and students score the work themselves. When teachers are given such responsibility for creating assessment systems that are both meaningful and reflective of their teaching priorities, the insights obtained from assessment provide ideas and information for future instruction.

Portfolios Enhance Students' Ownership of and Responsibility for Their Own Literacy Behavior

Too often, students view education as something that happens to them. Their passive involvement in school activities often results in students completing assignments required for promotion or graduation without any meaningful participation. Many students never develop the attitude that they are responsible for their own learning during the elementary and secondary school years, even though they are responsible for doing the work. However, this model dramatically changes when a portfolio process is used, because the process is built on the premise that the students own and are accountable for their work; responsibility for the contents of a portfolio resides with the individual student. Rather than externalizing the need for literacy improvement, the portfolio process requires that students become decision makers and acknowledge that their education is part of their identity. Students' successes and triumphs with learning as well as their disappointments, become internalized as their own, based on self-evaluation, and are no longer limited to assessment built on decontextualized grades, comments, or red marks from an external evaluator. The medium of the portfolio becomes the source for self-reflection and self-evaluation. When students are guided toward introspection, they become more committed to what they have done and what they have learned. Figures 2–6A and 2–6B provide a letter to a reader of a sixth-grade student's portfolio and indicate his specific writing goals for the next 2 months.

Educators have long recognized that children need to be sufficiently motivated to achieve meaningful and long-lasting improvement in literacy growth; however, implementation has been elusive. Frequently, motivation has been associated with rewards for short-term successful performance, instructional materials chosen with high interest themes, or through a positive, personal relationship between the teacher and the student. Rarely are unsuccessful readers and writers motivated to improve; rarely, if ever, do poor achievers think of literacy development as being a high personal priority of any benefit in their lives. In some cases, improvement has been noted in postsecondary young adults who find that literacy is a necessary survival skill in the adult world. Educators have reported seeing even the most disabled reader motivated to learn to read a driver's

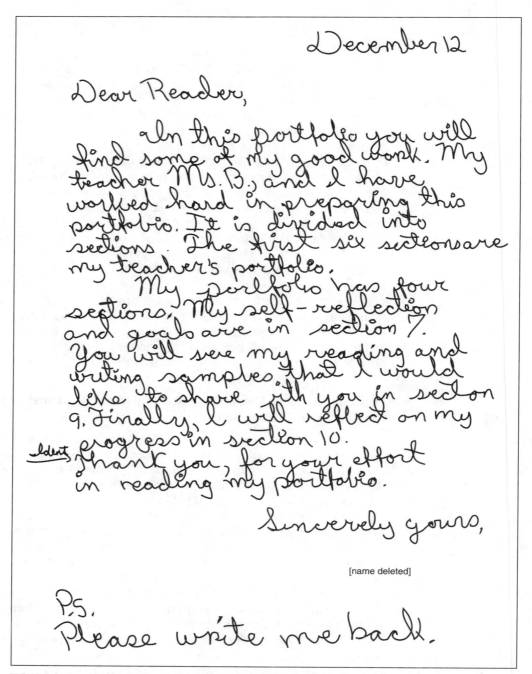

FIGURE 2–6A A 6th grade student introduces his portfolio.

manual to obtain a license; the importance and status attributed to driving are obviously powerful motivators. But reading and writing improvement throughout the grades have rarely been priorities in the lives of students who have been identified with low ability in reading and writing. Intrinsic motivation has been absent.

The portfolio movement recognizes that for meaningful improvement to take place in literacy, the student must be central to this process. The concept of children owning their literacy development is an outgrowth of the child-centered philosophy. According to Harp (1993), "for children to have ownership of their learning, they must have choice and direction in that learning" (p. 10). When students have meaningful decision-making power in the portfolio process, they can become intrinsically motivated to improve their

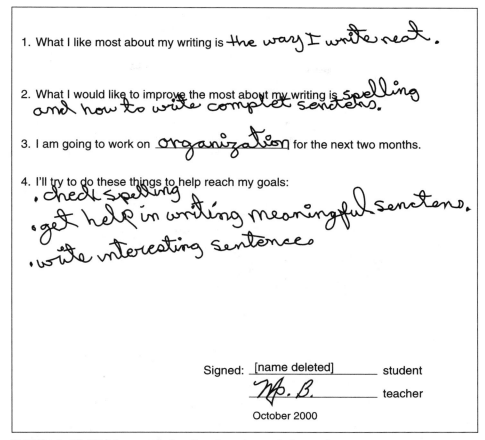

1. What I like most about my writing is the way I write neat.

2. What I would like to improve the most about my writing is spelling and how to write complet senters.

3. I am going to work on organization for the next two months.

4. I'll try to do these things to help reach my goals:
   • check spelling
   • get help in writing meaningful senctens.
   • write interesting sentences

Signed: [name deleted]   student
        Mp. B.   teacher
        October 2000

FIGURE 2–6B Writing goals for October through December.

literacy skills. When literacy learning becomes a priority for students, the likelihood of significant improvement is realized. Nothing is more satisfying for a teacher than to hear students reflect on themselves as readers and writers and note pride in their accomplishment. The portfolio process uniquely provides this opportunity.

Portfolios Promote Accountability by Fulfilling District and State Mandates for Literacy Evaluation

The renewal of public confidence in education is a key to developing a collaborative relationship and, therefore, documenting the incorporation of new standards in daily teaching and being able to document student outcomes in literacy instruction are of prime importance. Although many speak of the necessity for a global restructuring of schools, most community residents want to take pride in the quality of their local schools and want reassurance that the educational establishment is adhering to community values and graduating literate students. No child who graduates from school without the ability to read and write independently will ever be viewed as a school success, and the public wants the schools to demonstrate accountability for outcomes of literacy instruction.

Consequently, evaluating students' reading and writing ability is a priority in state-mandated testing programs. Virtually all states evaluate language ability. In 1992 to 1993, 45 states formally tested reading, and 35 states formally tested writing as part of mandated statewide evaluation programs (Barton & Coley, 1994). The portfolio movement is gaining national recognition as an additional, viable means of documenting literacy improvement and providing helpful information about the processes and products that are outcomes of literacy instruction. Portfolio use is becoming a reliable and valid form of assessment and is emerging as a part of district evaluation programs throughout the country.

There is a growing acknowledgment that performance-based assessment can overcome many of the perceived disadvantages of standardized testing. Many states are using a variety of assessment formats to balance their current programs, including the use of writing samples, performance events, and portfolios along with norm-referenced and criterion-referenced tests. To overcome limitations when standardized literacy tests are used, it is important that teachers be involved in the development of statewide evaluation programs that use portfolios and other authentic assessment techniques. The concern then becomes balancing authentic assessment and other indicators of student ability with the need for reliable measurement used in important decision making. A report from the National Association of State Boards of Education (Claycomb & Kysilko, 2000) simply states that "no one test can 'do it all' . . . and recommended that states consider ensuring fairness and curricular coverage and depth by implementing an assessment system with more than one test that balances performance assessment items with multiple-choice." (p. 9) According to Valencia, Hiebert, and Afflerbach (1994), this will take time, but it is worth the effort:

> It has taken decades and millions of dollars to create the assessment system we now have. It would be naive to believe that we could create an effective new system in just a few years. We need to move slowly and cautiously into these new arenas, but we must move. The alternative is to remain in an assessment environment that has not worked very well for any of us—least of all for students. (p. 299)

Portfolios Enhance Many Partnerships

These partnerships include collaboration between families and school, between teachers, and between teachers and administrators. Education is a partnership among students, teachers, administrators, and families and the more effective these partnerships are in communicating with each other, the more likely that educational procedures will result in joint approval. Parents have sometimes felt left out of the partnership. The portfolio concept provides a meaningful opportunity for parents to become more involved in their children's literacy growth through a dialogue with their children and the teacher using the portfolio as a centerpiece. One parent who was asked to write a letter to her son after viewing his portfolio commented, "I can really see how much your spelling has improved this year, and I truly enjoyed reading your poetry! I never knew you were such a talented poet!"

The reason for using a portfolio should be clearly explained to parents. Parents have always relied on letter grades and percentage scores as validation of their children's progress, and this traditional practice is not easily replaced. Individual teachers must inform parents about their use of portfolios and ask for their assistance with the practice. For example, when Wendy Eisenhauer, a third-grade teacher in Lynbrook, New York, began to use portfolios, she wrote to parents to explain the latest portfolio entries. She also asked that parents review their child's literacy portfolio and provide her with information from their perspective. Significantly, Eisenhauer asks parents for their assistance and feedback and she reports the most positive reaction to this approach, with no parent unwilling to assist.

When parents understand the portfolio process, they willingly assist teachers in understanding their children. One fifth grader's parent reviewed her son's portfolio and reflected both on his literacy progress and how she could help her son at home. One parent from Juneau, Alaska (Juneau School District, 1993), commented how the portfolio process enhanced her confidence in the teacher's ability to work effectively with her child: "I was glad to see the classroom teacher become just as aware of my child's attitude as I was. I know the teacher is better able to teach my child knowing this information."

Sharing portfolio information with parents is central to effective conferencing. Teachers report that parent conferences centered around discussing student portfolios provide concrete information that explains the student's level of achievement, the instructional goals and techniques, and the student's growth. Portfolios provide an occasion for parents to see their child grow and reflect on their learning. One parent noted that her child took more pride in her work and was willing to rewrite and edit her stories because they would be kept in her portfolio.

Another part of the educational partnership that has become increasingly evident is the number of children educated by instructional teams. This is particularly evident in inclusion classrooms where students with special education needs may be instructed by the classroom teacher, a special education teacher, an aide, subject specialists, and other support personnel. Given the present diversity of children in the schools, it is common practice to meet each child's needs by creating an instructional team consisting of many specialists who all work with one child. Frequently, a reading teacher, speech and language teacher, bilingual or English as a second language teacher, and a resource room teacher or other special educators work in conjunction. Psychosocial personnel (psychologists, counselors, and social workers) form other partnerships with classroom teachers. When these multidisciplinary teams collaborate to discuss a child—whether for diagnosis, program placement, monitoring the child's progress, or creating an individual educational plan (IEP)—examining actual work products provides tremendous insight into the child's capacity and performance. When children's progress and development are reviewed to determine if interventional services are appropriate, the portfolio process is an important tool in educational decision making.

The partnership between the school administrator and classroom teacher is also enhanced by the portfolio process. Because supervision is necessary for accountability as well as promoting teacher growth, building and district administrators search for ways to be of constructive assistance. Teachers are required to demonstrate what goes on in their classrooms and the outcomes of instruction. Student-produced portfolios are an excellent way for teachers to concretely show their curriculum goals translated into assignments, to provide samples of the level of student work produced, to demonstrate how this process contributes to their knowledge about children, and to describe how the process assists with instructional decisions. One elementary school principal, who supports the use of language arts portfolios, asked to be assigned to work with a group of children on their portfolios. She felt that she needed to understand more about the day-to-day realities of portfolio use in a classroom before she could meaningfully understand the process and interact appropriately with the teachers in her school.

CONCLUSION

The use of portfolios arises from a context of new thinking about how reading and writing should be taught, learned, and assessed. In Chapter 3 we will survey current applications of literacy portfolios. Chapter 4 contains a format for the use of a model literacy portfolio and describes a process for its implementation.

REFERENCES

Arter, J., & Spandel, V. (1992, Spring). Using portfolios of student work in instruction and assessment. *Educational Measurement: Issues and Practice*, 36–44.

Barton, P., & Coley, R. (1994). *Testing in America's schools*. Princeton, NJ: Educational Testing Service.

Claycomb, C., & Kysilko, D. (2000, Spring). Purposes and elements of effective assessment systems: State education standards. *Quarterly Journal of National Assessment of State Boards of Education*, 7–11.

Gooding, K. (1994, April). *Teaching to the test: The influence of alternative modes of assessment on teachers' instruc-tional strategies*. Paper presented at the meeting of the AERA, New Orleans.

Graves, D. (1992). Portfolios: Keep a good idea growing. In D. Graves & B. Sunstein (Eds.), *Portfolios portraits* (pp. 1–12). Portsmouth, NH: Heinemann.

Harp, B. (1993). The whole language movement. In B. Harp (Ed.), *Assessment and evaluation in whole language programs* (pp. 1–18). Norwood, MA: Christopher-Gordon.

Juneau School District (1993). *Language arts portfolio handbook*. Juneau, AK: Author.

Murphy, S., & T. Underwood. (2001). *Portfolio practices: Lessons from schools, districts and states*. Norwood, MA: Christopher-Gordon.

Paulson, F. L., Paulson, P., & Meyer, C. (1991, February). What makes a portfolio a portfolio? *Educational Leadership*, 60–63.

Seger, F. D. (1992). Portfolio definitions: Toward a shared notion. In D. Graves & B. Sunstein (Eds.), *Portfolio portraits* (pp. 114–126). Portsmouth, NH: Heinemann.

Valencia, S., Hiebert, E., & Afflerbach, P. (1994). Realizing the possibilities of authentic assessment: Current trends and future issues. In S. Valencia, E. Hiebert, & P. Afflerbach (Eds.), *Authentic reading assessment* (pp. 286–300). Newark, DE: International Reading Association.

Surveying Portfolio Use in Authentic Literacy Classrooms

KEY WORDS AND CONCEPTS

literacy products
literacy processes
writing portfolio
reading portfolio
benchmark portfolio
literature portfolio
electronic portfolio

integrated language arts or
    reading/writing portfolio
portfolio performance
cumulative record portfolio
showcase portfolio
collaborative portfolio
balanced reading

I asked Craig,* a fifth-grade student, how his school year had gone. He replied, "Let me show you my portfolio and then we can really talk." He returned with a large loose-leaf notebook entitled "My Fifth-Grade Portfolio." It was decorated with animals and contained many different entries, including: "About the author," cartoons and comics, class pictures and events, class autographs, writing pieces, artwork, letters from parents, and reactions to reading.

Craig was quick to point out that in addition to this end-of-year portfolio, he had a separate writing folder and another loose-leaf notebook that contained his reading log and all of his responses to reading done during the year. The portfolio made it quite easy to understand how fifth grade went for Craig. It was a year full of projects, with special emphasis on reading and writing poetry, and certainly it was a year of considerable growth and reflection about literacy.

It is evident both from Craig's perspective as well as from teachers' perspectives that a portfolio has become an important aspect of quality literacy instruction. Although the theoretical debates about how best to teach children to read and write continue, teachers have pragmatically adopted balanced literacy practices. A national survey of elementary teachers found that teachers do not take a one-sided approach to literacy instruction; they combine skills and strategies as well as immersion in enriched literacy experiences in eclectic programs of their own design (Baumann, Hoffman, Moon, & Duffy-Hester, 1998). Such programs combine the best of skill-focused instruction with real-life reading and writing opportunities. Even among literacy experts there appears to be more agreement about what constitutes quality literacy instruction than one would believe, given the provocative articles in the media. According to Flippo (1998), it is significantly "only the classroom teacher who works with a child every day [who] is in a position to know what is appropriate instruction for that particular child" (p. 38). Teachers have also benefitted from the ongoing debates over what are the best practices of the past (Reutzel, 1999).

Many teachers describe their literacy approach as being balanced. Although the definition of what is a "balanced" approach varies, there is a common understanding that "balance is a 'philosophical perspective' about what kinds of reading knowledge children should develop and how those kinds of knowledge can be best attained" (Fitzgerald, 1999, p. 100). Those who use balanced approaches consequently evaluate their underlying beliefs and choose methods to meet their goals, even if the methods arise from different schools of thought (i.e. literature-based immerson versus specific-skills teaching). Increased importance is also given to children's affective dimensions as being critical to literacy learning.

Consequently, today's classrooms most often exemplify the best of what we now know about quality literacy instruction. It's hard to find a class where children don't keep journals, don't peer edit, don't use rubrics, don't engage in author studies, don't enjoy and discuss quality children's literature, and don't use webs and maps to aid comprehension. Likewise, today's classrooms feature focused and strategic-skills instruction and guided reading, but often teachers do this by using a wide variety of instructional materials, including classic literature, popular children's literature, trade books, predictable books, newspapers and magazines, as well as the newly revised literature-based, basal readers. Likewise, many teachers use portfolios as a means to more authentically assess the literacy development of their students, to promote student self-reflection, and to provide essential information for more effective instruction.

This chapter provides a survey of current portfolio practices and will assist teachers by suggesting guidelines to either begin using a portfolio process or to help them reflect on current use of a portfolio system. A literacy portfolio is an important and dynamic ingredient in a state-of-the-art literacy classroom.

---

*Note: In order to prepare for the 2nd edition of this text, Craig, who has just graduated from high school, was interviewed again. I showed Craig the chapter introduction from the first edition of the text, and also showed him his fifth-grade portfolio. He was fascinated about the entries he chose to put in his portfolio and had a great time remembering that special year. The moral of the story—portfolios are worth keeping, and they certainly are a time capsule about a year in a child's life!

WIDE DIVERSITY IN PORTFOLIO USE

Literacy practices throughout the country demonstrate acceptance and variability in portfolio use. Many school districts and several states mandate portfolio use and find that this method of assessment actually portrays what children are truly learning. The "chameleon-like nature of portfolios" is a demonstration of their flexibility and elasticity as they are adopted by different professionals who have very different purposes in vastly different learning contexts (Murphy & Underwood, 2000, p. 15). All teachers who thoughtfully integrate portfolios into their classrooms, are faced with many questions, including the following:

- What goal do I have for this portfolio?
- What kind of portfolio should I use?
- What should be collected in the portfolio, and how should the contents be organized?
- How will I manage a portfolio process as part of literacy instruction?
- How will a portfolio enhance my literacy program?

Wiggins (1998) commented that failure to think through the purposes of a portfolio results in confusion over what should go into the portfolio, who owns the portfolio, and what value there is in keeping the portfolio going through successive years of instruction. There are many choices to be made, and because the portfolio format is so flexible, it lends itself to a variety of instructional, assessment, and evaluation purposes, but unless goals and processes are clarified, confusion can occur.

Individual teachers and school districts have adopted and customized the portfolio concept to meet their particular needs. Within the framework of state-mandated assessment systems and increased concern with accountability, harm can result from reducing educational accomplishment to a student's performance on a test. An informed public should recognize that "school performance is complex and assessments should be as well" (Rothstein, 2000). Portfolios have much to offer in literacy assessment and are being used to document performance-based, learning outcomes. Some educators truly believe that portfolios should replace standardized tests; for example, a New York City alternative high school has applied to the State Education Department to replace required Regents Exams with a graduation portfolio (Halloway, 1999). Former U.S. Secretary of Education, Richard Riley, also touted portfolio use when he said that "states should incorporate multiple ways of measuring learning, including portfolios of student work" (Wilgoren, 2000). Within the framework of documenting outcomes as part of the Standards Movement, portfolios have a meaningful place. Diez (2000) describes an application of portfolio use to illustrate the concept of "assessment as learning," and calls for assessment measures that serve student learning and describes how a seventh-grade teacher uses portfolios that require the daily collection of work and reflection about what is learned. Without such thoughtful application of assessment measures, Diez feels, that the promise of the standards movement will not be met.

A review of the literature and discussions with educators across the country reveal that different forms of portfolios with various formats are used, but many teachers use writing portfolios, reading portfolios, integrated language arts portfolios (often including emphasis on content areas), literature portfolios, and cumulative record portfolios. Courtney and Abodeeb (1999) recently reviewed the status of portfolio definitions and agreed that "portfolio" means different things to different people, but the underlying concept is that portfolios are selected collections and reflections of a learner's work over time.

Jenkins (1996) proposed another model for describing portfolios that focuses on whether the teacher or the student has primary responsibility for the assessment and creation of the portfolio. This model is helpful for describing all portfolios and distinguishes between *benchmark portfolios*, which are teacher-directed to document accountability for literacy progress, and *showcase portfolios*, which are student-directed to portray accomplishment, and *collaborative portfolios*, which combine aspects of both. Which kind of portfolio to use will depend on the underlying purpose of what the portfolio is being used for. Some portfolios are limited to use in individual classrooms, where teachers adopt the portfolio concept and modify it for their own particular purposes. Elsewhere, teams of teachers work together to promote consistency and continuity in practices. Other school districts prescribe the contents of portfolios and require that all teachers become involved in the same process, to promote standardization.

It is interesting to determine how a portfolio process begins in various settings, because this often reveals how many individuals value portfolios and the likelihood of portfolio use continuing through subsequent years. Some teachers have independently embraced the portfolio process through self-education (e.g., reading professional literature, sharing ideas with colleagues, attending conferences, taking college or in-service courses). These teachers find the use of portfolios to be an important part of their individual instructional programs. They create portfolios that are customized for individual classroom use. Students in such settings aren't likely to have the portfolio process continue through the grades and, consequently, although the process may be valued for an individual year, it will not have a long-term impact. Conversations with other teachers reveal that there is tension when portfolio use is mandated without teacher input, because some teachers perceive portfolios to be merely another unneeded educational fad. Other teachers fear that portfolios create an enormous time burden without having any real benefit. If teachers do not understand and endorse a prescribed portfolio process and do not appreciate its worth as an instructional and assessment tool, the process will also fail. Murphy and Underwood (2000) studied portfolio use that had significant impact in eight different locations across the country. In these locales, portfolios emerged as a response to political, pedagogical, and general interest as part of a change from traditional assessment practices. The striking feature these researchers found is that the form of each portfolio used is so individual as to make "portfolio assessment systems . . . inseparable from the people and situations in which they were made and used," and they consequently compare portfolios to an organic process shaped by individual social, ideological, cultural, and institutional aspects of each system (p. 281).

Calfee and Perfumo (1993) conducted a survey of portfolio practice in 150 different sites across the country and concluded that reactions to the portfolio concept are varied and complex and that portfolio practices sometimes resulted in "virtual anarchy" as a "pendulum swing" reaction to teachers' bias against traditional testing practices. Conversely, if portfolios are used as part of broad educational changes, then "this 'package' offers the opportunity for fundamental reform in U.S. schooling" (Calfee & Perfumo, 1993, p. 536). Thus, it seems clear that portfolio assessment needs to be part of a coherent theory of literacy teaching and assessment. The use of a portfolio is likely to falter if teachers, who are already burdened by the number of external mandates, see portfolios as an additional demand without direct benefit.

The use of a portfolio often reflects redirection in teaching processes and assessment. Careful thought and clear planning are needed for effective implementation. Therefore, it is recommended that teachers work together within their system and collaborate with their administration to agree on the purposes of the portfolio, choose a suggested framework for the contents of the portfolio, discuss the use of the portfolio, and share concerns about such issues as storage and time management, standardized assessment requirements, and balancing instructional priorities. Without collaboration between teachers and administration, portfolios will have neither continuity nor impact.

ISSUES TO DECIDE BEFORE BEGINNING A PORTFOLIO

Choosing Portfolio Contents: Balancing Process and Product

A literacy portfolio should include evidence of both literacy products and processes. Reading and writing involve the active participation of the student in reconstructing meaning. Portfolio contents must show evidence of both students' literacy products (the outcome of reading and writing activities, which might be in the form of essays, narratives, logs, and journals), and literacy processes, or strategies used during reading and writing. For example, teachers often want to know what students do when they encounter an important but unfamiliar word during reading. Traditional forms of reading assessment have long focused on literacy outcomes and do not provide this kind of process information. Because much of reading and writing involve internal, cognitive processes, evaluating students' literacy strategies is much more complicated and elusive than collecting literacy products, but can be addressed by the literacy portfolio process. Techniques such as self-reflective questionnaires, student-composed literacy biographies, informal reading assessments (especially running records and informal reading inventories), and teacher-student conferences provide important information about students' literacy processes.

Rhodes and Shanklin (1993) suggested that teachers can also be guided by two questions when they think about what to include in a portfolio:

1. What does this information reveal or demonstrate about a student's development?
2. How will this information help [me to] make instructional decisions for this student? (p. 421)

For example, if a teacher is trying to determine if student-selected poetry belongs in the portfolio, the teacher might decide that including poetry demonstrates that the student is learning a new genre. Paulson, Paulson, and Meyer (1991) provide eight guidelines to consider when teachers involve students in a portfolio process. Answering the question, "What makes a portfolio a portfolio?" they say that all portfolios:

1. Should contain information that demonstrates the student has become involved in self-reflection.
2. Reflect a process where the student is directly part of choosing the entries.
3. Should not be similar to students' cumulative folders, and should contain scores and other cumulative folder data only if they become meaningful as part of a portfolio collection.
4. Should document the student's activities, including the portfolio's purpose, goals, contents, standards, and judgments.
5. Can serve an instructional purpose during the school year, but the end-of-the-year portfolio should contain data that the student wishes to display.
6. May have a variety of purposes, with an almost universal purpose of demonstrating progress in the instructional program, but multiple purposes should not conflict with each other.
7. Should document the student's growth in terms of skills, school performance, interests, and attitudes.
8. Should be based on a support structure where students are shown portfolio models that demonstrate how collections are created and how other students reflect on the contents. (pp. 62–63)

Choosing Portfolio Contents: Who Decides?

Another decision involves determining who will be responsible for choosing portfolio entries. Jenkins (1996, p. 11) provides a useful survey for teachers to complete that will help them resolve this dilemma. She suggests choosing among student control, teacher control, and joint control as alternatives for taking responsibility about entry selection, portfolio access, product assessment, goal setting, conferencing, and sharing contents. If a portfolio is to be used primarily for accountability, then teachers may feel totally responsible for choosing entries that reflect accomplishment of developmental benchmarks. However, if a portfolio is used to celebrate and showcase student accomplishments, then the student's choice should prevail. Jenkins (1996) feels that a collaborative portfolio process combines the best of both benchmark and showcase portfolios. This collaborative model accomplishes three goals: (1) it engages children in self-assessment and goal setting, (2) it assesses progress, and (3) it collects data for instructional interactions. The Literacy Portfolio recommended in this text (see Chapter 4) endorses this collaborative model for purposes of improving teaching and learning. Figure 3–1 shows how a fifth-grade student made decisions about what to include in her portfolio.

This Is My Portfolio

My name is _A. C._

I am in grade _5th_ at _Munsey Park School_ School.

My teacher's name is _B.C._

I filled in this sheet on _March 21, 2001_

I started my portfolio on _September 2000_

This is how I organized my portfolio: _I picked out the writings that I enjoyed writing and the responses to reading of books I liked reading_

This is what my portfolio shows about my reading: _I read a lot and my favorite type of book is realistic fiction. It shows that I have a strong understanding of the things I read about._

This is what my portfolio shows about my writing: _I like to write about everything. I have trouble concentrating on only one part. I give lots of details._

This is what I think are the best things in my portfolio: _The paper about my grandma because I was the most descriptive in this paper._

FIGURE 3–1 A fifth grader's decisions about what to put in her portfolio. *Source:* From ALTERNATIVE ASSESSMENT TECHNIQUES FOR READING AND WRITING by Wilma Miller Copyright © 1995. Reprinted with permission of Center for Applied Research in Education/Prentice Hall Direct.

Providing an Organizational System

An essential component of any portfolio is an explanation of how the entries are chosen and the system by which they are organized. Students should include a table of contents or write a letter to the reader in which the contents and the reasons for specific entries are described. Figure 3–2 is a letter written by a third-grade student to her parents in which she describes her portfolio. (The reading test that is mentioned is a running record.) Careful organization of portfolio contents requires that both the student and teacher reflect on criteria for collection. No two students' portfolios will be identical, which is desirable. In fact, depending on the amount of independence given to the students, each collection will vary widely. Portfolio contents should reflect variation between students in terms of interests, attitudes, goals, strategies, and abilities. "Above all, a portfolio is a portfolio when it provides a forum that encourages students to develop the abilities needed to become independent, self-directed learners" (Paulson et al., 1991, p. 63).

TYPES OF LITERACY PORTFOLIOS CURRENTLY IN USE

Several fairly consistent patterns emerge from an informal survey of current portfolio practices. These are summarized and categorized in the balance of this chapter.

Writing Portfolios

The most widespread use of portfolios has been the writing portfolio, evolving from the writing folder. Writing instruction has changed dramatically in recent years. The writing process approach is a nationally recognized model of good writing instruction and, consequently, writing folders have proliferated. Rarely does one find a classroom where students are not engaged in composing a piece of writing over several days and then storing their work in folders. The contents of these folders vary to include such other writing-related items as writing skills checklists, self-editing guidelines, conference notes,

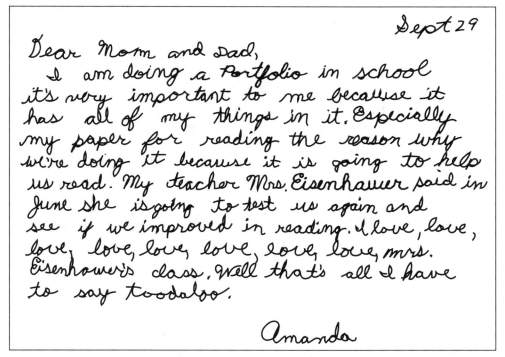

Sept 29

Dear Mom and Dad,
I am doing a Portfolio in school it's very important to me because it has all of my things in it. Especially my paper for reading the reason why we're doing it because it is going to help us read. My teacher Mrs. Eisenhauer said in June she is going to test us again and see if we improved in reading. I love, love, love, love, love love, love, love, mrs. Eisenhower's class. Well that's all I have to say toodaloo.

Amanda

FIGURE 3–2 Sample letter from a third-grade student introducing her portfolio to her parents.

feedback from other students, and teacher evaluations, but they share a common feature in that they are an outgrowth of the writing process philosophy of instruction. A piece of writing is the outcome of different stages that involve such activities as making lists, taking notes, attempting drafts, sharing with peers, conferencing, editing, revising work and, finally, publishing pieces. Students need a repository for their work as it evolves through these stages. Collecting writing pieces as works-in-progress gives teachers the opportunity to see the evolution of a piece of writing and provides insights about the process used by an individual student.

When students value the outcome of their writing efforts and take pride in their accomplishment, they want a place to store finished pieces in a semipermanent fashion for both display and review. The use of writing folders with collected students' work is a means of reviewing student work for display, conferencing, and communicating and sharing with families, and they are sometimes used for acquainting next year's teacher with the student's work. The final products of the writing process can be found in best works folders, where students choose the contents and are self-reflective when they decide why a piece is meritorious. A key distinction exists between the writing folder, as a collection of all work, and a writing portfolio, where contents are chosen for selected purposes (i.e., to show writing in various genre, to trace writing improvement) and are used by both teacher and student for reflection. Figure 3–3 contains a third-grade student's reasons for choosing entries for his writing portfolio. Later in this text we discuss how the contents of a writing portfolio can be a significant aspect of improved writing instruction.

Many state-wide testing programs now require the collection of actual writing samples; Kentucky and Vermont use state-wide, mandated writing portfolios. New Mexico also uses a portfolio system for state-wide assessment (Rael & Travelstead, 1993). Each school year, teachers are given criteria for good writing to use with their students, and they develop lessons using a writing process approach. Students' best efforts are col-

Tod,

I selected this France report because I used many techniques to make it. I feel this report is just like a grownups report because I put so much effort into it.

I think my writing improved so much because I make all my letter corectly.

The techniques I used to make my report were to feel like you were really in it. Now I am putting more facts into my reports.

My reports make me feel better because I learned so much.

FIGURE 3–3 A third-grade student shares his reasons for choosing an entry for his portfolio.

lected in writing portfolios, and the writing samples are then scored as part of the state-wide program using criteria that have been widely distributed.

The widespread use of word processing has facilitated students' writing. When all writing was handwritten, students who experienced graphomotor problems were physically limited in their ability to produce a large amount of writing or were certainly reluctant to recopy or revise. Older students often resisted the suggestion that they edit their writing because of the time and effort needed. Editing and revising are intensive and laborious without the use of a computer. As students use word processing for writing and with increased access to computers in the classroom or in computer labs, a marked increase in writing productivity has resulted. Students are motivated to write more with the aid of word processing, and their ability to produce legible copy with ease of revision is evident. It is noteworthy that some of the more technologically advanced schools have begun using electronic portfolios so that students' portfolios can be easily stored and saved. The use of technology motivates student performance, and electronic portfolios will undoubtedly be more widely used as more schools access technology.

Writing Portfolio Contents. A writing portfolio should contain evidence of both process and product (Hill & Ruptic, 1994; Rhodes & Shanklin, 1993; Tierney, Carter, & Desai, 1991). Writing process entries reveal how such strategies as drafting, composing, organizing, and editing are employed. Because many students have difficulty beginning a writing task, they are often helped by group brainstorming, lists of suggested topics, or referring to guiding questions. During the drafting phase, notes from conferences (with both peers and the teacher) may prove helpful. Evidence of the processes students use during writing can be found in word webs, story maps, semantic maps, pictures, and lists that assist organization and help maintain focus. Self-reflection about students' writing (often as answers to teachers' questions) as well as copies of their works-in-progress are also process entries. When students self-edit, they can be assisted by checklists and wall charts labeled with titles such as "What to Look for When I Edit." Often, students edit their works collaboratively in peer groups or by having another student sign off that the work has been reviewed by a peer. Rhodes and Shanklin (1993) suggest using the following writing process entries:

- Topics lists,
- Self-reflections,
- Webs and artwork,
- Writing strategy checklists,
- Conference guides, and
- Author's circle tapes and notes. (p. 420)

When deciding what product measures to include in a writing portfolio, a variety of age-appropriate writing projects (e.g., personal narratives, reports, persuasive essays, letters, poetry) as well as projects that integrate writing in different curriculum areas should be used that reflect daily writing activities. Many teachers now require students to respond to books they've read in various ways, including response logs and literature journals. These reflective reactions reveal how students construct meaning from what they've read and how they emotionally respond to literature. In the age of specific standard outcomes, teachers can be guided by curriculum objectives for each grade level that provide the different forms of writing that are expected at each developmental stage. Tierney et al. (1991) suggest a list of writing products that can be assembled to show evidence of work on underlying instructional goals:

- Written responses to literary components such as plot, setting, point of view, character development, and theme.
- Items that are evidence of development of style, organization, voice, sense of audience, choice of words, and clarity.

- Writing that shows growth in use of skills such as self-correction, punctuation, spelling, grammar, appropriate form, and legibility.
- Writing that illustrates evidence of topic generation. (pp. 73–74)

In the development of writing skills in young students, or in students who are just beginning to acquire English-language skills, the relationship between writing and illustrations is most important, and the inclusion of students' artwork as a supplementary form of expression is encouraged. Artwork not only personalizes a student's writing but also helps to communicate ideas or a sequence of events and often is a motivating factor. For older students, illustrations as well as diagrams, charts, and tables should be encouraged. Figure 3–4 provides a summary of what often constitutes a writing portfolio. The writing portfolio provides an excellent opportunity for students to self-reflect on their writing ability and specify their own writing goals (see Figure 3–5).

Management of Writing Portfolios. Even a well-conceived writing portfolio can be undermined by day-to-day management problems with such practical concerns as how portfolios are created, stored, and reviewed. When teachers question whether or not they should continue a writing portfolio, their concerns almost always relate to these issues, not to the fundamental worth of the process. Writing portfolios must be accessible to students and have ample storage with a secure pocket so that small items are not lost. Many suggest that a writing portfolio be divided into two phases: works-in-progress and published writing. Teachers often store these writing folders on open shelves in a convenient location, in cardboard or plastic filing boxes, or in file cabinets, or students can keep folders in their desks. Many teachers prefer to use an informal folder approach for work-in-progress and reserve the writing portfolio for those special pieces that are carefully selected and need to be saved. Some schools are now able to use digital portfolios, which eliminate cumbersome storage systems.

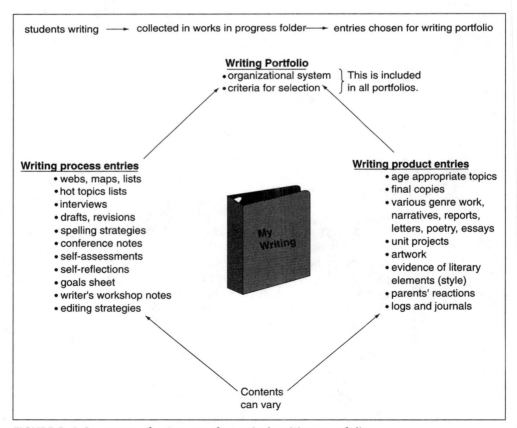

FIGURE 3–4 Summary of contents of a typical writing portfolio.

Writing Goals

Name: _Amanda_   Date: _October 25_

Content / style goal: _I would like to work on my opening paragraph and my ending paragrap. Also I want to work on not freezing when somebody says writing._

Action Plan: I plan to work towards achieving my goal by: _Writing the middle of my paragraph first and then work off of that for my beginning sentence. My other plan would be writing a word and then write off of that._

Converntions Goal: _I think I need to work on my puncuation, because sometimes I don't know if I need to put a comma or a periode._

Action Plan: I plan to work towards achieving my goal by: _I think I need to read my piece over and when I take a breath I need a comma instead of a period._

FIGURE 3–5 A fifth grader's writing goals to be included in the writing portfolio.

Ongoing monitoring by the teacher ensures that the goals of the portfolio process are met. It is extremely important to establish the portfolio's purpose and specify criteria for selection of entries. Collections that are too large become unwieldy, the contents can become devalued, and they don't accomplish any purpose. Wiggins (1998) cautions that most portfolios contain too much and that "far fewer samples are needed than people typically imagine" (p. 191). If a portfolio's purpose is clearly specified, then entries can be thoughtfully selected to coordinate with that purpose, thus eliminating less meaningful entries. Writing conferences are an excellent time for the teacher to guide a student in shaping portfolio contents. Regardless of whether teachers adopt portfolio practices for other uses, the writing portfolio clearly is essential for those who use a writing process approach. Chapter 8 provides helpful guidelines for teachers to use during portfolio conferences.

Reading Portfolios

There has been a major shift in our understanding of what constitutes literacy, with consequent changes in the manner in which instruction is conducted, and this logically impacts assessment processes. Changing theories about reading behavior have obvious implications for how we assess or diagnose students' reading ability. Tierney (1998) reviewed the need for rethinking literacy assessment and concluded that "developing better assessment practices requires more than simply choosing a new test or adopting a packaged informal assessment procedure" (p. 374), because assessment must be grounded in principles that recognize diversity and complexity in assessment processes. Fundamental to Tierney's (1998) new assessment principles for literacy is the importance of student self-analysis, and he feels that portfolios are appropriate springboards for accomplishing this goal.

Enlightened educators know that assessment must not be exclusively outcome-based in terms of numbers reported from standardized tests, but rather needs to include process measures that involve the student and provide insight about learning strategies children use; they should show how children construct meaning, what they think about when they read, and how they respond to reading. These current views about assessment make students more active participants and partners in the assessment process (Stiggins, 1997). The use of rubrics, often developed with the students and used independently by students, is an example of this new thinking (Skillings & Ferrell, 2000). Adding multiple measures of student performance enhances the diagnostic process (Hinchman & Michel, 1999).

Reading portfolios are a superb means to incorporate these new views of assessment, because they actively involve the student, reflect both reading process and product measures, and certainly incorporate multiple measures of assessment. The Literacy Portfolio (described in detail in Chapter 4) should be considered an excellent framework for creating a state-of-the-art reading assessment system. Courtney and Abodeeb (1999) also describe a diagnostic-reflective portfolio process used in a second-grade classroom that mirrors what we propose. A reading portfolio process is an opportunity to better understand strategies that students use in a wide variety of activities each day. The portfolio promotes the opportunities for students to engage in thoughtful reflection about what and how they read and, therefore, has important instructional implications for teachers. Chapter 5 will help teachers learn how a reading portfolio can promote better literacy instruction.

Reading Portfolio Contents. The contents of a good reading portfolio—one that will truly give the teacher and the student a full appraisal of reading ability—must incorporate both product and process measures. A review of the literature regarding reading portfolios also indicates that the contents can be divided into the following categories:

- Measures that reflect and analyze students' decoding and vocabulary skills;
- Measures that reflect and analyze students' comprehension skills;
- Measures that require students to write as a reaction to reading across content areas with different forms of text and for different purposes;
- Measures of students' reading interests and attitudes;
- Lists and logs of students' actual reading experiences;
- Projects or products that are the outcomes of reading assignments;
- Teachers' progress notes, conference notes, or observational notes about the student when the student is engaged in reading activities; and
- Appraisal of the students' reading skills outside the school environment.

Figure 3–6 summarizes the contents of a typical reading portfolio. Reading portfolios can include numerous types of entries.

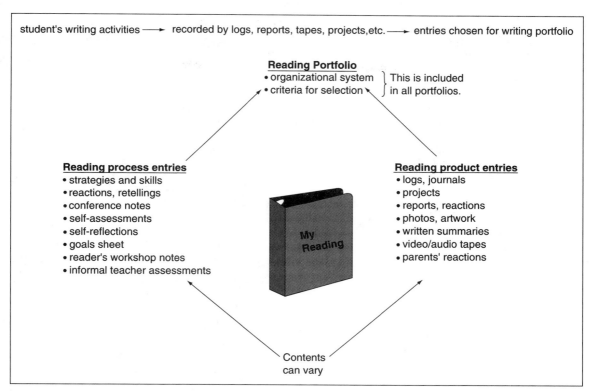

student's writing activities ⟶ recorded by logs, reports, tapes, projects, etc. ⟶ entries chosen for writing portfolio

Reading Portfolio
- organizational system ⎱ This is included
- criteria for selection ⎰ in all portfolios.

Reading process entries
- strategies and skills
- reactions, retellings
- conference notes
- self-assessments
- self-reflections
- goals sheet
- reader's workshop notes
- informal teacher assessments

My Reading

Reading product entries
- logs, journals
- projects
- reports, reactions
- photos, artwork
- written summaries
- video/audio tapes
- parents' reactions

Contents
can vary

FIGURE 3–6 Summary of contents of a typical reading portfolio.

Literature and Reading Logs. Classrooms that use literature-based approaches to reading frequently use a technique called a literature circle, so that a group of students can engage in meaningful discussions after reading. Depending on the age and experience of the students, or with some training, these groups can be student led. Portfolios frequently will contain tape recordings, reactions or notes from these literature discussion group meetings. Whenever literature is a central component to reading instruction, a literature log is helpful for recording and monitoring student reading and reactions of quality material.

In a reading log, students record what they read during school and at home and a reading log is included in almost all reading portfolios. This is a significant indicator of how much reading a student is engaged in; the type, difficulty, and variety of books being read; and the student's reaction to what is read. Many of the new state-mandated reading outcomes require extensive reading, and thus reading logs (as well as literature portfolios) are commonly kept. Many teachers have their students keep a simultaneous reading and writing log to reinforce that both forms of literacy are important (see Figure 3–7).

Reading projects. Teachers often give formal assignments for students to complete after they have finished a chapter or an entire book. These have taken the place of the traditional book report and are often in the form of projects (e.g., write an advertisement for the book, create a bookmark or book jacket). These projects provide insights into depth of comprehension and personal reactions.

Self-reflections/Self-assessments. Self-reflections can take many forms. Many teachers include self-assessment forms that help appraise the students' general perceptions of themselves as a reader, their reading interests, their goals, and their specific reactions to something that has been read. Some ask that students write a literacy autobiography that describes their individual history as a reader and also focuses on self-identified literacy goals for the year. Figure 3–8 shows how a fifth grader reflects on his last 3 years of reading progress. Students often keep a daily journal. A popular topic for an entry is

FIGURE 3–7 Typical contents of an integrated portfolio.

a personal reaction to something they have read. Teachers can also provide a reading response sheet to guide students in responding to their reading selections, as shown in Figure 3–9.

Documenting the use of decoding strategies. Teachers place a heavy emphasis on teaching decoding strategies, especially during the primary grades or when they work with students who struggle with fluency. Therefore, appraising a student's decoding strategies is frequently an important part of reading assessment. Analysis of these strategies is incorporated into reading portfolios in the form of informal inventories, running records, and miscue analysis. Taped, oral readings by the student, obtained at several points during the school year, may be included to show changes in reading fluency and document growth over time. In one third-grade class, the teacher, the students, and the parents found oral recording to be valuable, because this presents a clear demonstration of how a student's ability changes during the year. Figure 3–10 is a letter to parents prepared by the teacher, Mrs. Eisenhauer, explaining how they can use the taped reading to assist their children. Of particular interest is Mrs. Eisenhauer's emphasis on reading strategies, the use of content material (often thought to be more difficult for young children), and enlisting the parents' help.

Reading was a temporary thing because in third grade I stumbled a little and in fourth grade I got up to reading and now in fifth grade I've improved on my reading. I read different books that are harder.

FIGURE 3–8 A fifth grader's self-reflection on his reading progress.

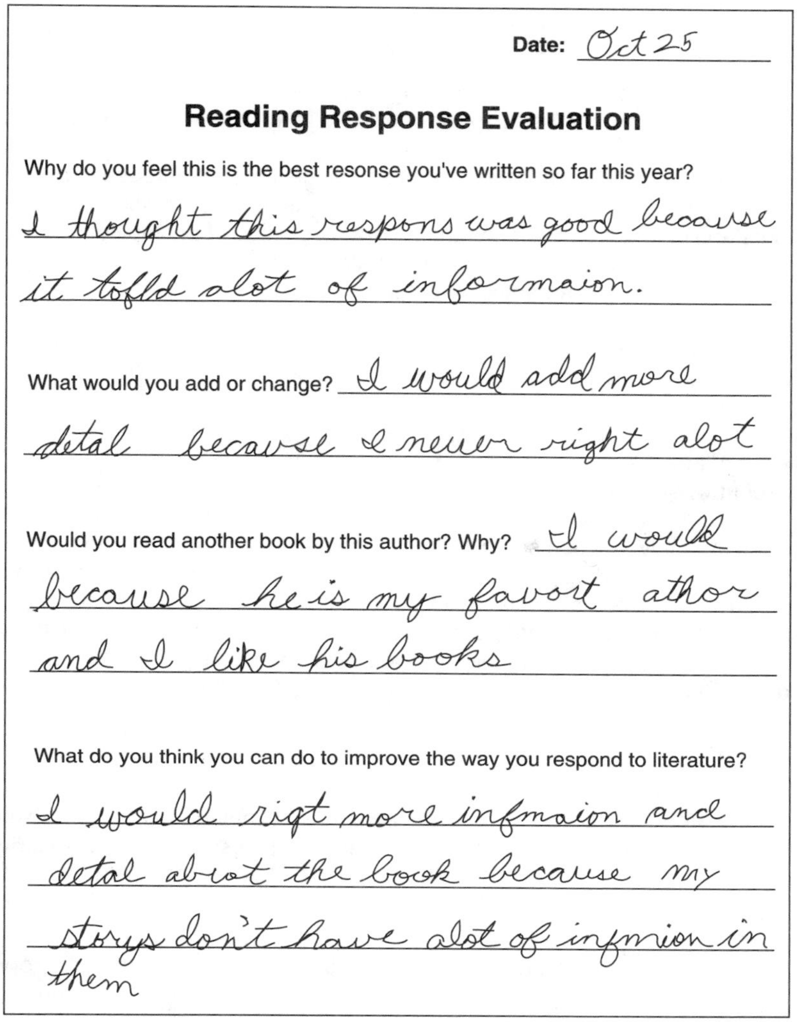

Date: _Oct 25_

Reading Response Evaluation

Why do you feel this is the best resonse you've written so far this year?

I thought this respons was good because it tolld alot of informaion.

What would you add or change? _I would add more detal because I never right alot_

Would you read another book by this author? Why? _I would because he is my favort athor and I like his books_

What do you think you can do to improve the way you respond to literature?

I would rigt more infmaion and detal abeot the book because my storys don't have alot of infmion in them

FIGURE 3–9 A completed reading response sheet from a third-grade student.

Observational data. Another source of valuable information for the reading portfolio is composed of observational data collected by the teacher. Goodman's (1978) concept of "kid watching" has given renewed attention to observing children and recording insights gained through informal assessment. Information such as the student's attention span, the student's individual work habits and preferences, and how the student relates to other learners can be gained only from observing the child at work. Making notes on small self-adhesive tags is an easy method of keeping track of individual student behavior and can be placed in the student's portfolio or contained in a teacher notebook. Other teachers use a clipboard to record their daily observations. Some teachers create an observational loose-leaf book with separate sections devoted to each child so that a chronology of behaviors can be documented throughout the school year. It is essential to allocate time to observe and document individual student behavior on a regular basis. Notes that the teacher takes after a conference with a student about the portfolio or an ongoing literacy project provide additional valuable information.

Content area projects. Because reading is an integral part of content learning, reading portfolio entries often include products that are the outgrowth of subject area assignments. The inclusion of research reports and other forms of content area studies (these can include pictures or multimedia displays) demonstrates to students that reading has practical significance in learning across the curriculum, exposes students to different

February 10

Dear Parents,

Your child has completed a third taped reading and evaluation of a reading response. We'd like to share it with you, so you can note the progress your child is making and continue to take part in our plans for improvement.

This time we taped a selection from our social studies text for the purpose of monitoring our strategies for reading factual material. We discuss reading techniques in school that will improve our recall and understanding of this type of material. At the beginning of the taping, I asked your child what techniques if any s/he uses before reading factual material. Listen carefully to see if your child mentioned any of the following prereading strategies:

1. Read the title or subject heading.
2. Think about everything I know about the subject before reading.
3. Look at any pictures, graphs, maps, etc.
4. Look at any words in bold type.
5. Predict what the passage will be about.
6. Think about what I'd like to learn about the subject.

Your child will probably mention some of these techniques, and you want to encourage him/her to use them while reading content area books for reports or for pleasure. Using them will help improve your child's recall and comprehension.

Enjoy this tape with your child, and please let me know where you see your child making the most progress and what areas you and your child feel you'd like to focus on next.

Your child and I thank you for your continued support and interest.

Mrs. Eisenhauer

FIGURE 3–10 Letter to parents of students in Mrs. Eisenhauer's third-grade class in Lynbrook, New York, informing them about using a taped reading. *Source:* From ALTERNATIVE ASSESSMENT TECHNIQUES FOR READING AND WRITING by Wilma Miller Copyright © 1995. Reprinted with permission of Center for Applied Research in Education/Prentice Hall Direct.

contexts for using their reading skills, and meaningfully incorporates research strategies into the reading curriculum. Thematic and integrated language arts units should be included in the portfolio collection.

Family information. Input from parents and families about portfolio contents is an additional welcome entry. To promote cooperation between the family and the school, parents should be actively included in the process. Some teachers do this by sending the portfolios home regularly. Students are encouraged to share their portfolios with their parents, and parents are asked to add an entry into the portfolio, noting that they have viewed the contents, discussed the portfolio with the student, and responded to the portfolio and their child's work. Many teachers find that a dialogue journal can assist them in understanding what important things a child is thinking about. Students especially find that this personal attention is rewarding (see Figure 3–11A, B).

Other reading portfolio contents. An organizational framework for a reading portfolio is essential, whether in the form of a table of contents or a letter to the portfolio reader. This helps entry selection, encourages students to take responsibility for choosing entries, and makes the ongoing monitoring and conferencing much more efficient. In Figure 3–12, Lisa provides a title and describes the contents of each "chapter" of her portfolio, and certainly demonstrates her organizational skills.

Use of standardized test data. A critical issue has been whether standardized test scores obtained both from district-wide testing programs and state assessment systems should be included in a reading portfolio. Many educators find that these traditional data add to a more complete picture of how the child functions as a reader. Others feel that such information is often unreliable, is not helpful in terms of instructional decision making,

> Dear Angela,
>
> I know this must be a very exciting month at your house. My brother is having a baby in March, and everyone is getting so excited. There are so many things to get ready for a new baby. Please tell me some of the ways your family is getting ready to welcome your new baby.
>
> Yours truly,
> Mrs. Murphy

FIGURE 3–11A Student teacher's dialogue journal with a third-grade student.

and contaminates an authentic assessment model. Regardless of a teacher's views about standardized tests, these measures are here to stay and are used in making high-stakes decisions. Teachers should know how a child functions on these tests. According to Johnson (2000), "Whether or not it is worthwhile use of instructional time, whether we like it or not, standardized, norm-referenced tests are having an incredibly powerful impact on U.S. schools right now" (p. 597).

Feb 8th

Dear Mrs. Murphy, Well we're running out of room to put all the baby's stuff so my dad is going to knock the wall down and make another room out of it. We all are so excited. I'm getting my own room soon and we're all going to take my momy on next Monday to toys "Я" us to buy more baby stuf and get a nice wooden crib to put in the baby's room.

FIGURE 3–11B Student's response to the dialogue journal entry in Figure 3–11A.

Name ___Lisa___ Grade __4__ Student Teacher _____ Date _____

My Portfolio
Table of Contents

Decide how you want to organize your portfolio. Sort everything in your portfolio and put them in piles that seem to go together in some way. Then try to think of a good title for each chapter. Include the books and stories you have read and all the different kinds of writing you have done.

Title for Chapter 1: ___Emma L.___

What I included in this chapter: ___~~Emma~~ L.___

In this chapter it included a report, or biography I wrote on Emma Lazuras.

Title for Chapter 2: ___Poetry___

What I included in this chapter: ___I included a poem about an ice cream shop and a poem about Autumn, and a halloween poem.___

Title for Chapter 3: ___retellings___

What I included in this chapter: ___in this chapter it included retellings that I made from stories I have read.___

Title for Chapter 4: ___Story Prompts___

What I included in this chapter: ___in this chapter it included a begining of a story, but then I finished it to make a Story Prompt.___

FIGURE 3–12 Sample portfolio contents of a fourth-grade student.

Before test data are included in a reading portfolio, it is strongly recommended that consideration be given to whether the data should be shared with a student, given the student's age, maturity, and reading level. Students who do not succeed on standardized tests can easily be defeated by having such data reproduced in their portfolio, which has been geared to documenting growth and success. Also, these data must be interpreted in the context of other information learned about the student through authentic assessment. For example, is the performance reported on standardized tests compatible with the work that the child has produced in the classroom setting? If there appears to be a significant discrepancy between standardized test scores and classroom performance (often in the direction of a depressed test score and better class performance), what explanation can be given for the divergence in performance data? Such factors as the child's language and experiential background, test-taking behavior, motivation, and attention span, as well as the content of the standardized test as compared with school curriculum, are all variables that must be considered because they can have dramatic impact on a child's test performance. Special consideration needs to be given to standardized tests taken by students with special education needs and students for whom English is not the first language. A more detailed discussion of portfolio assessment and these students is contained in Chapters 9 and 10.

In summary, a reading portfolio will reflect the goals of the reading curriculum, as well as the reading activities used in the classroom, and is highly individual, based on each child's interests, goals, and abilities. Such diversity is not only expected but is encouraged. According to Tierney et al. (1991), a good portfolio collection will demonstrate variety: "Collections will undoubtedly differ from classroom to classroom and from student to student depending upon teacher and student interests, cultural background, grade level, and many other variables" (p. 74).

Literature Portfolios

Many teachers and school districts now value the importance of incorporating quality literature into the instructional program, and it is evident that most standards-driven literacy portfolios now include evidence of the number of books read by children at each grade level and reflect the requirement that students read widely in various genre, and respond to literature in both cognitive and affective ways. Some teachers are unsure as to how to meaningfully document the extensive use of literature, whether it is part of the instructional program or as part of free-choice and recreational reading. Literature portfolios solve this problem. The prevalence of Author's Studies and literature-based learning centers also calls for a means of documenting students' wide reading. The dreary book report assignment has now been discarded for more meaningful reactions to literature that ask students to demonstrate that they've understood what they've read and encourage them to respond to the many important themes, ideas, and dilemmas represented in quality literature. Those teachers who use literature circles certainly value the importance of students discussing and reflecting on literature, but how to document this process is sometimes a challenge. Again, the literature portfolio is a superb solution.

Teachers in District 28 in New York City are required to use a portfolio to demonstrate students' attainment of the literacy standards which includes evidence that all students have read extensively each school year. At the elementary-school level, the students' portfolio must include the following:

Evidence of Reading Accomplishment

Entry #1—2–4 pieces of writing about literature read

Entry #2—2–4 pieces of writing about informational text read

Entry #3—Teacher certification that familiar texts were read aloud well.

Evidence of Quantity, Range and Depth

Entry #4—Teacher certification that 30 books were read, including 3 different kinds of books by at least 5 different authors; and 4 books on the same topic or of the same kind.

(The portfolios also include entries to document writing, speaking, listening, and even viewing!)

At the middle school level a similar portfolio requires students to again demonstrate range and depth in reading accomplishment. Among the required entries is documentation that the student has read at least 25 works, including works in 3 different genre, by at least 5 different authors; and at least 4 works by the same author or on the same topic. Entries can be in the form of: reading journals, literature logs, book reviews, and responses to literature. Again, the middle school journal also includes writing, speaking, listening and viewing exhibits.

Literacy Portfolios

Many educators now recognize that the language arts are most effectively taught in an integrated fashion, often employing such strategies as literature-based teaching, thematic teaching units, or reading and writing process activities. It logically follows that the portfolios contain evidence of reading and writing as well as other language arts activities. In many school districts literacy is properly viewed as the integration of reading, writing, speaking, and thinking, and thus literacy portfolios are used to reflect this more holistic view of literacy development. Likewise, for the purposes of documenting attainment of literacy outcomes, literacy portfolios take on an important role for accountability purposes.

A number of prominent literacy experts who have supported the use of portfolios describe total literacy collections. Valencia's (1990) article on portfolios was seminal in proposing a portfolio process that suggested a range of almost limitless entries; "the key [was] to ensure a variety of types of indicators of learning so that teachers, parents, students, and administrators [could] build a complete picture of the students' development," and the contents of a portfolio [grew] from curricular goals and instructional priorities (p. 339). Portfolio contents could therefore include a variety of language activities: reading logs, daily work, writing at various stages, class tests, checklists, unit projects, and audiotapes and videotapes. In another widely cited article about portfolio collection, Au, Scheu, Kawakami, and Herman (1990, p. 574) support the concept of an integrated portfolio. They describe six aspects of literacy that should be reflected in a portfolio: student ownership, reading comprehension, writing process, word identification, language and vocabulary knowledge, and voluntary reading. Further, they propose that the portfolio collection portray these literacy characteristics by containing an attitude questionnaire on reading and writing, a response to a literature task (including a checklist), a writing sample, a running record, and a voluntary reading log.

Rhodes and Shanklin (1993, pp. 416–418) suggest that teachers keep reading and writing folders that contain student-collected chronological entries of their ongoing work and that these folders should be reviewed with particular pieces selected and put into a Current Year Portfolio. Hill and Ruptic (1994, pp. 20–28) recommend a portfolio process that requires teachers to keep separate reading and writing collections of students' work. Suggested contents include attitude and interest surveys, logs, responses to reading and writing, and content area projects. These authors also advise teachers to keep an ongoing diagnostic notebook that records students' literacy development in both reading and writing. Farr and Tone (1994) also provide a very comprehensive and easy-to-use guide to creating portfolio collections and recommend various entries, with emphasis on the students' role in selection to reflect their interests and language applications. The portfolio process used at the Center for Reading and Writing, Rider University is described by Glazer and Brown (1993, pp. 34–37) and reflects the literature-based, language arts program employed in this clinical setting. Collected work samples are chosen by the students to reflect their accomplishments, and entries that contain data most helpful for planning instruction are also included.

Some school districts use separate portfolios for the emergent literacy stage and such portfolios can be considered more developmental in describing students' attainment of beginning reading and writing skills. Often these portfolios include developmental checklists in all language development areas and are completed by the teacher at critical points during the academic year to document progress.

Teachers in Juneau, Alaska, have used an integrated literacy approach and their Language Arts Portfolio echoes this philosophy by including assessment of reading, writing, listening, and speaking within a developmental framework (see Juneau School District, 1993). Consequently, a student's portfolio is an integrated language arts portfolio that presents a comprehensive assessment of that child's educational accomplishment in language arts. The portfolio used in Juneau contains the following entries collected during the four quarters of the school year: Student Reflection Letter, A Reading Continuum (a behaviorally oriented scale that assesses the student's development in essential skill areas), Reading Samples (using a running record form of analysis), Reading Attitude Survey, Writing Continuum (parallels the reading continuum concept as it pertains to essential writing skills), Writing Samples (scored according to district guidelines), Written Teacher Narrative (statement describes the student's performance and progress in reading, writing, listening, speaking, literacy interests, and suggestions for parents), and Speaking/Listening Narrative (a description of observed behavior in speaking and listening). Optional entries include favorite pieces chosen by the student, teacher anecdotal observations, oral language cassette tapes, developmental spelling lists, reading logs, and drawings and illustrations by the child. The Juneau portfolio collection is noteworthy both as an early example of district-wide portfolio adoption and for its attempt to document growth in all language areas.

Portfolio Performance or Demonstrations

An interesting aspect of portfolio use is the presentation or performance portfolio. Often this adds importance to the portfolio project or provides a conclusion to important, long-term effort. Students value the public display of their learning, especially when family and friends are invited as interested observers. Some teachers have students present portfolio projects in the form of a performance or oral report that often is assessed through the use of a collaboratively designed evaluation system called a rubric. Consequently, speaking and other communication skills become an important aspect of a student's ability to share information. Such a practice is part of a sixth-grade exit project used in the South Brunswick, New Jersey, schools to demonstrate that students are eligible for graduation and are prepared for middle-school work (see King-Shaver & Spicer, 1993). These projects integrate research skills, reading and writing ability, as well as speaking and presentation skills. Students are also reminded about the importance of listening, both when they are an audience for others' presentations and when they are involved in research that may include interviews. In this school district, community residents, local professionals, and students enrolled in teacher education programs at nearby colleges are all invited to participate as assessors, so that each sixth-grade student is individually evaluated by an "expert" trained in the use of a uniform scoring rubric.

In Long Island's North Shore school district—a district that endorses the use of integrated portfolios—a team of special education teachers in a middle school has students participate in a school-wide presentation of independent research in social studies that is incorporated into their portfolios. These teachers find that the oral/aural presentation format is especially important for their students who may be struggling with reading and writing skills. A successful oral presentation enhances the students' feelings of self-worth. It is evident that many school districts use a portfolio process that attempts to reinforce the interrelationships among all of the language arts.

Cumulative Record, Longitudinal Portfolios

Some school districts see the portfolio process as a collection designed not only to support the instructional program but also to promote accountability by adding to information contained in cumulative record folders and other forms of standard assessment information traditionally kept by school districts. Maintaining record folders (often called permanent record cards) has been traditional practice in compliance with state-mandated testing and record keeping, and it has also been useful in documenting longitudinal change and achievement over time. These records also follow children if they leave one school district and register in other districts within or out of state.

Districts that embrace portfolios as part of a district-wide, uniform assessment system do so with the belief that the authentic nature of the portfolio process is a true reflection of both instructional priorities and the actual achievement of students. However, restructuring district-wide assessment procedures is a formidable task replete with problems. The Lawrence/Inwood school district in New York is representative of school districts that are proponents of the portfolio process and have found them useful as part of longitudinal, cumulative records. This school district created a district-wide portfolio process through a series of committee meetings with both administrators and teachers. It was designed to reflect the concerns and reciprocal respect between teachers and administrators. New forms of literacy instruction were being used to emphasize reading and writing process strategies as well as extensive use of children's literature (Peppe & Petraglia, 1992). The result of this change in philosophy not only was seen in instructional practices but also created a necessity to change assessment to parallel and reflect the district's literacy practices. The district eventually adopted a reading-writing portfolio that was an outgrowth of several years' work and reflects the belief that teachers' observations, students' self-reflections, and analysis of classroom tasks are the most valid tools for language arts assessment. In the 8 years that the portfolio has been used there have been annual revisions, and recently the early childhood portfolio was separated from the portfolio used in upper grades. The Middle School English and Reading Departments created their own literacy portfolio from the outset.

The Lawrence/Inwood K–6 Reading/Writing Process Assessment Portfolio is contained in a sturdy, three-part folder with required core elements and encourages teachers to include other entries under an optional elements category:

Core Elements

- Language Literacy Profile (for use in kindergarten)
- Reading Development Checklist (grades 1 through 8)
- Record of Books Read
- Self-Assessment Form: Am I Developing as a Reader?
- Student Teacher Conference Log
- District Writing Folder—a standardized rubric to evaluate students' writing samples

Optional Elements

- Reading journals
- Audiotapes or videotapes of the student reading
- Photographic records
- Other projects
- Other formal and informal measures, including running records and anecdotal records
- Student interest inventory
- One-minute assessment taken three times per year

The elementary-grade folder was designed to be an end-of-year compilation of entries chosen from classroom portfolios kept for each child and accompanies the child from kindergarten through sixth grade. A Lawrence administrator and teacher proudly comment that after 8 years of portfolio use the portfolio process is alive and well. It is very evident that Lawrence has moved a long way from the traditional cumulative record system to a change in assessment strategies using a portfolio process based on mutual cooperation between teachers and administrators. One district administrator reported that the greatest asset of the portfolio process may be improved communication between teacher and family, especially during conferences in a district where parents are strongly involved in their children's education. The portfolios clearly show the parents the development of each child's literacy profile, which is well-known to the teacher.

District 28, a school district in Queens, New York City, with a highly diverse student population, recently mandated that all teachers keep a literacy portfolio for each child. This portfolio will follow the students throughout the elementary school years and is being implemented as part of documenting each student's growth toward reaching the NYC literacy standards. This portfolio system, used from kindergarten through middle-school years was previously briefly described under the literature portfolio discussion as it began with the need to document the number and kinds of books children read during each school year.

Other professionals in the assessment field have discussed the worth of using portfolios to document longitudinal change in literacy growth. Hill and Ruptic (1994) propose that a learning profile accompany students from kindergarten through grade 5 and be composed of representative samples from each year's collection. Rhodes and Shanklin (1993, pp. 418–419) propose that a permanent portfolio be assembled for students so that each new teacher can benefit from previous assessments. The number of items in such a permanent folder should be limited, or its usefulness will be outweighed by the unwieldy size of a long-term collection.

Several states and large school districts have instituted longitudinal portfolios. Murphy and Underwood (2000) describe portfolio projects in urban, suburban, and rural areas from the East Coast to the West that reflect both progressive and traditional forms of education. Vermont and Kentucky have mandated writing portfolios that are required of all teachers. (The Kentucky writing portfolio system will be described in greater detail in Chapter 6.) In these states children's portfolios are valued as a long-term index of the child's literacy development. Kentucky's portfolio system is especially important because it is linked to extensive educational reform efforts and called for changes in curriculum requiring activity-based instruction and interactive classrooms. This reform effort has been called "unprecedented in scope" and has involved all stakeholders in the education, legislative, and judicial branches (Murphy & Underwood, 2000, p. 183). The scores from children's writing portfolios are used in Kentucky as part of an Accountability Index to document what outcomes are evident as part of school reform, and before this "no one had ever linked portfolio assessment and accountability for classroom performance so tightly together before" (Murphy & Underwood, 2000, p. 185).

CONCERNS AND CONCLUSIONS

The use of portfolios is not without some significant concerns. For example, it is important to separate the effects of using a classroom portfolio process from using portfolios in larger assessment programs, which result in portfolios being used for making high-stakes decisions such as program placement, promotion, and graduation. Some educators feel the need to be especially cautious because of the serious ramifications of misinformed decision making. Issues that have been raised about large assessment programs that use performance-based techniques have addressed such areas as the reliability of limited sampling of student performance, concern about equity issues that result from assessment decisions, the opportunity for students in diverse communities to receive quality education, and the tension of creating systems that are sensitive to individual priorities and allow for wide variations but are still reliable and consistent (Pearson, 1994, pp. 218–227). Wiggins (1998) proposed a portfolio anthology process designed to overcome issues regarding the validity of other portfolio formats. These portfolios are created with three different forms of student work, including tasks (requiring integrated performance), prompts (open-ended writing questions), and tests and quizzes (from both district and state levels with various formats). These anthologies would be scored annually to determine if a student's performance had met benchmark outcomes for each grade level.

Researchers also caution that too much emphasis has been placed on how to create portfolios without understanding and analyzing how portfolios are actually used. Gomez and Graue (1994) reported that although portfolios have opened a new dialogue about teaching and learning, too much emphasis has been placed on the form of portfolios without analyzing the effects of their use. Their research describes current portfolio practice by a small group of teachers who were identified as being quality educators by peers, administrators, parents, and children. Unfortunately, the researchers found that assessment with portfolios often replicated much of traditional, standardized measures, because portfolios tended to be cumulative and linear, were permeated by the context of accountability, were quantitative rather than integrative, and focused on reporting data that all too often focused on students' deficiencies rather than their strengths. In summary, these researchers feel that any act of assessment is essentially interpretive and relies on the lenses of the observer, who creates meaning from portfolio contents. While portfolio assessment has promise, experts such as Gomez and Graue (1994) remind us that that use of portfolio assessment will likely be constrained by historical and social factors, by the different expectations of different schools and school systems, and certainly by what an individual teacher feels is important about teaching, learning, and students.

Arter and Spandel (1992) share similar concerns about the ability to draw accurate conclusions from portfolios. They caution that portfolios, as a form of performance assessment, can have a number of problems:

> The work in the portfolio may not really be representative of what the student knows and can do, the criteria used to critique the product may not reflect the most relevant or useful dimensions of the task, the work that a student puts in the portfolio may make the viewer wonder what is authentic about it, there may be aspects of the portfolio process that make a student unable to really demonstrate what he or she knows or can do, and the conclusions drawn from the portfolio can be heavily influenced by the person doing the evaluation. (p. 38)

Graves (1992) cautioned that educators should "slow down and learn" about portfolios before "rac[ing] to use portfolios with large populations" (p. 2). He suggested seven principles that should be heeded when a portfolio process is used:

1. Involve the students.
2. Help the staff keep portfolios of their own.
3. Broaden the purpose of portfolios.
4. Keep instructional opportunities open.
5. Re-examine issues in comparability.
6. Study the effect of school policy on portfolio practice.
7. Enlist the ingenuity of teachers. (p. 3)

These suggestions still appear timely and relevant. There is great benefit to be obtained from using portfolios as well as a great deal to learn and understand about the process. It is evident that portfolios are not simply folders that contain students' work. According to Harp (1996), teachers need to know that portfolios involve "a collection that is carefully, thoughtfully and critically evaluated," require an effective management system, and can be time-consuming (p. 140). The ability to record and store students' work in electronic portfolios will likely resolve some of the management concerns about portfolios, but they are also likely to raise new problems. Murphy and Underwood (2000), having extensively reviewed current portfolio practice, conclude that "portfolios have grown well beyond their infancy, that their promise has been at least partially fulfilled, and that there is a future for portfolios—even when they are taken beyond classroom walls" (p. 16). The impact of technology on portfolios is at its infancy. Some school districts are just beginning to use computer technology to create, store, and manage student records, and certainly technology has much to offer with portfolios. A brief Appendix that follows this chapter discusses electronic portfolios. Undoubtedly, literacy portfolios will continue to develop and will reflect the idiosyncratic contexts in which they are used for different purposes.

REFERENCES

Arter, J., & Spandel, V. (1992, Spring). Using portfolios of student work in instruction and assessment. *Educational Measurement: Issues and Practice*, 36–44.

Au, K., Scheu, J., Kawakami, A., & Herman, P. (1990, April). Assessment and accountability in a Whole Literacy Curriculum. *The Reading Teacher, 43*(8), 574–578.

Bauman, J., Hoffman, J., Moon, J., & Duffy-Hester, A. (1998). Where are teachers' voices in the phonics whole language debate? Results from a survey of U.S. elementary classroom teachers. *The Reading Teacher, 51*(8), 636–650.

Calfee, R., & Perfumo, P. (1993). Student portfolios: Opportunities for a revolution in assessment. *Journal of Reading, 36*, 532–537.

Cooper, J. (1993). *Literacy*. Boston: Houghton Mifflin.

Courtney, A., & Abodeeb, T. (1999, April). Diagnostic-reflective portfolios. *The Reading Teacher, 52*(7), 708–715.

Diez, M. (2000). Teachers, assessment, and the Standards Movement. *Education Week* (May 3), pp. 45, 49.

Farr, R., & Tone, B. (1994). *Portfolio and performance assessment*. New York: Harcourt Brace.

Fitzgerald, J. (1999). What is this thing called "balance?" *The Reading Teacher, 53*(2), 100–107.

Flippo, R. (1998). Points of agreement: A display of professional unity in our field. *The Reading Teacher, 52*, 30–39.

Glazer, S., & Brown, C. (1993). *Portfolios and beyond: Collaborative assessment in reading and writing*. Norwood, MA: Christopher Gordon.

Gomez, M. L., & Graue, M. E. (1994). *Possibilities, not panacea: A case for rethinking the processes of portfolio assessment*. Unpublished paper. University of Wisconsin-Madison.

Goodman, Y. (1978). Kid watching: An alternative to testing. *National Elementary Principal, 57*, 41–45.

Graves, D. (1992). Portfolios: Keep a good idea growing. In D. Graves & B. Sunstein (Eds.), *Portfolios portraits* (pp. 1–12). Portsmouth, NH: Heinemann.

Halloway, L. (1999). A tailored path to graduation. *New York Times* (Dec. 15), B1, 13.

Harp, B. (1996). *The handbook of literacy assessment and evaluation*. Norwood, MA: Christopher-Gordon.

Hill, B., & Ruptic, C. (1994). *Practical aspects of authentic assessment: Putting the pieces together*. Norwood, MA: Christopher Gordon.

Hinchman, K., & Michel, P. (1999). Reconciling polarity: Toward a responsive model of evaluating literacy performance. *The Reading Teacher, 52*(6), 578–587.

Jenkins, C. B. (1996). *Inside the writing portfolio*. Portsmouth, NH: Heinemann.

Johnson, M. (2000). Develop strategies for success in critical questions. *The Reaching Teacher, 53*(7), 597.

Juneau School District. (1993). *Language arts portfolio handbook*. Juneau, AK: Author.

King-Shaver, B., & Spicer, W. (1993). What is worth assessing? Authentic assessment in South Brunswick. *Focus on Education, NJASCD*, 38–44.

Murphy, S., & Underwood, T. (2000). *Portfolio practices: Lessons from schools, districts and states*. Norwood, MA: Christopher Gordon.

Paulson, F. L., Paulson, P., & Meyer, C. (1991, February). What makes a portfolio a portfolio? *Educational Leadership*, 60–63.

Pearson, P. D. (1994). Commentary on California's new English-language arts assessment. In S. Valencia, E. Hiebert, & P. Afflerbach (Eds.), *Authentic reading assessment: Practices and possibilities* (pp. 218–227). Newark, DE: IRA.

Peppe, R., & Petraglia, M. (1992, Winter). Toward a reading/writing assessment portfolio. *Holistic Education Review, 5*(4), 24–30.

Rael, P., & Travelstead, J. (1993). *Statewide student assessment requirements*. Santa Fe, NM: New Mexico State Department of Education.

Reutzel, D. R. (1999). On balanced reading. *The Reading Teacher, 52*(4), 322–324.

Rhodes, L., & Shanklin, N. (1993). *Windows into literacy*. Portsmouth, NH: Heinemann.

Rothstein, R. (2000). Tests alone fail to assure accountability of schools. *New York Times* (May 24), B12.

Skillings, M., & Ferrell, R. (2000). Student-generated rubrics: Bring students into the assessment process. *The Reading Teacher, 53*(6), 452–455.

Stiggins, R. (1997). *Student-centered classroom assessment*. Columbus, OH: Merrill.

Tierney, R. (1998). Literacy assessment reform: Shifting beliefs, principled possibilities, and emerging practices. *The Reading Teacher, 51*(5), 374–390.

Tierney, R., Carter, M., & Desai, L. (1991). *Portfolio assessment in the reading-writing classroom*. Norwood, MA: Christopher-Gordon.

Valencia, S. (1990, January). A portfolio approach to classroom reading assessment: The whys, whats, and hows. *The Reading Teacher, 43*(4), 338–340.

Wiggins, G. (1998). *Educative assessment: Designing assessment to inform and improve student performance*. San Francisco: Josey-Bass.

Wilgoren, J. (2000). Secretary of education proposes that teachers work all the year. *New York Times* (Feb. 23), A19.

Worthy, J., & Hoffman, J. (2000). Critical questions: The press to test. *The Reading Teacher, 53*(7), 596–598.

Chapter 3 Appendix

Literacy Portfolios in the Electronic Age

by

Mark Quigley, Ed.D. Social Studies Teacher
Garden City High School,
Garden City, NY

Carole Rhodes, Ed.D., Assoc. Prof. Education
Adelphi University,
Garden City, New York

with the assistance of

Jeffrey Nowak, Ph.D., Assistant Professor
Indiana-Purdue, Ft. Wayne, IN

The implementation of literacy portfolios is explored in depth throughout this book. This Appendix describes the use of electronic portfolios (e-portfolios) in literacy classes. (Note: Here, the terms "electronic portfolio" and "digital portfolio" are used interchangeably.) Making e-portfolios "happen" is a matter of motivation, determination, and technological sophistication as well as availability of resources and energy. E-portfolios provide many benefits for both teachers and students because they require minimal storage space; are very durable; can be easily updated; are highly portable and duplicable; lend themselves to high-interest presentation; can include artifacts in many media types (audio, video, graphic, and test); and provide easy accessibility. Perhaps a prime advantage is that e-portfolios provide a concrete way for students to apply technology skills in a meaningful, purposeful way. A current trend in e-portfolio development is to make them Internet accessible, which means that once a portfolio is published on a Web site, viewers can "see" a portfolio any place in the world that has Internet access.

What is an e-portfolio and why should I use it?

A portfolio is a systematic collection of student work and an e-portfolio, as all good portfolios, is not a haphazard collection. Rather, it is a reflective tool that demonstrates accomplishment of a specific goal in a different form, which allows students to collect and organize portfolio artifacts in many types of media (audio, video, graphics, written work, scanned images, and any student product that demonstrates learning). All of a student's work can be put into a computer format or digitized for the portfolio. Audio files, picture files, video captures, and scanned writing can be linked to a student Web site and an Internet address allows fellow students, teachers, and friends to view the portfolios via the Internet. Preparing material for the Internet can be time consuming, but the Internet provides a more permanent and accessible record. The use of e-portfolios may provide a solution to the problem of creating, updating, managing, and storing large amounts of information and they can ultimately eliminate the need for physically storing and transporting bulky paper portfolios.

Students often find that creating a Web-based e-portfolio is fun and they are very enthusiastic about developing the portfolio because they can easily share it with their peers in the most up-to-date format. An additional benefit of e-portfolios can be found in the inclusion of hypertext links, which allow clear connections between reflections and artifacts within the portfolio. In order to use e-portfolios, technology resources and familiarity with their use are essential. Schools must have appropriate recording technologies that are accessible and understandable to all potential users and group viewing systems that allow for the social activity of interpreting performances.

The ability to store a wide variety of contents cannot be underestimated. Original writing from students may be collected easily in notebooks and files and then digitized (by use of scanning equipment) and entered into a computer file. But what about samples of oral reading, a three-dimensional model, artwork, a sketch, an animation, and other response type activities? E-portfolios make it possible to include examples of all these different media in a portfolio.

For cross-curricular purposes, the e-portfolio provides an easy way for students (particularly once they are taking many classes with different teachers) to document their literacy progress in multiple classes and can assist with team collaboration. For example, a project done for a social studies class may contain examples of a persuasive piece of writing that would be appropriate for a language arts class as well. In a paper format, the student would have to duplicate the work for both teachers and classes, but in an electronic format the student can simply add a link to the entry on his or her Web site. Doing so also helps students and teachers see interdisciplinary connections between literacy and in all subject areas. Teachers can better understand and provide appropriate instruction for their students when they see how students perform in a variety of settings.

What technology is useful in the creation of an e-portfolio?

There are numerous commercial computer software packages that make creating a portfolio relatively easy. These programs are essentially computer database packages that provide a friendly interface that is less intimidating than typical database programs. However, for the adventurous educator, any "off the shelf" database package has the capacity to store and categorize the typical files of a digital portfolio. These packages can include Microsoft Access and Filemaker Pro, to name two. The teacher creates a template for the portfolio for distribution to students in the classroom. Essentially, this template is an empty database format with all of the areas defined for different computer file formats, such as audio, video, and written work. Students can then be guided to use the format for the assembly of their portfolio.

The use of a database package may be intimidating—another package to consider would be a presentation program. Typically, these programs are designed to present information to an audience using text and pictures and are being used more frequently in the classroom by both teachers and students. Two popular presentation packages are Microsoft PowerPoint and WordPerfect Presentations, which allow for the user to integrate text, graphics, scanned images, sound files, and video files into one computer file. Both products also use a feature known as a hyperlink to create connections to the Internet and other computer files. Ultimately, students can integrate different presentations from different subjects into a cohesive portfolio reflecting all their course work. Even a word processor program, such as Microsoft Word or WordPerfect, can be used to develop a simple e-portfolio.

The wide use of Internet resources is clearly apparent in today's classrooms and the Internet already contains the necessary features for e-portfolios such as text, graphics, sound, and video. Any Web page development package can be used to create a Web-based portfolio; two popular packages are Microsoft FrontPage and Netscape Composer. Because of security issues revolving around Internet use, all educators should be cautioned to use good judgment when students publish their portfolios on the Web. For example, the use of an access code for opening a portfolio file would mean that it could be viewed only by those who have permission to do so.

Just do it!

The easiest way to begin the e-portfolio process is to start with a word processor. Written work is the backbone of any portfolio and by typing directly into a computer, a student is well on the way to developing an e-portfolio. Next, buy and install a scanner on the computer for entering pictures and graphics. Adobe Photoshop is a valuable program because it will allow students to fix any problems with photos in a digitized format. A scanner can be used to convert handwriting samples or artwork to a digital picture which can be integrated into a Web page. Photographs can also be scanned into a computer. If a student has previously typewritten work, an Optical Character Recognition software package can be used to scan in the work without requiring the retyping of the entire paper. A digital camera can be used to take photographs of artwork or models or any other work students wish to include in their portfolio. These photos are already digitized and can be integrated immediately into a Web page. Storing sound files or video files requires special software to convert them to a digitized format. Preparing student work for an e-portfolio is relatively easy once the proper equipment has been installed on a computer.

E-portfolio applications

E-portfolios can be used in many ways. Consider the case where students start out in a school where the teachers assist them in creating an e-portfolio. If primary-grade students are taught and assisted to scan and save images of their work in digital format, a record of their progress over time can be made, backed-up, stored, retrieved and, when necessary, transferred. Add the inclusion of teacher progress reports, reflections, and evaluations of student growth over the course of the year, and a multidimensional picture of students' development would now exist. In addition, embedding digital audio and video records of students in the e-portfolio taken with a digital camera could assist parents and subsequent teachers in viewing the many aspects of students' academic, psychomotor, speaking, and social abilities. This full picture of student accomplishments could have many applications from a team Committee on Special Education meeting, to parents and students celebrating the evidence of growth and learning over time at graduation, to teachers acquainting themselves with students well before the beginning of a new school year.

There are also other benefits that will be attained by students as they are guided in the process of further developing their respective e-portfolios. Some benefits result from the many aesthetic and technological aspects of these kinds of e-portfolios that can broaden students' thinking and creativity and allow for the demonstration of their multiple abilities. As students progress through the grades, more ownership over the task of creating and storing educational artifacts may be placed on them. Student ownership of the educational process is fostered when they are given more responsibility for organizing the artifacts in their e-portfolio. It is becoming increasingly evident that many students possess technological skills that often are difficult for their teachers and parents to master, and the e-portfolio is a wonderful opportunity to utilize these skills in an educationally sound process!

Another benefit to this format for archiving student work is related to student mobility issues. Students often move from school to school within in a school system or even from school system to school system across many miles. Individual school district curricula and differences between state requirements can easily result in there being incongruence between what is offered and expected for students who move from one location to another. The e-portfolio offers the new school administration and personnel the opportunity to view a realistic and authentic assessment of a student's current educational accomplishments. For example, if it became necessary for "Grant's" family to move to another state in the middle of his sixth-grade school year, his e-portfolio could be instantaneously forwarded to the new school system and easily reviewed there. Grant's current educational status could be authentically assessed on matters such as performance-based proficiency and in the context of the available offerings of the new school system. Therefore, even before he arrives on the school property, a good understanding of Grant's abilities and needs may be assessed via an examination of the available artifacts (i.e., drafts, final copies, logs, journals, reports, goal sheets, conference notes, essays, video presentations, art work), thus allowing for appropriate educational offerings and services to be arranged.

Conclusion

So are e-portfolios something so new and profound that they will drastically change how the educational enterprise operates? Perhaps this will not occur to a sizeable degree because the e-portfolio is in one sense merely another means by which student achievement can be recorded, assessed, and celebrated. At the same time, however, using digital media for a student portfolio allows for ease of storage, back-up, and transmittal that makes it worth consideration. In addition, students reap the extra benefits of technological skill enhancement and increased ownership over the educational process. The benefits of archiving student progress via the creation of digital student portfolios make this new technology not just enticing but promising!

REFERENCES

Barrett, H. (1998, October). Strategic questions: What to consider when planning for electronic portfolios. *Learning & Leading With Technology*, 6–13.

Lankes, A. M. D. (1995, December). Electronic portfolios: A new idea in assessment. *ERIC Digest*, ED 390377.

Sheingold K., & Frederiksen, J. (1994). Using technology to support innovative assessment. In B. Means (Ed.), *Technology and education reform*. San Francisco: Jossey-Bass.

A Model Literacy Portfolio

KEY WORDS AND CONCEPTS

interest inventory   summative portfolio
student portfolio   permanent record portfolio
cumulative portfolio   teacher portfolio
baseline portfolio

A new teacher taking a graduate literacy class recently posed a dilemma. She said that her school requires that students spend a great deal of time preparing for the standards-based literacy test that is used throughout the state and she feels that too much time is being spent on test preparation. Although she's heard a great deal about portfolio assessment and values the authentic nature of this process, she hears other teachers' concerns that it's too time consuming, especially in the current climate for standards-based teaching and test preparation. She questions whether she can fit a portfolio process into her packed curriculum and whether the effort is worthwhile.

Her concerns are important and require a thoughtful answer. This chapter describes a model portfolio process, a literacy portfolio, and is our response to this teacher's concerns.

GOALS AND PURPOSE OF A LITERACY PORTFOLIO

Much has been written about portfolio use, and attention has focused on the various forms of portfolios that teachers have begun using as an integral aspect of language arts instruction and literacy assessment. More recently, a great deal has been written about the mandate for more standardized testing as an antidote to failing schools and low standards. How to balance mandated testing within a context of meaningful school reform is a question worthy of ongoing debate. However, it is our firm belief that literacy portfolios can be a valuable aspect of a quality literacy program and, combined with mandated assessment, can provide teachers with information and insights needed to improve instruction. This chapter describes a model literacy portfolio that we recommend. We describe the ideal contents, discuss a process for using it, and then present some important issues that need to be clarified before a portfolio process can be successfully implemented.

The primary purpose of the literacy portfolio is to improve literacy instruction by authentically assessing the child's development in reading and writing. The literacy portfolio can become the anchor of a quality literacy program that encompasses literacy assessment, literacy teaching, and literacy learning. An effective literacy portfolio enables the teacher to monitor a child's progress and affords ample opportunities to gain insights into strategies that the student uses. Additionally, it sets the environment for collaborative learning so that the child and teacher can work together toward improvement in reading and writing. Students' involvement in self-assessment, setting priorities, and assuming greater responsibility for their literacy development all provide for a maximal educational experience. Information obtained through the portfolio process becomes an important aspect of sharing assessment with children, their families, and other members of their instructional team and clearly documents the outcomes of a literacy program that are essential as part of the renewed emphasis on accountability and raising standards.

Specific purposes of the Literacy Portfolio (LP) include the following:

- Provides opportunities for realistic and authentic assessment of a student's literacy abilities by observing the student during reading and writing.

- Promotes collection of actual student work that gives the teacher a direct opportunity to see the application of reading and writing skills in the broad context of daily performance. Such information can be used to ascertain whether the student has reached the literacy standards that are specified for the given grade level and stage of development.

- Creates a collaborative relationship between the teacher and student so that shared instructional goals are appropriate and relevant to actual student needs and priorities.

- Creates an opportunity through portfolio conferencing for direct one-to-one instruction that maximizes the quality of teaching through individualized and focused group instruction.
- Assists the student in developing metacognitive and self-reflective reading and writing skills and strategies that encourage responsibility for ongoing development.
- Creates a climate of recognizing the student's strengths in reading and writing ability, rather than focusing on weaknesses or deficits.
- Provides insight that will prove invaluable for jointly establishing appropriate literacy goals and choosing effective instructional strategies.
- Promotes the sharing of information about the student's actual reading and writing strategies with other members of the instructional team and interested parties.
- Incorporates the child, the teacher, and the family in joint assessment, collaboration, and learning.

The concept behind a literacy portfolio process is that literacy instruction will be enhanced by selectively collecting student work that reflects daily reading and writing behavior used in the classroom, by the descriptive and analytic evaluation of this collection by both the teacher and student, and by the judicious use of other informal assessment techniques. It is both frustrating and discouraging for teachers to merely lament the imposition of state assessments and the disproportionate time school districts are expending on test preparation. It would be more worthwhile for teachers to collectively reflect on the quality of their literacy programs and provide students with opportunities for mastering the skills and strategies that are appropriate for their grade levels. By establishing portfolios, the teacher and student learn to:

- Accurately evaluate the current status of the student's literacy behavior.
- Reflect and take pride in the student's changing literacy behavior.
- Establish appropriate literacy goals for instruction.
- Choose effective methods of literacy instruction.
- Communicate more effectively with others (e.g., parents, school district personnel) and provide a complete and accurate description of how literacy is progressing.

Ultimate accountability for literacy teaching is achieved when the teacher understands the individual student's reading and writing strategies and competencies and correspondingly when students understand the importance of reading and writing in their lives.

NEW ROLES FOR TEACHERS AND STUDENTS

The portfolio is built on the underlying belief that literacy learning is enjoyable and has practical and personal significance. Quality literacy instruction employs methods that are interesting, dynamic, and compelling and results from the teacher's understanding of what strategies students use in daily encounters with print, what students enjoy reading, and what is meaningful to students. As students become proficient in reading and writing, they increase opportunities for both academic and personal success.

Students need to be actively engaged in their own literacy development; they can no longer be passive recipients of information and indifferent participants to a sometimes unmotivating instructional program. Therefore, an essential aspect of the literacy portfolio process is the collaborative partnership between teachers and students to determine literacy goals. It is through guided self-reflection—best accomplished before and during the portfolio conference—that students take pride in their developing reading and writing ability. Too often in the past, assessment was external to the teaching-learning process and had little practical impact on daily instruction. Student's opinions and attitudes about what was important to learn and how they learned best were rarely incorporated in instructional decisions. When engaged in the portfolio process, students reflect on their reading and writing and they establish appropriate goals for continued accomplishment that will have meaning in their lives. Instructional decision making is the end result of a self-evaluative, collaborative process.

The teacher has a very important role when a literacy portfolio process is used. Teachers must be keenly aware of each student's reading and writing profile (past and current performances) and must be knowledgeable about literacy methodologies so they can translate assessment data into goals and effective methods of instruction. Teachers must know the state and local standards that have been specified for literacy at each grade level and the progress that the child is making toward reaching them. Consequently, each teacher must develop skills for diagnosing reading and writing ability and must be familiar with a wide range of sound methodological approaches to maximize literacy learning. Although this diagnostician/teacher role sounds quite formidable, it is the most effective model for meeting students' needs. Figure 4–1 contains a conceptualization of the process in which literacy portfolio assessments interface with instruction, reflection, goal setting, and literacy opportunities. Each phase of the model obviously affects and informs the other stages.

When teachers begin to think about the development of a literacy portfolio process, they should ask themselves several basic questions:

1. What are the reading and writing strategies that students should be developing, given their age, grade placement, level of ability, and where are they in terms of meeting the grade-level standards?

2. What reading and writing opportunities and activities are appropriate, given the students' interests and abilities and goals for literacy development during this school year?

3. What specific literacy products should the students and I review that come from daily activities and reflect student learning opportunities?

4. What behavior and activities should I observe on an ongoing basis that will help inform me about the strategies used by the students?

5. How can I translate the assessment knowledge I have gained from working with the students, observing the students, jointly evaluating the portfolio contents, and using other informal assessment techniques into effective whole class, guided group, and individualized instruction?

FIGURE 4–1 Model of a literacy portfolio assessment process.

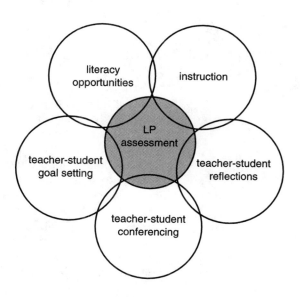

One aim of the portfolio process is to give the teacher an opportunity to reflect on the outcomes and opportunities for dynamic language-based learning for all students in the classroom. It is our sincere belief that a quality literacy program incorporates the following:

- Students should be given opportunities to enjoy quality literature appropriate for their age and development by reading work in different genres.

- Students should be given opportunities to expand their conceptual base as well as enhance language development through exposure to literature, both fiction and nonfiction.

- Students should be given the opportunities to grow in written expression through direct instruction in individual, small-group, and large-group settings; daily writing in various forms in all curriculum areas, especially using journals and logs; writing for various purposes and different audiences; and by seeing the reciprocal relationship between the reading and writing processes.

- Students should be shown how reading and writing have personal importance in their daily life, both in school and at home.

STARTING A LITERACY PORTFOLIO

Collecting and Selecting Student Work

Students are told to collect their daily literacy work in "work-in-progress folders." These folders become the repository of different projects and products that the students review to select entries for the portfolio, but students need to be guided in determining how to choose the entries. It is most important that the teacher help the students understand that the purpose of the portfolio process is for both the teacher and students to assess ongoing literacy strategies and growth, as well as to document how each student changes over time. Work produced in all subjects should be considered for the working folders. Some teachers require students to write in journals each day and to keep written work in separate writing folders.

Obviously, it is vital that the teacher has a firm understanding of the portfolio's purpose and once the purpose is clear, it becomes easier to determine what the contents of the portfolio should be. It is our belief that a good portfolio documents both reading and writing development throughout the school year. Several techniques are useful in assisting students to have a real understanding of what a portfolio is and what it looks like. Teachers and students are encouraged to review portfolios from other grades or from previous classes. Teachers can also invite students from a previous year to share their portfolios with the new class. The students and the teacher should reflect on the students' opportunities for using reading and writing throughout the school day and brainstorm the possible products that can be used to show literacy ability.

Students need to be guided in how to select products from their work in progress and reading and writing folders for the more carefully defined and selective literacy portfolio. Some teachers list core contents and provide students with a sheet of suggestions to guide their selections. Teachers should conduct minilessons to demonstrate the decision-making process that students should use when choosing portfolio entries. Some teachers model the process and show their students how they reflect when choosing entries for their own portfolio. Other teachers use individual teacher-student conferences, peer groups, or a buddy system to ensure that students have the opportunity to share with others who are also part of the portfolio creation process. It is essential that students realize that a portfolio consists of *selected* entries and that these entries have been chosen for a *specific* reason.

We recommend that at least four times per year, students be required to choose entries for their individual literacy portfolio and participate in a formal conference with the teacher to discuss selections and review the portfolio. The literacy portfolio evolves through four sequential phases. Materials are added or deleted based on the portfolio focus of each phase. The focus of these four portfolio phases will vary slightly throughout the school year:

- Portfolio 1 creates the *baseline portfolio* in which the student's literacy ability, interests, and background are determined and the initial goal-setting process is begun.

- Portfolios 2 and 3 are *developmental* and are used for monitoring progress toward meeting literacy goals, redefining goals as appropriate, and determining the most appropriate methods and materials for literacy opportunities.

- Portfolio 4 is *summative*, because it reflects on the entire year's work and growth in literacy development.

Prescribing the specific contents of a literacy portfolio should not pose a dilemma. It is essential that the contents reflect each teacher's priorities and be sensitive to individual student needs as well as to differences among students, school environments, and literacy philosophies. The following section provides suggestions that are culled from a theoretical understanding of factors that promote quality literacy instruction and reflect a review of instructional practices in different types of classrooms in varied locations. The suggestions are not meant to create a standardized portfolio but are provided to guide teachers who are just beginning to implement a portfolio process. We highly recommend that teachers within a school district collaborate with each other as well as with administrators and, most important, with their students to create the outline for a literacy portfolio. It is important to balance the concern that portfolios reflect individuality with the concern that they also incorporate consistent features to promote focus and longevity.

Student Portfolios

We recommend that students' portfolios contain the following entries (see Figure 4–2):

Introductory Letter. Students should write a brief statement that describes the purpose of the portfolio and how the contents are organized. This can also be facilitated by including a table of contents created by the student or provided by the teacher when core contents are mutually agreed on. Students should date each entry so comparisons can be made to determine growth and change. Many teachers and students have developed portfolios that are easy to read, review, and update by using loose-leaf notebooks, with the different sections identified by section markers.

A Self-Reflective Piece of Writing. One entry should reflect the students' awareness of themselves as readers and writers. It can be written exclusively for the portfolio (some teachers use a survey/questionnaire format), or it can be a piece chosen from the working folders accompanied by a self-reflective essay. Many teachers have found it helpful for the initial self-reflective writing to contain information about the students' interests and attitudes as well as their expectations for the school year. In some schools these expectations are translated into goals, but in others they are related to state standards. Figure 4–3 is a writing goals sheet that was completed by a fifth-grade student at mid-year.

It is helpful, especially with younger students, to have this self-reflection include a statement about why the piece was chosen. The focus is on students becoming aware of their own literacy skills so they can comment on their development through the year. Self-reflection can focus on literacy goals that have been met and on changes in literacy ability, and it can also be used for analytic thinking about specific literacy projects. For example, a student might answer these questions:

"What piece of writing do you feel most proud of and why?"

"What have you read that has had a strong impact on you? How did it affect you?"

Teachers can also review commercially available materials such as those contained in Bader's (2002, pp. 11–14) informal reading inventory, which includes student priority

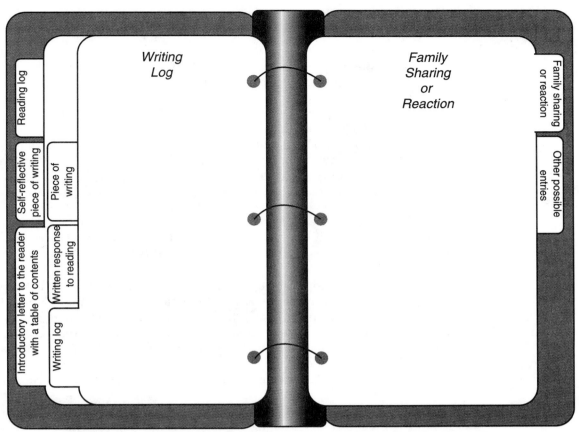

FIGURE 4–2 Contents of a student's literacy assessment portfolio.

Writing Goals for Richard for February through March

1. What I like most about my writing is

that my spelling is getting better.

2. What I would like to improve the most about my writing is

sentence structure.

3. I am going to work on *organization* for the next two months.

4. I'll try to do these things to help reach my goals:

use spelling checks
use language skills checklists
write interesting sentences.

Signed: _____ student

_____ teacher

Feb. 1

FIGURE 4–3 A writing goals sheet completed by a fifth-grade student.

surveys; Rhodes's (1993, pp. 2–31) text that contains interviews and attitude surveys that are appropriate for students of different ages and also are translated into Spanish; Vizyak's (1996) text that focuses on primary grade students; forms provided by Sharp (1989, p. 27); and strategies suggested by Miller (1995), Clemmons, Laase, Cooper, Areglado, and Dill (1993), and Fiderer (1995). There are a plethora of commercially available portfolio books that provide checklists, forms, and structure for teachers to use when they begin a portfolio process. Obviously, such materials can be a good starting place for those new to the process, but they need to be thoughtfully reviewed before being adapted to the teacher's own goals.

For young, emergent readers or students with limited literacy skills, artwork and pictures can be included along with dictated narration to explain the illustrations. Students are encouraged to use art to decorate their portfolios, to personalize them, and to make them distinctive and representative of their interests. A reflective or descriptive piece might be included to describe the illustrated portfolio jacket.

Reading Log. In a good literacy program students are encouraged to keep track of the amount and kind of reading that they are doing in school and at home. A reading log can be used to document books students read. Additionally, more schools are inviting parental participation in at-home literacy projects through sharing books with their children, listening to their children read aloud, or reading to them. The logs can reflect this as well. The log of books read can be accompanied by a chart that analyzes the entries according to genre. This encourages diversity in reading choices and can also guide reading selections.

Some teachers require a reaction to each book read, whereas others simply ask students to note their daily reading. Analyzing or reporting on books read can be individualized based on the student's age and level of sophistication. Tedious, old-fashioned book reports should be avoided if a love of literature and reading are to be encouraged and developed. Teachers should encourage students to respond and make personal connections to what they read.

Writing Log. Parallel to the reading log, students should keep records of their writing that can be analyzed in terms of how often they write, the forms of writing they use, and their audiences. Providing students with diverse writing opportunities promotes frequency and range in writing. Some educators suggest that students integrate reading and writing logs to reinforce the understanding that reading and writing are integral and related aspects of literacy. Whether lists are integrated or separate is not as significant as the necessity for keeping track of how much and what kind of reading and writing students do daily.

Again, for the emergent reader or the student with limited English proficiency, artwork and dictated stories with captions can supplement the writing contributions.

A Written Response to Reading. The form of written response will vary, given the age and ability of the student and the formats the teacher employs. At the primary level, the entry might be in the form of a story grammar, a story frame, a web, or a picture with a dictated reaction or a response using invented spelling. At the intermediate level, the response to literature is more likely to come from a literature response journal, a learning log, or a teacher-directed assignment. Some teachers have successfully used innovative forms of reporting about books such as annotated bookmarks, book jackets, or book advertisements. These entries will depend on the instructional program and the kinds of assignments and literacy opportunities that are part of the reading program. For example, teachers might suggest to their students that responses include a statement about a reading selection that had a significant impact on them or a reaction to what they've read explaining why they liked or disliked a book. Having students make self-to-text connections has become an important goal in well-informed literacy programs.

Students should be encouraged to respond to both fiction and nonfiction reading material. Students might be asked, "What have you recently read where you learned something new?" or "What reading have you done that provided interesting information?" In classrooms where nonfiction trade books are routinely used as well as selections from appropriate newspapers and magazines, students will have a wide range of reading selections from which to choose. Students can also respond to thematic projects or reading they've done for an integrated unit that includes several curriculum areas.

Teachers should be aware that when students respond to reading, they construct meaning based on their individual understanding, attitudes, background, and beliefs. Additionally, modes of responding to literature should vary from fact-based, cognitive reactions (summaries) to emotional and aesthetic reactions (impressions of how a theme or character impacts on their lives). When students truly enter into the world of a book, their reactions can be quite personal and compelling.

A Writing Sample. A selection from the student's ongoing writing should be included in the portfolio along with a statement of why the particular piece was chosen. Figure 4–4 contains a fourth-grade student's explanation for choosing an essay about basketball for her portfolio.

In classrooms that have adopted the writing process strategy, the student should include drafts to show how a piece of writing has evolved from brainstorming or list making, to draft stages, to revised copy, and finally to the edited and published piece of writing. By including work that is part of each stage, students demonstrate how they've applied writing and editing techniques, whether they were done individually or collaboratively. Figure 4–5(A,B,C) shows how a student's story was created from a character web, to a plot web, to the finished story. These entries clearly show that the student uses organizational skills to "map" a story before writing. If peer conferencing is part of the process used, then conference notes can be included. For publishing, some teachers require students to share a piece of writing with others to reinforce the concept of the

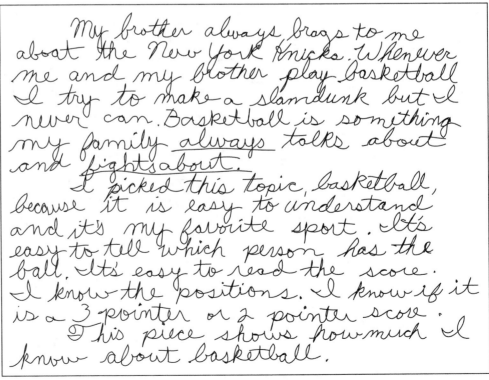

FIGURE 4–4 A fourth-grade student's self-reflections on her basketball story.

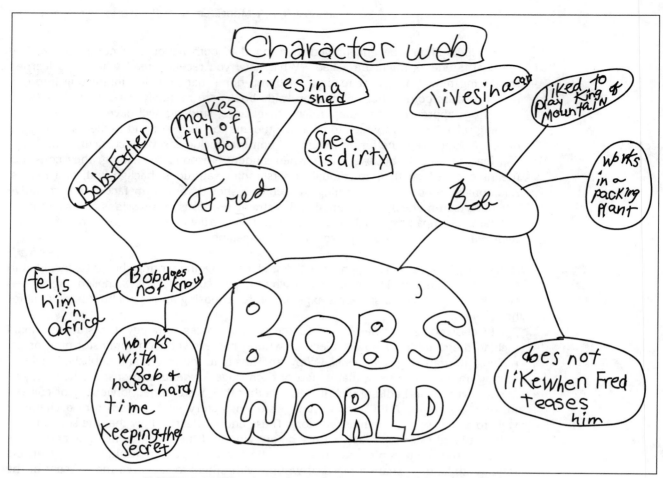

FIGURE 4–5A Fourth-grade student's story development character web.

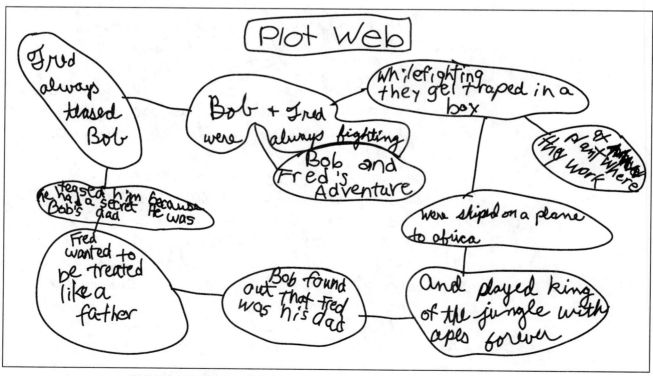

FIGURE 4–5B Plot web.

classroom as a community of learners. If this has occurred, then other students' reactions to the piece or a self-reflection about how the writing was shared and received should be incorporated. This provides an opportunity for students to concretely reflect on changes in their writing ability. The use of collaboratively designed rubrics also aids students in self-evaluation and gives them specific guidelines to consider.

Depending on the students' age, interests, and ability, this aspect of the portfolio can be refined to include such assignments as writing in a new genre (attempt at poetry or fable writing), writing that incorporates content area learning (from a project or learning log entry), students' choice of their best work, or work that shows how the students' writing has changed.

Family Sharing or Reaction. Growth in literacy is best accomplished when both the child's family and school personnel collaborate on learning. Information from the home should be incorporated in the portfolio because it shows the teacher's interest and concern for involving the child's family. This reinforces the idea that literacy is important both in and out of school. Information from the family can also inform the teacher about changes in the student's literacy ability that the parents see outside of school. In essence, parents need to be active partners in promoting literacy growth and having them review and contribute to a portfolio is a tangible way of reinforcing this.

Parents may be asked to complete a questionnaire, respond generally to the portfolio collection, or respond to a specific entry. It has become quite popular to have parents sign "contracts" to read with their children at home. For example, the Fort Wayne, Indiana schools have a 20-minute "Read-to-Me" community-wide program called Everybody Reads. A portfolio can document this important out-of-school activity. Family involvement also results in an additional benefit of making the family well-aware of the instructional program and of the teacher's interest in each individual child.

For the emergent reader, a family member might be asked to provide a portfolio entry that describes the student's language skills at home, important family activities, or family news. Parents can be asked to participate in reading and writing activities with the child, and then write a brief note describing books shared, trips to the library, a TV program or movie that was watched and discussed, or their child's reaction to school activities and related at-home projects. For an older student, the family can collaborate by providing reactions, sharing news about relevant events or activities, discussing the application of literacy skills used outside of school and, most especially, praising the student's efforts. All of these can be included in the portfolio to reinforce the family's interest in the child.

Bob's World

Welcome to Bob's World! Bob is just like anybody else except he went on a big adventure that nobody else would ever go on. His friend Fred went with him. Here is the story.

Bob was 34 years old and worked in a packing plant. He worked with a guy named Fred who liked to tease him and make him feel bad. Bob hated Fred when he teased him. Fred teased Bob because Bob had no where to live and so he lived in his car. Fred was 55 years old and he lived in a dirty shed which he thought was better then living in a car. When Bob got mad he used to yell "Fred lives in a dirty shed!" Then Fred got mad so they always got in to big fights and wrestled until they got tired. This happened all the time at work. The only thing they both liked to do was play King Of The Mountain.

One day Bob and Fred were wrestling and all of a sudden they fell into a big box at the packing plant. They were still fighting in the box when they felt the box start to move. The box was being shipped somewhere and they couldn't get out!

They tried to get out but they couldn't so they went to sleep. The next morning Bob and Fred found out that they were shipped to Africa. A bunch of monkeys saved them and brought them back to the jungle. At first it was cool for them because the monkeys liked to play King Of The Mountain too. Soon they got scared that they would be trapped in Africa forever. Fred got very sick one day and told Bob that he always teased him because he had a secret. Bob asked Fred what the secret was. Fred thought that he was dying so he told Bob the secret. Fred told Bob that he was really his father and not just someone he worked with and that he wanted Bob to treat him like a father and not a friend. Bob was so surprised. They found out the next day that Fred was not going to die and so they spent the rest of there lives together playing King Of The Mountain with the apes in the jungle.

FIGURE 4–5C Finished story.

Many school projects can be used to enlist parental support of literacy development: book clubs and sales, shared reading activities, read-a-thons, projects that require interviews with family and community members, and parent volunteers in the classroom. All these activities can be incorporated into the portfolio.

Other Possible Artifacts. The list of additional entries for the portfolio is almost endless. Some include audiotapes or videotapes recorded while the student reads aloud or presents a project. Audiotapes can be used to document and appraise students' reading fluency, and videotapes not only are fun to make and watch but also provide a dynamic record of literacy events in progress. Special educators, in particular, find that because change in their students is often quite gradual, a videotape or audiotape record can demonstrate progress that can be noted only over longer periods of time.

Photographs of a student-created model, diorama, or any three-dimensional project are delightful inclusions. To "lighten" the portfolio collection, teachers can encourage students to keep a joke page, cartoon collection, or other entries that are personal and fun. Pictures from home or meaningful memorabilia can likewise give the portfolio a personal flair.

Integration of literacy activities with content areas should be emphasized, to document how reading and writing are used across all subject disciplines. In middle schools, instructional teams frequently plan unit and project work to include reading and writing activities in such areas as social studies, science, health, and even mathematics. These interdisciplinary learning activities reinforce how reading and writing are important in all content areas and should be included in the portfolio. Instructional team members should collaborate on goals and contents of middle-school portfolios and coordinate their efforts to promote diverse literacy opportunities.

Teacher Portfolio

More schools are requiring teachers to informally assess each child's reading progress (running records are widely used). What to do with this informal data can be a problem. We believe that teachers should create individual portfolios for their students to document each child's literacy profile. Figure 4–6 contains a summary of the suggested contents for a teacher portfolio. Various means of collecting and storing the information can be used for the teacher portfolio. Again, many teachers use a loose-leaf notebook, with individual sections for each child or separate file folders, because they are convenient and flexible for storing information. Teachers should choose diagnostic techniques that they are comfortable using and find beneficial for appraising reading and writing skills and strategies. Chapters 5 and 6 will provide guidance in suggested means of assessing students' reading and writing development. The following is offered as a suggested outline for the contents of a teacher's record-keeping portfolio for individual student evaluations.

Background Data Sheet. It is vital for teachers to be familiar with each child's background. Without knowing the child's family and school history, the teacher cannot fully understand the child. Frequently, this information can be collected by reading a student's permanent record folder; by checking with the school nurse, other faculty, social worker, psychologist, or guidance counselor; and through conversations with the child and family members. Rhodes (1993) offers excellent suggestions for interviewing parents and children, writing letters to the family, and providing questionnaires that the child and family can complete. The aim is to provide information about literacy involvement at home as well as to learn about special circumstances that might impede or enhance a student's development. The following are important topics to consider as background knowledge about each child:

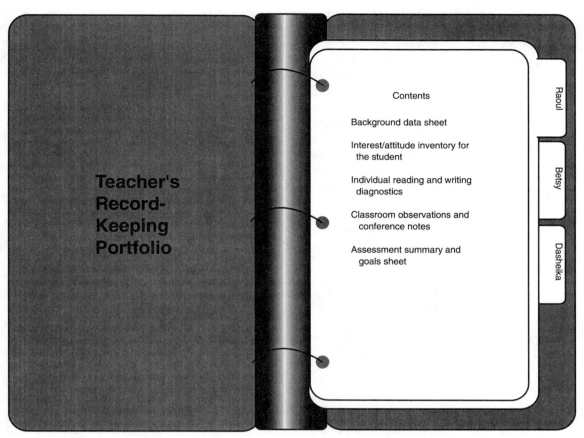

FIGURE 4–6 Contents of a teacher's record-keeping portfolio.

- Health and developmental history
- Family background

  People with whom the child lives
  Special family circumstances
  Parental employment, interests, or talents
  Places that the child has lived and visited

- Language background

  Language spoken by the family
  Child's language development history

- Child's school history

  Schools attended
  Achievement
  Interventional help
  Results of testing

Because so many of our students are now taught by teams in order to address their learning needs (e.g., special education assistance, or ESL classes), input from other team members is essential for having a complete picture of how the student is functioning in different contexts. Multidisciplinary teams benefit from reviewing a student's portfolio, and thus students' portfolios should reflect not only the general education curriculum but special services as well. Teachers comment that having portfolios available at Individual Education Plan (IEP) conferences and parent conferences is very helpful to clearly determine the child's instructional needs and progress.

Interest/Attitude Inventory. This can be used to learn more about the individual child with respect to interests as well as attitudes about reading and writing. For beginning readers, the inventory can be administered orally, and family members can assist the teacher in recording the child's responses. For older students, the information can be collected through a brief list of questions, an incomplete sentence inventory, focused interviews, and conferences. The interest inventory is a good focal point for the first portfolio conference with the child.

An interest inventory should be used to learn more about the child's hobbies (collections), interests (leisure activities, sports activities, and clubs), favorite activities (television programs, favorite books, and movies), and emotional responses to school and learning. Bader (2002) provides an outline for an interview with a child's family as well as an unfinished sentence test that can be used to reveal underlying student attitudes. Rhodes (1993) also provides surveys and inventories about reading and writing that achieve the same purpose. Figure 4–7 contains an example of Bader and Wiesendanger's (1994) unfinished sentence inventory that was completed by a fourth-grade student. It is interesting to see that the child who completed this survey has a positive attitude about herself and school, enjoys reading, likes to swim, and has humanitarian concerns. During a conference, when discussing the child's interests, this information provides a great opportunity to suggest related, high-interest, recreational reading.

Individual Reading and Writing Diagnostics. Various informal appraisals can be made of a child's reading and writing skills. Some school districts have devised their own developmental checklists. Most schools administer standardized tests that present reading and language arts achievement in terms of norm-referenced scores that are useful for program placement and evaluation. However, more process-oriented measures should be used to profile each student's reading and writing abilities.

Many published informal techniques are available for locating helpful diagnostic techniques (e.g., Miller, 1995; Rhodes, 1993) and running records are used widely. The administration of a reading diagnostic in the form of an informal reading inventory (IRI) is most helpful for obtaining essential information about a child's reading strategies, including reading fluency, decoding strategies, vocabulary skills, comprehension strategies, and the various levels of reading ability for classroom instruction and independent reading. Although administering, scoring, and evaluating an IRI are time-consuming, with experience, most teachers can efficiently complete the essential aspects of such inventories in a short amount of time. The information gathered from the IRI is too valuable to overlook, and time must be allocated for its use. Running records and miscue analysis are also widely used diagnostic techniques for reading fluency and can be incorporated into this part of the teacher's portfolio. Chapter 5 provides information on various reading assessment strategies.

A writing diagnostic is another essential aspect of a literacy profile. As more states now assess writing as part of mandated testing, it is strongly recommended that teachers be aware of the form of writing assessment used in their state. Chapter 6 provides more information about writing assessment and how it can promote better teaching. Clearly, teachers have many choices to consider in writing assessment: they can use the system adopted in their individual state (often a form of holistic scoring); use rubrics created by teachers working collaboratively; employ checklists of writing behavior expected at different developmental levels; or create an analytic scale with their students. We encourage teachers to examine these informal techniques and choose an assessment that is compatible with their instructional approach as well as with district and state requirements. Students must become familiar with the forms of writing required on state and district tests and teachers should be familiar with the manner in which their students will be assessed.

With the widespread acceptance of rubrics for both reading and writing, many students are now accustomed to this form of assessment and rubrics can simply be attached to a writing sample to document a student's writing ability. Also, depending on

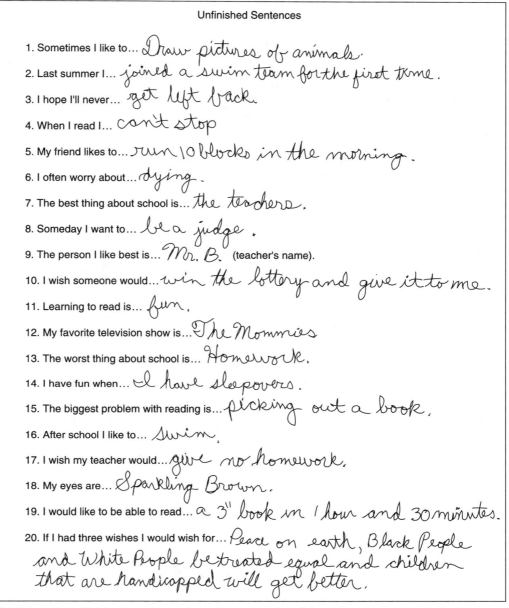

Unfinished Sentences

1. Sometimes I like to... *Draw pictures of animals.*
2. Last summer I... *joined a swim team for the first time.*
3. I hope I'll never... *get left back.*
4. When I read I... *can't stop*
5. My friend likes to... *run 10 blocks in the morning.*
6. I often worry about... *dying.*
7. The best thing about school is... *the teachers.*
8. Someday I want to... *be a judge.*
9. The person I like best is... *Mr. B.* (teacher's name).
10. I wish someone would... *win the lottery and give it to me.*
11. Learning to read is... *fun.*
12. My favorite television show is... *The Mommies*
13. The worst thing about school is... *Homework.*
14. I have fun when... *I have sleepovers.*
15. The biggest problem with reading is... *picking out a book.*
16. After school I like to... *Swim.*
17. I wish my teacher would... *give no homework.*
18. My eyes are... *Sparkling Brown.*
19. I would like to be able to read... *a 3" book in 1 hour and 30 minutes.*
20. If I had three wishes I would wish for... *Peace on earth, Black People and White People be treated equal and children that are handicapped will get better.*

FIGURE 4–7 Unfinished sentence inventory completed by a fourth-grade student. *Source: From Bader Reading and Language Inventory* (p. 186), by L. Bader and K. Wiesendanger, 1994. Upper Saddle River, NJ: Merrill/Prentice Hall. Reprinted by permission of Prentice Hall.

the writing program used in the classroom, a writing evaluation can focus on the strategies used during the writing process (listing, drafting, conferencing, and editing) and can be used to determine the quality of the written product based on realistic expectations given the child's age, language background, overall ability, and exposure to quality instruction. Any diagnostic should assess the child's ability to express ideas in written form; understand a rhetorical task and use appropriate written forms; organize and develop ideas; use language effectively with good elaboration; use acceptable syntax; form letters to promote legibility; be aware of language conventions and mechanics (e.g., capitalization, punctuation, spelling); and use editing strategies.

Individual literacy assessment should be administered early during the first phase of the annual instructional program to be included in creation of the *baseline portfolio* and then be repeated toward the end of the school year to determine growth and provide information for the *summative portfolio*.

Classroom Observation and Conference Notes. Each student should be routinely observed during a variety of reading and writing activities. Such observations help the teacher know more about the child's strategies and study habits, including the ability to focus, attend, sustain interest, work independently, work cooperatively, apply skills to actual reading and writing assignments, be involved in oral discussions, and demonstrate metacognitive reflection. During portfolio conferences, the teacher adds insights to these observational data through one-on-one dialogue. Teachers' reflections after conferencing with students should be accurately and succinctly recorded.

Assessment Summary and Goals Sheet. All of the preceding data should facilitate specifying appropriate goals for each student. The goals should be developed collaboratively. The teacher should discuss the student's objectives and then coordinate these objectives with activities that promote acquisition of targeted strategies and outcomes. When goals are discussed, the teacher should keep in mind each student's priorities. For example, if a student wants to read longer books, then activities to promote sustained reading should be considered. Likewise, a program to enhance vocabulary growth can best be undertaken if the student sees this as important. The teacher should be aware of the student's interests so that instruction incorporates use of high-interest materials. A summary of the teacher's assessment and targeted goals should be carefully noted in the teacher's portfolio.

THE PORTFOLIO PROCESS

The teacher's portfolio and the student's portfolio should complement each other. Figure 4–8 shows a chronological scheme of how these two portfolios can be created simultaneously and inform each other. The purpose of the *first portfolio* is to assemble baseline data and is used to discuss expectations and to establish initial goals. Literacy opportunities (e.g., reading and writing activities, projects, assignments) are suggested and discussed so that the goals are realistic and attainable. The *second and third portfolios* are developmental and provide evidence of progress toward attainment of goals and for revision and refinement in instructional methods and literacy opportunities. Student self-reflections as well as ongoing observation and insights by the teacher are essential aspects of these portfolios.

Toward the end of the school year, the teacher and student together select and create the *final portfolio* that is the outgrowth of the entire year's portfolio process. At this point, the teacher may wish to readminister the IRI and writing diagnostic used for the first portfolio to reveal changes in reading and writing ability. Both the student's and the teacher's reflections are used to summarize the student's progress throughout the year. It is also appropriate to discuss expectations for the future that may be passed on to next year's teacher, as well as possible summer literacy opportunities. An end-of-the-year family conference is encouraged for several reasons. Obviously, having family members participate in the process will enhance literacy development at home and will also inform the family about the child's progress that year.

The exact timing of the four portfolios should be determined by the particular school context. Before formal conferences, teachers should give students ample time to make their final portfolio selections from the material in their working folders. Some schools require that portfolios be given a grade, and students should clearly understand the criteria for the evaluating a portfolio collection. To help students be comfortable and familiar with portfolio conferences, a sample conference format should be developed collaboratively. Some educators have found it helpful to conduct a demonstration conference so that students can observe the process and become at ease and prepared before their own individual conference. The scheduling of formal portfolio conferences

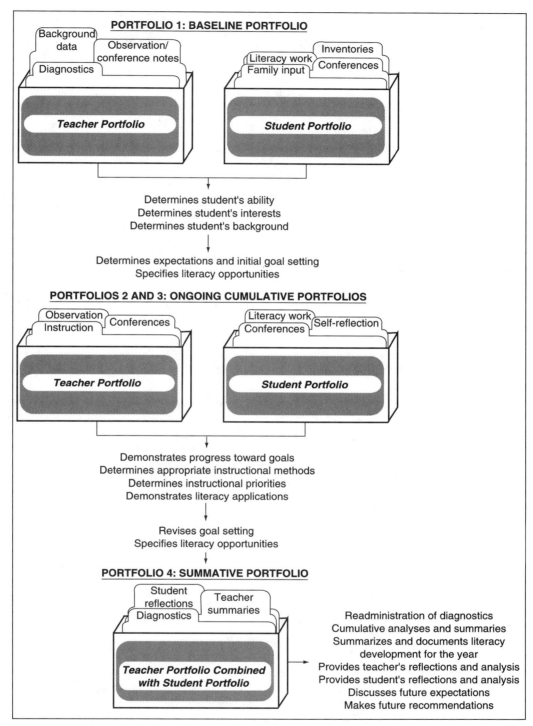

FIGURE 4–8 Chronological application of a Literacy Portfolio process.

often coincides with marking periods and parent conference days. The portfolios are obviously a rich source of information that can be used for student evaluation in the language arts and interdisciplinary work as well as for sharing with the student's family. Teachers report that the evidence of literacy ability contained in portfolios facilitates assessment in the language arts. More information about conferencing with students and families is provided in Chapter 8.

At the end of the school year, if the portfolio becomes part of a student's permanent record or will be transmitted to next year's teacher, then a formal summary report should be created from the teacher's portfolio and combined with the student's portfolio into a permanent record portfolio. If the portfolio will be returned to the student at the end of the school year, then a summary letter from the teacher to the student and the family should be inserted into the student's portfolio.

Issues to Be Decided Regarding Portfolio Process

Many important issues regarding the adoption of a portfolio process need to be addressed before the implementation phase. In a helpful article about using portfolios, Mitchel, Abernathy and Gowans (1998) suggest that teachers simply divide the portfolio plan into the following stages:

1. Describe the focus of this portfolio assignment.
2. Describe the procedure for content selection.
3. Describe [the] guidelines [used] for adding materials and building the portfolio.
4. Describe feedback and evaluation procedures. (p. 385)

The following questions are presented to assist in the development of a portfolio process that successfully integrates literacy instruction with assessment issues. These questions clarify some of the dilemmas teachers encounter when they consider using a literacy portfolio process in their classrooms. Highlighting these issues may assist and promote informed decision making. Figure 4–9 is a summary of this self-survey.

How Does the Portfolio Process Complement the Philosophy of Literacy Instruction?
Several trends in literacy have had a profound impact on classroom instruction. In an optimum situation, the use of a portfolio process will not be perceived as an add-on but will be incorporated as an ongoing part of the literacy curriculum. The underlying philosophy of literacy instruction and the methodological choices that result should be understood. A portfolio process will work best when:

- Literacy instruction reflects the view that the language arts are intrinsically related to each other and that there is a reciprocal, supportive relationship between instruction in reading, writing, speaking, and listening.
- Literacy instruction uses authentic tasks that demonstrate to students that being literate adds value to their life, is personally enjoyable, and has practical utility.

---

1. How does the portfolio complement the philosophy of literacy instruction?
2. What should be included in the literacy portfolio?
3. Who decides which entries go into the literacy portfolio?
4. How should portfolios be stored and managed?
5. How can teachers learn to use literacy portfolios?
6. How are portfolios graded and used as part of evaluation, including report cards?
7. What happens to the literacy portfolio at the end of the school year?
8. How can a portfolio be used as part of school district accountability?
9. How can we balance consistency and reliability with the need to create flexible portfolios?
10. What if you try portfolios, and they "flop"?

FIGURE 4–9 Self-survey for teachers to complete before beginning a literacy portfolio process.

- Literacy instruction addresses the individual child's level of ability, readiness for learning, interests, and background. While grade-level expectations for meeting curricula goals should be considered, the teacher focuses on the individual child by knowing what the child is ready to learn, how the child learns best, the child's own goals, and what the child enjoys learning.

- Integrated language instruction incorporates all aspects of the curriculum, using quality literature (both fiction and nonfiction) with a wide variety of subject area content, often thematically presented, and engages students in active individual and collaborative group participation.

- The underlying instructional philosophy reflects the view that students, parents, and educators are all partners in helping students become literate and independent learners; therefore, all members of this triad have important roles and responsibilities for enhancing literacy.

- The philosophy of instruction demonstrates that students' self-reflection and ownership of their literacy behavior are essential aspects of the portfolio process. Students learn and improve when their thoughts and feelings are respected and when they are guided in knowing how to use metacognitive strategies.

- Instructional strategies reflect the most current holistic views that literacy revolves around reconstructing and producing meaning, which is best reinforced in the context of genuine literacy environments. Skill instruction is to be undertaken as reinforcement after primary language activities are practiced in a meaningful context.

Many teachers use basals as the primary mode of instruction, and inexperienced teachers often rely on the prescriptive nature of basalized instruction as a starting point in their teaching careers. Guided reading in small groups led by the teacher and focusing on skill building is quickly gaining in popularity and often relies on basals, graded books, or anthologies for reading content. Basal readers have undergone dramatic transformation. When teachers choose basal instruction, it is hoped that they do so because the newer programs incorporate quality reading material and provide variety in genre and content. In such programs, a literacy portfolio process can be used, especially if core books and chapter books are added to the reading materials. But the primary method of instruction—the quality and content of what children read, how writing instruction is conducted, and the manner in which skills are reinforced—needs to be carefully examined and perhaps revised, otherwise the portfolio process will become only a clerical attachment to a reading/writing program and, therefore, will be perceived as irrelevant by both teachers and students.

What Should be Included in the Literacy Portfolio? For a literacy collection to be meaningful, it should reflect the variety of instructional assignments that are the essential activities in day-to-day literacy instruction. Therefore, entries for the portfolio should be authentic, naturally evolving from ongoing activities, not contrived to fulfill some notion of a stilted, mandated, literacy collection that does not reflect actual classroom practice. Entries should also reflect the instructional priorities of a program. For example, one teacher who does a great deal of work with poetry in her class of gifted children uses the children's poetry as the central focus of their portfolios. Anyone reading a child's portfolio from this class would be struck by the number of entries that are selected to reflect individual and collaborative attempts at poetry writing and reading.

Consistency in portfolio collections, both in terms of contents and means of analysis, increases portfolio validity and reliability. Although some professionals are concerned that standardization in a literacy portfolio collection undermines the individuality of a portfolio, it is clear to us that each child's portfolio will be a unique compilation of what is important to that child and a given teacher, during that time in the child's life, in a given classroom. The notion of standardization needs to be carefully balanced with sensitivity toward instructional priorities and individualization.

All literacy collections need to contain entries that reflect both literacy processes and literacy products. Obtaining products is quite easy (e.g., lists of books read, narratives ready for publication), but it is vitally important that the collection provide information to gain insights about the underlying processes and strategies that children use. All literacy collections need to be based on selection criteria. Although a chronology of entries is important for documenting growth and change, unless the collection is created through a process of critical reflection, it will be too large and unwieldy for meaningful use. Central to the collection should be a system of organization so that both the student and anyone reading the portfolio will know why specific entries were chosen and how they are arranged.

Who Decides Which Entries Go Into the Literacy Portfolio? The literacy collection is the product of collaboration between students and teachers. Children need to be shown models of portfolios to see how others have created a literacy collection. The goals, uses, and criteria for entries for the portfolio collection should be jointly developed and well-understood by the students. Folders of ongoing work are the raw materials for the literacy portfolio selections.

Collaboration between children is also recommended. Research on peer tutoring, peer conferencing, and collaborative learning demonstrates that when children work together and communicate with each other, there are many positive outcomes. Students should be encouraged to share their literacy collections and assist each other in evaluating their work. This process is directly related to other classroom practices that are frequently used as part of the writing process, reading workshops, and literature response circles. Meaningful feedback from others helps students decide which entries to consider for inclusion. In classrooms where peer groups are part of an ongoing instructional program, such collaboration will be a natural outcome. If such collaboration is not regularly undertaken and students have little experience working with each other, then ample time needs to be devoted to helping children work together in meaningful and supportive ways.

As noted earlier, parents are also involved in the portfolio process. Students need a responsive audience for their work, and parents often can supply needed instructional reinforcement. Teachers report that parents have told them that portfolios provide a concrete means of learning about their child's school activities, and discussion about school contributes to the sense that learning is a valued priority for the family.

Ultimately, it is the teacher's job to collaborate with the student on the selections for the portfolio. The teacher guides the young child through the process and helps older students by posing key questions and focusing their thoughts.

How Should Portfolios Be Stored and Managed? A great deal of the literature about portfolios reflects an inordinate concern over management issues and focuses too extensively on the how-to of portfolio collection. There are simply no right answers to the management questions that will prove appropriate for all teachers in all classrooms. School districts that have implemented a portfolio process have found it necessary to modify the process each year based on teachers' experiences.

Teachers are encouraged to explore various management possibilities on a trial-and-error basis and share their experiences with colleagues. Many schools are just beginning to fully utilize the wide possibilities of using computer technology in the classroom. It will be exciting to see if the use of electronic portfolios will eliminate some of the more cumbersome aspects of portfolio collection and storage. However, the following guidelines provide helpful considerations regarding storage and management:

- The child's age must be considered. Obviously, young children produce literacy products that are rather large and, therefore, the binder must be of adequate size. Students of all ages want to personalize their collections and show their own individuality.

- Privacy is an important issue for many children, regardless of age; parameters need to be established to ensure appropriate confidentiality. The classroom environment needs to support the concept of respect for each other's work. Nothing is more distressing for children than to have their collections lost or mishandled or for a personal, private log to be read by another.

- The folder should be sturdy enough to withstand frequent use but not so costly as to prohibit replacement from wear and tear. Folders, binders, envelopes, storage bins, baskets, cartons, and file cabinets have all been used for portfolio storage.

- The portfolio should be kept in an area where it is easily accessible to the students and the teacher. This might be in each child's desk, on a designated shelf, or in a central file area. Regardless of where the folders are kept, students must be able to locate their own folders independently and feel secure that the contents will be treated with respect.

- A time management system needs to be created. Students need to know when and for how long they can work on their portfolios. For the portfolio to be meaningful, students should have regular access to them. Some days they may use their folders only for storing works in progress; other days they may need to review prior entries. Time needs to be allocated for the students' review of the portfolio before conferences with the teacher. To make the most of valuable conference time, the focus and format of conferences need to be established and known to students and the teacher. Developing and displaying a calendar for portfolio conferences and sharing the agenda for these conferences make time allocation much more manageable.

How Can Teachers Learn More About Literacy Portfolios? It is important that teachers who are involved in portfolios have a support system, ideally within their own buildings or districts, for sharing information with friends and colleagues. Networks can be established by taking local college courses, summer courses, and in-service classes. Several newsletters assist in putting teachers in touch with each other and provide helpful information. It is vital that teachers using a portfolio process have the support of their school administration. We also recommend that teachers request that portfolios and authentic assessment be topics for in-service education in terms of courses, consultants, and speakers. Ultimately, the best way to learn about portfolios is to start using the process and learn from experience.

It is also interesting to note that portfolio use is now being used in higher education. Many teacher education programs use portfolios as an exit criterion for graduation from the program. Prospective teachers are encouraged to keep showcase portfolios to use on job interviews. Some in-service teachers are now learning to use electronic portfolios to document learning over time. As more teachers become familiar with the portfolio process as part of their own education, it is likely that they will value it and use it as an important part of their own instructional program.

How Are Portfolios Graded and Used as Part of Evaluation Including Report Cards? The issue of evaluating portfolios is complex and controversial. Some teachers feel strongly that portfolios should be celebrated and examined to provide insights about the quality of students' work in order to make better instructional decisions. These teachers believe that portfolios should not be graded. Others feel that students perform best when they know specifically what is expected of them and that students want evaluative feedback. Therefore, they believe that portfolios should be graded.

The concern over evaluation in our society is increasingly apparent. It is essential that appropriate feedback be provided for students when portfolios are used, regardless of whether they are graded. Students invest a great deal of time and energy in their portfolios and should be rewarded with appropriate teacher feedback. Such feedback can be communicated through teacher conferences, conferencing with other students, notes from the teacher, self-evaluations, and checklists. If a portfolio is graded, students should be aware of this, along with the evaluation criteria, during the initial planning stage. Teachers should work with their students to create rubrics so that entries or the entire portfolio can be evaluated cooperatively, using jointly developed criteria. Teachers who do not believe in reducing an entire portfolio to a letter grade or a numerical score should provide students with analysis and thoughtful comments regarding the portfolio work. Students both want and deserve this kind of information from their teachers. We also highly recommend that the report card system be evaluated in light of the portfolio process so that information on the report card can reflect and include portfolios.

What Happens to the Literacy Portfolio at the End of the School Year? The decision about what to do with the portfolio at the end of the year will be determined by the goals established for the literacy portfolio. Several models based on different purposes for the portfolio collection are described below:

1. A literacy portfolio established for exclusive use by the classroom teacher. This portfolio is not used after the instructional year. The teacher may return the portfolio to the student with a special celebration at the end of the year. The teacher should write a summary to the student and family describing the literacy program and the student's growth and performance. Teachers may decide to keep several student portfolios each year to use as exemplars with subsequent classes and, obviously, students need to provide permission for teachers to do so.

2. A literacy portfolio established as part of permanent record keeping. A literacy portfolio that is part of the permanent record either will be kept in a central location in the school (along with other permanent records) or will be passed from teacher to teacher throughout the grades for review and additions. This permanent record portfolio is useful in noting the change in literacy skills over time. It is also useful in familiarizing each new teacher with the individual student's profile of literacy behaviors, which can help in establishing appropriate curricular goals for the new school year.

3. Variations and combinations of types 1 and 2. After engaging in an effective portfolio process for a year, teachers probably will want to share the wealth of information contained in a student's portfolio with next year's teacher. Even if a school district does not designate literacy portfolios as an aspect of permanent records, teachers within buildings may still find it useful to pass along student's portfolios. Unfortunately, this process is often not replicated when students are promoted from an elementary building to middle school or junior high school. If the district does not formally provide permanent storage and transmission of student portfolios between teachers and buildings, then teachers should request this. Obviously, portfolios that are transferred between teachers and buildings need to be carefully reviewed so that entries provide insights and meaningful information with appropriate examples. In the preceding discussion describing literacy portfolio contents, we recommended that teachers create a summary of each student's literacy profile. Such a condensed profile would prove most informative for subsequent teachers.

How Can a Portfolio Be Used as Part of School District Accountability? If a school district contemplates using a portfolio process for monitoring students' literacy development, this should be coordinated with other record-keeping and testing programs that are mandated by the district or the state education department. Large-scale assessment systems are moving toward more authentic and performance-based forms of measurement, and portfolios are recognized as making an important contribution to this movement. Some states mandate, whereas others recommend, that student portfolios be used as part of longitudinal evaluation. Data collected from review of individual portfolios containing standardized writing tasks have already been used in many school districts to monitor the effectiveness of instructional programs, track developmental trends in writing, and provide an indication of overall student achievement. According to Simmons (1992), who has done extensive consulting with districts on portfolio assessment, the time is ripe for using portfolios in large-scale assessment:

> Portfolio assessment has now developed sufficiently at the individual level to be adapted to large-scale settings. To fail to do so, or to settle in the process of change for only the most superficial or highly constrained forms of portfolios, can only perpetuate the inequalities and inaccuracies of the past. (p. 113)

The use of portfolios helps to balance test results that are often influenced by socioeconomic factors and, therefore, has great potential and benefit in helping to see students' actual performance ability.

How Can Consistency and Reliability Be Balanced With the Need to Create Flexible Portfolios? There is concern that if educators jump on the "portfolio bandwagon," portfolios will ultimately become products of standardized and rigid mandates. While attempting to demonstrate authentic student accomplishment, portfolios can easily reflect formalistic views of what constitutes a "good" portfolio, which would likely be composed of uniform checklists, typical lists of students' reading, and uniform writing products. Such portfolios would hardly overcome the concerns many educators have voiced about standardized testing and evaluation systems. Commercial kits are now available that provide teachers with sample checklists and forms to be reproduced to create portfolio collections. Such commercial products may be worth considering as starting points, but they may produce a portfolio process that is essentially insensitive to the diverse concerns of schools and classrooms all across the country. Gomez and Schenk (1992) have viewed advertisements that promote the use of "handy folders," "a portfolio storage box," a prescribed list of activities that can be "administered at selected intervals throughout the school year," and "scoring guides and training packages," and commented that

> The tacit promise of these professional workshops and products is the development of a generic set of tools that all teachers can acquire and apply to the collections of work of all children in their classrooms. Such efforts not only echo the problems of standardized tests . . . they make an individual teacher's scrutiny of a student's work appear scientific and plausible . . . and ignore a fundamental dimension of their use—an understanding of the ways teachers construct meanings from these collections of materials. (p. 4)

A good portfolio should reflect the goals and curriculum of individual children, teachers, and educational programs; therefore, uniformity and standardization are suspect.

Flexibility in portfolio contents is desirable, but there is a perception that portfolio evaluation lacks rigor because teacher judgment can be highly biased or reflective of undemanding local standards. There is also concern about producing reliable results when a variety of portfolio entries are scored as part of large assessment systems. The issue of interrater reliability is of paramount concern when portfolio entries are evaluated as part of state-wide testing programs that can result in high-stakes decisions. More research needs to be done on scorer reliability when portfolio contents reflect diversity. Experience with holistic scoring of writing samples demonstrates that training scorers has a very positive effect on the reliability of scoring outcomes. If portfolios are to be used reliably in state-wide assessment systems, then certainly some level of standardization in terms of suggested contents and means of assessment is needed. In large-scale programs, the use of selected entries, prompted responses, uniform scoring rubrics, and adequate training for scorers is necessary but should be distinguished from the evaluation of portfolio contents for other purposes.

If portfolios are to be used primarily to document individual student growth, to monitor the effectiveness of local instructional approaches, and as an intrinsic part of a methodological approach to literacy instruction, then diversity of contents and scoring systems is not only expected but appropriate and desirable.

What if Portfolios Are Tried and They "Flop?" Contributions from teachers using portfolios (described in Chapter one) indicate that the process is one of experimentation, revision, and refinement. Even experienced teachers find that their second-year portfolio process was different from that of the first year, and they expect the process to be modified each successive year. For example, one teacher found that her choice of passages for a running record was boring to the students, and therefore counter-productive, whereas another teacher found that she needed to communicate more effectively with parents earlier in the school year.

Every teacher knows that each year contains triumphs and mistakes. Truly, the portfolio process is a learning experience for both teachers and students and, therefore, if the process is less than successful one year, it should be analyzed and discussed to determine why. Some teachers are overly ambitious at the outset and should be cautioned to set modest goals and expand the process in small stages. Shared planning and decision making are highly recommended. Teachers should not use portfolios in isolation, and every teacher should have at least one colleague with whom to share and reflect.

CONCLUSIONS

In the current political climate, it would be naive to think that portfolios will replace standardized testing. However, there is growing realization about the limitations of standardized tests and how their imposition changes the instructional process. It is much more realistic and helpful to promote portfolio use to supplement information gathered for mandated testing programs and to thereby improve teaching. Teachers who have not used a literacy portfolio process naturally approach its implementation with a good deal of trepidation. There are many unanswered issues, ranging from theoretical concerns about balancing authentic assessment practices with mandated standardized tests, to practical issues of how to efficiently use a portfolio as part of daily literacy instruction. Although the literacy portfolio process is known to have many advantages, teachers undertake the use of portfolios with the realistic concern that their workload may be increased in terms of more time spent observing students, working with individual students through conferences, note taking, and record keeping. If teachers do not see important advantages in literacy portfolios, such added work will be too burdensome to offset the benefits. Portfolio use not only changes the *quantity* of a teacher's involvement with students but certainly affects the *quality* of this involvement. When teachers use a portfolio process they must recognize the changing roles and responsibilities for both themselves and their students, otherwise portfolio use will be reduced to a fad that is quickly abandoned.

Teachers should also recognize that there may be no simple answers to their many questions about literacy portfolios. Hopefully, the suggestions contained in this chapter offer some guidelines for portfolio use. However, the literacy portfolio is still a relatively new strategy that needs to be tried and tested in many different contexts in classrooms across the country. The "perfect" portfolio is elusive, if not unattainable, and the process is far more important than the product.

REFERENCES

Bader, L. (2002). *Bader reading and language inventory* (4th ed.). Upper Saddle River, NJ: Merrill/Prentice Hall.

Bader L., & Wiesendanger, K. (1994). *Bader reading and language inventory* (2nd ed.) Upper Saddle River, NJ: Merrill/Prentice Hall.

Clemmons, J., Laase, L., Cooper, D., Areglado, N., & Dill, M. (1993). *Portfolios in the classroom—A teacher's sourcebook.* New York: Scholastic.

Fiderer, A. (1995). *Practical assessment for literature-based reading classrooms.* New York: Scholastic.

Gomez, M. L., & Schenk, J. (1992). *What are portfolios? Stories teachers tell.* Paper presented at the meeting of the AERA, San Francisco.

Miller, W. (1995). *Alternative assessment techniques for reading and writing.* West Nyack, NY: The Center for Applied Research in Education.

Mitchel, J., Abernathy, T., & Gowans, L. (1998). Making sense of literacy portfolios: A four-step plan. *Journal of Adolescent and Adult Literacy, 41*(5), 384–86.

Rhodes, L. (1993). *Literacy assessment—A handbook of instruments.* Portsmouth, NH: Heinemann.

Sharp, Q. Q. (1989). *Evaluation: Whole language checklists for evaluating your children.* New York: Scholastic.

Simmons, J. (1992). Portfolios for large-scale assessment. In D. Graves & B. Sunstein (Eds.), *Portfolio portraits* (pp. 96–113). Portsmouth, NH: Heinemann.

Vizyak, L. (1996). *Student portfolio—A practical guide to evaluation.* Bothell, WA: Wright.

Using Portfolios to Promote Learning and Literacy

Using the Literacy Portfolio to Assess and Guide Reading Development

KEY WORDS AND CONCEPTS

anecdotal notes
balanced literacy
observation checklists
student attitude survey
literacy collaborative
tapes and digital cameras
running record
informal reading inventory
  (IRI)
high-stakes testing

literature questionnaires
story retelling
think-alouds
four-block scheduling model
reciprocal teaching
reading lists
journals and logs
story frames
Venn diagrams
reading rubrics

The following letter was sent by a 5th grade student after she read several books by the same author Chris Van Allsburg for an authors study. It indicates her enthusiasm as well as the depth of her comprehension of the material. Spelling errors are indicated and provide additional areas for instruction.

Dear Chris Van Allsburg,

Hello! My Name is Cristina R., and I just love your books. You are very talented to be able to write and illustrate like that. I have read many of your books, such as "The Wreck of the <u>Zaphar</u>," "The Widow's Broom," and "The Polar Express." Yet, my favorite is "The Garden of Abdul Gasazi." I love all the <u>betutiful</u> illustrations! They almost seem to make the story come alive! I especially like the end because you do not reveal if the dog <u>really</u> becomes the duck.*

> *Now, if you don't mind, I'd like to ask you a few questions:*
>
> *#1   Why did you use the same dog in "The Widow's Broom," and "The Garden of Abdul Gasazi?"*
>
> *#2   At what age did you start drawing?*
>
> *#3   What do you do in your spare time?*
>
> *#4   Where do you think you got <u>you</u> talents from?*

Thanks!

Sincerely,
Cristina (5th grade)

————————

Note: All underlined words were spelled incorrectly by the student.

THE READING ASSESSMENT ENVIRONMENT: HIGH-STAKES TESTS VERSUS MULTIPLE MEASURES

In classrooms where basals, workbook activities, and skill sheets are the major focus of the reading program, reading evaluations are often based on a formal standardized test, now referred to as high-stakes testing, where a single test score is used to make decisions which will significantly impact children's lives. "High stakes testing means that the consequences for good (high) or poor (low) performance on a test are substantial . . . inflate the importance of the test . . . (and affect) important decisions such as promotion or retention" (IRA Board of Directors, 1999, p. 258). Many educators are concerned about this singular emphasis, which has been strengthened, and perhaps reinforced, by the current movement for educational reform and accountability. Coleman (2000) raises the issue of educational discrimination and states that high-stakes tests do "more harm than good to the very students who need the most help," and warns that this practice is actually "dangerous," because test scores are not perfect measures and, therefore, should not be the sole criterion for decision making.

Reading performance in literature-based and balanced reading classrooms is often assessed so as to reflect a broad spectrum of students' learning progress, with many informal measures added. In the letter to author Chris Van Allsburg at the beginning of this chapter, which was written by a fifth grader and included in her portfolio, the teacher can evaluate various aspects of the student's comprehension of the books she read for an author study, and assess and assist her on skills that might need attention (for example, the underlined items indicate spelling errors the student made that need correction.) In terms of critical thinking, Cristina appears to relate well to the subtleties in Van Allsberg's writing, as indicated by her comments on specific details, and her ability to read critically and draw high level conclusions, such as noting that the same dog appears in all of Van Allsberg's books (which sent many of us scurrying to see if we could find the dog hidden in the illustrations—a real challenge!) Additionally, Christina indicates enthusiasm and a desire to read and know more about the creative style of the author.

The literacy portfolio contains the representative works of each student that have been selected by both student and teacher, along with shared comments about literacy experiences, ongoing projects, completed units, logs, reports, and accomplishments that indicate the progressive nature of the student's learning and reading growth. Together the teacher and student inspect, analyze, and reflect on the use of written language, the fluency of guided reading, and interest in and comprehension of literature so that a thorough understanding of literacy progress and achievements emerges. Meaningful and appropriate literacy goals are jointly determined. Because reading is a complex and multidimensional process, when assessing and evaluating students, one must look at both cognitive and affective dimensions, including reading interests, motivation, feelings of self-esteem, and positive or negative attitudes toward reading. The objective is to note, over time, the students' skills and abilities to comprehend critically, read fluently, self-correct, effectively respond to literature discussions, and integrate and evaluate ideas and concepts that are both textually explicit (literal) and textually implicit (interpretative, critical).

CHANGING PATTERNS OF READING INSTRUCTION

Teachers who implement a literature-based, thematic, or balanced literacy approach to teaching reading and writing have a variety of effective assessment strategies at their disposal. Balanced literacy (a fairly new term) refers to programs that integrate skills, use guided and independent reading, organize students in small and large groups, implement four-block instruction, and employ process writing. This integrative model is replacing whole language in many classrooms. Fitzgerald (1999) calls balanced literacy the "hottest topic in reading education" (p. 100) and describes it in terms of three categories of reading—local knowledge, global knowledge, and love of reading—all of which are equally important and, thus, balanced in terms of classroom instruction and attention. Smith (2000) succinctly describes balanced literacy as instruction that instills a love of reading through high interest books and multiple responses to stories while deliberately teaching needed skills. According to Stoicheva (1999), children become more proficient readers when there is a combination of motivating literature, student engagement, and explicit, systemic skills teaching.

Four-block scheduling describes a model that is similar to balanced literacy. When using this approach, class time is divided evenly between guided reading, self-selected reading, writers' workshop, and working with skills. Skills can include word study, decoding, comprehension skills, and other strategies. There is equal emphasis on skills, cognitive strategies, and the ability to respond and relate to literature. Nichols (2000) examined this model to determine the effects of educational reform on instructional time, and states that four-block scheduling is an attempt to use allocated time more efficiently. He cites studies that indicate that "only 38 percent of the average school day involves actual academic activities" (p. 134); therefore, more efficient models of instruction are necessary.

Purdue University has established a literacy collaborative, a school-wide program that is designed to increase literacy achievement in students in grades K–2 and advocates a model similar to four-block scheduling described in the previous paragraph. It has four blocks or four contexts within an integrated framework for reading and writing, which also include linkages to families and community. Purdue's model of reading Instruction includes:

1. Reading aloud to children
2. Shared reading
3. Guided reading and reading workshop
4. Independent reading

The four contexts for writing include:

1. Language experience and shared writing
2. Interactive writing
3. Guided writing and writers' workshop
4. Independent writing

Students' accomplishments can be exhibited in a literacy portfolio. A sample of each component for reading and writing should be included; for example, students could answer questions such as, *What and where did you read aloud? With whom did you share your reading? What skills do you have to work on as indicated from the reading workshop? Include a list or log of the books you read independently.*

READING ASSESSMENT STRATEGIES AND PORTFOLIO CONTENTS

As previously discussed, high-stakes testing and the prevalent use of standardized literacy assessment has caused many parents and teachers to be concerned about some of the directions educational reform has taken. They object to the concept of the scores of one test determining the fate of students, especially in terms of literacy abilities. Here are just a few admonitions:

- High-stakes testing is the primary instrument that justifies keeping minority children in lower end tracks and explains their eventual failure. (Ruiz et al., 2000)
- Literacy practices involve the interrelated use of oral language, reading, and writing, which are altogether different when decomposed into discrete separate skills. (Street, 1995)
- High-stakes testing does more harm than good to the very students who need the most help, and this practice is actually "dangerous" because test scores are not perfect measures and, therefore, should not be the sole criteria for decision making. (Coleman, 2000)
- "Test-o-crats" outlaw recess and see reading aloud as a "frill." High-stakes testing has nothing to do with education. Children must read to find a machine-scorable objective (title, author, illustrator), whereas adults read for enjoyment, to be transported to another place, or experience others' feelings. (Ohanian et al., 2000)
- Because meaning is embedded in sociocultural contexts, the interpretations depend on the context (Barton, 1994). High-stakes testing has significant consequences for good (high) or poor (low) performance on a test, inflates the importance of the test, and affects important decisions such as promotion or retention (IRA Board of Directors, 1999).

Joining the ranks of those who caution against this type of assessment is the prestigious American Educational Research Association, which in the past, has rarely taken a stand on controversial educational issues (Viadero, 2000; see also www.aera.net). Although educators are apparently concerned (and often appalled) by the potentially damaging emphasis on one test score, this trend is not about to change in the near future. It is very popular, in fact, with the current educational reform and accountability movements whose proponents are politicians, school boards, and some parents.

The above citations from various educational specialists are provided to reinforce the need to counteract the singular, high-stakes, approach to assessment and to encourage the creation of literacy portfolios. The literacy portfolio frees the teacher from an either/or bind or the qualitative-quantitative quandary. All sorts of data go into the literacy portfolio, even objective testing information! But students' knowledge and abilities in reading are enhanced by other indicators of their skills and abilities.

Teachers use numerous techniques to assess, analyze, monitor, and appraise reading behavior. The literacy portfolio includes both process and product measures, many of which are informal and holistic and include ongoing observations of students applying their reading skills in authentic classroom situations. The process includes the observation of and recording actual literacy behaviors, practices that can identify strengths and weaknesses, reading patterns, cueing systems, oral and silent reading fluency, and comprehension and help the teacher plan for appropriate instruction based on these assessments. For example, Figure 5–1 is a reading assessment profile that teachers are required to include in literacy portfolios in the Lawrence, New York, schools to provide necessary information about students' reading development. Likewise, in this district students are required to do some self-analysis about their reading development by completing the form shown in Figure 5–2.

The following formal and informal reading assessment strategies are suggested for inclusion in a portfolio.

Anecdotal Notes

During whole-class, small-group, or minilesson time, while students are actively engaged in a reading activity, the teacher should circulate about the room, observing and taking notes as the students read silently or with partners, confer, discuss books, share their knowledge of story elements, or retell stories. During shared book activities, the teacher can focus on a particular child and record specific reading behaviors (e.g., vocabulary growth, the ability to synthesize), become engaged in discussions, self-correct, predict, and make judgments. Informal, anecdotal notes provide authentic and useful information that may be recorded in a notebook, on loose-leaf paper, or on self-adhesive notes that are transferred at a later time to the appropriate student's record page. Figure 5–3 is a copy of an anecdotal reading record that a student teacher entered after observing a student learning English as a second language (ESL).

Observation Checklists

There are many different types of checklists, all of which allow for structured observations of specific skills, behaviors, and strategies. These checklists can be designed to look at particular oral reading and word identification competencies; to note comprehension strategies, strengths, and weaknesses; or to observe a student's ability to predict, and set a purpose for reading as shown in Figure 5–4. Shearer and Homan (1994) suggest that structured checklists be used as a starting point, to be followed later by interviews and conferences. Assessment information can be used for small-group or direct instruction. (Once again, this demonstrates how assessment and instruction cannot be separated.) Teachers find checklists useful because items can readily be added or deleted, and they are easy to design. Literature checklists may focus on comprehension of text, metacognitive abilities of the student, and the student's understanding of the story structure, setting, character, and plot. Comments and summaries can be written at the end of a checklist.

Sharp (1989) describes checklist models that range from early readers' language usage to identifying students' prior knowledge and thought processes in their interpretations. Checklists using metacognitive insights can be implemented at various times of the year to examine progress and recognize when new strategies are incorporated into the child's literacy repertoire. Rhodes and Shanklin (1993) suggest a checklist model with a focused format that includes *before reading* (i.e., uses captions to make predictions), *during reading* (i.e., is aware when text doesn't make sense), and *after reading* (i.e., recalls important information) (p. 237).

Reading Development Checklist
Teacher/Student Assessment Sheet

Student _____   Year _____

Teacher _____   Grade 1 2 3 4 5
                                                                  (circle)

The Reading Development Checklist has been designed to record a child's reading development based on the teacher's professional observations.

This checklist should be completed twice a year; the first time during the month of October and the second time during the month of May.

Key

E—Evident: The student consistently demonstrates the attitude or behavior.
F—Frequently: This attitude or behavior is frequently present.
R—Rarely: This attitude or behavior is rarely present.
NE—Not Evident: The student has not yet demonstrated the attitude or the behavior. It has not been observed by the teacher.
NA—Not Applicable: This attitude or behavior is not developmentally expected at this time.

Note: The *Evident* and *Not Evident* categories are *not* intended to represent pass or fail status.

Reading Participation

| | October | | | | | | May | | | | |
The Child	E	F	R	NE	NA		E	F	R	NE	NA
▨ listens to others.											
▨ participates meaningfully in class discussions.											
▨ completes assignments.											
▨ reads beyond required assignments.											

Comments (optional): _____

_____

_____

_____

_____

Recommendation (check if applicable):

_____ Reading support services are recommended.
_____ Reading enrichment is recommended.

FIGURE 5–1 Sample reading assessment profile. *Source:* Lawrence Public School Office of Curriculum & Instruction.

Am I Developing as a Reader (K–2)?

Name _____   Grade_____

Date _____   Teacher _____

1. I listen to others.	Yes	No	Sometimes
2. I like to read.	Yes	No	Sometimes
3. I look at pictures in a book to help me understand the story.	Yes	No	Sometimes
4. I ask questions about stories I do not understand.	Yes	No	Sometimes
5. I like when people read to me.	Yes	No	Sometimes
6. I talk to the class about books I have read.	Yes	No	Sometimes
7. I like to retell stories.	Yes	No	Sometimes
8. I like to write.	Yes	No	Sometimes

FIGURE 5–2 Sample student self-analysis. *Source:* Lawrence Public Schools Office of Curriculum & Instruction.

Baskwell and Whitman (1988) caution that although checklists are useful, they can be cumbersome and lengthy, and the fact that they "are written in a linear, sequential fashion often misleads people into thinking that is the order in which things must happen" (p. 17).

Literature Questionnaires

Literature questionnaires are designed to determine how children react to reading materials. Such questionnaires include items that relate to or question attitudes toward reading or appreciation of poetry, fables, and folktales; understanding of other cultures; and knowledge of various literary genres that are enjoyed and read most frequently. A questionnaire with an incomplete sentence format, as in Figure 5–5, allows for self-reflection and can touch on various issues, attitudes, and information, which could be useful for conference discussions.

Other questionnaires might be of the more traditional question and answer type, such as the following:

- Do you prefer reading fables or poetry?
- Who is your favorite character in a mystery?
- What would you like to learn next? What is your reading goal?
- What kind of books do you like best?
- What do you like to do on weekends and after school?

Am I Developing As An Independent Reader? (3–5)

Name _____ **Grade** _____ **Date** _____ **Teacher**_____

Choosing My Books	Yes	No	Sometimes
Do I choose books I can read?			
Do I choose different kinds of books?			
Do I listen to the suggestions of others when it comes to choosing books?			

I choose books from:

____home   ____public library   ____book club

____classroom   ____stores   ____other

____school library

Reading Books

When I read by myself I feel . . .

_____

_____

_____

_____

_____

FIGURE 5–2B *Source:* Lawrence Public Schools Office of Curriculum & Instruction.

Audio/Videotapes and Digital Cameras

Audio- and videotaping can be quite valuable in sharing reading behaviors with children and their parents. Teachers record students while they read both familiar and unfamiliar stories. Strategies and fluency can then be analyzed. Does the student self-correct? Use pictoral clues? Is the reading early in the year (October) different from the flow of reading heard on a later tape (March)? Taped comparisons can be made when a student selects a passage from a favorite book and when the teacher selects the material. Children can record each other during a reader's workshop or shared reading time or when they read to another, perhaps younger, child. Figure 5–6A is a youngster's self-assessment of his taped reading. In some schools, the parents are sent the tapes of their child reading several times during the school year. Figure 5–6B is a parent's enthusiastic written reaction after listening to a child's taped reading. In other schools, tapes are considered a significant part of the literacy portfolio and are sent along with additional work to the next year's teacher. When the child goes on to middle school, the tapes, along with other literacy portfolio contents, can be sent home. Parents (and the students) often

Anecdotal Reading Record

Date _March 16_   Time _10:45_

Name _Alex_

Subject _Reading_

Setting _Reader's Workshop_

Reading Activity _Read story—discuss_

Observations _Alex was attentive but did not actively participate. He listened but didn't volunteer any answers to questions._

Significance _Alex has an interest in reading but still has trouble interacting with the group. His English has improved greatly, but he rarely volunteers._

FIGURE 5–3 An anecdotal reading record completed by a student teacher for a student learning English as a second language.

treasure them, because they can listen (or see) the child grow in reading ability over the years.

Videos are an equally powerful assessment tool. Children can be taped with video or digital cameras in their shared reading group, during the whole group interactions, or for specific purposes such as a final unit project. Sometimes teachers videotape individual children during the administration of an Informal Reading Inventory at the beginning and end of the year to demonstrate (e.g., to parents, other teachers) students' reading behaviors and progress.

Story Retelling

An effective way of monitoring metacognitive processes for comprehending reading material is through story retelling. This appears to be replacing more traditional, structured, literal comprehension questions. Emergent readers, as well as older students, can use this strategy productively. They listen to a story and retell, or recall and reconstruct important parts of the story. To make story retellings more effective, Polakowski (1993), a teacher in New Jersey, indicates that directions must be clearly explained to students and include these steps: (1) Tell students they will be asked to retell the story; (2) for portfolio purposes, the story should be read from beginning to end without interruptions; (3) for assessment purposes, the child retells the stories without teacher prompts (the book is closed during the retelling).

Through retellings, kindergartners and first graders internalize linguistic structures, activate their auditory memory, and demonstrate various levels of listening comprehension. In grades 2 and up, story retelling assists the teacher in understanding how students reconstruct meaning from text, what elements of text are significant to them, and if they are aware of story elements such as plot, setting, and characters. Figure 5–7 depicts a story retelling done graphically using a Bubble Map, indicating the story elements from the book *The Witch Has an Itch* (Guthrie, 1990).

OBSERVATION CHECKLIST
METACOGNITIVE STRATEGIES

Student _____   Grade _____

Examiner _____

	Obs. I Date ____		Obs. II Date ____	
	DA*	NI*	DA*	NI*
1. Links prior knowledge before reading.	_____	_____	_____	_____
2. Develops purpose for reading.	_____	_____	_____	_____
3. Uses titles and/or illustrations to predict content/events.	_____	_____	_____	_____
4. Verifies predictions.	_____	_____	_____	_____
5. Develops questions to guide reading.	_____	_____	_____	_____
6. Creates visual representations of key concepts (web, outline, etc.).	_____	_____	_____	_____
7. Summarizes.	_____	_____	_____	_____

Summary

_____

_____

_____

_____

Recommendations

_____

_____

_____

_____

*DA = Developing Adequately.
 NI = Needs Improvement.

FIGURE 5–4 A sample observation checklist for structured observation. *Source: Linking Reading Assessment to Instruction* (p. 155), by A. Shearer and S. Homan, 1994, New York: St. Martin's Press. Copyright © 1994 by St. Martin's Press. Reprinted by permission of Lawrence Erlbaum Associates.

1. I don't like to read about _____.

2. When I read about other cultures _____.

3. I think it's interesting when I read about other people's problems because

   _____.

4. In the book I'm reading now, the part that really got to me is _____.

5. During discussion time, I like it best when _____.

6. The most difficult book _____.

FIGURE 5–5 A sample literacy questionnaire for students' use.

Name: Date:

Listen to your tape as many times as you want. Then answer the questions below.
Use the Good Reader's Lists to help you.

What do you notice about your reading?

I went back and fixed the words I read.

What do you feel you do well?

I try to sound out the words

What did you do when you came to a word you weren't sure of?

I sounded it out and if I didn't know it I asked the teacher

What did you do when you didn't understand what you read?

I go back.

FIGURE 5–6A A student's self-assessment of his taped reading. *Source:* Courtesy of Wendy Eisenhauer, Lynbrook, New York, school district.

This taping is a great gauge for me. It has terrific timing insofar as it allows me to participate and correct any bad habits Joey may have developed. It has given me an opportunity to understand and know exactly what Joey is doing and how he evaluates himself. This is a very informative tool.

FIGURE 5–6B A parent's reaction to a child's taped reading. *Source:* Courtesy of Wendy Eisenhauer, Lynbrook, New York, school district.

Retellings can be tape-recorded, given orally, or written as summaries. Teachers analyze the tapes and keep records of the child's retelling. Figure 5–8, developed by Polakowski and colleagues (1993), is a story retelling assessment sheet that includes story structure, theme, plot and text difficulty.

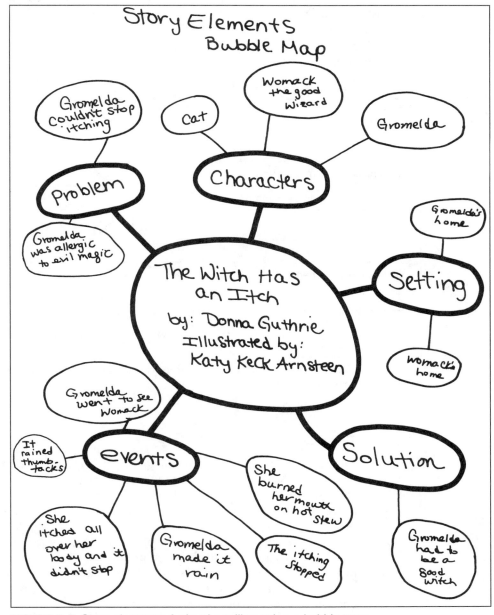

FIGURE 5–7 Story elements: A visual retelling using a bubble map.

Child's Name _____ Grade _____ Date _____

Teacher _____ Book Title _____ Author _____

___ Story was read to child

___ Child read alone

Text Difficulty

___ High Predictability

___ Moderate Predictability

___ Advanced Predictability

Response

___ Oral Retelling

___ Pictorial Retelling (Attached)

___ Written Retelling (Attached)

Story Structure	Includes	After Prompt	Comments
Setting/Characters Starts retelling at beginning of story			
Names main character(s)			
Names other character(s)			
Tells when story happened			
Tells where story happened			
Theme Identifies goal or problem			
Plot/events			
Includes all major events			
Tells events in sensible order			
Resolution Tells how problem was solved or goal was met			

Evaluative Comments:

_____

_____

_____

FIGURE 5–8 Sample story retelling assessment sheet. *Source:* Courtesy of the South Brunswick, New Jersey, school district.)

Think-alouds

Another way of observing metacognitive processes is through the use of think-alouds (see Figure 5–9). Students are taught to predict, confirm, and elaborate as they verbalize their thinking processes before, during, and after reading. Predictions are based on previewing the text and prior knowledge of the topic. During reading, students confirm predictions and describe whatever difficulties or confusions they encounter with unknown words, comprehension, plot, and so on. After reading, students are encouraged to verify their predictions, summarize what they've learned, and verbally elaborate on and react to the text. According to Thompkins and McGee (1993), "The purpose of think-aloud activities is not to teach students how to talk about strategies . . . but to encourage them to be more aware of the different kinds of strategies they might use when reading" (p. 261).

1. Teacher models several examples of think-aloud strategies.
2. Students often work in pairs or groups to verbalize their strategies to one another.
3. Enhance students' comprehension.
4. Help children see their thinking, operationally. They verbally express their thought processes.
5. As students think aloud or state what they are thinking, they are constructing meaning from the text.
6. Teacher assesses students' ability to access prior knowledge, see if a selection makes sense, and make inferences and predictions.
7. Collaborative activities (peer interaction) are especially useful as students tell *why strategy was used, how it is used, and when to use it successfully.*

FIGURE 5–9 How to conduct a think-aloud. *Source:* Based on the theories of J. F. Baumann, 1993.

Think-alouds can be a time-consuming and highly subjective technique. Myers and Lytle (1986) suggest a think-aloud model that includes six categories for teachers to consider as children verbalize their thought processes: monitoring, signaling, analyzing, judging, reasoning, and use of prompts. It may also be helpful to focus on the following areas when evaluating think-alouds:

1. The quality of the student's literal understanding of what was read. How many important features did the student comprehend and attend to?
2. The student's ability to differentiate between the relative significance of information presented.
3. The strategies employed during reading. Does the student use context clues and look for compound or root words when encountering an unfamiliar word?
4. Do certain patterns recur?
5. Note the student's emotional involvement with the text and ability to relate material to life experiences.

Running Records

Because it is critical for teachers to profile how students read and to monitor their progress, Clay (1993) suggests an assessment procedure, called a running record, which has gained wide acceptance. Running records allow the teacher to directly monitor students' decoding skills and are an important addition to the literacy portfolio because they specifically note and record a child's oral reading strategies. Although they may seem arduous at first, running records become easier with practice and take only 5 to 10 minutes to administer to each student. Most teachers take about three training workshops to become familiar and comfortable with this assessment technique. The conventions are rather simple: The teacher notes everything the child says and does while reading; all the correct words and the all the miscues are recorded. Clay notes that "As your ear becomes tuned-in to reading behaviors and you gain control over the recording conventions, your records will become more and more reliable" (p. 24).

Teachers are trained to use a kind of shorthand to note how the child reads and what is said. The record page contains four columns across the top: (1) the text, (2) the running record (check marks for each word read correctly, (3) E (Errors), and (4) SC (Self Corrections). The letters MSV appear in the E and SC columns and when a child makes an error it is circled and analyzed as either: M = the meaning or the message influenced the error or the student brought a different meaning to the author's text; S = syntax or structure of the sentence influenced the response; V = the visual information influenced the error.

Interpreting the Running Record. A running record is used to determine how children read, how they gain information from written text, and the kinds of errors or miscues they make. One examines the responses to ascertain the following:

- Do students use visual cues or rely on letters and sounds?
- Do they make predictions?
- Are their responses appropriate?
- Are there patterns to their miscues?
- How do they use meaning?
- How is print processed?
- What higher order problem-solving skills are applied?
- Were there self-corrections?
- What patterns can be seen?

Any text can be used as reading material but it should be a familiar text that the youngster has read before. Text should contain 100 words or less. Many teachers use books from suggested state and national book lists.

Scoring Running Records.

$$\text{Score} = \frac{\text{total words correctly read}}{\text{no. of words in book or sample read}} \times 100 = \underline{\hspace{1.5cm}} \%$$

95% or more means the book is easy for the child and is on the independent level.

90% to 94% of words read accurately means book is at the instructional level.

90% or less means the book is too difficult for the student to read.

Some teachers keep a sheet of lined paper next to the text and maintain a record by placing a check for each word read correctly. When there is a miscue—a reversal, substitution, repetition, or omission—it is counted as an error. However, if the child self-corrects, it is not counted as an error. Other teachers duplicate the passage(s) being read and record each miscue on their copy as the child reads.

Informal Reading Inventories (IRIs)

IRIs are similar to running records. Although IRIs can be teacher made, many well-constructed IRIs are available through major publishers. (Some basal programs provide an IRI as part of their packet of materials.) IRIs are comparable in that all have graded word lists to determine sight vocabulary and graded story passages, ranging from preprimer up through 8th or even 12th grade. The student is asked to first read the stories orally and then to read others silently. Literal and inferential comprehension questions are asked after each selection is read. IRIs such as the Bader Reading and Language Inventory (Bader & Wiesendanger, 1994) distinguish between comprehending and recalling and assess students' ability to retell as well as recall answers.

While the student reads orally, decoding strategies and fluency are assessed. Most IRIs include interest inventories and attitude surveys; some (Miller, 1995) include self-assessments, cloze procedures, semantic inventories, and phonic surveys. When completed, an IRI provides the teacher with knowledge about the child's reading behaviors and attitudes, as well as the student's independent, instructional, and frustration reading levels.

The *independent level*, also called recreational or pleasure reading level, indicates where the child is most comfortable with written material and therefore makes almost no errors. Library books checked out for enjoyment (as opposed to informational and reporting purposes) should be on this level. It is usually 1 year below the instructional level.

Word recognition = 99%   Comprehension = 95%

The *instructional level* is often referred to as the teaching level, especially if one is using a graded or basal reader. The student finds the reading material challenging, but neither too difficult nor too easy.

Word recognition = 90%   Comprehension = 75%

The *frustration level* is where reading performance breaks down. Vocabulary and concepts are much too difficult and the child shows signs of anxiety and frustration.

Word recognition = below 90%   Comprehension = below 50%

Reading/listening capacity level is the level of comprehension a youngster achieves when the material is read to the student. Listening capacity is useful to determine if poor readers have the ability to comprehend but are unable, for a variety of reasons (e.g., insufficient prior knowledge, poor decoding skills, emotional issues), to read and comprehend effectively on their own.

These distinctive reading levels are useful to gain an understanding of how a child reads in different situations, to determine how interests can be matched with books and, overall, to determine instructional goals for individual students.

When scoring an IRI, teacher judgment plays a large and subjective role; one point is deducted for a major miscue (substitution, mispronunciation) and a half-point is deducted for minor miscues (insertion, omission). Miscues are considered minor when meaning has not been affected by the error.

Additionally, IRI results provide insightful information for literacy conferences with students and parents. Figure 5–10 is part of a student teacher's IRI summary report that discusses the reading behaviors, motivation, strengths, and weaknesses of Spencer, a 10-

---

Strengths and Weaknesses in Reading

I was pleasantly surprised by the IRI. Spencer did very well in all facets of the test. He has an excellent sight vocabulary. He was reading words on the list a few grade levels above his own. He also showed promising decoding skills.

Spencer decoded words from the word list such as *antibiotic* and *contrary*. He succeeded in reading twenty-one words on the seventh-grade level correctly. I stopped there, because he had reached his frustration level. On the sixth-grade level, he did very well, saying twenty-three words correctly. The sixth-grade level proved to be his instructional level. At this point I began to wonder why he was in a low reading group. I discovered no glaring weaknesses while observing the word list portion of the IRI.

We began on the fourth-grade level for the oral reading passages. I wanted to begin with an easy reading passage, for I was still biased by the reading group placement. He answered the questions without a flaw. We discussed the passage, and he admitted to finding it easy. This was good, for he had seemed nervous, as if expecting something highly difficult.

This time I noticed four miscues, mispronunciations, and an omission, and two repeated words. On the questions, his only mistake was forgetting Bill Clinton's hometown. Some answers to higher level questions were adequate, yet uninspiring. This lack of creativity surfaced throughout the testing.

The sixth-grade level showed a dramatic dropoff. He just barely answered the questions. He had trouble with the higher level questions. His comprehension skills do not measure up to his sight vocabulary and decoding skills. He seemed rattled and acted irritated. I decided he'd had enough.

The silent reading part confirmed my view that comprehension is his weakest area. I contributed the dropoff to its being harder and Spencer's being less interested in the material.

I discovered that Spencer is a better reader than I would have previously guessed. I think he has been compared to his very bright classmates. Spencer did very well when motivated; the Alcatraz passage is a great example. Since I administered the IRI, Spencer has come up to me several times to discuss the prison.

FIGURE 5–10 Part of an IRI summary report: The student's reading strengths and weaknesses. *Source:* Courtesy of Scott Starkey.

year-old fifth grader, and includes recommendations to help Spencer become a more effective reader (see Figure 5–11).

IRIs may include spelling tests, interest inventories, and self-assessment reports (see Figure 5–12). These contribute to understanding the student's literacy repertoire and assist teacher, child, and parents in selecting appropriate books of interest. In Figure 5–12, the student says he likes scary stories; therefore, books could be suggested that deal with suspense and mysteries, such as *On the Edge* (Cross, 1985), *The Case of the Vanishing Corpse* (Newman, 1978), *A Kind of Thief* (Alcock, 1992), *Encyclopedia Brown Tracks Them Down* (Sobol, 1971), or the various *Harry Potter* books (Rowling, 2000).

We suggest that an IRI be given to all students in the Fall and again in the Spring, if possible. It is especially useful for noting growth and change in children with reading difficulties and for collaboratively setting instructional goals. The teacher can monitor reading progress and see which strategies have been learned and applied and which still need additional guidance. The summary sheet and fairly detailed recommendations for future instruction should be included in the literacy portfolio, along with the student's self-assessment of reading achievements and future goals, preferably in narrative form.

Reciprocal Teaching

The reciprocal teaching strategy both assesses and teaches comprehension through metacognitive monitoring (Figure 5–13). The teacher demonstrates four structured comprehension approaches, and then students take turns modeling themselves after the teacher and guiding other students to use the technique (Berliner & Casanova, 1986). The four strategies for reciprocal teaching are: (1) generating questions, (2) summarizing, (3) clarifying, and (4) predicting. The teacher assesses students' ability to use this struc-

---

Recommendations

Spencer has definite potential to be an outstanding reader. His greatest weakness was comprehension; arguably the most important aspect of reading. He was not deficient in this area, but compared to other areas, this one lagged behind. Fortunately, the weakness is now identified, and remediation can begin. There are a number of different strategies to improve comprehension. The remediation is twofold. Some of the strategies are direct teaching strategies, while another is to teach Spencer to change his own approach to reading.

Some of the different direct procedures include predicting, prereading, cloze procedure, guided questioning, and story mapping. Each strategy could be used during in-class reading.

Prereading activities attempt to activate the student's problem solving and motivation. Motivation is a key help for Spencer. The reading segment on Alcatraz brought this to my attention. When interested, he can do very well. Drawing on background knowledge before reading awakens curiosity and thus makes the reader more focused. This heightened attention is necessary, for without it Spencer misses much of the material.

I would also teach Spencer about the use of analogies. Analogies help students make inferences when they read. Again, an appropriate analogy can help awaken prior knowledge.

If we are reading out loud, guiding questions may help stimulate comprehension. Questioning is a beneficial comprehension strategy, for it encourages reader interaction with the test. These questions again can be derived from the student's prior knowledge. Students using questioning strategies (QARs) do better than their peers. These questions would help keep him focused on the important material.

The cloze procedure could help Spencer enhance his predicting skills. The teacher should be careful to recognize the wide range of possible answers. The problem with the cloze procedure is that it is choppy and interferes with the flow of the story. This could cause a lack of enjoyment. Pleasure is a necessary component of reading.

Story mapping is yet another important skill that could be tried. The student must organize the story into a web. The mental, or visual, representation can stimulate the student in a new way. Spencer may prosper from this type of practice. It is impossible to know, unless it's tried.

FIGURE 5–11 Part of an IRI summary report: Recommendations for student. *Source:* Courtesy of Scott Starkey.

Name **Richard**   Grade **4**   Teacher ***D. Basilone** Date_____

SELF-ASSESSMENT DEVICE
(Intermediate-Grade Level)

1. What does a person have to do to be a good reader?

   Read alot.

2. Who is my favorite author? Why do I like to read books or stories written by him or her?

   RIstine he was good horror stories

3. What are the three best things I have read this semester? Why did I like them?

   earth and Lights out Garfield

4. What are the easiest and hardest things about reading for me?

   Made up Words

5. What kinds of books and stories would I like to read in the future?

   Long ones

6. What does a person have to do to be a good writer?

   Spell good

7. What kinds of writing have I done this year?

   Short Stories

8. What kinds of writing do I like to do the most?

   Computer writins

9. What piece of writing would I like most to do over to make it better?

   Final Escape the last breakout to happen in jail.

10. What kinds of writing would I like to do in the future?

    none

11. What are the easiest and hardest things for me about writing?

    easy story; editing hard

12. What do I need to work on the hardest to improve my writing?

    Spelling

---

* Student Teacher

FIGURE 5–12 A 10-year-old ESL student's self-assessment sheet. *Source:* From ALTERNATIVE ASSESSMENT TECHNIQUES FOR READING AND WRITING by Wilma Miller Copyright © 1995. Reprinted with permission of Center for Applied Research in Education/Prentice Hall Direct.

tured process to become successful, insightful, and independent readers who are aware of their metacognitive processes and understand when and which strategies are being implemented. Most significant, according to Berliner and Casanova (1986), is the students' facility to monitor their own comprehension and to become more cognitively informed about their own thinking processes and how they comprehend text.

Directions: Follow the steps below in order. **"R"** before the directions means you will read. **"W"** means you will write the answer to a question. To complete this assignment, you will read pages _____ in your text.

R   Read the title of the section and subtitles. Then skim the first paragraph.

W   What is this going to be about?

_____

_____

W   What are two questions you have on this topic that can guide your reading?

_____

_____

R   Now read the first section.

W   What words were unfamiliar to you?

_____

_____

W   What do you think these words mean?

_____

_____

R   What was unclear to you as you read this passage?

_____

_____

W   Write a summary of this section.

_____

_____

_____

FIGURE 5–13 Reciprocal teaching guide. *Source:* From *Linking Reading Assessment to Instruction* (p. 149), by A. Shearer and S. Homan, 1994, New York: St. Martin's Press. Copyright © 1994 by St. Martin's Press. Reprinted by permission of Lawrence Erlbaum Associates.

ASSESSING CHILDREN'S READING PRODUCTS

In order to be effective, the literacy portfolio must contribute to the thorough understanding of each child's literacy strengths and weaknesses. It should be viewed as a dynamic and viable vehicle for designing instruction based on each child's competencies and performance as indicated by the artifacts in the portfolio.

Reading assessment includes the teacher's observations and the assessment of the student's artifacts or collections, which could include story maps, story frames, story grammars, reading lists, journals (character journals, reading response journals), reading conference logs, personal reading goals, and reflective self-assessment reports, all of which are carefully deliberated on by both teacher and student. Because the reading process is not as tangible as the writing process, writing is often used as a tool to describe reading. The portfolios, therefore, contain a variety of written materials that exhibit the student's response, understanding, and reflection on material the student has read. Analysis of specific accomplishments, goals to improve specific areas of weakness, attention to the student's products, reflections and a self-evaluations are all essential outcomes.

Reading Lists

Reading lists kept by students provide information as to the types of literature being read and when books were completed. Reading lists are an easy form of record keeping that can be used in conjunction with logs and journals.

In Figure 5–14, the teacher can see at a glance that in less than 2 months, Renée has self-selected books that include poetry and fantasy, as well as a multicultural dictionary. Additional books by the same authors could be suggested to Renée. As the year progresses, the book list indicates Renée's reading interests and the extent of her reading involvement, which helps the teacher guide and plan her instructional directions.

Journals and Logs

We have discussed the variety of journals and logs that children can maintain as both a record and a response to their reading. Journal entries should be read and evaluated by the teacher because they provide valuable insights into students' understanding and reaction to what they read. This insight is especially valuable for determining appropriate instruction to meet individual student needs. Character journals indicate that students understand a book on the creative-thinking level and can express themselves through the voices of the characters in the stories. The student in Figure 5–15 humorously describes herself, in a carefully written letter, as a conquering soldier who had a laughing fit. The teacher can discuss spelling and homophones (*threw* versus *through*), acknowledge the careful self-corrections (*hysterical*), and note the mechanics of writing (indentation for paragraphs, etc.).

Books I Finished Reading

Name: *Renee*

Title	Author	Completed
1. *A Light in the Attic* This was a fun poem book. The pictures are silly too.	S. Silverstein	Oct. 3
2. *Jambo Means Hello* I learned lots of African words.	M. Feelings	Oct. 17
3. *Charlotte's Web* I cried when Charlotte died, but I loved this book.	E. B. White	Nov. 20

FIGURE 5–14 A sample basic reading list.

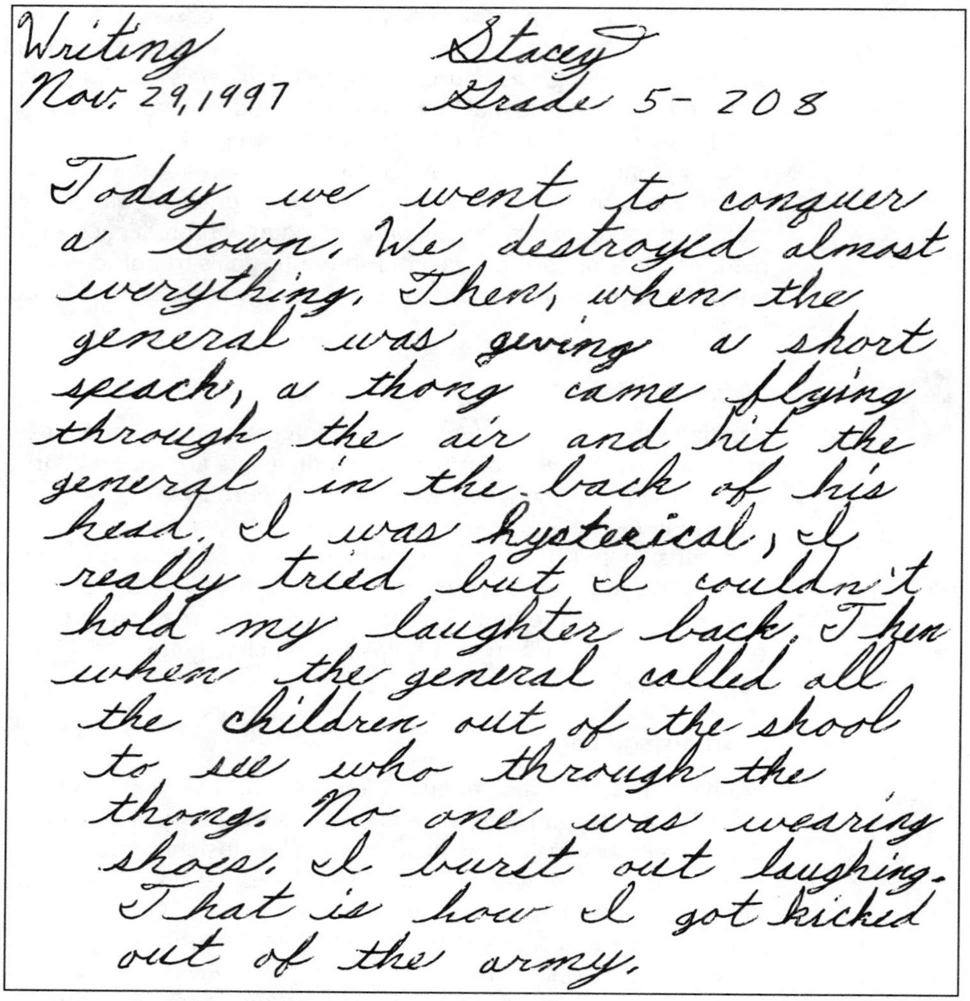

Writing   Stacey
Nov. 29, 1997   Grade 5 - 208

Today we went to conquer a town. We destroyed almost everything. Then, when the general was giving a short speach, a thong came flying through the air and hit the general in the back of his head. I was hysterical, I really tried but I couldn't hold my laughter back. Then when the general called all the children out of the shool to see who through the thong. No one was wearing shoes. I burst out laughing. That is how I got kicked out of the army.

FIGURE 5–15 A character journal entry by a fifth grader.

Story Frames and Related Items

Story frames, story grammars, story maps, and story boards provide insights into a student's understanding of plot, character, ability to predict, and sequence. In Figure 5–16, a story board created by a fifth grader from an inner-city school indicates how well the story was understood. This child appropriately sequences the story and understands the multicultural tale that took place in another century and setting. The youngster's artistic ability should also be applauded and encouraged.

When using content books and nonfiction, a *KWL* (What I know; What I want to know; What I learned) lesson can be helpful in reviewing background information, setting goals, and then evaluating the student's comprehension. Figure 5–17 illustrates what one struggling fifth grader learned from a book about golden retrievers. It is clear that although he didn't answer the questions he posed before reading, he did obtain some information from the text and can read additional material to answer the other questions.

Venn Diagrams

Venn diagrams are a popular tool for comparing stories and can be used with primary as well as intermediate- and middle-school students. Two circles each detail the unique characteristics, ideas, or concepts under consideration, and the intersecting part shows the commonalities and similarities. Students can compare two pieces of literature or two authors' styles and then create a Venn diagram to visually indicate this information. The

FIGURE 5–16 A story board created by a fifth grader.

third grader's Venn diagram in Figure 5–18 shows her understanding of the similarities and differences between two books of fantasy, *Jumanji* (Van Allsberg, 1981) and *Where the Wild Things Are* (Sendak, 1963). In Figure 5–19, a fifth-grade student contrasts and compares two different cultures, China and the United States, after reading *In the Year of the Boar and Jackie Robinson* (Lord, 1984) as part of a multicultural unit. Further readings to overcome stereotypes and learn more about Asian American literature and experi-

FIGURE 5–16 *Continued.*

ences might be suggested, such as *Dragonwings* (Yep, 1975), *Grandfather's Journey* (Say, 1993), or *Tales from Gold Mountain: Stories of the Chinese in the New World* (Yee, 1990).

Student Attitude Surveys and Self-Evaluations

Self-reflecting tools help to determine how students perceive themselves as readers (Figure 5–20). Students should ultimately learn to write narrative self-assessments (rather than completing a fill-in-the-blank form) to provide depth and insights on where

KWL: Golden Retrievers

What I know	What I want to know	What I learned
1. They have golden hair.	1. How old can they get until they die?	① males are about 61 cm (24 in) high
2. They're dogs.	2. Do they pull when you walk them?	② They are powerfull dogs
3. Can be trained to be mean.	3. What country did they come from?	③ They are hunting dogs.
4. Family dog.		④ The name yellow was dropped and changed to golden.
5. They shed a lot.		⑤ females are smaller then males.
6.		⑥
7.		

FIGURE 5–17 A fifth grader's KWL.

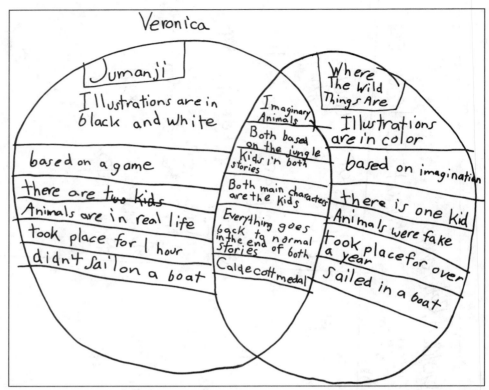

FIGURE 5–18 A Venn diagram by a third grader comparing two books of fantasy.

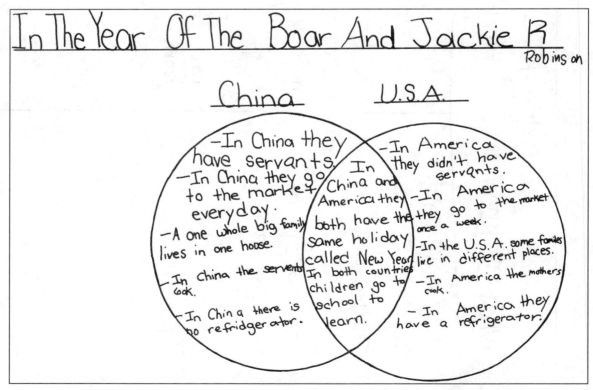

FIGURE 5–19 A Venn diagram by a fifth grader showing cultural comparisons.

Reading Attitude Inventory/Interview

Begin the discussion with "tell me about your favorite book" (or your favorite author) to get the conversation going. Please elaborate on the following questions and prompts (probe with "why?" or "tell me more" to get children talking).

1. How do you feel when your teacher reads a story to the class?

    I feel like there's an adventure and I would stop whatever I do and stick it in my desk and just listen to her. (S.B.)

2. How do you feel when someone gives you a book for a present?

    I like books and it's one of my number one things to do—read! (J. W.)

3. How do you feel about reading books for fun?

    I feel great, because books are like puzzles. Your mind and your books are hooked together like a puzzle. (Z. G.)

4. How do you feel when you are asked to read to others in the class?

    Nice! Once I read a whole book to the whole class. (A. L.)

5. How do you feel when you are asked to read to your teacher?

    I feel good—it's sort of like putting your heads together. (Z. G.)

FIGURE 5–20 A sample student attitude survey showing various students' responses.
Source: Courtesy of Juneau, Alaska, school district.

they've been and where they want to be. Figure 5–21 reveals the poignant self-evaluation that was put into a portfolio created by a student with a reading disability who was being tutored. It is evident that this student knows that he has trouble with comprehension, but finds more satisfaction with writing, which would be a fine way to motivate reading. It is unfortunate to hear that any teacher yells at a child. The tutor learned far more from this child's self-evaluation than she learned from the classroom teacher. Some schools also ask for a reflective literacy autobiography: When did the students first start reading? Are they reading more now than a few months ago? What are their disappointments? What strengths do they see, and what areas do they want to improve?

Reading Rubrics

To clarify and guide students in terms of what is being looked at and assessed, rubrics help teachers focus on specific reading strategies, which are then rated on a progressive

6. How do you feel about going to school?

It's fun and I always want to be in school. (A. S.)

7. How do you feel about how well you read?

I feel good because I get to read to myself whenever I want to read. I don't have to have a parent read to me. (O. M.)

8. How do you think your teacher feels when you read?

I've been in her class this year and last year and I've done amazing in reading. (A. B.)

9. How do you feel when you read to your family? Who do you read to? When do you read?

I like it because we read stories to each other. (C. D.)

10. How did you learn to read?

My grandpa taught me. He read me stories and then I caught on to them. (S. M.)

FIGURE 5–20 *Continued.*

Self-Reflection on Myself as a Reader and Writer

I don't think that I am a very good reader. I am good at sounding words out but sometimes I don't know what I am reading. I don't really like my language arts class. It is really boring and really hard. Some of the stuff we read makes me confused and I get mad. When I get mad the teacher yells at me. I don't like to read. I like to write a little more. I come up with some good stuff to write about but sometimes I don't write it like I want to hear it. I wish I could be a good reader and a good writer. I will try more.

FIGURE 5–21 Reading self-evaluation by a fifth-grade student with reading difficulties.

scale, ranging from specific itemized strengths to specific itemized areas of weakness. Vizyak (1996) has revised her first-grade rubrics many times over the years. They are now fairly extensive and include predicting, recognizing print inconsistencies, knowing when meaning is lost, fluency and automaticity in reading, comprehension of text, and enjoyment of literature (see Figure 5–22). Figure 5–23 is a different kind of reading rubric used by a fifth-grade teacher to score a student's written response after reading.

Reading Rubric Grade 1

Name _____

Date _____

Shows Comprehension of Text

1	2	3	4	5
Relies on story being read by teacher or with others Retells with very little detail; sequences pictures to tell simple story Does not include inferred information when summarizing Does not differentiate real/make-believe Does not connect story events to experiences in life		Reads independently and/or relies on story being read with others Retells story in own words including characters, setting, and sequence of events Begins to include inferred information when summarizing Differentiates real/make-believe Connects story events to own life experiences		Reads independently Retells story accurately and sequentially in own words and elaborates Includes inferred information when summarizing story Differentiates real/make-believe and fiction/nonfiction Connects story events to experiences in own life and elaborates

Comments:

Shows Appreciation/Enjoyment of Literature

1	2	3	4	5
Shows limited interest in being read to Shows little interest in books Participates minimally in oral reading of familiar stories Limited use of classroom library		Enjoys being read to and wants to hear favorite stories repeatedly Reads when directed to books Participates in oral reading of familiar stories Uses classroom library when directed		Selects books he/she wishes to have read aloud and requests favorite stories repeatedly Voluntarily reads Leads oral reading of favorite stories Voluntarily uses classroom library

Comments:

FIGURE 5–22 Part of a developmental reading rubric used for first-grade students by Adams County Five Star School District, Colorado.

Reading Responses   Title of Book _____ Name _____

	5	4	3	2	1
Understanding of Reading	• An insightful understanding of key issues in the reading • Draws significant conclusions about issues	• A strong understanding of issues in the reading • Draws solid conclusions about issues	• An adequate understanding of issues in the reading • Draws satisfactory conclusions about issues	• A partial understanding of the issues in the reading • Lacks conclusions about issues or forms inaccurate ones	• A minimal understanding of issues in the reading • Lacks conclusions about issues or forms inaccurate ones
Use of Support Information	• Accurate and appropriate use of a variety of examples and references to the text. Support for ideas and opinions is precise and thoughtfully selected	• Accurate and appropriate use of examples and reference to the text to support ideas and opinions	• Satisfactory use of examples and references to the text to support ideas and opinions	• Uses few details or examples from the text to support ideas and opinions	• Lacks details or examples from the text to support ideas and opinions
Organization	• Logical and effective organization of ideas	• Logical organization of ideas	• Adequate organization of ideas	• Weaknesses in organization of ideas	• Lacks organization of ideas
Quality of Expression	• Rich, effective language • Skillful use of sentence variety • Consistent use of accurate conventions	• Specific descriptive language • Sentence variety • Minimal errors in conventions that do not interfere with communication	• Appropriate language • Some sentence variety • Satisfactory use of accurate conventions • Errors do not interfere with communication	• Occasionally uses inappropriate or incorrect language • Sentence makes sense but has little variety • Errors in conventions may interfere with communication	• Inappropriate or incorrect language • Lacks accurate sentence structure • Errors in conventions that interfere with communication

Date _____ Rating _____ Comment _____

Suggestions _____

FIGURE 5–23 Reading response rubric used by a fifth-grade teacher.

It is clear from this rubric that both the comprehension of the material and the student's writing ability are important.

READING ASSESSMENT CONCERNS AND CAUTIONS

A thoughtful teacher must ask, "What's the purpose of all of this assessment?" We firmly believe that better assessment guides the teacher to set appropriate goals for each student and consequently to create reading opportunities and experiences that will help the child enhance literacy skills and strategies. Calkins (2001) feels that better teaching is the result of better assessment:

> Assessment is the thinking teacher's mind work. Assessment is the stance that allows us to learn from our students and thus to teach them. Assessment is the compass with which we find our bearings and chart our course, and the map on which we do this. (p. 137)

Regarding the student's reading products, what does the teacher do with these collected "treasures" in each child's portfolio? Are all of equal merit? How can the teacher equitably assess the worth of what each student believes is precious and in which each has ego-investment? The metacognitive process of reflection and self-assessment is not only empowering but can assist the teacher as students analyze their own growth and development.

To fairly assess the contents of literacy portfolios in terms of reading progress, caution and discretion must be wielded so that subjective judgments do not undermine the climate of trust that has been established nor the philosophical underpinnings of literacy and assessment that are espoused in this book. Strickland (1995) emphasized that "schools must provide low-risk learning environments" (p. 299) for successful learning to take place. There cannot be a mismatch between instruction (how we teach) and assessment (how we judge children's works). The portfolio process should contain enough selective and appropriate teacher and student materials so that fair, collaborative, and constructive analysis and evaluation of reading behaviors and progress can be exercised.

CONCLUSIONS

Reading assessment should incorporate guided reading. It entails keeping records of students' works, extensive teacher's notations, and the students' formal and informal observations and evaluations. The goal of assessment is to understand each student as an individual and as a reader, and to change instruction so that each student can improve and move forward in reading and learning. It answers these questions: What do students know? What do they need to know to be more effective in their reading and critical thinking skills? Previous and ongoing works are scrutinized, and the teacher and student together can determine the goals that have been met and set new goals for short-term and long-range learning. Ultimately, an in-depth reading profile emerges. Both student and teacher can identify and understand the student's reading preferences; where, and if, motivation is lacking; strengths in fluency, vocabulary, and metacognitive awareness of reading strategies; self-monitoring ability; insights and critical comprehension abilities; and growth in appreciation of literature. Always in the forefront are these questions: Does the child read often and with pleasure? Can the child use print to find information? Do formal test scores reflect the type of work the child is doing in class? Does the portfolio provide evidence of continual learning and progress? As the portfolio is perused the teacher provides guidance and strategies to each child so that growth, solutions to problems, and enhancement of learning will be apparent. As all educators know, and as Hornsby and Sukarna (1986, p. 142) caution, it is the promotion of individual achievement, not competitive assessment, that is most important. Better assessment ultimately leads to better reading progress for our students!

REFERENCES

Barton, D. (1994). *Literacy: An introduction to the ecology of written language*. Oxford, UK: Blackwell.

Bader, L., & Weisendanger, K. (1994). *Bader reading and language inventory*. Upper Saddle River, NJ: Merrill/Prentice Hall.

Baskwell, J., & Whitman, P. (1988). *Evaluation: Whole language, whole child*. New York: Scholastic.

Berliner, D., & Casanova, U. (1986, January). Should you try reciprocal teaching: Yes! *Instructor*, 12–13.

Clay, M. (1993). *An observation survey of early literacy achievement*. NH: Heinemann.

Coleman, A. (2000). None of the above: Rejecting the false choice about high-stakes testing. *Education Week* (August 2), 42, 45.

Fitzgerald, J. (1999). What is this thing called "balance?" *Reading Teacher, 53*(2), 100–107.

Hornsby, D., Sukarna, D., & Parry, J. (1986). *Read on: A conference approach to reading*. Portsmouth, NH: Heinemann.

International Reading Association Board of Directors. (1999). High-stakes assessments in reading. *Reading Teacher, 53*(3), 257–263.

Myers, J., & Lytle, S. (1986). Assessment of the learning process. *Exceptional Children, 53*, 138–144.

Miller, W. H. (1995). *Alternative assessment techniques for reading and writing*. West Nyack, NY: Center for Applied Research in Education.

Nichols, J. D. (2000). Scheduling reform: A longitudinal exploration of high school block scheduling structures. *International Journal of Educational Reform, 9*(2), 134–147.

Ohanian, S. et al. (2000). Agora: The impact of high-stakes testing. *Journal of Teacher Education, 5*(4), 289–292.

Polakowski, C. (1993). Literacy portfolios in the early childhood classroom. In *Student portfolios*. South Brunswick, NJ: South Brunswick Schools.

Rhodes, L., & Shanklin, N. (1993). *Windows into literacy*. Portsmouth, NH: Heinemann.

Ruiz, R. et al. (2000). Agora. The impact of high stakes testing. *Journal of Teacher Education, 5*(4), 289–292.

Sharp, Q. (1989). *Evaluation: Whole language checklists for evaluating your children*. New York: Scholastic.

Shearer, A., & Homan, S. (1994). *Linking reading assessment to instruction*. New York: St. Martin's.

Smith, C. (2000). Trends in the reading curriculum. University of Evansville. *NetWords*, pp. 6–7.

Street, B. V. (1995). *Social literacies: Critical approaches to literacy in development, ethnography and education*. London: Longman.

Strickland, D. S. (1995). Reinventing our literacy programs: Books, basics, balance. *The Reading Teacher, 48*, 294–302.

Stoicheva, M. (1999). Balanced reading instruction. http://www.indiana.edu/~eric_rec/.

Tompkins, G., & McGee, L. (1993). *Teaching reading with literature*. New York: Merrill.

Viadero, D. (2000). In short. *Education Week*. (August 2), p. 8.

Vizyak, L. (1996). *Student portfolios: A practical guide to evaluation*. Bothell, WA: Wright.

Children's Literature References

Alcock, V. (1992). *A kind of thief*. New York: Delacorte.

Cross, G. (1985). *On the edge*. New York: Holiday House.

Guthrie, D. (1990). *The witch has an itch*. New York: Simon & Schuster.

Lord, B. B. (1984). *In the year of the boar and Jackie Robinson*. New York: HarperCollins.

Newman, R. (1978). *The case of the vanishing corpse*. New York: Atheneum.

Rowling, J. K. (2000). *The Harry Potter Series*. New York: Scholastic.

Say, A. (1993). *Grandfather's journey*. Dallas: Houghton Mifflin.

Sendak, M. (1963). *Where the wild things are*. New York: HarperCollins.

Sobol, D. (1971). *Encyclopedia Brown tracks them down*. New York: Scholastic/Four Winds.

Van Allsberg, C. (1981). *Jumanji*. Dallas: Houghton Mifflin.

Yee, P. (1990). *Tales from Golden Mountain: Stories of the Chinese in the new world*. New York: Macmillan.

Yep, L. (1975). *Dragonwings*. New York: HarperCollins.

Using the Literacy Portfolio to Assess and Guide Writing Development

KEY WORDS AND CONCEPTS

indirect measurement
direct measurement
performance-based
   assessment
rubrics
holistic scoring

benchmarks
anchor papers
exemplars
analytic scoring
primary trait scoring
writing process approach

New York State began to use a writing competency test for fifth-grade students in the early 1980s. The test format required that all fifth graders write two different pieces in response to specific prompts. Each piece would be read and given a score from 1 to 4 (4 being the highest) by two raters. Thus, a student's score would fall on a continuum from 0 to 16. The first group of fifth graders to take the test did so with great anticipation and eagerly awaited the results. When the data were reported to the students, one student named Robert was told by his teacher that he got a 14 on the test, without any further explanation. He shared this news with his parents. When they asked him what he thought the score meant and what his teacher had to say about his writing, he answered "All I know is that Brian got a 16, and I think I write better." Robert's teacher did not explain the scoring system to Robert or his parents and did not comment further about Robert's writing. The value of this assessment opportunity was lost to the teacher, to Robert, and to Robert's family. If writing assessment is to have value, it must have meaning and purpose for all who participate—and with the increased pressure for more literacy assessment on national, state, and local levels, this is more important than ever!

INTRODUCTION

Today's teachers have learned the value of writing in their classrooms, not only because students should be effective writers as an important part of functional literacy but because writing has many purposes. Writing is more than a tool—it has utility in learning all subjects, it reveals a great deal about students' understanding, reactions, and cognitive strategies, and it also has personal meaning. According to Smith (1982), "Writing touches every part of our lives, and not even the illiterate escape its consequences . . . I propose to take the general utility of writing to be axiomatic; it has earned its place in any culture in which it is found" (p. 7). Writing has been found to be useful as a means of communication, for producing a permanent record, and as an art (Smith, 1982).

Renewed Emphasis on Writing Creates Controversy

The renewed interest in writing in our schools is the result of several trends. In the 1970s, the public became particularly concerned about the quality of literacy instruction, and attention not only focused on the national indicators that depicted poor literacy attainment but also highlighted the deficient writing skills of many high school graduates. In the 1980s, educators began to view reading and writing as parallel aspects of children's literacy development and saw that reading and writing instruction shared cognitive dimensions that were not only linked together but reinforced each other. Consequently, reading and writing began to be taught simultaneously. Educators began writing instruction at the emergent stages of literacy development, and writing was emphasized throughout the grades in all curriculum areas. In the 21st century, newer theories of integrating the language arts now provide teachers with strategies for incorporating both reading and writing activities into daily instruction as part of balanced reading programs, guided reading, literature-based teaching, and thematic units.

The work of Calkins (1983, 1986, 1994), Graves (1983) and others popularized a newer theory of writing instruction that many have called the process approach to writing. According to Burns, Roe, and Smith (2002), this approach is child-centered; students take ownership of their writing by creating their own pieces, are aware of audience, develop their writing through stages and, finally, share their writing through publication in a supportive community of authors. Most important, it is recognized that writing is ongoing and recursive and requires writing every day. (Burns, Roe, & Smith, 2002, p. 309). Classroom strategies that emerged from this new approach have included writing workshops, the widespread use of journals, writing activities applied to all curriculum areas, peer editing, conferencing, computer-assisted writing instruction, students responding to literature, and recreating meaning through writing. In recognition of the importance of students editing their own work, teachers have adopted writing portfolios to facilitate the students' ability to work on a piece of writing through various stages. The writing folder, in which the students' work was collected, is undoubtedly the forerunner of writing portfolios.

Currently, the recognition of the importance of writing as integral to children's literacy has caused renewed concern about how best to teach and assess writing. State-wide assessment programs now require more measurement of writing to determine if students are meeting more stringent literacy standards. This has had a profound impact on classroom instruction. One teacher recently complained about the time spent in preparation for state-wide literacy testing in her middle-school literacy classes; her principal requires that she have her struggling readers and writers practice for the New York State language arts exam (given in the spring) for 2 out of 5 days each week. The form of practice consists of worksheets. Test preparation does not replace good teaching, and many are concerned that instructional time is being lost to meaningless drill and practice. Newspaper accounts tell of the alarming number of New York teachers who do not want to teach fourth grade, because that is the elementary school level for the administration of reading and writing tests. These teachers say that the overemphasis on testing ruins their instructional programs, creates tremendous stress on the students and, furthermore, the teachers are being held responsible for low test scores that, if they are at all reliable, reflect cumulative learning over many years. In many classrooms, teachers are caught in the crossfire between knowing what good writing practices are versus the mandate to drill students, with the expectation that drilling will produce higher test scores. Consequently, the many controversies regarding how best to teach and assess writing persist:

Mechanics Versus Content. Teachers have long faced the dilemma of whether written work should be evaluated for its correctness or for the quality of ideas and content. Although an essay that contains many mechanical errors can easily be red-penciled and criticized, to do so negates the thoughts, feelings, and valuable content that may be revealed in the writing. In the past, students became discouraged and didn't enjoy writing because they feared extensive criticism when assessment focused on mechanics.

Focus on correctness has never ensured good writing. A piece of writing can exhibit good technical skills without being interesting, persuasive, artistic, or compelling. Thoughtful educators are now more inclined to examine a piece of writing for its assets rather than deficits, which is a model that encourages students by acknowledging accomplishments instead of highlighting weaknesses. Although the use of writing rubrics and holistic assessment systems are attempts to balance the importance of content with concerns about form and mechanics, what constitutes good or acceptable writing is still debated. Many educators are concerned that the standards movement values correctness of form over quality of content.

Process Versus Product. Enlightened educators often are interested in the underlying cognitive process that children use when they write (commonly exemplified by concerns about organization, elaboration, and language use), and thus are less likely to focus exclusively on the product. The strategies students use when they compose, such as the ability to self-edit, may ultimately be more important than attention to the writing product. According to Bratcher (1994), we have seen a paradigm shift in that "We no longer emphasize the products of writing to the exclusion of the process. Grading students' writing has always been a cause for concern, but with the emphasis on teaching through a writing process approach, an assessment dilemma persists" (p. 5). According to Bratcher (1994),

> On the one hand, we are committed to teaching writing as a process. . . . On the other hand, we are locked into school situations that require us to translate our response to our students' writing into letter grades or even numbers. But there is hope: teacher/grader schizophrenia can be overcome by choosing grading options that match our teaching purposes. (p. 6)

The process and strategies that students use as they compose are now valued for the insights they provide teachers about how students reflect, organize, and construct meaning, and thereby enable teachers to become more effective.

Genre Influences Writing Assessment. All forms of writing are not equivalent—each genre requires different knowledge and strategies and ultimately succeeds because of different dynamics. Highly descriptive and colorful language used effectively in a poem would obviously be less appropriate in a business letter. A student's ability to write a friendly letter to a pen pal (now often replaced by computer e-mail) cannot be assessed in the same manner as an independent research report. Writing assessment needs to be responsive to differences in writing forms. This is especially important as classroom strategies encourage written expression in many genre, including personal narratives, reports, essays, letters, poems, and articles.

The recognition of the importance of writing in different forms is reflected by writing assignments that require students to compose using different formats. Likewise, many of the new standards for literacy provide specific guidelines for the forms of written expression that are appropriate at different developmental levels. For example, one New York City school district provides all third-grade teachers with these monthly themes to focus on: September—journal writing; October—personal narrative; November—writing descriptions; December—letter writing; January—persuasive writing; February—fiction book report; March—biographical book report; April—writing directions; May—fantasy narrative; and June—poetry. Many teachers now use writing rubrics to customize writing assessment to the particular genre that the students are employing. (Examples of rubrics are found throughout this book, especially in this chapter in Figures 6-2, 6-3, 6-22, 6-23, and 6-27.)

Evaluation Versus Description. Another dilemma for teachers is the necessity for reducing extensive analytic and descriptive comments to a grade. At the emergent literacy levels, parents and administrators may be satisfied with a thoughtful description of how a child is developing as a writer; at the upper levels, however, they want more precise assessment in the form of grades. Report cards from grades 2 through middle school usually require teachers to reduce complex information to a letter grade. How to reduce the thoughtful analysis of writing into a letter or number that can be recorded on a report card is difficult, and certainly students' efforts, as well as the success of their products, should be part of the grading equation.

Sensitivity to Individuals Versus Meeting Uniform Standards. Classrooms are now more heterogeneous than ever before. New patterns of immigration have resulted in large numbers of English as a second language (ESL) learners in classrooms at every grade level in every school district across the country. School districts experiencing rapid growth in development are especially challenged by the need to provide for children of newly arrived immigrants as well as others seeking better housing and employment. Additionally, the legal mandate to incorporate students with special education needs into the general education curriculum is no longer a theory but a reality, and inclusion programs are widely used, with fewer self-contained, special education classrooms. Consequently, the range in students' abilities, their learning profiles, and their literacy needs is more diverse than ever before! But within this context, the schools are being held even more accountable for demonstrating results. The standards movement speaks to the concern that students should not be promoted from grade to grade without meeting developmentally appropriate standards at each level. Many people feel that the schools have not been sufficiently rigorous and believe that by establishing and publishing uniform standards, all will know the requirements at each level, and thus education will become more rigorous.

Unfortunately, the concern with meeting standards becomes very complicated when the concept is applied to actual students in real schools. Is it fair to measure all students by the same yardstick considering their vastly different educational opportunities, diverse learning profiles, and abilities? Special educators, for example, have been trained to assess students from a developmental perspective to determine if appropriate change and progress are taking place, without the expectation that all students will meet a standard of performance at each grade level. The concern with uniform standards seems to negate the reality of learners with differing patterns of growth, rate of development, and academic profiles. Teachers must be sensitive to individual differences and want to encourage rather than discourage growth. Should the writing products of all students be assessed according to whether they meet uniform, grade-level expectations, or should the individual progress of a student be the key factor? In many states there are mandates that no student be exempted from state tests even if they are second-language learners or identified as having learning disabilities and other special needs. How these students will be treated if they do not reach the expected level of performance is unknown, but early indications seem to reveal reliance on such traditional practices as retention, mandatory summer school attendance, more regimented teaching practices, and "certificates of attendance," rather than high school diplomas. These practices will not appropriately address the dilemma.

Indirect Versus Direct Assessment. Another concern has revolved around whether writing should be assessed through indirect or direct measurement techniques. Indirect measurement is based on the theory that writing ability is composed of subskills (i.e., spelling, punctuation, sentence structure) that can be appraised through tests which measure knowledge independent of actual writing. Direct measurement relies on the analysis of the writing product itself to determine if it meets the criteria for good writing. Underlying the choice between the two approaches is the debate over which subskills constitute good writing, as well as what criteria should be used to analyze a writing product. The pendulum has swung to the side of recognizing that the best way to assess students' writing is by directly looking at their writing performance. The measurement of writing through the use of standardized tests using multiple-choice questions has fallen into disrepute and has been replaced or augmented by performance measures.

New Forms of Writing Assessment Gain Acceptance

Direct Measurement Using Performance-Based Assessment. Direct writing assessment requires examination of the writing product and process. Now commonly referred to as performance-based assessment, direct writing assessment often involves the use of rubrics, rating scales, and holistic scoring systems. These direct measures often replace the older indirect methods, but they too have drawbacks: inefficiency caused by hand scoring and labor-intensive work, subjectivity of scorers, lack of interrater reliability, differing opinions about what constitutes good writing, and debates over how to prioritize different writing traits. Some researchers feel that direct measures of writing are best designed at the local level and that scoring systems, even those designed for large-scale assessment programs, must be created and administered by teachers. When these systems are used in state testing programs, there is concern about the training and expertise of the scorers to promote reliability in their ratings, which may have significant consequences. Holistic scoring, analytic scoring, and primary trait scoring have all been devised to assess students' writing samples.

Holistic scoring is based on the concept that the assessment of a writing sample should be based on the general or total impression, not the demonstration of different subskills. Writing samples are read quickly and separated into distinctive categories and usually assigned score points from 1 to 4, indicating the overall quality of the writing along a continuum from unsatisfactory to excellent. This sorting process is quick, efficient, and applicable for screening students for special help. It is common to see holistic scoring systems used extensively in state-wide assessment programs where a very large amount of student work needs to be reviewed in little time. Kentucky uses a state-wide writing assessment system and evaluates students' work in annual portfolios. The holistic scoring system used defines student work as falling into these categories: novice, apprentice, proficient, and distinguished (see Figure 6–1). Raters are given behavioral

Kentucky Writing Assessment

Kentucky's educational goals include helping all students reach proficiency as writers. When writing portfolios are assessed in 4th, 7th, and 12th grades, these definitions of writing ability are used to help with the scoring process.

You can use them with your students and children to help them understand how to become better writers.

Novice

- Limited awareness of audience and/or purpose.
- Minimal idea development; limited and/or unrelated details
- Random and/or weak organization
- Incorrect and/or ineffective sentence structure
- Incorrect and/or ineffective language
- Errors in spelling, punctuation, and capitalization are disproportionate to length and complexity

Apprentice

- Some evidence of communicating with an audience for a specific purpose; some lapses in focus
- Unelaborated idea development; unelaborated and/or repetitious details
- Lapses in organization and/or coherence
- Simplistic and/or imprecise language
- Some errors in spelling, punctuation, and capitalization that do not interfere with communication

Proficient

- Focused on a purpose; communicates with an audience; evidence of voice and/or suitable tone
- Depth of idea development supported by elaborated, relevant details
- Logical, coherent organization
- Controlled and varied sentence structure
- Acceptable, effective language
- Few errors in spelling, punctuation, and capitalization relative to length and complexity

Distinguished

- Establishes a purpose and maintains clear focus; strong awareness of audience; evidence of distinctive voice and/or appropriate tone
- Depth and complexity of ideas supported by rich, engaging, and/or pertinent details; evidence of analysis, reflection, insight
- Careful and/or subtle organization
- Variety in sentence structure and length enhances effect
- Precise and/or rich language
- Control of spelling, punctuation, and capitalization

FIGURE 6–1 Holistic scoring guide from Kentucky Writing Program. *Source:* from the *Holistic Scoring Guide*, used by Kentucky Writing Program's Regional Writing Consultants. Used with permission of the Kentucky Department of Education, Frankfurt, Kentucky 40601.

descriptors of what constitutes each level of accomplishment, so that, for example, whereas a "novice" has incorrect and/or ineffective use of language, a "distinguished" writer uses precise and/or rich language (Kentucky, 1999).

Several newer techniques have refined holistic scoring. *Writing rubrics*, for example, are scoring guides that describe qualities of writing at different levels of competency and have facilitated the ability to clearly discriminate between different levels of performance.

Rubrics have gained wide acceptance, as seen in their use in such different contexts as large, standardized, state-wide assessment systems and in teacher/student-created rubrics for reviewing classroom assignments. Rubrics are easy to design and can be created collaboratively by teachers and students to reflect the specific characteristics of good writing in various forms and in response to different assignments. It is interesting that the rubric shown in Figure 6–2 created by the teacher and students to assess and guide the writing of a persuasive essay uses marine life names instead of numbers to rate the quality of the work, which is in keeping with the theme of the essay. Figure 6–3 shows a rubric in a different form that was developed for third graders' narrative pieces that were written to document that the students had mastered a third-grade writingstandard.

Benchmarks, or *anchor papers* (papers that exhibit the traits expected for each scoring point), can be used and are helpful to provide assistance to scorers, whether teachers or students, so that writing can be compared with a known standard. Developmental rating scales are being widely used to evaluate the work of beginning writers. The scales provide teachers with specific descriptions of appropriate behavioral indicators for the students' level and grade. For example a "pre-emergent" kindergarten student at the beginning levels of writing would be expected to:

Island of the Blue Dolphins by Scott O'Dell
Rubric for Persuasive Writing

Criteria	Dolphin	Sea otter	Starfish	Sand crab
Spelling	My writing has no spelling errors.	My writing has only one spelling error.	My writing has less than 5 spelling errors.	My writing has 5 or more spelling errors.
Grammar	My writing is grammatically correct.	My writing has only one grammatical error.	My writing has less than 5 grammatical errors.	My writing has 5 or more grammatical errors.
Punctuation	All punctuation is correct. Quotation marks are appropriately used.	My writing has only one punctuation error.	My writing has less than 5 punctuation errors.	My writing has 5 or more punctuation errors.
Support of Opinion (1st Paragraph)	My writing clearly states my opinion and my reasons for having this opinion	My writing clearly states my opinion.	My writing mentions my opinion.	My writing does not state my opinion.
Connection to Author (2nd Paragraph)	My writing clearly states what the author believes and gives evidence through citation.	My writing states the author's opinion and tells about it in the novel.	My writing mentions the author's opinion.	My writing does not state the author's opinion.
Comparing myself to Scott O'Dell (3rd paragraph)	My writing concludes that my opinion does or does not match the author's and I explain why.	My writing concludes that my opinion does or does not match the author's.	My writing has a conclusion that tells more about the author's and/or my opinion.	My writing does not have a conclusion.

FIGURE 6–2 Rubric used by a fifth-grade class to assess writing.

Standard: Narrative Procedure   Assignment Grade
_____

Name: _____

Assignment: _____

Narrative Procedure Rubric

I. *Standards*   *Scoring Guide*

1. Captures reader interest	4	3	2	1	0
2. Provides correct sequence of events	4	3	2	1	0
3. Includes the most important details	4	3	2	1	0
4. Excludes unnecessary details	4	3	2	1	0
5. Provides a definite ending	4	3	2	1	0

II. *Conventions of Writing*   *Scoring Guide*

1. Proof of the 5-step writing process	4	3	2	1	0
2. Uses correct punctuation	4	3	2	1	0
3. Uses correct grammar	4	3	2	1	0
4. Spells words correctly	4	3	2	1	0
5. Uses sequence clue words	4	3	2	1	0

Teacher Comments:
_____

_____

_____

_____

_____

FIGURE 6–3 Rubric for third-grade writing standard.

- Draw a picture
- Dictate to a scribe
- Begin to develop awareness that print has meaning
- Attempt to imitate print
- Draw or write shapes/scribbles that resemble letters
- Write randomly on a page

However, at the first-grade level, the same student would be expected to:

- Use several ideas or events in their stories
- Choose topics to write about (often with guidance)
- Use pictures to illustrate ideas

- Write in multiple sentences (although sentence structure is just beginning to develop)
- Use upper and lower case letters
- Use some punctuation
- Put spaces between words
- Use "temporary" spelling, with some correct sounds representing words

Exemplars are pieces of writing that meet the highest standards and clearly demonstrate the characteristics of excellent writing; they can also be used for comparison and guidance. *Anchor* papers (specific samples of student work) are often provided for teachers who are involved in grading as part of state-wide assessment programs. In Kentucky, teachers can use an independent learning module put on a computer disk to review samples of students' work at various levels of achievement before scoring students' papers. Another example of the use of exemplars is having students examine professional writing to determine the traits of excellent work. For example, students who were preparing travel brochures as part of a social studies unit analyzed commercial travel brochures to determine the characteristics that make them appealing, informative, and successful.

Analytic scoring systems are used to provide a more in-depth profile of an individual's writing ability. Here, the components of good writing are specified and prioritized, and a student's work is analyzed to determine to what extent it exhibits the targeted traits. The total score is composed of the sum of subscores, although different systems have been developed to proportionately weight various aspects of writing based on their comparative importance. Figure 6–4 is an example of an analytic scoring system for students to use as part of self-assessment and provides an opportunity for the student to determine if a specific trait is a "strength" or "weakness." Analytic systems are similar to the informal writing evaluation that classroom teachers have traditionally used to review and mark student writing products. However, they provide more guidance by prioritizing the importance of different writing characteristics as well as by promoting a set of uniform characteristics. The use of analytic systems, although more time consuming, is helpful in informing teachers what specific characteristics students use in their writing, and can therefore inform the teacher about areas in which students need help. Some educators caution that the use of analytic scoring can reduce writing assessment to error counting, rather than noting accomplishment and strength.

A less frequently used system, but one that has often been combined with analytic scoring, is *primary trait scoring*. This system is based on the realization that different forms of writing require different components. Thus, the qualities of an excellent business letter should not be used to rate another form of writing, such as a friendly letter or a personal essay. Primary trait scoring analyzes a particular piece of writing to determine if it succeeds according to its purpose, for its audience, in a given situation. This system has been used both with rubrics and with analytic scoring so that a guide can be customized to a given assignment and form of writing.

WRITING INSTRUCTION AND LEARNING

Far too many teachers admit that they lack confidence in their ability to effectively teach writing. This may be attributable to their own negative experiences as writers in school, their lack of confidence in their own writing ability, the absence of meaningful writing in their daily lives, their perception that writing is difficult, and poor teacher preparation. However, many teachers are now becoming better educated about writing instruction. Consequently, they recognize the importance of writing in their classrooms and are more willing to try writing process approaches. They also realize that writing has many important and practical applications as well as providing insights into the language and thought processes that their students use. There is no question that the proliferation of

Writing Portfolio Assessment
Author's Self-Assessment/Conference Form I

Student: _____

Title/Descriptor: _____

| | Conference with Classmate | Date |
| Conference with Classmate | Date |

Analytical Annotation Guide

Scoring Features	The Big Picture	What Is Scored	Strengths +	Needs −	Comments About Writing Strengths and Needs
Purpose/ Audience	How much • you know what you want to write and why you are writing • the people you write for understand what you write • the voice or tone you use fits the purpose of the pieces	1. The author understands who will read his/her writing			
		2. The author's reasons for writing are clear			
		3. The author shows how he/she thinks and feels about the topic			
Idea Development Support	How many details and examples prove your main ideas	4. Important ideas are developed			
		5. Examples help the main idea			
		6. Examples fit in with the main idea			
		7. Details make the idea clearer			
Organization	How much • you stay with your plans • what you write all fits together	8. The beginning and ending are solid			
		9. The order of ideas goes easily from one to another			
		10. Transitions help the flow of ideas			
		11. The piece of writing is easy to read and understand			
Sentences	How much you use different sentence lengths, different kinds of sentences, and clear subjects and predicates	12. Sentences have different lengths and structures			
		13. Sentences express complete thoughts			
		14. Sentences have subjects and predicates			
Language	How you use a variety of words that make your meaning clear	15. Words say what the author means			
		16. Words are used correctly			
Corrections	How you demonstrate good • spelling • punctuation • capitalization	17. Control of spelling			
		18. Control of punctuation			
		19. Control of capitalization			

FIGURE 6–4 Example of an analytic scoring system for student self-assessment. *Source: Kentucky Writing Portfolio Teacher's Handbook,* January 1999. Used with permission of the Kentucky Department of Education.

state-mandated writing assessment has had a marked impact on today's classrooms and if state-wide assessment systems can be credited with any positive curricular outcomes, it may be the renewed attention to incorporating writing as an important part of daily classwork.

Teachers certainly are being mandated to require more writing in their classrooms to better prepare students for literacy tests that require actual writing. Consequently, there is more writing going on in today's classroom, including: writing applied in all curriculum areas, writing as a response to literature, writing for transactional purposes, writing for enjoyment, and writing to personally connect students with what they have learned and what they have read. More teachers are also better informed about how to thoughtfully review students' writing, as shown by the widespread use of rubrics in classrooms at all grade levels. (Note: I recently spoke to a college professor who had attended a national conference on Assessment in Higher Education. He described an innovative practice he learned about for assessing student work called "rubrics." I remarked that if he had been an elementary-school or secondary-school teacher, he would have known about this for many years. Apparently, college professors outside of education are now beginning to catch on to effective pedagogical and assessment strategies!)

WRITING FOLDERS AND PORTFOLIOS

Writing portfolios are a superb means by which to nurture, guide, reflect on and, most important, *celebrate* children's growth in writing. Writing portfolios are not likely to replace other means of assessing writing in state assessment programs, but their use has gained in popularity as they have become incorporated in some state assessment systems. More important, they have become an essential tool for classroom teachers. There is renewed emphasis on writing as an important aspect of literacy instruction (both because it *is* important and because it is being tested), and this has resulted in the widespread use of folders and portfolios to collect student writing.

Although writing folders originally were a simple way to store students' work in progress, literacy portfolios now reflect the more analytic process that promotes self-reflection and guides instruction, as described in the preceding chapters. It is truly unusual to find a classroom at either the elementary or secondary level where a writing collection is not kept by students. Many teachers encourage their students to save their daily writing in work-in-progress folders. Classes that use a writing process approach value how a piece of writing is the result of many drafts. By saving the students' writing, the teacher, students, and families have a collection that can demonstrate developmental changes and promote self-reflection. The work for the writing folder often is chosen collaboratively and is especially valued. Pieces can be selected to demonstrate specific characteristics of writing, examples of different genre, writing used in various curriculum projects, a personal response to reading, or change over time. The selections are then put into best works or showcase portfolios that are designed to demonstrate writing accomplishment. These portfolios can be created exclusively for writing work or can be combined into reading and writing portfolios. Unfortunately, some of the writing folders currently in use are simply unwieldly collections of all daily writing and do not lend themselves to thoughtful reflection. To be meaningful, portfolios require a selection process.

Inside the Student's Writing Portfolio

The contents of a literacy portfolio have been described in previous chapters, but to succinctly summarize current practice, Figure 6–5 contains an overview of the contents of a comprehensive writing folder from which a reflective portfolio can be created. It is vital that teachers remember that any portfolio collection must have a specific purpose and focus that will guide students' choice of entries.

- ■ "Hot topics" list/writing ideas
- ■ Self-reflections
- ■ Goals sheet
- ■ Artwork, webs, maps, organizers
- ■ Lists, drafts, revisions, final copies
- ■ Writing in many forms: reports, narratives, poems, letters, etc.
- ■ Writing record/log
- ■ Writing journal
- ■ Spelling strategies
- ■ Editing strategies, checklists
- ■ Author's circle notes/peer conferences
- ■ Teacher conference notes
- ■ Family reactions

FIGURE 6–5 Contents of a student's writing folder.

Students' Self-Reflections, Self-Evaluation and Goal Setting. Students' self-reflections are very important to the portfolio concept. The ability to engage in thoughtful self-reflection will be affected by students' age, skill level, and training. The process of getting students to think about their writing, however, should begin at the emergent literacy level, where they need both encouragement and modeling to learn what is expected of them as part of this self-reflection. Self-reflection certainly is possible even with young children!

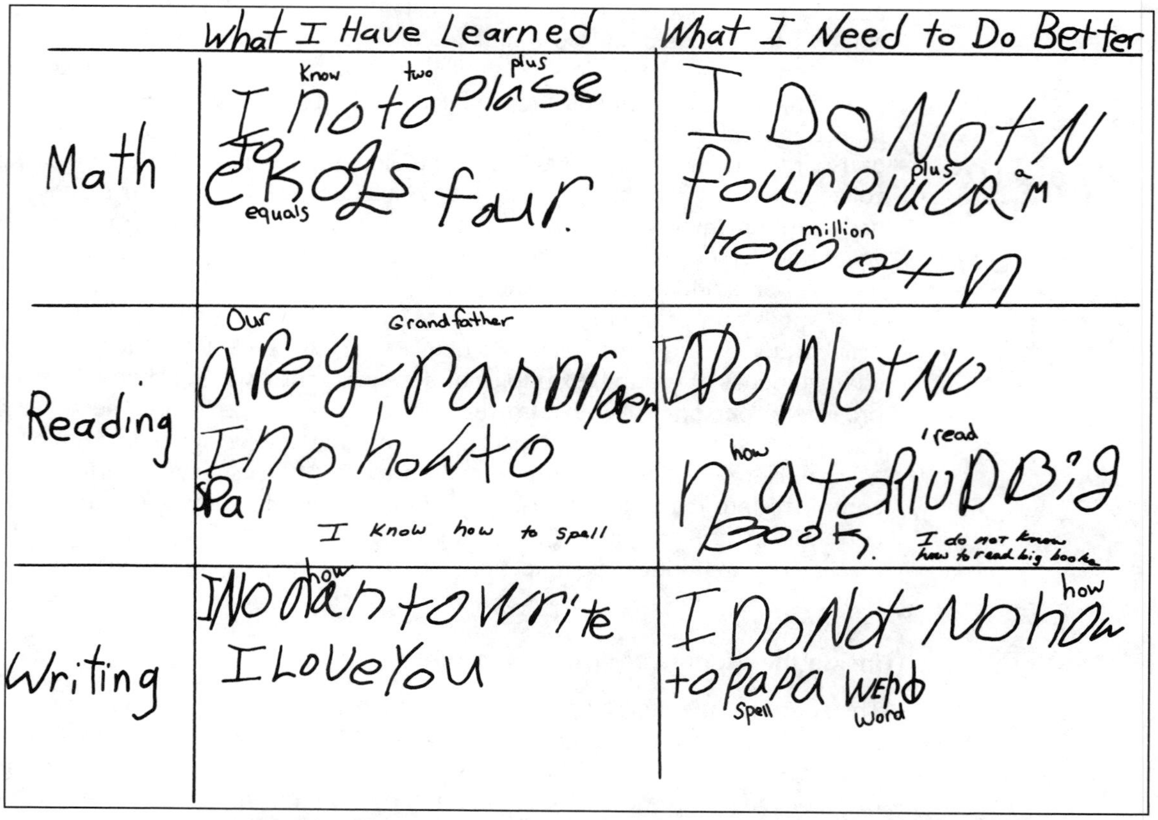

FIGURE 6–6 Student's self-reflections from a beginning reader and writer from South Brunswick, New Jersey.

Figure 6–6 contains a rubric format for the self-reflections of a beginning reader and writer and demonstrates the first attempts to have a young student view herself. This same example shows that this first grader knows how to write "I Love You" but also reveals that she does not know how to spell words. It is important that teachers acknowledge the student's expectations, and it would be appropriate to share with this student that spelling is an important goal and that correct spelling will develop throughout the year. This would support this student's concern and provide reassurance that spelling is an area to be worked on. One second grader put her thoughts in narrative form (Figure 6–7).

Figure 6–8 shows the more advanced self-reflections of a seventh grader from the Lawrence, Long Island, school district at the end of the school year. This essay was prompted by a review of the entire year's portfolio. In this middle school, a portfolio evaluation and conference were used in place of a final English exam. During a conference, it would be important for the teacher to reinforce this student's positive feelings about herself as a writer of short stories, share the concern about writer's block, and discuss her feelings about being published. Reflections can come in various forms. Figure 6–9 is a self-reflective poem that was written by a gifted fifth grader who also discusses writer's block and the intense frustration that it causes. Obviously, this student's teacher should respond to his intense frustration. Providing personal essays written by well-known writers who also experienced writer's block would be comforting and might even provide some suggestions for addressing the dilemma. Writer's block would also be a good topic for a lesson, so students can explore various strategies to overcome the dilemma. Many students have found the following techniques to be helpful: discussing topics with peers, using "hot topics" lists, revising or extending a finished piece, reading other students' published work, and doing related reading. One teacher had the class compile a list of suggestions entitled "Things I Can Do When I Get Stuck," which all students kept in their portfolios.

Related to the process of self-reflection is the students' ability to take self-reflection to the next level and set goals for themselves. The progression from generalized reflection to more analytic self-evaluation and then choosing appropriate goals will take time, training, and often a great deal of guidance from the teacher. When students can meaningfully engage in such collaboration, they take greater responsibility for their own literacy development and instruction becomes more meaningful. Obviously, this is a complicated and sophisticated process and needs to be made developmentally appropriate for students of different ages and ability levels.

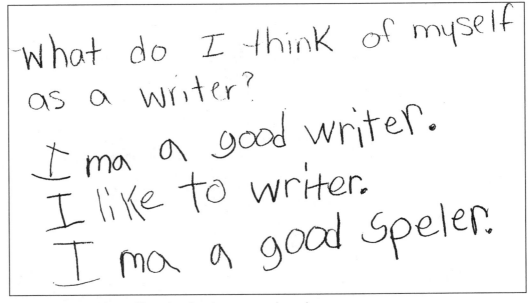

FIGURE 6–7 Writing self-evaluation by a second grader.

Final Essay: Writing Self-Evaluation

My mom has always pushed me to write. She thinks that I have a natural talent and she wants to make sure that I develop it. I on the other hand, don't really try to develop my writing. Once in a while I might write a story for the fun of it. My mom has tried to make me keep a diary, and a journal for the books that I have read, but I am always forgetting. I write though, because once a week I write letters to my father. Also, for holidays and my mom's birthdays I write stories and give them as gifts.

The type of writing that I like to do the best, are short stories. My ideas come in the spur of the moment, and if I feel like it, I might write a story. Once I got an idea from a picture that I drew. Sometimes I might have just finished reading a book, and I might be changing something that happened in it, and from that an idea might spring.

I really get frustrated when I am writing, and I get a writer's block. I might have the best story, and know how it will end, but in the middle I will get stuck. I usually get really fed up if I can't get over a writer's block. What I do is, get up, walk around, and then go back to the story. It is all worth it when I finally come up with a great story.

The only time I have been published was in the elementary school newspaper. I would sometimes write a poem, story, joke, or recipe. Now in the Middle School, the newspaper only writes about things that are going on. I haven't been published since. It is great to be published, to see the words that I wrote on paper! I love the proud feeling that I get and I hope that I have the opportunity to be published again someday.

FIGURE 6–8 End-of-year self-evaluation by a seventh-grade student.

Goals sheets can be used to aid the process and they can take many forms. They can be completed by the students and then collaboratively reviewed during writing conferences. Figure 6–10 contains the writing goals of a third-grade student who wants to work on neatness and is eager to use cursive writing. Figure 6–11 shows that a seventh grader wants to write in different genre and improve his use of language. This is an instructional message for the teacher; future lessons should provide exposure to different forms of writing and examples of expressive language in published works.

Early in the year, it is important for the teacher to create an atmosphere in which students think of themselves as writers and begin to develop a metacognitive awareness about how they approach writing. Figure 6–12 (p. 161) is an example of a survey that a student completed in which he clearly thought about himself as a writer. Based on this student's answer to question 12, where he says that he sometimes can't think of "good ideas," a good minilesson would be to work on personal narratives that focus on first-hand experiences and create a "hot-topics" list for future reference. It would be important

---

This is a blank page.
I do not know anything to write.
My mind is a huge brick wall blocking the path to my ideas.
Therefore, my mind is blank.
I do not have the ignition key or the ignition.
My mind is a big blob of clay.
Shapeless, useless.
And I have no hands to mold it into something useful and valuable.
I do not have the kindling to start the fire.
I only have two negative wires so I can not spark the light.
My mind is a big block of ice.
Frozen.
It is a disease without a cure.
But not death in the place of life.
Death in the place of writing.

FIGURE 6–9 "Writer's Block," a self-reflective poem written by a gifted fifth-grade student.

Writing Goals Sheet

Student Name _Katie_____ Date _10/24_____

1. What I like most about my writing is _it's interesting._

2. What I would like to improve the most about my writing is _neatness._

3. I am going to work on _neatness_____ for the next two months.

4. I'll try to do these things to help reach my goals: _take my time and try to be neater_

Signed: _Katie_____ (student)

_____ (teacher)

(She thinks she needs to improve her cursive handwriting.)

FIGURE 6–10 Writing goals chosen by a third grader.

to explore with this student his admiration for two writers, Roald Dahl and Michael Crichton, and the specific characteristics that make them so popular. During a conference, the teacher could assist this student by recommending other authors whose writing is similar in style. This student could also be aided by the use of graphic organizers, which provide details to elaborate a general topic. Figure 6–13 shows how one student used a graphic organizer before writing a piece, then did a rough draft, and finally produced a final piece about his grandfather as a response to the topic "Someone Who Inspires Me."

A less complex and less introspective form of self-evaluation can be started with students reviewing their own work by using a checklist. Figure 6–14 includes questions about both story content and mechanics; Figures 6–15 and 6–16 show other forms of self-editing guides.

As more teachers incorporate writing workshops into their classrooms, they encourage students to collaborate and assist with editing and revising. Figure 6–17 is a peer evaluation chart used in District 6 in New York City for third-grade students to use when they work in groups to help them listen to each other's writing and provide feedback.

WRITING PERFORMANCE

Circle the appropriate letter for each item below.   (G equals GOOD EFFORT and N equals NEEDS to WORK HARDER ON THIS.)

1. Writing folder upkeep (Use of goal-setting calendar, class note taking, upkeep of skills and spelling list, keeping well-organized collection of all drafts).   G   Ⓝ

2. Use of writing process (evidence of revision, conferring, editing).   G   Ⓝ

3. Amount of writing submitted.   Ⓖ   N

4. Amount of writing completed.   Ⓖ   N

5. Trying new types of writing.   Ⓖ   N

6. On-task behavior during writing.   Ⓖ   N

7. Ten-week goal(s) accomplished.   Ⓖ   N

Based on the above assessment, I believe that my overall writing grade for this ten weeks should be:

My writing goal for the coming ten weeks is:

Write various things (Yes)
I have accomplished this goal. I have writtin a poem, essay & story
To be able to creat sentences which contain vivid language

FIGURE 6–11 The writing goals of a seventh grader in a writing performance self-evaluation.

Having students complete an end-of-year reflection for the writing portfolio is an important strategy for students so that they can truly see and acknowledge their progress throughout the year. It is also a wonderful opportunity for the teacher (and the students' families) to celebrate and praise the students' accomplishments. If meaningful progress has not been made during the school year, this end-of-year review presents an important opportunity for the teacher and students to candidly discuss why change has not occurred. There are many reasons why students do not make the progress that we would hope for. Surprisingly, even the least motivated students may find writing an important outlet for their thoughts and feelings, but hard work is needed for change to occur. If a student has made best efforts and has been provided with quality instruction, but progress is not meeting expectations, then this may be the time to refer the student to appropriate ancillary services, either for more extensive diagnosis or for individual or small-group assistance. (Note: Each semester I teach a graduate course on addressing and treating literacy disorders. My graduate students, who are all teachers, seem to be perpetually amazed by the extent of students' problems with producing grade-appropriate writing and too often feel that it is a reflection of an undiagnosed learning disability. When I ask that they reflect on whether or not the child has been exposed to consistent,

Name _____   Date _____

Teacher _____   Grade _____7_____

WRITING SURVEY

1. Are you a writer? _____Yes_____

    (If your answer is YES, answer question 2a. If your answer is NO, answer 2b.)

2a. How did you learn to write?

    I learned to write from my teacher and my parents.

2b. How do people learn to write?

    _____

    _____

3. Why do people write?

    To communicate and express their feelings.

4. What do you think a good writer needs to do in order to write well?

    They must be creative and check their writing-

5. How does your teacher decide which pieces of writing are the good ones?

    She looks to see how much effort was put into the writing and how the ideas were put into writing-

6. What kinds of writing do you like to do?

    I just right the best thing I can think of, regardless of what kind it is-

FIGURE 6–12 A middle school student's writing self-evaluation survey.

quality writing instruction, invariably and unfortunately the answer is "No." The answer to their concerns is evident; for students to succeed in writing, especially those students who struggle with reading and writing, quality, consistent writing instruction is essential!)

Selecting Writing Exhibits

The writing portfolio should develop from the assignment of daily writing and the products that result to the collection of student writing in individual writing folders, to the more formal and refined writing portfolio. Again, the writing portfolio is a selected collection of student work that is chosen to reflect the specific purpose of the portfolio (see Figure 6–18). For example, work selected for a showcase portfolio is likely to be very different from that of a developmental portfolio as compared to a writing portfolio that is created to demonstrate work in a genre, or a portfolio where the contents are specified by local or state assessment requirements.

7. How do you decide what to write?

The best ~~idea~~ idea I get is what I wrote

8. Do you ever revise or edit a piece of writing? If so, describe what you do.

I check my first copy for spelling or grammar mistakes. Then I read it over to find places where it would sound better worded differently. I correct my mistakes in the next copy—

9. Do you ever write at home just because you want to? Yes
If so, how often do you write at home (just because you want to)?

I don't write at home (just because I want to) very often. But once in a ~~____~~ I do.

10. Who or what has influenced your writing? How?

All my teachers have influenced my writing by teaching me new words and techniques.

11. Do you like to have others read your writing? Sometimes Who?

My parents and teachers because I trust their advice on how to improve my writing—

12. In general, how do you feel about writing?

I like to write if I get good ideas. It can be boring and frustrating if I can't come up with any—

FIGURE 6–12 *Continued*

Benchmark portfolios are being used to document that students have accomplished the grade-level curriculum standards. Therefore, benchmark portfolio contents are clearly chosen to reflect specific kinds of writing. Teachers in District 28, Queens, New York, have worked hard to align their writing portfolio to the requirement that all teachers show evidence of their students' writing in various genre. Figure 6–19 specifies the form of writing that is required at various points for each grade level. From the writing stored in work folders, students select particular pieces for their writing portfolios that will document their work in each form of writing.

Many of today's portfolios are developmental and are designed to show the student's progress throughout the school year. Such a portfolio can be created by simply having the teacher and student select one writing exhibit each month and clearly dating it. Other portfolios are used to celebrate "best work," and thus the teacher and student would select exhibits that demonstrate accomplishment that might be showcasing various strategies

13. Among the published authors you know about (books you have read or that teacher/parent has read to you), who do you think is a good writer?

> I used to read alot of Roald Dahl books and I think he is. Now I like Michael Crichto.

What makes him or her a good writer?
(Why do you like his or her writing/books?)

> His stories are imaginative and they keep me interested.

14. What do you really like about your writing?

> I like my writing because it is an example of how I feel and what I'm thinking.

What would you like to improve about your writing?

> I would like to keep my stories tied together and make them more enjoyable for others to read.

FIGURE 6-12 *Continued*

(e.g., the use of dialogue) or writing in different genre (e.g., a business letter for an older student). If a writing portfolio is used to exhibit subject area learning (e.g., the outcomes of an independent research effort), then the exhibits can be assembled accordingly. Portfolio exhibits must be chosen with reflection and care, and it is most helpful if a student completes such statements as "This piece is in my folder because . . . " as part of the selection process. All writing portfolios should be clearly organized. Students enjoy completing a Table of Contents, because they are familiar with this system and it makes their work look more professional. Often a "Letter to the Reader" is a helpful tool students can use to articulate the purpose of the portfolio and describe how contents were chosen and organized. Considering the amount of time and pride that goes into the creation of a portfolio, students are eager for a response from the portfolio reader.

Students are accustomed to saving their writing pieces, but few are adept at transforming their folder collections into writing portfolios. Students must be educated (both by modeling and training) about the differences between their work folders and the portfolio. Therefore, it is essential that the teacher and student have a clear understanding of what kinds of exhibits should be chosen from the folder for the portfolio. Again, the purpose of the portfolio will guide the collection.

Inside the Teacher's Writing Portfolio

As part of the portfolio process, we recommend that teachers keep a writing portfolio for each child, or record their ongoing observations, conference notes, and other insights about each child in a notebook. (This is obviously similar to the literacy portfolio process described in Chapter 4.) The goal of this teacher portfolio is to profile a student's writing progress, processes, and strategies, with the outcome of better instruction. Also important to this process is teacher encouragement, so that students gain self-confidence and are motivated to write. Figure 6–20 is a summary of the typical contents of a teacher's writing portfolio for a student.

Teachers are now keenly aware that they have many options to choose from regarding how they analyze their students' writing, both in terms of the writing product itself and the process. Bratcher (1994) and Jenkins (1996) have written excellent texts for

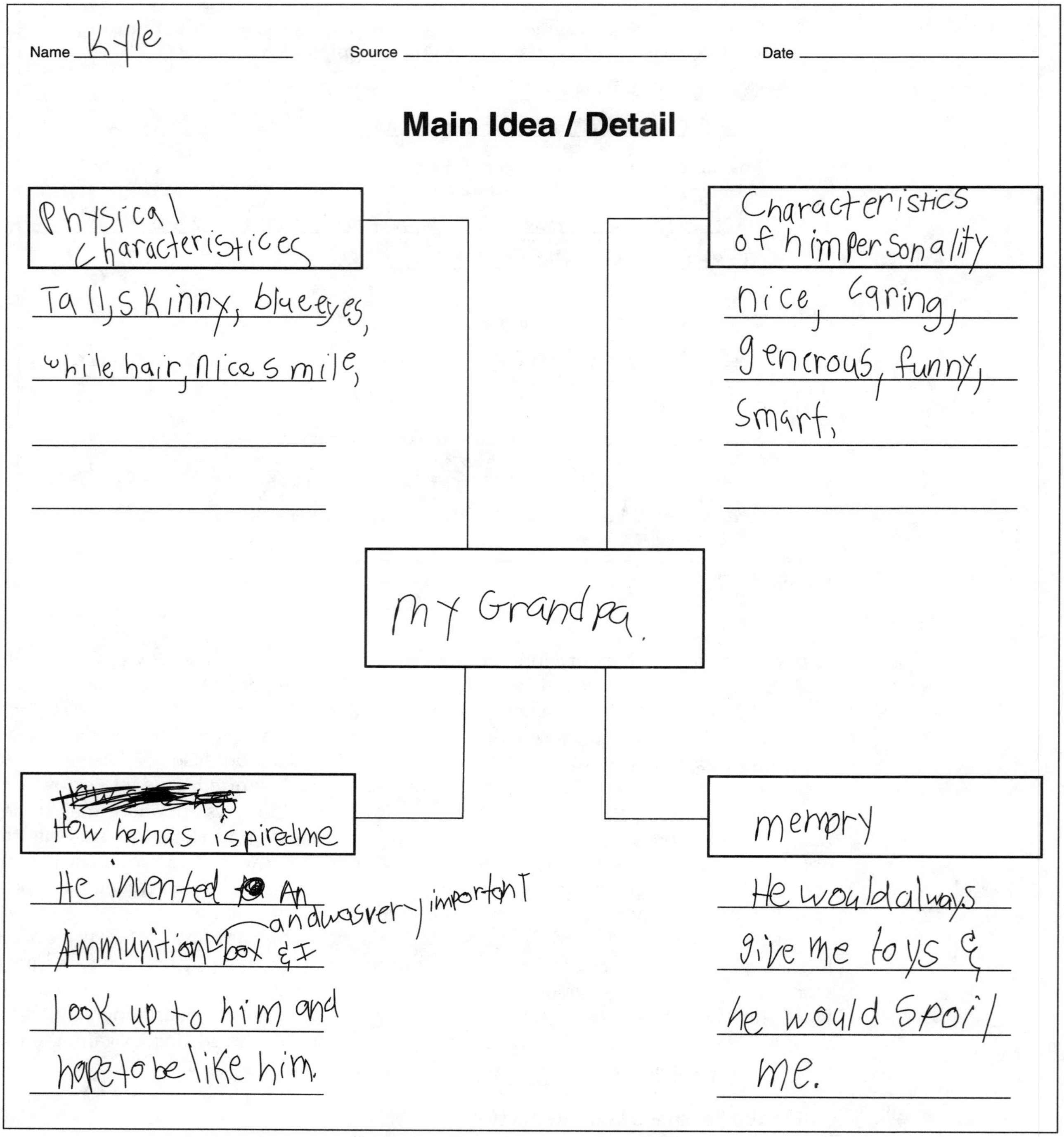

Name Kyle _____   Source _____   Date _____

Main Idea / Detail

Physical Characteristices
Tall, skinny, blue eyes,
while hair, Nice smile,
_____
_____

Characteristics of him personality
nice, caring,
generous, funny,
Smart,
_____

My Grandpa.

How he has ispiredme
He invented An Ammunition box & I and was very important
look up to him and
hopeto be like him.

memory
He would always
give me toys &
he would spoil
me.

FIGURE 6–13A Sample use of graphic organizer.

teachers who want to learn more about how children develop into writers. These authors provide elaborate descriptions and examples of different kinds of analysis teachers can do with children's writing products and processes. The use of writing conferences is also a most effective means to provide students with feedback and assistance. Harwayne (2001) provides excellent guidance to help teachers conduct supportive writing conferences as a wonderful way to respond to children's writing. Likewise, Atwell (1998) informs us about conducting writing conferences with adolescent learners.

The person who Inspires me is mygrandpa. My ~~grandfather~~ Grandpa Inspires me because he is smart, Kind, giving, special, and many other reasons, my Grandpa ~~dosent~~ doesn't not only Inspires me, but he is one of my mentors.

MyGrandpa Inspires me alot. Some day, I wish I could accomplish ~~and~~ what my grandpa ~~Achieved~~ achieved, ~~and he~~ What did he achieve? My Grandpa is nice, considerate, ~~and~~ giving & many other things.

My Grandpa is one of the smartest ~~person~~ people I Know. He invented an ~~Ammition~~ ammunition box & even ~~meet~~ met Golda Meir. MyGrandPa has been all over the world and he gave me coins from those places.

My Grandpa Inspires me alot for many ~~oth~~ reasons. Mygrandpa is smart, (nice) ? Another word and many other things. Mygrandpa truly inspires me.

FIGURE 6–13B Rough draft.

The following writing assessment techniques are highlighted because they provide the means for teachers to readily analyze and reflect on students' writing as part of their classroom program.

Anecdotal/Observational Notes. The ongoing observation of students while they write provides excellent insights into writing strategies. To assist the teacher in daily observation, it is often helpful to create a list of target areas that the teacher wants to observe in order to fully understand how the student approaches writing. Figure 6–21 contains a

The person who inspires me is my Grandpa. My Grandpa inspires me because he is smart, kind, giving, and special. My Grandpa not only inspires me, but he is one of my most special mentors.

One day, I wish I could accomplish what my Grandpa has achieved. He invented an ammunition box. He even met Golda Meir. My Grandpa has been all over the world. He has given me coins from all of the places he has visited.

My Grandpa inspires me in many ways. He is a special person to anyone who meets him. He is intelligent, kind, and considerate. I hope that I make him

FIGURE 6–13C Final piece.

Name: _____

Self-Evaluation of Story Writing

Put an X next to the statements that are true about your writing.
__ This sounds good when I read it to myself.
__ I said what I wanted to say.
__ I think the reader will be interested in it.
__ This topic is worth reading and writing about.
__ There is a beginning to my story.
__ There is a middle to my story.
__ There is an ending to my story.
__ When someone else reads my story, I think they will be able to understand it.
__ The order of the sentences make sense.

Name: _____

Mechanics Self-Check List

Put an X next to statements that are true about your writing.
__ I put periods or other punctuation marks at the end of sentences.
__ I used commas when necessary.
__ I started each sentence with a capital letter.
__ A reader could read my handwriting.
__ I reread this story for misspelled words.
__ I checked the spelling of the words I am unsure about.
__ I started every paragraph by indenting.

FIGURE 6–14 A third-grade student's self-evaluation checklists.

simple writing checklist developed by Lindy Vizyak, a first-grade teacher in Colorado (see Vizyak, 1996). The teacher's concerns reflect goals at the emergent stages of literacy and also are compatible with the first-grade curriculum framework. The teacher's comments are kept in chronological order on the child's writing portfolio.

Development Checklists and Rubrics. Many school districts have developed checklists, rating scales, or rubrics for literacy skills that correspond to different developmental levels and that are especially helpful for determining if a student is meeting grade-level expectations. Figure 6–22 is an example of a developmental writing rubric that is used by the Adams

Nonfiction (Written or Interview)

1. What did you like about this piece of writing?
2. List three things that you did well.
3. What might you change if you did this piece again?
4. Did this piece tell what you know? Why or Why not?
5. Was there something that you could have done that would have been more meaningful? Why or Why not?

Personal Narrative (Written or Interview)

1. What did you like about this piece of writing?
2. List three things that you did well.
3. What might you change if you were to do more revision on this piece?
4. What do you plan to work on in your next piece of writing?

FIGURE 6–15 Writing self-evaluation for elementary grades. *Source:* Developed in the Plainedge, New York, school district.

Writing Workshop
Editing and Evaluating Yourself as an Author

Rate Yourself
3—often   *2—sometimes*   *1—not yet*

1. I use a dictionary to check my spelling.
2. I organize my paragraphs.
3. All sentences in my paragraphs support the main idea of the paragraph.
4. I express ideas clearly.
5. My sentences are grammatically correct.
6. You can hear a voice in my piece.
7. My work has a focus.
8. I use exciting vocabulary (metaphors, similes, showing words).
9. I apply the mechanics of writing (punctuation, capitalization, etc.).
10. I use quotations in dialogue.
11. I use details to support my ideas.
12. I write with a sense of audience.

FIGURE 6–16 A student self-editing guide for elementary grades. (*Source:* Developed in the Plainedge, New York, school district.)

County Five Star School District in Colorado to evaluate first graders. With the increased emphasis on literacy standards, many school districts and state education departments are providing teachers with grade-level expectations for literacy attainment. Teachers should obviously familiarize themselves with these expectations (often reproduced as a checklist of literacy behavior) to help them plan their writing curriculum and to assess their students.

State-Generated Writing Analysis Systems. Writing ability has become a very important aspect of demonstrating accountability and, therefore, assessing writing is an important aspect of literacy assessment mandated by state education departments. Different states have developed their own systems for scoring students' writing samples. It is important for teachers to be aware of the system employed in their state so that their assessment practices include analysis of the competencies that their students will be expected to demonstrate. One teacher, for example, encouraged her students to take risks and use vivid imagination when writing. She was dismayed when a student was penalized in a state assessment for not writing a realistic set of directions for watching a pet. Instead, this student described the care and feeding of his "pet," a fire-breathing dragon. Although the writing displayed a wonderful sense of humor, some evaluators felt that it did not respond to the task, and certainly students should be able to demonstrate practical writing as well as more imaginative work.

Many states use holistic scoring to rate the large number of writing samples that must be reviewed. In New Mexico, sixth-grade students are given a standard writing prompt, and their efforts are scored based on a set of criteria, with score points ranging from 1 through 6 (see Rael & Travelstead, 1993). To assist scorers in using this system, they are provided with rubrics and anchor papers so that the scoring of narrative, expository, and descriptive papers is based on uniform criteria throughout the state. Some state systems also furnish exemplars to assist scoring by providing examples that show excellence. Figure 6–23 is a scoring rubric used to assess expository pieces done by sixth-grade students in New Mexico. It is particularly helpful because it details the criteria to be used for the different points as part of holistic scoring.

Analytic Scales. New York State uses a holistic scoring system samples for the writing samples collected as part of the fourth-grade English/Language Arts exam. In the past, the state generated an analytic worksheet for teachers to use to guide them toward the assessment

Peer Evaluation Chart to Be Used by Students in Small Groups—Grade 3

Writer's Name: _____   Date: _____

Topic: _____

	First Reader's Name:	Second Reader's Name:	Third Reader's Name:
1. What part is most interesting? Why?			
2. Is any part confusing? Which?			
3. Do ideas or events follow each other in an order that makes sense? Are they logical?			
4. Is there enough detail? If not, where should the writer add detail?			
5. Are illustrations or examples needed to back up statement or opinion? Where?			
6. Should any sentence be omitted? Which one(s)?			
7. Is the opening interesting? Is there a better way to begin?			
8. Is there a better way to end?			

FIGURE 6–17 Peer evaluation chart. *Source:* District 6, New York City.

of important characteristics of good writing. This analytic worksheet was particularly helpful to establish instructional priorities. Figure 6–24 is an adaptation of this helpful system.

Figure 6–25 illustrates how this system can guide instruction. This descriptive essay was written by a fifth-grade student in response to a prompt to describe his best friend. A quick review of this essay shows it to be rather simplistic and concrete, with weakness in several areas. A more detailed analysis shows that the student also has many strengths. Figure 6–26 provides a sample analysis of this essay using the worksheet. When doing detailed analysis of writing that will lead to individualized instruction, it is important that teachers prioritize instructional goals so as not to overwhelm students. In the sample analysis, it seems that the primary goals should relate to organization and

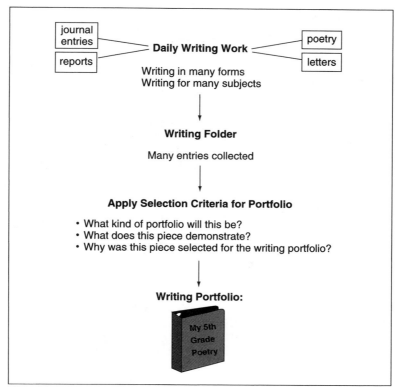

FIGURE 6–18 Selection process for a writing portfolio.

use of more vivid language. It should be noted that suggested teaching techniques include making use of oral discussion, related reading, and peer editing. When teachers use analytic systems such as this worksheet, they too often emphasize all that is wrong with a child's writing. It is vital to emphasize that even the poorest writer shows mastery of some basics, which should be acknowledged as a starting place from which to work.

Rubrics. The use of rubrics has been described previously, and several examples can be found in other parts of this book. It is important to emphasize that rubrics are best created in a collaboration between teachers and students. Rubrics can be customized for specific assignments, because the evaluation criteria may be quite different with different forms of writing. Figure 6–27 is an example of a rubric created by students and teachers in the Plainedge, New York, school district to evaluate an independent research project that is an important part of the fifth-grade curriculum. Both the teacher and the librarian are involved in scoring the students' research papers and in the research process.

Authoring Process. As more teachers adopt the use of a writing process approach in their classes, their students learn that a finished piece is the product of many stages from prewriting (e.g., brainstorming, listing) to drafting, sharing, revising, editing, and publishing. Consequently, teachers should note how well the students use the strategies appropriate for each phase of the process. Figure 6–28 shows an evaluation system developed by Cohen that can be employed to determine how a student succeeds with four stages of the writing process. Most important, this emphasis on process, not product, will assist teachers in determining where in the writing process the student is "stuck" and where instruction should begin. Acknowledging and reviewing the process of composing (not just writing) provides insights for the teacher into how a student thinks, understands, relates, and reflects.

Months	Kindergarten	1st Grade	2nd Grade	3rd Grade	4th Grade	5th Grade	6th Grade	7th Grade	8th Grade	9th Grade
Sept/Oct	Narrative Writing	Narrative Writing	Narrative Writing	Narrative Writing	Narrative Account-Memoir	Narrative Account-Memoir	Narrative Account-Memoir	Memoir	Memoir	Memoir
Oct/Nov	Responding to Literature	Responding to Literature	Responding to Literature	Responding to Literature	Response to Literature	Response to Literature	Response to Literature	Responding to Literature	Responding to Literature	Responding to Literature
Nov/Dec	Informational Writing	Informational Writing	Informational Writing	Informational Writing	Report Writing	Report Writing	Report Writing	Report Writing	Report Writing	Report Writing
Jan/Feb	Narrative Writing	Narrative Writing	Narrative Writing	Narrative Writing	Narrative Account-Fiction	Narrative Account-Fiction	Narrative Account-Fiction	Narrative Account-Fiction	Narrative Account-Fiction	Narrative Account-Fiction, Reflective Essay
March	Functional Writing	Functional Writing	Functional and procedural Writing	Functional and procedural Writing	Narrative Procedure	Narrative Procedure	Narrative Procedure	Narrative Procedure	Narrative Procedure	Narrative Procedure
April	Poetry	Poetry	Poetry	Poetry	Poetry	Poetry	Poetry	Poetry	Poetry	Poetry
May/June	Informational Writing	Informational Writing	Informational Writing	Informational Writing	Report Writing	Report Writing	Persuasive Essay	Report Writing	Report Writing	Report Writing

FIGURE 6–19 Sample benchmark portfolio for types of writing, K–9. *Source:* District 28, Queens, New York.

■ Anecdotal/observational notes
■ Developmental checklists (state- or school district-generated)
■ Analytic measures of student's writing ability, such as

    Profile of student's writing process

    State-recommended analysis

    Writing rubrics (developed by teacher and class or school district)

    Criterion-referenced evaluations

    Assessment of different forms of writing: personal narratives, reports, stories, etc.

    Assessment of spelling, handwriting, mechanics

■ Conference notes with child
■ Writing goals
■ Conference notes with family
■ Family communications

FIGURE 6–20 Contents of a teacher's writing portfolio for a student.

Name _____   **Date** _____

Writing Checklist—Grade 1

Spelling

_____ Student uses random letters or copies randomly.
_____ Student uses correct beginning sounds.
_____ Student uses correct ending sounds.
_____ Student uses correct middle sounds.
_____ Student uses vowels (not necessarily correctly).
_____ Student uses correct vowels.
_____ Student spells common words (*in, the, you, and,* etc.) correctly.
_____ Student appropriately copies words from charts, books, lists.
_____ Student spells harder words correctly.

Language

_____ Student capitalizes the beginning word of a sentence.
_____ Student capitalizes *I*.
_____ Student capitalizes names.
_____ Student includes end punctuation marks (.?) in writing.

Handwriting

_____ Student uses spacing between words.
_____ Student writes legibly.

Comments

_____

_____

FIGURE 6–21 A first-grade writing checklist. *Source:* From *Student Portfolios* (p. 50) by L. Vizyak, 1996, Bothell, WA: The Wright Group. Copyright 1996 by the Wright Group. Reprinted by permission.

Writing Rubric—Grade 1

(Assessment Criteria)

The District Expects Most Students to Achieve Level 3 by the End of the School Year

1	2	3	4	5
Message Quality [Generates Drafts]				
▪ Has difficulty generating ideas ▪ Writes only a single thought about a topic		▪ Generates ideas with increasing ease ▪ Develops a topic by writing several sentences		▪ Develops a topic by adding a variety of evidence or details ▪ Organizational plan begins to emerge (beginning, middle, and end)
Drafts and Edits				
▪ Lack of letter–sound correspondence (spelling) interferes with message ▪ Writes with difficulty ▪ Does not consider capitals or periods		▪ Uses beginning, medial, and ending consonants ▪ Writes some vowels ▪ Uses some correctly spelled high-frequency words ▪ Writes with increasing ease ▪ Begins to use beginning capitals and periods appropriately		▪ Writes beginning, middle, and ending sounds ▪ Writes many vowel sounds correctly ▪ Uses many correctly spelled high-frequency words ▪ Spelling does not interfere with message ▪ Writes fluently ▪ Makes few errors in beginning capitals and periods
Communicates in Developmentally Appropriate Form				
▪ Prints illegibly ▪ Writing contains many reversals and incorrect letter forms; doesn't differentiate between upper and lower case ▪ Does not consistently write top to bottom, left to right ▪ Does not space between words		▪ Prints legibly enough for others to read ▪ Writing contains some reversals; most letters are correctly formed; may contain some random caps ▪ Writes top to bottom, left to right ▪ Usually spaces between words		▪ Prints letters of equal size and appropriate spacing ▪ Letters are formed correctly ▪ Writes top to bottom, left to right ▪ Always spaces between words

FIGURE 6–22 A developmental writing rubric used by Adams County Five Star school district, Colorado.

New Mexico Portfolio Writing Assessment—Expository Scoring Rubric

Strong Command of Exposition Score Point 6	Generally Strong Command of Exposition Score Point 5	Command of Exposition Score Point 4
Has an effective opening and closing that tie the piece together	Has an opening and a closing	Generally has an opening and closing
Relates to the topic and has a single focus	Relates to the topic and has a single focus	Relates to the topic and has a single focus
Well-developed, complete response that is organized and progresses logically; writer takes compositional risks resulting in highly effective, vivid responses	Key ideas are developed with appropriate and varied details; some risks may be taken and are mostly successful; may be flawed, but has sense of completeness and unity	Development may be uneven with elaborated ideas interspersed with bare, unelaborated details
	Organized and progresses logically, but there may be a lapse	Some responses are organized with little, if any, difficulty moving from idea to idea; other responses may ramble somewhat with clusters of ideas that may be loosely connected, but an overall progression is apparent
Very few, if any, errors in usage	Few errors in usage	Some errors in usage, no consistent pattern
Variety of sentence and/or rhetorical modes demonstrates syntactic and verbal sophistication; very few, if any, errors in sentence construction	Syntactic and verbal sophistication through a variety of sentences and/or rhetorical modes	May demonstrate a generally correct sense of syntax; avoids excessive monotony in syntax and/or rhetorical modes; may contain a few errors in sentence construction
Very few, if any, errors in mechanics	Few errors in mechanics	May display some errors in mechanics but no consistent pattern

FIGURE 6–23 A scoring rubric to assess expository writing by sixth graders. *Source: New Mexico Portfolio Writing Assessment, Teacher's Guide, Grade 6, (p. 50.), Santa Fe, NM: New Mexico State Department of Education.*

Figure 6–29 shows how a student teacher, Maureen Murphy, employed this system to describe how a second-grade student used the process strategies. It is important to note that analysis and description are used to guide instruction. The student being analyzed is Monica, who is 7 years, 6 months old and in the second grade. She is described as a friendly and cooperative child, who is not at the very top of her class, but appears

New Mexico Portfolio Writing Assessment—Expository Scoring Rubric

Partial Command of Exposition Score Point 3	Limited Command of Exposition Score Point 2	Inadequate Command of Exposition Score Point 1
May not have an opening and/or closing Relates to the topic and usually has a single focus; some responses may drift from the focus	May not have an opening and/or closing Some responses relate to the topic but drift or abruptly shift focus	May not have an opening and/or closing May state a subject or a list of subjects; may have an uncertain focus that must be inferred
Some responses are sparse with clear, specific details but little elaboration; others are longer but ramble and repeat ideas	Details are a mixture of general and specific with little, if any, elaboration, producing a list-like highlight response	Details are general, may be random, inappropriate, or barely apparent
Some responses have elaborated details but are interrupted by organizational flaws/lapses or by lack of transitions	Attempt at organization; some attempt to control details but few, if any, transitions	Some lengthier papers are disorganized and difficult to follow; may show no sense of planning
May display a pattern of errors in usage	May display numerous errors in usage	May have severe problems with usage including tense formation, subject–verb agreement, pronoun usage and agreement, word choice
May demonstrate excessive monotony in syntax and/or rhetorical modes; may display errors in sentence construction	Excessive monotony in syntax and/or rhetorical modes; may contain numerous errors in sentence construction	May contain an assortment of grammatically incorrect sentences; may be incoherent or unintelligible
May display a pattern of errors in mechanics NOTE: Errors may interfere with readability	May display numerous serious errors in mechanics NOTE: Errors may interfere somewhat with comprehension	May display severe errors in mechanics. NOTE: Errors may interfere with comprehension.

FIGURE 6–23 *Continued*

bright and able. She works hard to meet literacy challenges with enthusiasm. Based on an informal reading inventory, Monica is a successful second-grade reader. Monica's class devotes approximately 45 minutes each afternoon to writer's workshop. She's had good exposure and experience with the writing process and truly seems to enjoy and look forward to the writing part of each school day.

Name _____   Grade_____   Date_____

Priority Items   Diagnostic Comments/Suggestions for Teaching

1. Task/Content

- Responds appropriately to the requirements of the task (audience, purpose, form, etc.)
- Provides sufficient information to respond adequately to the task (ideas, explanations, examples, etc.)
- Selects appropriate information for focus or emphasis
- Maintaining a consistent point of view

2. Organization

- Unifies the piece by means of appropriate generalization
- Supports generalization and conclusion by providing reasons, details, examples, etc.
- Makes logical connections

3. Sentence Structure

- Avoids sentence fragments
- Avoids run-on sentences
- Uses sentences of varied types and lengths

4. Language

- Uses specific, vivid words
- Forms words correctly
- Uses words accurately
- Avoids unnecessary repetition

5. Mechanics/Usage

- Developing spelling skills
- Uses punctuation correctly
- Uses capital letters correctly
- Usage
  Subject–verb agreement
  Verb tenses
  Pronoun references
  Other:
- Improves handwriting

FIGURE 6–22 New York State writing product analysis sheet for elementary grades.

CONCLUSIONS

The use of writing portfolios is no longer theory; it is accepted and expected practice. The major challenge for many teachers is to elevate their students' writing folders into a more selected portfolio, and then to use portfolios as a vehicle for improving instruction

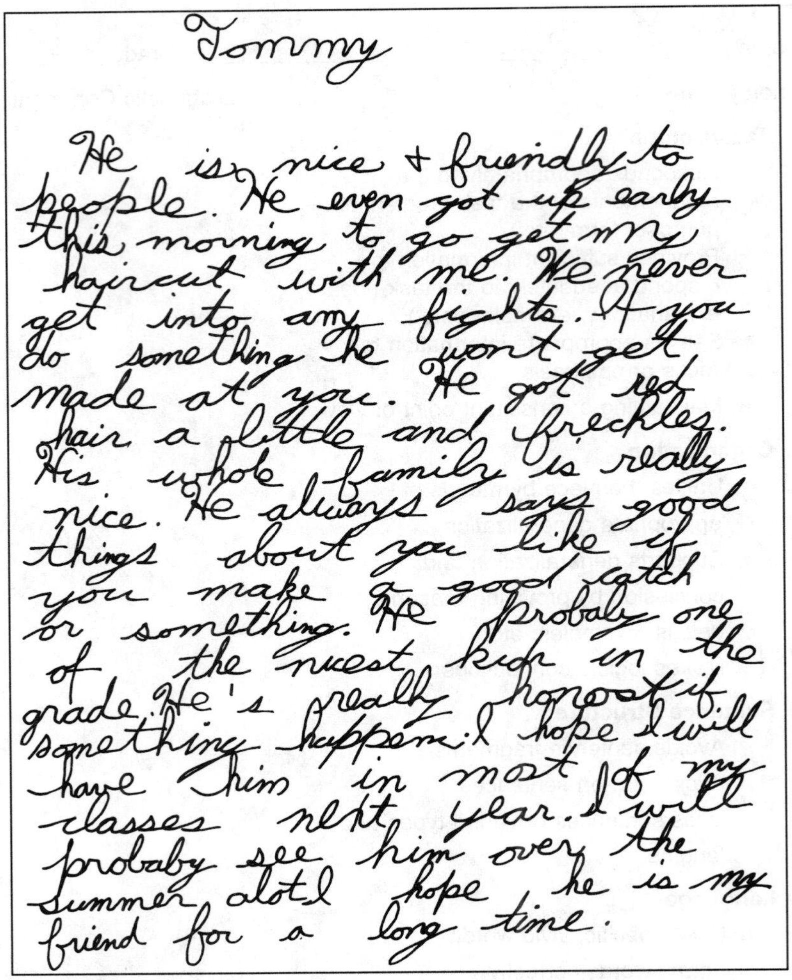

Tommy

He isn nice + friendly to people. He even got up early this morning to go get my haircut with me. We never get into any fights. If you do something he wont get made at you. He got red hair a plittle and freckles. His whole family is really nice. He always says good things about you like if you make a good catch or something. He probaly one of the nicest kids in the grade. He's really honest if something happens. I hope I will have him in most of my classes next year. I will probaly see him over the summer alot. I hope he is my friend for a long time.

FIGURE 6–25 Sample descriptive essay by a fifth-grade student.

and working more individually with their students. In today's political and social climate, teachers are especially concerned about having their students demonstrate that they meet state standards for specific literacy behavior, and certainly it is important that teachers be able to document that they have included the standards in their literacy program. This concern with accountability must be balanced with teachers' professional judgment and good sense so that writing instruction and assessment do not become tedious drill and practice for test preparation. Writing portfolios provide a superb means both to note and celebrate students' accomplishments and to document how students progress in writing throughout the year. The strength of the writing portfolio lies particularly in the process of self-reflection and collaboration as well as in the use of the process to guide instruction.

Several themes emerge from this chapter. Teachers should emphasize self-reflection, which needs to be modeled early in literacy instruction and throughout the grades. Collaboration must also be encouraged through classroom strategies so that students learn that they benefit when they work with others. In particular, students should share their writing and self-reflections with their families. Teachers need to develop strategies

1. **Task/Content**

   This student has a clear understanding that he is supposed to describe his best friend in detail.

   The student provides a great deal of information about Tommy including personal characteristics, physical description, background about his family, and examples of times they have enjoyed together. He maintains a consistent point of view and seems to have a good sense of his audience.

   No specific intervention seems indicated.

2. **Organization**

   There are significant problems with the organization of this piece of writing. The student does not organize his thoughts but tends to simply list them as they come to mind. The writing lacks topic sentences and does not display any organizing statements.

   Teaching should focus on getting this student to link related ideas. Using a map or web would be helpful techniques before writing. This student should be encouraged to list his ideas and then group related thoughts under an appropriate organizer, i.e.,

   How Tommy looks
   > freckles
   > red hair

   Personality
   > friendly
   > nice to people

   Oral discussion with a peer would be helpful before writing.

   Once this student can organize his thoughts into logical categories, then attention to paragraph development can follow.

3. **Sentence Structure**

   This student writes in well-formed, declarative sentences and seems to be quite aware of sentence structure. (Note capital letters and large periods.) There is one example of a run-on sentence.

   While organization of the writing should be the primary instructional goal, it would be helpful to expose this student to a variety of sentence structures. Providing examples of descriptive pieces with variety in sentence structure would be appropriate reading.

4. **Language**

   This student's language usage seems concrete and simple for his grade level. In particular he overuses the word *nice*. He appears to form words correctly.

   This student's oral language is probably more vivid than his written language. Oral discussion should focus on using a variety of words to convey specific, vivid pictures, and certainly, substitutions for the overuse of *nice* can be developed. Again, providing reading that uses vivid language would aid awareness of descriptive language.

5. **Mechanics**

   The student seems to have appropriate spelling skills for this level, given that he restricts language usage to simple words. The words *probably, mad,* and *honest* are misspelled. He uses terminal punctuation and begins each sentence with a capital letter. In one sentence he omitted the verb, and use of appropriate verb tense needs to be developed.

   There is little evidence that the student used self-editing, and this should be developed at this grade level. Creating a checklist of items to edit would be a helpful strategy. Peer and self-editing need to be emphasized as part of this student's writing program.

FIGURE 6–26 Analysis of the "Tommy" essay using New York criteria.

to accomplish the school-family link, including periodic conferences (which often include the student or are even student-led), portfolios that are sent home, letters to parents, photos that circulate, and exhibits for all to attend.

Portfolios can contain a wide range of materials, and there is no one correct way to create a portfolio process in a classroom. However, literacy portfolios should reflect actual classroom experiences. They should also contain writing products and other

STUDENT _____ TOPIC _____

TEACHER _____ LIBRARIAN _____

WRITTEN LIBRARY RESEARCH PROJECT RUBRIC—GRADE 5

	3	2	1	0
Library skills	You always located information independently. You summarized and paraphrased the information very well. You managed your time.	You usually located information independently. You showed an ability to adequately summarize and paraphrase your information. You used your time fairly well.	You sometimes located information independently or with a teacher's help. You usually copied from source. You need to manage your time.	A teacher had to guide each step.
Note taking	You always recorded meaningful information related to topic using index cards and abbreviations.	You usually recorded meaningful information related to topic using index cards and abbreviations.	You sometimes recorded useful information. You made limited use of index cards and abbreviations.	You need to record much more information.
Outlining	You always used logical sequencing and grouping of ideas. You used the correct format.	You usually used logical sequencing and grouping of ideas. You usually used the correct format.	You demonstrated adequate sequencing and grouping of ideas. You need to improve your format.	You need to revise your outline.
Form	You have shown that you have used the writing process extremely well. Your opening and closing paragraphs are excellent. You used specific, accurate details and examples. You have a title page and cover.	You have shown a use of the writing process. You have a good opening and closing paragraph. There is some use of details and examples. You are missing either a title page or cover.	You need some revision before it is of publishable quality. You are missing either title page or cover.	You need to use the writing process to be of publishable quality. Check requirements.
Content	You have shown that you have done extensive and full research.	You have done solid research with some gaps.	Your topic needs to be more fully developed or explored.	You need to do much more research to fully develop your topic and to show that you understand your topic.
Bibliography	You have used excellent types and quality resources. You used at	You have used acceptable sources and correct form.	You have some errors in form. You have an inadequate number or type of resources.	Needs to be revised.

FIGURE 6–27 A rubric created by students and teachers to evaluate an independent research project. *Source:* Courtesy of the Plainedge, New York school district.

Four Stages of the Authoring Process

1. Prewriting: rehearsing and drafting
2. Conferencing and revising
3. Editing
4. Publishing

Rating System

0 Did not observe the use of the strategy

1 Having difficulty with the strategy

2 Developing the use of the strategy

3 Using the strategy successfully

1. Prewriting Strategies: Rehearsing and Drafting

The student is able to

- Understand the task
- Choose an appropriate form of writing
- Use appropriate beginning strategies: draws pictures; uses webs, story maps, etc.; lists; generate and discuss ideas
- Select a focus
- Generate appropriate and relevant ideas and details
- Put initial ideas on paper
- Sustain focus
- Work independently where appropriate
- Work cooperatively where appropriate
- Seek help where appropriate
- Produce a rough draft

Strengths noted: _____

Difficulties noted: _____

Teaching strategies: _____

2. Conferencing and Revising

The student is able to

- Share ideas
- Generate further, relevant ideas

FIGURE 6–28 Evaluation of a student's use of an authoring process. *Source:* Developed by J. Cohen, Adelphi University.

entries that reveal the writing process. Student self-selections and their reflections are essential components of the process. Additionally, students should be given time to think about their portfolio contents and be accountable for creating an organizational system (e.g., table of contents, letter to the reader) that is coherent and clear. Of course, expectations for students will differ at different grade levels. Conferences are essential and must be held regularly so that the teacher and student collaborate and both can benefit from reviewing portfolio contents.

- Use feedback from classmates
- Use feedback from teacher conferences
- Modify draft
- Sustain focus

Strengths noted: _____

Difficulties noted: _____

Teaching strategies: _____

3. Editing

The student is able to
- Self-edit with attention to organization/coherence, word choice, spelling, punctuation, capitalization, grammar/sentence structure, etc.
- Seek appropriate resources
- Assist with editing others' work

Strengths noted: _____

Difficulties noted: _____

Teaching strategies: _____

4. Publishing

The student is able to
- Produce a final work in an appropriate time frame
- Produce a legible piece
- Produce a piece that has a good appearance and use graphics appropriately (artwork, illustrations, etc.)
- Take pride in finished work
- Share with others

Strengths noted: _____

Difficulties noted: _____

Teaching strategies: _____

FIGURE 6–28 *Continued*

The essential outcomes of this writing portfolio process are to enhance students' self-esteem, promote metacognitive reflection, and guide instruction. In today's standards context, writing portfolios are also a means to document the students' actual writing in meaningful day-to-day activities. Portfolios are unlikely to replace state-mandated writing assessments (although many states include an actual writing sample in their system and several states actually incorporate portfolios as part of documenting growth), but they can supplement information from standardized literacy assessment with more authentic samples of student work. Many teachers have begun to collect students' work

1. Prewriting—Rating, 3

Monica is very good at planning her topics and focusing on what she needs to do to accomplish her task. The class was given an article for research about an animal. Monica handled the task of nonfiction writing with ease. Her strength is her lack of any problems in attempting the rough draft stage.

Monica should continue to receive positive reinforcement for her excellent beginning strategies and should read a variety of written forms of expression to expand her writing genre choices.

2. Conferencing and Revising—Rating, 3

The class uses peer conferencing after a rough draft is done. Again, Monica meets this phase successfully. In fact, she is one of the children who the other children most like to have a conference with because she is good at sharing ideas and posing questions that help the other students with their products. Monica also makes judgments in a nonthreatening manner.

Monica should continue to receive positive reinforcement for her excellent strategies at this stage. She should continue to be used as a resource for other students in the class.

3. Editing—Rating, 2

Monica is presently in second grade. The editing she exhibits independently is indicative of a child who is beginning to learn an editing process and continues to show growth. Her writing ability shows good spelling for this level. She uses sound–symbol correspondence as her primary spelling strategy. The sentence structure in her stories still seems choppy and shows problems with run-on thoughts. Her writing has progressed from the beginning of the year, when her sentences usually were only three to four words long.

Small group editing lessons and individual writing conferences will help Monica. She's just beginning to use self-editing strategies on a limited basis. Each editing lesson should have a simple focus with an appropriate strategy highlighted based on her recent writing. Monica should be encouraged to develop a list of skills that she can refer to when she self-edits.

4. Publishing—Rating, 3

This is a student who looks forward to completing her stories and seeing them bound with a story cover. The final products are completed neatly and in a timely manner. In this classroom, the teacher displays the finished stories on an open book rack. During snack time, I've observed Monica rereading her finished stories and sharing her stories with a friend. These stories are definitely a source of pride for her.

Monica should receive positive reinforcement for her completed work. It may be necessary to slow down her productivity at a somewhat later point so that she doesn't overemphasize the number of stories completed. Sharing stories with her family and with classmates should be continued. Monica may enjoy developing a pen-pal relationship with another second grade student from a different school to broaden her experiences and audience.

FIGURE 6–29 Authoring process evaluation for a second grader completed by a student teacher, Maureen Murphy, Adelphi University.

in portfolios, but they are still unsure how the contents should be used. Several different techniques may be used to analyze the writing contents of portfolios. Clearly, the portfolio process is an important tool in literacy teaching and can be a potent force for change. According to Jenkins (1996),

> The potential of portfolios to change the way we view ourselves, our children, and our curriculum will be realized only if we pursue a course of patient, persistent inquiry and continual reflection. Portfolio assessment is an evolutionary process of self-renewal that requires resolve, knowledge, and the belief that it makes a difference in children's lives. (p. 241)

REFERENCES

Atwell, N. (1998). *In the middle.* Portsmouth, NH: Heinemann.

Bratcher, S. (1994). *Evaluating children's writing.* New York: St. Martin's.

Burns, P., Roe, B., & Smith, S. (2002). *Teaching reading in today's elementary schools.* Boston: Houghton Mifflin.

Calkins, L. (1983). *Lessons from a child.* Portsmouth, NH: Heinemann.

Calkins, L. (1986). *The art of teaching writing.* Portsmouth, NH: Heinemann.

Calkins, L. (1994). *The art of teaching writing* (2nd ed.). Portsmouth, NH: Heinemann.

Graves, D. (1983). *Writing: Teachers and children at work.* Portsmouth, NH: Heinemann.

Harwayne, S. (2001). *Writing through childhood.* Portsmouth, NH: Heinemann.

Jenkins, C. B. (1996). *Inside the writing portfolio.* Portsmouth, NH: Heinemann.

Kentucky writing portfolio (1999). Writing Portfolio Development, Teacher's Handbook. Kentucky Department of Education. http://www.ael.org/rel/state/ky/kyasesmt.htm.

Rael, P., & Travelstead, J. (1993). *Statewide student assessment requirements.* Santa Fe, NM: New Mexico State Department of Education.

Smith, F. (1982). *Writing and the writer.* New York: Holt, Rinehart & Winston.

Vizyak, L. (1996) *Student portfolios.* Bothell, WA: Wright.

Using Standards-Based Porfolios and Other Assessment Tools to Promote Curriculum Goals

by
Giselle O. Martin-Kniep, Ph.D.
President, Learner-Centered Initiatives, Ltd., CEO,
Center for the Study of Expertise in Teaching and Learning

KEY WORDS AND CONCEPTS

standards

learner outcomes

standards-based assessments

indicators

learning and assessment opportunities

standards or outcome-based portfolio

curriculum- or content-driven portfolio

The last 10 years have seen many changes in the questions that researchers, educators, and policy makers are asking about testing and assessment. Many of these questions relate to the design and implementation of authentic literacy assessments in the context of state and national standards at the classroom, school, and school district levels. This chapter addresses some of these questions at the classroom level.

Much of the material in this chapter is based on my work with hundreds of teachers in school districts in the United States and abroad. This work focuses on helping teachers enhance their professional practice by engaging in such activities as assessing the distance between what they teach and what they should teach, as defined by state and national standards; designing curriculum and assessment experiences that support students' attainment of state and national standards; expanding their repertoire of assessment strategies to include performance, portfolio, and process assessments; and systematically studying their own practice through action research activities.

ASSESSMENT DEMANDS POSED BY THE STANDARDS

The current movement to identify district, state, and national standards is predicated on several key arguments, one of which is that schools have placed undue emphasis on educational inputs (e.g., course hours, credits, numbers of courses), without sufficiently defining outputs or expected results. Another argument is that there is far too much variability in content, expectations, and grading practices across classrooms, schools, districts, and states. A third argument is that standards offer teachers and schools the opportunity to focus on students by defining what they should know and be able to do in clear and explicit terms.

The identification of state and national standards has its merits. It is difficult to dispute the merits of articulating what we want students to know and be able to do. After all, how can we possibly envision the improvement of schools in the absence of clarity about what they should accomplish? Although the development of standards is a complex and political process (i.e., deciding "whose" standards will serve as criteria for success in a pluralistic society), it is critical that the standards used to judge success are made explicit. State and national standards are often defined broadly and in performance terms. The following are some examples:

> Students will demonstrate competence in the stylistic and rhetorical aspect of writing (Language Arts).
>
> Students will understand the concept of region (Geography).
>
> Students will understand the biological and cultural processes that shaped the earliest human communities (History).

Standards are a necessary but insufficient condition for improving schools. Along with such standards, schools need support systems and structures that enable teachers to address them and students to attain them. In fact, much needs to be done to support an educational system that strives for excellence without compromising equity.

First, teachers need significant time and assistance in incorporating the standards into their curriculum, instruction, and assessment practices. To do this, they need time to study and internalize the standards. They need to systematically assess the extent to which their current practices are aligned with the standards and, if they are not, they need opportunities to rethink such practices and incorporate new ones.

Second, teachers need assistance in transforming their lessons so that they can help students to apply the content and skills they have learned, because standards emphasize *understanding* and *application*. Third, because a relatively small number of standards encompasses large bodies of content, teachers need help in restructuring their lessons to increase their depth and rigor. The principle of "less is more" applies here in that, in standards-based classrooms, teachers often must reconfigure what used to be a large array of lessons into relatively few units.

Accompanying the implementation of standards is the pervasive and longstanding use of standardized tests. These tests are grounded in a 70-year-old tradition of externally imposed assessments designed to differentiate and sort students.

The use of standardized tests as the primary means to monitor educational attainment has raised many questions. The problems accompanying the reliance on these tests have been documented extensively (see Kohn, 2000; Madaus, Haney, & Kreitzer, 1992; Popham, 2000). Standardized tests tend to narrow the curriculum and impair the educational opportunities of students who test poorly on these measures.

There is much evidence that traditional tests are largely unreliable and often are not valid bases for making judgements about an individual's literacy development (Darling-Hammond, 1991; Stallman & Pearson, 1990). Some of the problems of traditional tests include the following:

a. They assess too narrow a range of literacy activity.
b. They are given too infrequently and not always at appropriate times in the school year.
c. They are too disconnected from curriculum and instructional practices to assist in planning instruction.
d. They encourage teachers to teach to narrowly defined outcomes and discourage teacher-learner collaborative evaluation of literacy learning.
e. They tend to discourage students whose test scores indicate that they are behind their peers.

The use of standardized testing for high-stakes decisions and program evaluation often drives teachers toward curriculum and instructional practices that enhance the teaching of isolated skills and knowledge tapped by these tests rather than toward integrated knowledge-in-use elicited by authentic assessment. To think that teachers will not do all they can to enable students to perform well on tests that are used to assess teaching and schools is, at best, naive. Ironically, many of the standardized tests currently in use in states like New York were originally designed to drive instruction in pedagogically sound ways (i.e., the New York state fourth- and eighth-grade writing tests). In many cases, however, such tests foster a decontextualized and contrived approach to writing that is far removed from the natural act of writing as an expression of one's thinking. In many cases, the writing tasks and tests are not as narrow or decontextualized, yet teachers perceive that the best way to prepare students to do well on such tests is to have students drill and practice each skill and content item in isolation. As in many other cases, perceptions, however unfounded, often replace and become reality.

A sound assessment system strikes a balance between (1) the use of standardized performance tasks that are not necessarily authentic but that elicit a broad range of outcomes, and can be used for program and state-wide evaluation and (2) the use of fully contextualized and authentic classroom-based assessments that demand that students produce high-quality work, even if such work was not produced under standardized conditions. Teachers should use a variety of assessment tasks and processes to elicit many different outcomes and to address different assessment purposes. Some of these tasks and processes may be authentic, whereas in some cases, the use of conventional tests might be advisable. In yet other cases, assessment data may be easily obtained from the learning opportunities themselves. For example, one could videotape a debate in which students discuss the merits and shortcomings of specific historical figures. The debate could be used as both an opportunity for students to discuss different points of view and as a means to assess outcomes such as students' ability to communicate ideas orally or students' use of different research sources to analyze and present historical issues or events.

Rather than thinking in terms of which type of assessment is needed, teachers should concentrate on appropriately matching specific learning standards and indicators with appropriate assessment tasks and measures. They should also realize that different students will prefer different kinds of assessment modalities and, therefore, teachers should consciously attempt to provide all students with at least some opportunities to make their learning evident by using the students' preferred learning modality.

DESIGN AND IMPLEMENTATION OF STANDARDS-BASED ASSESSMENTS

The design of standards-based assessments includes five key elements: (1) standards or outcomes, (2) indicators, (3) learning opportunities, (4) assessment tasks, and (5) scoring criteria and rubrics.

The design process itself is recursive, rather than linear, with teachers often moving back and forth from one element to another. It is not uncommon, for example, to use indicators as the basis for the development of standards and rubrics, and to then redefine the learning opportunities to ensure that the student has enough background information and skills to succeed in the assessment (see Figure 7–1).

Standards or Learner Outcomes

The phrase "learner outcomes" preceded the standards movement and is commonly associated with a movement known as Outcome-Based education. In practice, outcomes and standards are interchangeable and share the same meaning, although I often distinguish them by stating that outcomes are often internally or teacher-generated, whereas standards are externally generated by districts, states, or expert panels.

Outcomes or standards are statements that describe what students are able to do, know, or value as a result of their schooling. These statements provide teachers with a framework from which to make informed decisions about how to best use available curriculum resources. They also shift teachers' attention from what they need to teach to what students need to learn.

Standards are derived from educational goals, which are representations of shared cultural and societal values related to the purpose of education and schools. Sample goal statements include: "Students will be critical thinkers," "Students will be effective communicators," and "Students will be responsible citizens in a democratic society." Goal statements respond to the question, "What will students be educated as (or for)?" Standards can be generated for a specific grade level (i.e., seventh-grade students will write a business letter); for a program (i.e., students in this class will explore and effectively use the narrative and expository genres), or for the end of schooling (i.e., upon completion of 12th grade, students will know how to effectively write, listen, and speak for social interaction).

Standards/Outcomes: What do I, the state, or the nation want students to know and be able to do?

Indicators: What will that outcome or standard look like in my classroom? grade level?

Learning Opportunities: What do I need to teach, or have students experience so they will attain the standards or outcomes?

Assessment: What do I need to collect or administer to prove that students have grown toward and/or achieved desired standards or outcomes?

Standards/Rubrics: How will I communicate what mastery or accomplishment means? How do I help students recognize the difference between high-quality and low-quality work?

FIGURE 7–1 Design framework.

Teachers can develop or refine their curriculum by identifying the state or national standards they need to address, by generating their own outcomes for students, or by combining both approaches. Identifying standards for specific units is often facilitated by a process called curriculum alignment, gap analysis, or mapping. Through this process, teachers correlate their curriculum units, lessons, and assessments to the standards to determine the specific standards that will support different units or lessons.

To generate their own outcome statements, teachers often find it useful to imagine their best students and then describe these students' learning at the end of the year. Good outcome statements: (1) describe what students ought to know, and are able to do; (2) are stated in result-focused, observable, measurable, or inferable terms; (3) are developmental; (4) are reflective of broad goals; (5) are comprehensive and broad enough to be interdisciplinary; (6) are flexible in terms of how students attain them; and, (7) are specific enough to form the basis for outcome indicators and performance standards. Based on my experience with teachers in many school districts, some of the most typical outcomes related to literacy have included:

1. Students will communicate in writing using a variety of genres to meet different purposes and for different audiences.

2. Students will communicate orally using a variety of genres to meet different purposes and for different audiences.

3. Students will read and listen attentively for information and understanding by anticipating, summarizing, interpreting, analyzing, and evaluating contextual information, including various literary types, other written material, and media.

4. Students will appreciate the relationship between diverse languages and cultures.

5. Students will explain how their writing changes in order to take into account the differences among audiences.

6. Students will use writing as a strategy for personal learning and clarification of thinking.

Standards Indicators

Indicators are statements describing the specific knowledge, characteristics, and performances that are likely to demonstrate students' attainment of standards. Indicators for specific grade levels are often called benchmarks. Indicators for specific subjects are often known as content standards. An example of a standard and its respective indicators is presented below:

Standard: Students will use reading, writing, listening, and speaking for literary response and expression.

Indicators:

1. Students will recognize some features that distinguish the genres and use those features to aid comprehension.

2. Students will understand the literary elements of setting, character, plot, theme, and point of view and compare those features to other works and to their own lives.

3. Students will use inference and deduction to understand the text.

4. Students will evaluate literary merit.

Using standards to develop curriculum and assessment tasks is difficult for teachers for several reasons. Current curricular and pedagogical strategies vary widely and may not be consistent with the use of broad standards. Too often these standards appear to favor the discrete teaching of isolated skills, and the delivery of self-contained activities that often are not intrinsically linked to one another. Growing curricular demands, as well as the necessity to address the needs of very different kinds of learners who receive support within and outside the classroom, make it difficult for teachers to design integrated curriculum units that allow for an in-depth exploration of topics through a limited but significant number of learning and assessment opportunities. Finally, it is more convenient to reuse existing and discrete lesson plans, teachers' guides, and packaged instructional systems than to develop a year-long curriculum around standards and to ponder the extent to which daily and weekly activities are likely to result in their attainment. Fortunately, literacy instruction is undergoing significant changes, and more and more teachers are changing their instructional strategies in reading and writing and are increasingly comfortable with thematic, integrated curricular units that lend themselves to a variety of new assessment opportunities.

Learning and Assessment Opportunities

Learning opportunities are generated as the teacher asks: What kinds of experiences and learning opportunities must I provide so that my students can attain what I want from them? Learning opportunities should be stated in sufficiently general terms so that they allow for the emergence of "teachable moments" and to avoid their becoming redundant to lesson plans. At the same time, they should be specific enough so that teachers can use them as a way to lay out the scope and sequence of their curriculum. Needless to say, learning opportunities ought to be informed by district- and state-mandated curriculum guidelines as well as current research on effective literacy instruction.

Following are some examples of learning opportunities associated with the outcome "Students will interact with different kinds of reading material with understanding":

1. Ask students to write reading responses on a weekly basis.
2. Provide students with varied kinds of literature throughout the school year, including autobiographies, fiction (novels and mysteries), poetry (cinquains, haiku, and poetry-free verse), fantasy, and nonfiction.
3. Provide guided and independent opportunities for students to read samples of literature and analyze, in writing, plot structure, methods of characterization, importance of setting, creation of mood, use of theme, and author's purpose.

The adequate use of performance-based and portfolio-based assessment in authentic learning situations requires that teachers provide students with multiple and ongoing learning opportunities that support literacy development so that students: (1) experience the inherent connections among reading, writing, listening, and speaking; (2) read and write in realistic contexts and for diverse purposes and audiences; (3) experience and value the process of writing, not only for the sake of writing more and better but as a means to clarify their own thinking; and (4) relate their backgrounds and experiences to the material presented. In short, authentic learning opportunities demand sustained and in-depth work on the part of teachers and students. Such opportunities are often missing when teachers rely on compartmentalized and skills-based literacy programs that have been the basis of traditional basal reading programs.

If teachers rely on teacher-centered pedagogical approaches or use fragmented lessons that emphasize rote learning of isolated facts, they will struggle with the design of standards-based curriculum and assessment tasks. Given the inherent obstacles facing the use of authentic literacy assessments, teachers should aim at designing a limited number of standards-based assessment tasks per year and devote at least 2, if not 3 years to the design and implementation of student portfolios for specific outcomes, rather than assume that they can generate comprehensive portfolios or tasks for every curriculum unit.

Authentic Assessment Strategies and Tasks

Assessments include tasks, measures and processes that can be used to document students' progress and achievement of the standards. In general, assessment can be used for the following purposes:

1. To determine what students know, are able to do, and value. This purpose can be accomplished through:

   (a) diagnostic assessment: used to determine knowledge/skills before (baseline) or during instruction.

   (b) formative assessment: used for instructional or curricular decisions regarding students' needs; to communicate expectations, achievements, and progress to students, parents, and communities; and, to help all students learn and to intervene to prevent students from failing.

   (c) summative evaluation: used to determine achievement and produce grades.

2. To help teachers improve upon their instructional practice.

3. To determine curriculum and/or program effectiveness.

4. To develop means by which schools, districts, communities, and states can hold themselves accountable for focusing on the needs of learners.

Teachers need to ascertain the specific purposes for which their assessments will be used. At the classroom level, they should use assessments primarily to meet the first two purposes mentioned, so that they can monitor students' learning and improve upon their own professional practice.

In the process of continued curriculum, instruction, and assessment refinement, it is important for teachers to seek a parsimonious system, that is, one in which a few assessment tasks are required to assess a large number of standards. In terms of literacy portfolios, teachers would be wise to use portfolios as a means to showcase students' literacy skills and their application across the curriculum.

Performance Standards, Scoring Criteria, Rubrics, and Exemplars

Explicit standards and scoring criteria provide teachers and students with powerful images and pictures of what is deemed to be of high quality. This is important because all too often, we assign work without really knowing what it is that students will produce. When teachers accompany their assignments with clear and descriptive performance criteria and, when necessary, support that criteria with rubrics and models, they make it possible for students to identify the attributes of exemplary work and monitor their own performance and achievement.

Beyond their usefulness in the classroom, clear standards and criteria allow other stakeholders (i.e., parents, supervisors) to understand what teachers value in students' work or performance and, in turn, help to justify and validate grades. Related to the latter, the use of exemplars, scoring criteria, and rubrics result in an assessment system in which a teacher's judgment becomes more reliable and defensible.

The process of identifying performance standards is recursive or cyclical. Teachers begin this process by describing the attributes of a product or process that is considered exemplary. For example, in defining the attributes of an excellent oral presentation, teachers may generate criteria such as the following:

> The material presented was well-researched, accurate, and relevant; the presentation was well-organized and supported by visuals or media which clarified or accentuated the most important points; the presentation was thought-provoking and interactive, drawing where appropriate on the audience's questions or comments; the presenter was assertive, clear, and understandable; the student provided both a context or introduction, and a closure or conclusion to the presentation.

These criteria can be further refined by incorporating the language of specific standards and indicators and translating them into language that is student-generated, or, at least, is clearly understood by students. The criteria can also serve as the foundation for the development of a scoring rubric, that is, a scale that differentiates levels of student performance on a task or process.

Two of the most commonly used kinds of scoring rubrics are holistic and analytic rubrics. Holistic rubrics capture the whole of a product, are defined on a rather narrow scale, rely on multiple descriptors, and are limited in value in terms of providing precise diagnostic information. However, they are efficient means for sorting student work into comparative and discrete levels of achievement along a continuum from poor to excellent.

The following is an example of a holistic writing rubric for a project using novels developed by Richard Caravella, a participant in the Long Island Performance Assessment Project, and his fifth-grade students:

4   The project includes all required components. The ideas are developed fully using details and examples from the novel. All opinions are fully supported by specific examples. The project is presented in an organized manner and stays on the topic. The project has no spelling or mechanical errors. The student used a variety of interesting words from the novel. The project is neat, easy to read, and was presented in a clear manner.

3   Most parts of the project are complete. Many of the ideas are developed using some details and examples from the novel, but not all ideas are fully supported. Some opinions are supported by specific examples. The project is mostly organized and stays on the topic, although some parts are hanging loose. The project has very few minor spelling and mechanical errors, but these are not distracting. The student used several interesting words from the novel. Most of the project looks neat, is easy to read, and was presented in a clear manner.

2   The project includes few required components. The ideas are developed with very few details and examples from the novel. Most of the opinions are not supported by specific examples. The project looks disorganized and is hard to follow. The project has some spelling and mechanical errors that distract the reader. The student used a few interesting words from the novel. The project was not very neat, was difficult to read, and was not presented in a clear manner.

1   The assignment did not include any required component. The ideas are not developed at all. Opinions are too general and are not supported by specific examples. The project is poorly organized and is difficult to follow. Spelling and mechanical errors are so numerous that they interfere with meaning. The student did not use any vocabulary from the novel. The project was difficult to understand and was not presented clearly.

An analytic rubric describes and scores each of the task or domain attributes separately, uses limited descriptors for each attribute, uses a scale that can be both narrow and broad, and allows for specific diagnostic feedback. These rubrics include well-defined dimensions of good writing that should apply across a range of topics within broadly defined genres. Analytic rubrics translate well into providing personalized instruction geared toward addressing specific student needs. They are obviously useful for diagnostic purposes, whereas holistic rubrics lend themselves to efficiently grading and making comparisons between different levels of achievement.

Figure 7–2 contains an example of an analytic rubric for a first-grade writing sample that was developed by two primary-school teachers, Lorianne Perrelle and Jane Lemak. Rubrics can be generic, addressing writing or reading in general, or task-specific.

Figure 7–3 is an example of a specific writing rubric written by a second-grade teacher and her students, which allowed everyone to share an understanding of the important traits in a piece of writing as well as the characteristics that will be used to grade the writing.

More often than not, analytic rubrics are better starting points than holistic rubrics for both teachers and students because they allow for a clear and separate articulation of each of the scoring dimensions. Such articulation provides students with very specific feedback on the strengths and weaknesses of their products and processes.

Rubrics can be created to assess processes (e.g., cooperative learning, discussions, critical thinking exercises, habits of mind), products (e.g., portfolio, research paper, museum exhibit, investigation, story, poem), and other artistic products, and per-

	One	*Two*	*Three*	*Four*
Picture	"Simple" picture	"Good" picture	Very good picture that goes with the story	Great picture that goes with the story and adds detail
Legibility	Author cannot "read" the story	Only the "author" can read the story	Someone else can read parts of the story with help from the author	Someone else can read the story
Focus	Does not tell a story	Tells a story	Tells a whole story, but not all "complete" sentences	Two or more "complete" sentences that tell a whole story
Use of conventions	Does not use capitals, periods, and question marks	Tries to use capitals, periods, and question marks	Sometimes uses correct capitals, periods, and question marks	Uses correct capitals, periods, and question marks

FIGURE 7–2 Analytic rubric for first-grade writing.

formances (e.g., oral presentations, story-telling performances, debates, panels). Unfortunately, in the absence of multiple samples of students' work, it is difficult to generate precise scoring rubrics or to even precisely determine how many levels of performance should be described. Thus, teachers should assume that initial rubrics are subject to significant revision. After using a rubric for the first time, teachers can refine it by stacking students' work into piles that share similar characteristics. By analyzing and describing how the stacks are different from one another, teachers can enhance the description of the rubric levels and help students use them to monitor their work, as well as to provide more specific instruction based on students' needs.

When teachers begin to use rubrics, they may encounter a variety of problems. One of these is that rubrics can be anxiety-producing for students when used too early and without student participation. When the rubrics are formulaic and narrowly defined, they can also dilute the characteristics of authentic tasks, or be constraining in terms of allowing students to use their imagination and creativity. This tends to happen when teachers define work or performance in terms of quantitative descriptors that may inhibit the range of performance.

When unaccompanied by models, rubrics may not fully convey what we want students to do. On the other hand, when teachers systematically use rubrics with accompanying exemplars and anchor papers (i.e., examples of performance for the intermediate levels of a rubric or scale) to provide students with visual representations of quality work, there is an overall increase in students' performance. This increase results in the welcomed situation of having to raise the standards for subsequent generations of students.

Exemplars are models that can be used by teachers and students to depict desired attributes of quality in products and performances. These models embody standards and scoring criteria that provide teachers and students with powerful images and pictures of what is considered to be of high quality. If used systematically and throughout the instructional process, exemplars can guide students' thinking, planning, development, and performance.

Name: _____
Title: _____

Writer's Workshop Criteria

4	3	2	1
My story . . .	My story . . .	My story . . .	My story . . .
idea is very exciting and interesting to the reader.	idea is very good.	idea is OK.	idea is boring to the reader.
has lots of added details.	has some added details but needs more.	has few added details.	has no added details.
makes sense. My reader won't have any questions.	makes sense. My reader may have few questions.	makes little sense. My reader will have some questions.	doesn't make sense. My reader will have many questions.
creates a crystal-clear picture for my reader.	creates a clear picture for the reader.	creates a little bit of a picture for the reader.	doesn't give the reader any pictures.
will make my reader feel happy, sad, surprised, . . .	will give my reader some feelings.	will give my reader little feelings.	doesn't give the reader any feelings.
has a great beginning and ending.	has a good beginning and ending.	Has a beginning or ending that's OK.	doesn't have a beginning and/or an ending.
has many interesting words.	has some interesting words.	has few interesting words.	has many dull words.
has almost no proofreading mistakes.	has few proofreading mistakes.	has some proofreading mistakes.	has lots of proofreading mistakes.
has many neat and detailed illustrations.	has some neat and detailed illustrations.	has few neat and detailed illustrations.	has sloppy illustrations.

FIGURE 7–3 A writing rubric for second graders. *Source:* Courtesy of Lorraine Perrego, Hudson Valley Development Project.

Teachers need to use multiple and different exemplars to provide students with an opportunity to internalize attributes of quality, rather than perceive the work to be done as driven by a formula. Using one, and even two, exemplars often leads to students treating the exemplars as recipes and copying them. Therefore, teachers should show students at least three different exemplars that depict very different approaches to producing quality work. In addition, teachers should draw from three different *kinds* of exemplars. One kind refers to products or processes produced by students in the teacher's class in the current or previous years, or by students in the same grade level but in other classrooms. Another kind refers to exemplars from students in subsequent grade levels or in schools that represent a higher educational level. Finally, teachers can also use products and performances produced by people outside schools in the context of engaging with authentic experiences (i.e., professional published work, commercial brochures, political debates, public performances,).

To reconcile the use of criteria, standards, exemplars, and rubrics, we need to summarize the distinctions between these terms. *Criteria* refer to the different conditions that performances or products must meet to be considered of high quality. *Standards* define what students should know and be able to do and incorporate criteria; standards characterize exemplary performance, whereas *exemplars* depict standards. Standards are not the same as expectations, which refer to what we hope for and believe students should produce. It is very possible that no student will reach the standards for a given performance or product on a given grade. However, failure to reach such standards does not mean they should not be used as a means to "stretch" our students. The use of analogies such as the Olympics might be helpful in conveying the difference between standards and expectations; not every competitor will earn the perfect 10 but that does not mean one shouldn't try. Obviously the goal here is to assist students in improving their individual performance through self-analysis and understanding of what successful products look like, rather than to foster unhealthy competition or set unrealistic and unattainable goals. Students' sincere efforts to meet desired standards of quality need to be acknowledged, even if students have not yet met with success in their reading and writing.

Teachers must decide how they will translate standards into expectations in terms of grades. For some rubrics, it is possible to have a one-to-one correspondence between the rubric and the grade; for others, the conversion might entail equating a lower point on the rubric to the top grade. Nonetheless, reconciling assessments and grades requires much more than technical solutions. In essence, grading is a normative process informed as much by political and philosophical issues as by technical concerns. Consequently, rational grading and reporting mechanisms can be defined only after having substantive conversations with students, parents, teachers, administrative staff, and policy members regarding the use and value of grades and report cards. These conversations would have to be based on the shared understanding of standards and learner outcomes, with accompanying representative student work.

THE ROLE OF PORTFOLIOS IN DOCUMENTING STANDARDS

A portfolio is a collection of students' work that exhibits students' efforts, progress, achievements, or all of these in one or more areas. This collection is special because it is guided by a clearly established purpose and has a specific audience in mind. Unlike a district folder of a student's writing in different grade levels, this collection represents a personal investment on the part of each student; this investment that is evident through the student's participation in the selection of the contents, the criteria for selection of the items in the collection, the criteria for judging the merit of the collection, and the student's self-reflection.

When they are guided by standards, portfolios can provide a multidimensional view of students' development and achievement. They can be designed to show evidence of effort (all drafts leading to a completed product); corrections of test errors; progress (baseline or sample of work done prior to teacher's intervention and parallel exit task); and achievement (examples of best work).

Portfolios can supplement the existing array of assessment tools that teachers have at their disposal. There are several good reasons for teachers to consider using portfolios to document students' progress and attainment of the standards.

1. *Focus on authentic performance, or knowledge-in-use.* Portfolios include all kinds of evidence of learning, not just the kind of evidence that is derived from traditional assessments, such as tests and quizzes. A portfolio could include, for example, a PowerPoint presentation or a summary of feedback the class gave a student for an oral presentation. In fact, portfolios are well-suited to document students' abilities to use what they have learned.

2. *Students' access to structured opportunities for self-assessment and reflection.* Portfolios enable students to reflect on their progress, learning, and achievement related to the standards.

3. *Evidence of thinking.* Related to students' reflection and self-assessment, portfolios include evidence of students' thinking about the merits and shortcomings of their work as well as the processes followed to complete tasks and projects. Such thinking is absent from traditional testing practices and enables teachers to discover misconceptions, identify gaps in understanding, and learn about how different students engage with the same assignments.

4. *Validation of a developmental view of learning.* Portfolios allow teachers to witness and document growth. When portfolios include early samples of students' work as well as end-of-year samples, teachers and students can assess growth over time. This can help teachers contextualize students' scores in standardized tests.

What Are the Different Types of Portfolios and What Purposes Do They Serve?

This book has discussed a variety of portfolio designs. In this chapter, I would like to highlight the distinctions between two different kinds of portfolios that can be used to document students' learning of the standards (Martin-Kniep, 2000). A *standards-based portfolio* can be structured to provide specific evidence of students' attainment of learning standards. In this kind of portfolio, teachers ask students to collect or produce evidence of their growth or attainment of outcomes or standards. Examples of the kinds of outcomes and accompanying artifacts in an outcome-driven portfolio are listed below.

■ *Perseverance*: entries could include work that shows that you are persistent; a project that took at least 1 week to complete, with an explanation of the steps taken to complete it; or a paper that includes drafts and revisions, additions, or other changes, along with a justification for those changes.

■ *Mathematical representation/communication*: work in which you use a graph, table, chart, or diagram to inform others; or a write-up of a complex problem, with an explanation of all the steps you used to solve it.

■ *Reading/writing*: a piece of writing for which you could have changed the ending to improve it, along with a description of the changes that could be made; work that shows you have improved as a reader of literature; a log that shows the range of books you have read; a selection of book notes from different kinds of books.

■ *Communication in another language*: a piece of work that shows that you can initiate and sustain face-to-face conversations in French; a translation of a dialogue you heard in German; or a letter written to a pen pal in Spain.

■ *Collaboration*: a sample of work done with at least one other person in class, accompanied by a description of how each group member worked together and evidence of the group members' individual contributions to this work.

■ *Historical understanding*: a project that you developed in class to demonstrate the relationship between the past and the present.

■ *Analysis skills*: writing that analyzes a situation or a document.

A standards-based portfolio would list the specific standards for which students have to collect or produce evidence, such as the following:

■ *Read, write, listen, and speak for information and understanding*: one or more pieces of work that show you can gather information from a variety of sources and use that information to present an argument. You may consider including a product you created as a result of your research, a report you wrote, feedback from a lesson you taught the class, or your process journal on the research report you wrote last marking period.

- *Read, write, listen, and speak for literary response*: one or more pieces of work that show you can read, evaluate, use, and write material from different genres. You may consider including a literature log, a book review, or your notes for a Socratic seminar.

- *Read, write, listen, and speak, for critical analysis and evaluation*: one or more pieces of work that show that you can investigate issues or questions and use critical thinking and writing skills to produce work. You may consider including a research report, a persuasive letter you wrote after investigating a critical issue in our community, or the questions you wrote in preparation for the interview of Vietnam War veterans.

- *Read, write, listen, and speak for social interaction*: one or more pieces that show that you can listen and communicate with others in a variety of contexts and for different purposes. You may consider including your written reflections from a cooperative group project, the questions you wrote after a classroom discussion, or your process journal on the newspaper you developed in small groups.

As can be seen in the preceding examples, in a standards-based or outcomes-based portfolio, the teacher provides the students with a list of outcomes or standards or generates such a list with them. The students choose from among their work to select the pieces that provide the best evidence of their progress toward or attainment of these outcomes.

A *curriculum-* or *content-driven portfolio*, on the other hand, is structured so that students choose artifacts or pieces that they associate with specific units or text chapters. For example, a science teacher may ask students to compile the following artifacts: one lab write-up per marking period, two end-of-unit tests, 3 consecutive days' notes, and their first and last research reports. As a result, curriculum-driven portfolios tend to be much more standardized than outcome-driven portfolios.

Although most teachers prefer the idea of outcome-driven portfolios, they often begin their use of portfolios with tightly controlled curriculum-driven portfolios. The reason for this apparent paradox is that teachers often want to maintain a tight grip of the portfolio structure and selection activities until they and their students become comfortable with them and can develop familiar routines for incorporating them into their assessment repertoires.

There are marked differences in teachers' abilities to effectively design and use portfolios. According to Stowell and Tierney (1994), teachers' use of classroom portfolios can be understood in terms of two different continuums. One continuum may be termed *student-centered* (or *inside-out*) versus *teacher-directed* or (*outside-in*); the other might be termed *bottom-up* versus *top-down*. The first continuum represents the range of differences that may exist in terms of the basic purposes of the portfolio, its management, and perceived outcomes. The second continuum represents the range of differences that may exist in how portfolios are mandated, derived, analyzed, and used. A third continuum might be termed *standards-based* versus *curriculum-based*. When they are initially exposed to portfolios, teachers tend to like the idea of student-centered, standards-based, and bottom-up portfolios. However, more often than not, their first attempts at designing and implementing these assessments result in teacher-directed, curriculum-based, and top-down portfolios. My own work with teachers in multiyear projects centered on the use of student and teacher portfolios (Martin-Kniep, 1999) has revealed that teachers' first-year portfolio designs tend to be teacher-directed and curriculum-based. As teachers become increasingly familiar with standards and the assumptions underlying the use of authentic assessment, and as they develop more practice in terms of assisting students in the analysis and reflection of their learning, their portfolio designs become more student-centered, standards-driven, or inside-out.

Students' Role in the Assessment Process

When designing portfolios, teachers need to consider the extent to which the portfolio will be driven by the teacher or by the students, that is, who will decide what goes into the portfolio—the teacher, the students, or both? A standards-based or outcome-based portfolio tends to be more student-driven than a curriculum-driven portfolio in that the student has more freedom to choose appropriate evidence in the former. However, even an outcome-based portfolio can be teacher-driven when the range of pieces from which students can select is very limited. This would be the case if a teacher asks students to select a piece that shows that they are artistic and there were only one or two opportunities throughout the year for students to include anything that called for an artistic representation.

Students are likely to be more motivated to learn if they feel they are in control of their own learning. Such perceived control can be attained by involving students in the design or the use of classroom-based assessments.

There are a number of strategies for involving students in the design and use of authentic literacy assessments, including: (a) articulating desired learning outcomes for units or other portions of a course with the teacher; (b) identifying the forms of evidence or means by which students will demonstrate their knowledge, skills, or understandings (i.e., a skit, poem, research paper); (c) identifying processes/timelines for producing evidence of performance or work (i.e., a team-developed collage or performance that is done over 1 week vis-à-vis an individual report produced over a 3-day period); (d) defining performance standards (i.e., audience engagement, use of sources, good introduction); (e) developing scoring rubrics; (f) reflecting upon and evaluating their work; and (g) presenting their work to their peers and assessing their peers' work.

When teachers involve students in the assessment process, they often discover that students are indeed more motivated and seek higher levels of performance. The use of reflection and self-evaluation questions and activities results in teachers discovering aspects of students' learning that have been otherwise hidden. As teachers learn to value and foster such reflections, students, in turn, become better self-assessors and increase the quality of their learning.

STANDARDS-BASED PORTFOLIOS VERSUS STANDARDIZED PORTFOLIOS

Serious concerns can be raised about the use of portfolios beyond the classroom. As portfolios become a widespread application of authentic assessment, more individual teachers, school districts, and even state-mandated evaluation programs are considering their adoption. The use of portfolios for large-scale assessment requires comparability across classrooms and portfolio contents to support credible arguments about reliability and validity. Such portfolios are currently being used in states such as Vermont, Kentucky, Pittsburgh, Hawaii, and Maryland. However, their use raises the question: How can a portfolio be individually reflective of many different classroom practices and yet provide evidence of both validity and reliability? Although reliability can be attained through the standardization of assessment protocols and rubrics, such standardization often creates contrived assessment task conditions and undermines the authenticity of the task.

Additional concerns with standardization include the use of portfolios to determine whether students have met graduation or promotion criteria. The measurement community is struggling to produce sufficiently explicit and shared means to determine the validity and reliability of these portfolios, thus raising the possibility that these assessments might not hold up to legal challenges when promotion or graduation are denied.

It is doubtful that standardized portfolios can truly depict the range and quality of students' work in the context of producing authentic work. In short, it may well be that standardization and authenticity lie at two opposite extremes of an assessment continuum. An added problem in making valid judgements about student performance based on standardized portfolios relates to separating student performance from the context and support which surrounded that performance. Portfolios are constructed in a social context. As indicated by Gearhart and Herman (1995),

Portfolios contain the products of classroom instruction, and good classroom instruction according to pedagogical and curriculum reforms involves an engaged community of practitioners in a supportive learning process . . . Exemplary instructional practice supports classroom performance. (p. 3)

Whereas a specific teacher may have little difficulty teasing out students' performance and initiative from the context surrounding these, others who are outside that classroom would not be able to do so. Recent evaluation studies conducted on Vermont's use of portfolios (Koretz, Stecher, Klein, & McCaffrey, in press) and on the use of elementary portfolios in several schools in California (Gearhart et al., 1993) confirm that teachers vary dramatically in their understanding and use of specific assessment tasks and prompts and on the amount of support and scaffolding they provide to support students' performance.

Strategies for Supporting Teachers' Design and Implementation of Portfolios at the Classroom Level

In many school districts, professional staff are beginning to explore a portfolio process as an integral part of both classroom and district-wide assessment. Similarly, many teachers have learned about portfolios and are eager to try them out. In both situations, teachers need guidance in how to initiate a portfolio process. Without guidance in how to phase in such a program, teachers may be overly ambitious, unfocused, or may quickly discard a good concept out of frustration.

The set of guidelines that follow are designed to counter some of the barriers and constraints to the use of authentic assessment, and to help teachers use portfolio assessment in their classrooms.

Steps for Setting up Portfolios at the Classroom Level

1. *Decide upon a primary purpose and audience for the portfolios.* If you cannot make a decision among two primary audiences or purposes, develop two different portfolios. Some teachers like the idea of having students create a school portfolio and a home portfolio.

2. *Identify the standards or outcomes that will drive the portfolio design.* Decide if the curriculum will be outcome-driven or curriculum-content driven. Select the outcomes or curriculum areas that the portfolio entries will seek to make evident.

3. *Start small and in a focused fashion.* Begin with a short list of outcomes or with a narrow scope for content. Limit the use of portfolios to one class if you intend to use the portfolio for evaluation purposes. Give yourself 1 to 2 years to experiment with different kinds of portfolio entries and approaches.

4. *Inform parents of your plans to use portfolios and include a schedule or time line for sharing students' work.* At the beginning of the year, let parents know you will be keeping students' work to help students develop collections of their work. Let parents know how and when they will see their children's work.

5. *Create your own portfolio and use it to model the use of portfolios.* Model everything you want students to do with their portfolios, beginning with describing the reasons behind your entries. You can create a portfolio that showcases you as a learner or a curriculum and assessment designer, or one that incorporates your history as a teacher, the range of roles and responsibilities you have, or your goals and strategies to attain them.[1]

---

[1]Teachers can greatly benefit from the development and use of professional portfolios. See Martin-Kniep, G. (1999).

6. *Incorporate the portfolio into your classroom routines*. Set up a place and filing system for portfolios (e.g., filing cabinets, milk crates, small cartons, pizza boxes). Identify possible portfolio contents (with or without students) and a schedule for selecting them. Link contents to the learning outcomes you identified in #2. Decide which contents will be required or optional and identify who will do the selection.

7. *Generate criteria for selecting and judging contents* (preferably with students). Integrate criteria into classroom activities. Encourage students to make selections on a regular basis (once per month or per marking period) and discuss ways in which they can update their portfolios. Promote the sharing of selections and reasons among students. Even if you decide not to grade the portfolio, you need to be clear about what you are looking for and about the qualities that differentiate portfolios. Begin with a working portfolio and shift later to a showcase and growth portfolio.

8. *Incorporate reflection and self-assessment into the portfolios*. Reflection is central to the development and use of portfolios. It needs to be modeled, cultivated, and taught. Take the necessary time to help students recognize what you mean by thoughtfulness, and make reflection a habit in your classroom. Have students assess their work on a regular basis using criteria generated in class. Showcase good and poor examples of portfolio choices and reasons.

9. *Give students ownership over their portfolios*. Student-centered portfolios allow teachers to learn about how students think about their work and what they value. Such portfolios enable students to monitor their growth and achievement and to use their portfolios to generate and refine upon learning goals.

10. *Share portfolios*. Portfolios allow teachers and students to share their work in ways that others can understand and learn from. Encourage students to share their portfolios with their peers and with their parents, either individually or as a group (e.g., Portfolio Night, student-led portfolio conferences). Develop a strategy for allowing teachers in other grades to access and use student portfolios.

Strategies for Supporting Teachers' Design and Implementation of Authentic Literacy Assessments Within a School and District

At the school and district levels, there are a number of strategies for offsetting some of the barriers and constraints to the use of authentic assessment. One of these strategies involves the creation of action research and collaborative input from groups of teachers. An environment that allows teachers to transform their beliefs and practices requires active participation in a community in which teachers can experience themselves as learners, as thinkers, as professionals. Such a community could provide teachers with opportunities to work on projects that allow them to connect curriculum, instruction, and assessment. It would encourage them to use collaborative inquiry and research to reshape their teaching in ways that are most comfortable to them. In such a community, teachers would receive constructive feedback in a nonthreatening and supportive environment. In turn, teachers would be able to make connections between the changes in their teaching and the changes in their students' attitudes and performance.

Another strategy involves the systematic use of state or national standards or exit outcomes for the district, and their use in developing and aligning curriculum, instruction, and assessment. The identification of exit outcomes should be informed by a vision of what the learner should know or be able to do, and such a vision should be informed by the needs of different stakeholders in the educational system, including parents, teachers, administrative staff, and students.

Once standards or outcomes are identified, professional staff can articulate existing curriculum, assessment, and reporting systems, and identify areas in need of change. In addition, efforts should be made to define grade-level responsibilities related to their teaching and assessment in order to eliminate unnecessary duplication and redundancy. Finally, time should be allocated for teachers within and across grade levels to systematically study children's work and to use it as the basis for generating commonly shared expectations for students' work and performance.

A different strategy for supporting teachers' use of authentic literacy assessment involves having teachers identify and compare students' portfolios as well as samples of work that they consider exemplary. An ongoing dialogue centered on quality student work can lead to the shared identification of performance standards, the creation of libraries of exemplars and anchor papers for rubrics, and to the formation of communities of teachers, students, and community members who have a shared understanding and appreciation of school-related work.

CONCLUSION

When used together, the strategies discussed in this chapter can begin to offset some of the barriers to the use of authentic and standards-based assessments and can assist in the development of learning communities of teachers. These communities, in turn, can help teachers improve their understanding of students' learning and achievement. In short, enabling teachers to expand their uses of assessment is likely to benefit both teachers and students.

REFERENCES

Aschbacher, P. R. (1994). Helping educators to develop and use alternative assessments; Barriers and facilitators. *Educational Policy, 8*(2), 202–223.

Combs, A. W. (1991). *The schools we need: New assumptions for educational reform*. Lanham, MD: University Press of America.

Darling-Hammond, L. (1991). The implications of testing policy for quality and equality. *Phi Delta Kappan, 73,* 220–225.

Dyson, A. H., & Freedman, S. W. (1990). *On teaching writing: A review of the literature* (Occasional paper No. 20). Berkeley: University of California, Center for the Study of Writing.

Freedman, S. (1991, May). *Evaluating writing: Linking large-scale assessment testing and classroom assessment* (Occasional paper No. 27). Berkeley: UC Berkeley, Center for the Study of Writing.

Fullan, M. G., & Stiegelbauer, S. (1991). The new meaning of educational change (2nd ed.). New York: Teachers College Press.

Gearhart, M., & Herman, J. L. (1995 Winter). Portfolio assessment: Who work is it? Issues in the use of classroom assessment for accountability. *Evaluation Comment.*

Gearhart, M., Herman, J. L., Baker, E. L., & Whittaker, A. K. (1992). *Writing portfolios at the elementary level: A study of methods for writing assessment*. (CSE Technical Report, 337). Los Angeles: University of California, Center for Research on Evaluation, Standards, and Student Testing.

Glaser, B. G., & Strauss, A. L. (1967). *The discovery of grounded theory: Strategies for qualitative research*. New York: Aldine.

Kniep, W., & Martin-Kniep, G. O. (1995). Designing schools and curriculums for the 21st century. In J. A. Beane (Ed.), *Toward a Coherent Curriculum: ASCD Yearbook.*

Alexandria, VA: Association for Supervision and Curriculum Development.

Kohn, A. (2000). *The case against standardized testing: Raising the scores, ruining the schools*, Portsmouth, NH: Heinemann.

Koretz, D., Stecher, B., Klein, S., & McCaffrey, D. (1994). *The Vermont Portfolio Assessment Program: Findings and Implications*. Educational Measurement: Issues and Practice, 13(3).

Lamme, L., & Hysmith, C. (1991). One school's adventure into portfolio assessment. *Language Arts, 68,* 620–629.

Linn, R. (1993). *Educational assessment: Expanded expectations and challenges*. (CSE Technical Report, 351). Los Angeles: University of California, Center for Research on Evaluation, Standards, and Student Testing.

Madaus, G. F., Haney, W., & Kreitzer, A. (1992). *Testing and evaluation: Learning from the projects we fund*. New York Council for Aid to Education.

Martin-Kniep, G. O. (1995). *What do the "cultivated" assessment-related questions and measures of teachers tell us about what they can do in the area of student assessment?* Paper presented at the American Educational Research Association annual meeting, San Francisco.

Martin-Kniep, G. O. (1999). *Capturing the wisdom of practice: Professional portfolios for educators*. Alexandria, VA: Association for Supervision and Curriculum Development.

Martin-Kniep, G. O. (2000). *Becoming a better teacher: Eight innovations that work*. Alexandria, VA: Association for Supervision and Curriculum Development.

Martin-Kniep, G. O., Sussman, E. S., & Meltzer, E. (1995). Action research as staff development: A collaborative inquiry into alternative assessments. *Journal of Staff Development, 16*(4), 46–51.

McDonnell, L. M., & Elmore, R. F. (1987). Getting the job done: Alternative policy instruments. *Educational Evaluation and Policy Analysis, 9*(2), 133–152.

Moon, J. (1992, October 28). Common understanding for complex reforms. *Education Week*, p. 23.

Moss, P. A. et al. (1991, April). *Further enlarging the assessment dialogue: Using portfolios to communicate beyond the classroom*. Paper presented at the annual meeting of the American Educational Research Association, Chicago.

Noble, A. J., & Smith, M. L. (1994). Old and new beliefs about measurement-driven reform: "Build it and they will come." *Educational Policy, 8*(2), 111–136.

Popham, W. J. (2000). *Testing! Testing! What every parent should know about school tests*. Needham Heights, MA: Allyn & Bacon.

Resnick, L. B., & Resnick, D. P. (1992). Assessing the thinking curriculum: New tools for educational reform. In B. R. Gifford and M. C. O'Connor (Eds.), *Changing assessments: Alternative views of aptitude, achievement and instruction* (pp. 9–350). Boston, Kluwer.

Richardson, V. (1990). Significant and worthwhile change in teaching practice. *Educational Researcher, 19*(7), 10–18.

Sarason, S. (1982). *The culture of the school and the problem of change*. (2nd ed.). Boston: Allyn & Bacon.

Soodak, L. C., & Martin-Kniep, G. (1994). Authentic assessment and curriculum integration: Natural partners in need of thoughtful policy. *Educational Policy, 8*(2), 183–201.

Stallman, A. C., & Pearson, P. D. (1990). Formal measures of early literacy. In L. M. Morrow, J. K. Smith (Eds.), *Assessment for instruction for early literacy* (pp. 7–44). Englewood Cliffs, NJ: Prentice Hall.

Stiggins, R. J. (1991). Relevant classroom assessment training for teachers. *Educational Measurement: Issues and Practice, 10*(1), 7–12.

Stiggins, R. et al. (1992, June). *Assessment literacy: The foundation of sound assessment policy and practice*. Paper presented to the ECS/CDE Assessment Conference, Boulder, CO.

Stowell, L. P., & Tierney, R. L. (1994). Portfolios in the classroom: What happens when teachers and students negotiate assessment? In L. M. Morrow., J. K. Smith, and L. C. Wilkinson (Eds.), *Integrated language arts: Controversy to consensus* (pp. 78–94). Boston: Allyn & Bacon.

Sharing Literacy Progress With Students, Families, and Others

KEY WORDS AND CONCEPTS

collecting   teacher-parent conferences
collaborating   teacher-parent-student conferences
consulting   teacher-student conferences
communicating   teacher-teacher conferences

My 6-year old son, David, is a cooperative child who has had his share of trouble learning to read. During the first half of first grade, he attended a reading intervention program and did well enough to graduate from it. I was scheduled for a parent-teacher conference and I dreaded going, because my son was not having a great year.

The teacher began the conference with the flat observation that David's reading had improved, but this was the last encouraging word I heard. During the ensuing half-hour, she failed to mention his attitude in class, his relationship with peers, his level of cooperation, his achievement in subjects that didn't require much reading and writing, and his ability in specialty areas. What bothered me the most was that she did not tell me anything about David as a child, or a person, even if it was "What a pain in the neck he can be!" Instead, she spent the whole conference telling me his handwriting is messy and how many spelling mistakes there were in his writing. But my back really went up when she showed me a drawing he had done to prove how carelessly he had created it and how messy it was. This was the last straw! Finally, I composed myself and carefully expressed my feelings that she had not said one positive thing about my son.

I think I made an impression. That night David's work came home with supportive comments from the teacher. Other notes came home with compliments about the expressiveness of David's pictures.

What's the moral of the story from my perspective? I did feel that I was heard at the conference, even though I had a strong and noncompliant demeanor. But I realize that my son has had problems in first grade—he rushes through work, he's young for first grade, and he does not have academic self-confidence. However, any concern this teacher had was communicated only in terms of criticism and annoyance, and there was no understanding of David as a person or acknowledgment of his efforts. This teacher's negative judgment of David during the conference may not have been spoken aloud in class but was communicated to me and to David just as forcefully as a loud-speaker announcement. Why couldn't we have discussed David and come up with some positive ideas? I hope my ruminations have some value for other parents.

This is a mother's written description of a very distressing spring conference about her son's literacy progress with his elementary school teacher.

CONFERENCING: A VALUABLE, CONSTRUCTIVE TOOL

Many educators and parents are understandably concerned and confused about the increased emphasis on testing as a result of the standards movement. Some have raised strident voices in reaction to this movement, and truly fear the consequences of reliance on standardized testing, which too often results in a single assessment determining high-stakes decisions such as graduation and promotion. Others wonder what has happened to "child-centered" education and whether the new focus in their children's education will now be totally reliant on testing and quantitative reporting. Without becoming embroiled in debate, it is significant to note that performance-based assessment is also a vital part of this educational reform movement.

We subscribe to Tierney and colleagues' view, that the nature of the assessments teachers use should create a relationship between assessment and instruction that is "natural, ongoing, and constructive" (Tierney, Readance, & Dishner, 1995, p. 482). Advocates of balanced literature programs, the use of thematic units, literacy circles and reading to enhance cultural awareness and critical thinking can adapt to the newest accountability movement by embracing portfolios and welcoming students, parents, and other concerned parties into the assessment process. It is essential that if the public is to have confidence in what schools are accomplishing and if parents are to have a full understanding of how their children are doing, then assessment and outcomes must be shared in an environment of trust, understanding, and mutual respect. Portfolios can be used to combine authentic assessment data with the required standardized information that schools must provide. Portfolios contain students' work products, which are qualitative and authentic, indicating students' learning experiences and reflections, and also contain various test results, which are quantitative. Both aspects are essential components for accurate and meaningful student evaluations. Portfolio implementation may quell the resistance many teachers have because "standards fail to fit with their current practice" (Edmondson, 2001, p. 623). Most certainly, portfolios can become the centerpiece to shared conferencing that involves both students and parents as essential members of the education process.

The Role of Portfolios in Conferencing

According to Courtney and Abodeeb (1999), the literacy portfolio, a purposeful collection of students' work, should always be "diagnostic-reflective" (p. 709). It provides a conceptual coherence to performance-based assessment. It presents a clear compendium of each student's reading and writing progress and accomplishments, leads to students developing appropriate goals, and allows teachers to reflect upon and adapt their teaching strategies when necessary. Conferencing allows the teacher to personally interact with the individual student in order to determine the success of various instructional strategies and the student's mastery of basic skills and coherent learning. Conferences are essential for all types of classrooms and various instructional models, whether literature-based, basal, four-block, thematic, or balanced literacy programs, and they are a vital and useful device whenever portfolios are implemented to assess literacy and performance goals. The demands for performance-based assessment, both formal and informal, are necessary for all school-related activities and are crucial for special populations, those with language, learning, emotional, or behavioral problems, as well as children in traditional or literacy-focused classrooms. Conferences are the vehicle for collaborative exchanges and allow for parents, students, and teachers to review the products of students' actual learning and progress. "Formal" literacy portfolio conferences should optimally be held three to four times per year with students, parents and, whenever possible, other concerned members of a child's instructional team. The contents of the portfolio should be the centerpiece of the conference.

The literacy portfolio has several attributes that facilitate meaningful conferencing:

- It is a collection of actual student work, products of literacy strategies that provide the teacher the opportunity to see application of reading and writing skills in the broad context of daily performance.

- It creates a collaborative relationship between the teacher and the student so that instructional goals are appropriate and relevant to actual student needs and priorities.

- It provides for realistic and authentic assessment of a student's literacy achievements.

- It assists the student in developing metacognitive and self-reflective reading and writing strategies which encourage responsibility for ongoing development.

- It provides insights that allow for jointly establishing appropriate literacy goals and choosing more effective instructional strategies.

- It indicates students' current status as well as their changing literacy behaviors.

- It allows opportunities to share information about students' actual reading and writing performance with other members of the instructional team.

- Through one-on-one conferencing, it allows for immediate individualized instruction and focused group instruction later on.

- The conferences incorporate all the stakeholders—the child, the teacher, and the family—in joint assessment, collaboration, and learning.

Therefore, the reporting and sharing of portfolio contents, which reveal students' progress, is critical. Conferences thus become a vital element in the transmittal of information and for incorporating others into ongoing decision making about how best to improve students' reading and writing. Gill (2000) indicates that "Reading conferences may be more important than has heretofore been recognized. Conferences give teachers opportunities to assess students' reading as well as to provide individualized instruction" (p. 508). Several strategies and factors come into play that are essential for success in conducting a conference.

The Four Cs of Conferencing

Successful conferences are crucially dependent on the four Cs: collecting, collaborating, consulting, and communicating.

Collecting. Collecting refers to the selection of materials from reading and writing folders that will be perused by the student and discussed with the teacher. Students should be taught to save their material, store it in folders, and then select carefully and reflectively from a plentiful collection the materials they wish to include in their literacy portfolio. Choices based on these deliberations should be placed into the portfolio and discussed during the conference. De Fina (1992) clarifies the distinction between a folder and a portfolio: The folder is a collection of *all* works, whereas the portfolio represents *selective choices* of artifacts after careful reflection.

Collaborating. It is anticipated that a community of readers and writers will emerge from classrooms in which there is a strong shared literacy focus. Students learn to interact with one another in a collaborative manner when there is sharing of books and ideas, dynamic reading response groups, and ongoing communication with the teacher. Collaboration moves along a continuum from creating rubrics to evaluating learning in a cooperative fashion. During the conference, the teacher and student establish goals, look for trends and patterns, discuss recreational reading interests, and acknowledge writing growth and accomplishments. The collaborative spirit of the conference promotes the child's metacognitive awareness and results in focused self-reflections and self-evaluations. Collaboration extends beyond the classroom and should include the family as well. A three-way teacher-parent-student conference, which Hornsby, Sukarna, and Parry (1986) call "the guts of the [reading] program" (p. 59), is an outgrowth of this collaborative process.

Consulting. Conferencing provides an opportunity for the teacher to consult with the student, parent, and others within a focused framework. This is not merely a "How's it going?" informal question time. It is a planned dialogue—a discussion, a conversation, a time to question, explain, reflect, and understand. When consulting with students and parents, much can be discovered; assessments are made, appropriate strategies for teaching can be identified, and future directions for literacy performance are determined. The teacher consults with the various participants: (1) parents, who gain additional unambiguous, authentic knowledge and feedback; (2) other teachers or specialists, who work with and know the child (i.e., science coordinator, resource room teacher or reading specialist) and can share helpful information which might require further attention; (3) administrators for future placement, individual testing, additional services or schedule changes; and (4) of course, the student.

Communicating. Effective communication is the essence of all learning but is especially crucial when assessing the literacy process. Children communicate in various ways—orally and in writing, in small and large groups, with peers when engaged in cooperative learning, and in conferences with the teacher.

Whatever the type of literacy program—balanced, traditional, best practices, or project oriented—all literacy approaches should have at their foundation a communication ideology where students and parents are all kept informed about how literacy growth is progressing. As part of the portfolio process, students need to communicate, thoughtfully and persuasively, their reasons for making particular selections in written and oral formats. Can students effectively express how this month's "best work" selection differed from the one chosen last month? Similarly, can the teacher communicate and demonstrate interest in students' growth and instructional needs in a supportive manner?

During conferences teachers must transmit and share information in an open and nonthreatening fashion. How different this is from the actual experience of the parent who wrote about her conference experience in the opening vignette of this chapter. Written communications can also occur in the form of newsletters or weekly or monthly notes to the family. These are included in the literacy portfolio and are discussed during conference time.

The teacher facilitates the four Cs: collecting, collaborating, consulting, and communicating through careful preplanning, active listening, and guided questioning. The conference process provides a focus for the students' introspective and reflective thought processes and leads to self-regulation and self-monitoring, which are essential strategic skills (Biemiller & Meichenbaum, 1992).

Planning and Implementing Effective Conferences

There are various conference formats that will be discussed in greater detail later in this chapter. They are:

   a) teacher-parent conferences
   b) teacher-parent-student conferences
   c) teacher-student conferences
   d) teacher-teacher conferences

It is essential that the teacher understands the focus of each type of literacy conference. Conferencing provides a format and structure wherein the teacher can assess performance: Are students implementing what they have been taught? Can they "show" proficiencies? Traditional assessment and standardized tests furnish a one-dimensional look at knowledge, an impersonal numerical judgement, or a single source of information. Conferences provide a multidimensional picture of the child. Using the literacy portfolio as the focal point of the conference, students are able to exhibit and demonstrate—through real products—the essential proficiencies that have been taught and learned. Much confusion and misinformation is avoided when parents, teachers, and students together review the actual products in the portfolio—drafts, final copies, logs, journals, reports, goal sheets, conference notes, projects, essays, art work, videos—all of which display the child's competencies.

Parents often approach school conferences with varied concerns and mixed reactions. Many parents are uneasy when an annual conference focuses exclusively on standardized or classroom test scores, and many parents do not have the background knowledge and familiarity with seemingly esoteric terminology to truly understand what teachers are sharing regarding technical data. Further, if the child's achievement is seen as below average, the parents may believe that blame is implied and feel responsible and guilty for their child not achieving at the expected level. Misunderstandings, rather than shared responsibility, are often the result. Even parents of students who have achieved at grade level ability or beyond may be disappointed by traditional conferences. Although they feel proud of their child's numerical achievement, blanket praise does not translate into a clear, individualized assessment of the child's particular talents, levels of success, or areas that need to be strengthened. All parents profit when the teacher presents concrete documentation through a portfolio that captures each child's proficiencies and unique personal accomplishments. Additionally, parents can share valuable insights about their children that may not be apparent to the teacher in the school environment, but can contribute to more effective learning. There is no better bond between teacher and family than that built upon the parents' feelings that the teacher truly knows their child, cares about the child, and has the insights needed to help the child develop and build necessary literacy skills.

The frequency of conferences depends on the teacher and school policy. Some educators suggest every 8 weeks, others believe conferences can be successful if held at the beginning, middle, and end of the year. They can be formally scheduled in advance or be impromptu as the need arises. It is optimal for literacy portfolios, especially those built on the Literacy Assessment Portfolio model, to be assembled and assessed four times per year. Conferences can be scheduled, formalized, and integrated into the portfolio at these times (Wiener, & Cohen, 1997).

The key to conducting an effective portfolio conference is the teacher's careful examination of, and reflection on, the child's portfolio before the conference is held. The following questions and concerns about literacy and learning should be addressed prior to the meeting:

Generic Conference Questions for the Teacher

1. Does the student build on prior knowledge (schema)? What evidence supports this?

2. How does the student implement higher order thinking skills?

3. Does the student reflect on what has been read? Is this evident through response journals, story maps, or self-assessment forms?

4. Has the student's repertoire of knowledge expanded? What data indicate this growth?

5. Are reading and writing substantiated by reports, response journals, lists, logs, and stated goals? Are reading and writing strategies being developed and applied in all curriculum areas?

6. Has the student become an active participant in the community of literacy learners? Are there anecdotal notes or other records of this?

7. Are student goals realistic and reflective of prior learning and achievement?

8. Can the student use a variety of resources for finding information and is the student developing independent learning strategies?

9. Are ideas being expressed in coherent and precise prose?

10. Has self-selected, leisure time or recreational reading increased? Is there confirmation through logs, reports, etc.?

These questions allow the teacher to assess literacy progress that goes beyond test scores and indicates performance-based, authentic skills and abilities that are embedded in daily reading and writing activities.

Conferencing and literacy portfolios are not the exclusive domain of balanced or integrative literature based classrooms. Conferencing is important regardless of the classroom arrangement, teaching style, or reading approach. In more traditional reading classrooms, as well as in programs that are more innovative, teacher-student and teacher-student-parent conferencing is equally effective. The personal interactions with the child and family allow for the exploration, assessment, and discussion of reading skills and knowledge, writing progress, accomplishments and goal setting strategies. Sharing, monitoring, questioning, encouraging, guiding, and evaluating are the components of this conference process. No one test score can compare with the richness of this information!

The conference guidelines in Figure 8–1 can be used to make conferences most effective. The conference allows for a positive relationship to develop between student, teacher, and parent. It is a time to provide guidelines that inform the family as to how they can assist and be partners in helping the child become a successful learner. The climate should not intimidate but should be comfortable for families to freely ask questions and share concerns. Flexibility is suggested. If necessary, arrange for very early morning

1. Keep topics limited.
2. Have a scheduled time for each student.
3. Set an agenda that is known to students.
4. Keep notes on the meeting (to build an anecdotal history).
5. Review only two to four literacy portfolios per day.
6. Always model good reading and writing behaviors.
7. Be an active and attentive listener.
8. Do direct teaching and minilessons on deficits as they occur during the conference. If several areas need assistance and time is limited, note the weaknesses and demonstrate those tasks, strategies, and concepts soon after in small groups or individually.
9. Determine if students have implemented ideas, concepts, and information previously taught.
10. Be sure that students know what is expected, what rubrics will be used, and by what standards they are judged.
11. Encourage student reflection and self-assessment.
12. Create a collaborative conference climate.

FIGURE 8–1 Teacher-Student conference guidelines.

conferences with refreshments so that working parents can attend before work, or evening conferences for those who cannot attend during the day. Collins (1994) reports on schools where teachers are encouraged to be creative in scheduling conferences. Some accommodate parents by arranging home visits when necessary, weekend conferences at community centers, or even meeting with parents at fast-food restaurants. If possible, in the absence of an actual meeting, a friendly and encouraging telephone call, a "conference call," can establish an open line of communication.

CONFERENCE MODELS

There are four basic types of conferences:

1. Teacher-Parent: Informational and/or evaluative
2. Teacher-Parent-Student: Assess, share curriculum goals, evaluate growth
3. Teacher-Student: Small group or individual
4. Teacher-Teacher: Additional information, insights, modify instruction

Although conferences are often discussed as if they are all the same, it is important to identify and distinguish for whom, as well as the various ways, conferences can be organized. We will share information on each of the basic conference types indicated above. All are designed to be positive interactions, to share goals and information in a cooperative manner, and to help students grow and learn more effectively. All conferences must be carefully planned in order to be optimally effective.

Teacher-Parent Conferences

Conferences with parents, guardians, or other caregivers should be informative. They must be made aware of the reading and language arts standards of the state and school district. For example, in the Northwest Allen County School Corporation in Fort Wayne, Indiana (a suburban community), the *Standards Handbook* published by the Indiana Professional Standards Board is sent to every child's home for each and every subject so that all parents can be informed. Local and district goals and their assessment standards should also be shared with parents. Teachers in the Fort Wayne Community Schools (a larger, urban community) must inform all parents in writing of the strengths and weaknesses of their child on the Indiana Statewide Teaching for Educational Progress (ISTEP), a high-stakes state reading and math test that is given in grades 3, 8, and 10. However, information is only one conference goal; the others are to assess each child's performance, to share tangible evidence of progress, to compare current and past work through concrete examples of accomplishments, and to note where assistance is still needed.

The crucial and significant role that parents play in the education of their children cannot be overstated. Educators have always known—and are now making inroads in convincing policy makers—about the importance of funding projects that create partnerships with parents for children's school success. Unfortunately, Minnesota, Virginia, and Iowa are the only states which currently require elementary school teachers to take classes in parental involvement. Morrow and Paratore (1993) cite numerous research studies which confirm and emphasize the gravity and significance of parental involvement, ranging from the importance of parents reading to their children, to intergenerational programs in schools, to intercultural programs promoting diversity in schools and communities. Conferencing involves parents, families, and guardians interacting congruently with children and teachers, and thus contributes to school and community harmony as well as the enhancement of student learning.

For parental involvement to be truly significant, interaction should be carefully planned and integrated into the classroom structure. A good example of this is a conference approach used at the Franklin Early Childhood Center in Woodmere, New York. Staff at this school give parents a conference sheet with cartoon-like drawings, which the parent goes over with the kindergarten child at home several weeks before the conference. Various behaviors are depicted on the conference sheet (e.g., "I share books with friends"); the parent discusses these first with the child and then at a joint conference involving the parent, child, and teacher. This format clearly focuses discussion on important areas of concern that can be elaborated on in greater detail during the conference (see Figure 8–2).

It must be emphasized that families newly arrived from other countries or families for whom English is not the primary language can find schools alien and frightening. Economically disadvantaged families and families of color may also feel unwelcome in schools that appear to be dominated by White, middle-class individuals (Olson, 1990). Schools should work toward lessening discomfort and bridging gaps created by feelings of cultural differences. Families must be helped to feel that their diversity is respected and can be a welcome part of the educational process, otherwise they will not attend conferences or other school programs. Finders and Lewis (1994) point out that the diversity in social and cultural backgrounds of parents are viewed as a problem rather than valued as positive attributes. Teachers and administrators must make the effort to create a welcoming school climate in which parents become partners in their children's education. Bilingual parent volunteers should be used to overcome language barriers, and if recruited as teacher's aides, they can facilitate better understanding of the school program.

Again, schools have their own culture, language, procedures, and expectations that can be intimidating to multicultural, multiethnic communities. Ethnocentric biases must be realized and challenged, and the entire school community must learn to become sensitive to diverse values, family systems, and traditions. Parents and other family members must feel welcomed and respected. Only then will parents be comfortable enough to participate in conferences and other school-sponsored projects. School, home, and community must form a partnership, with the goal being the enhancement of children learning.

Conferences with parents and other caregivers should be informational and evaluative. At the conference, teachers should share the philosophy, structure, activities, and goals of the class so that parents know the learning experiences in which their children are engaged: What journals are to be taken home? Is the child working on a specific project? What books are children expected to read at home? How long should parents read

To the parent(s)

Please review these kindergarten goals with your child and add any comments in the allotted space. Please bring this "contract" to school with you at conference time. We are looking forward to sharing our mutual expectations for your child's school success.

Comments:

FIGURE 8–2 Kindergarten teacher-parent conference form. *Source: Courtesy of Franklin Early Childhood Center, Woodmere, NY.*

to the children, and should they be listening to their children read? How can the family become appropriately involved? The Lawrence/Inwood Public School District, Long Island, New York, assists parents with such questions by distributing a parent's handbook called *Reading Process*, where the district's literacy approach is explained in nonprofessional terms, stages of literacy development are described and, most important, specific ways for parents to support their children's literacy at home are listed. Such booklets can be distributed and discussed during conferences.

Teacher-Parent-Student Conferences

Conferences must do more than inform parents; they must also assess the student's performance. As parents confer with the teacher and their child and examine and discuss the contents of the portfolio, they see tangible evidence of progress, comparing current and past performance. It is important for children to be present at conferences so they can exercise their metacognitive awareness as they reflect on their work and explain to their parents how the portfolio is representative of their growth, why a certain piece was included, or what they were trying to accomplish. This concrete demonstration of skills and problem-solving abilities is much more meaningful to parents than a single numerical grade. When students participate in the conference, the portfolio can be the centerpiece. Barbara Colton, a fifth-grade teacher from the Manhasset, New York, school district, has her students build portfolios all year and participate in conferences with their parents. The students clearly understand that the purpose of the conference is to show the parents their learning progress and curriculum work as demonstrated by their choice of portfolio entries. Colton finds that this process is both rewarding to the students and provides great satisfaction to the parents.

The conference is an ideal time to share expectations. Because accountability is stressed and standard curriculum goals are a national trend, it is important that parents be made aware of typical or normative literacy behaviors for students at grade level. Understanding this will facilitate parents' acceptance of the grading practices of the school district.

When conferencing with parent and student, in addition to discussing the student's work samples, the teacher shares anecdotal notes, records of the youngster's reading preferences and dislikes, interactions during peer editing, performance on running records, and other informal reading inventories. Figure 8–3 shows a teacher's observations about Christopher, a beginning reader. There is a great deal of positive information here that can be shared with the family during a conference about this child's beginning reading strategies and how Christopher can be assisted at home. For example, Christopher relies on picture clues to assist decoding, which is a typical beginning reading strategy that can be reinforced by appropriately using picture books at home.

Figures 8–4A and B show two parent-teacher conference reports for the same child in the first and second grades. Accomplishments are noted and shared. Jennifer's growth with journal writing is reported, phonics application is noted, and her reading behaviors are discussed. In the second-grade report, it is noteworthy that the first-grade teacher was consulted about the child's adjustment. In the second-grade class, the parent and teacher and child had three portfolio conferences during the school year in which they were able to specifically review Jennifer's progress and collaborate on ways to continue to boost her confidence.

Lindy Vizyak uses a student conference session form shown in Figures 8–5A and B for her first graders to discuss both fiction and nonfiction books. The information on these forms is clear, detailed, and easy to share with families.

A different student conference record is shown in Figure 8–6. This conference was held with a bilingual youngster who has various literacy problems but very much enjoys the Curious George books and other funny stories. Showing the parents the Curious George books and suggesting other humorous, easy-to-read material are all likely to help Chris's parents feel they can be useful in contributing to his future learning by finding appropriate books for him to read at home.

When parents leave a conference, they should have knowledge of their child's work in progress; current skill applications and abilities; and strengths, needs, and accomplishments in reading and writing as well as other learning and social behaviors. Having some print material that parents can take home to support what has been discussed (a summary report, work samples, district publications, etc.) is another good idea.

Teacher-Student Conferences

Teacher-student conferences can be held individually or in small groups. Both are useful in different ways. Teachers often have a spontaneous or informal conference with students in what Jenkins (1996) refers to as the "assess-as-you-go conference." This is different from a more formally planned portfolio conference, which often coincides with the end of marking periods, with report card dates, or with the end of the semester. During student conferences, the teacher listens a lot and asks guided questions, evalu-

Teacher's Comments
Reading: A Guide for Observation

NAME: _Christopher_ GRADE: _1_ DATE: _____

Reads willingly	*Attempts to read. Curious about books & print.*
Expects reading to make sense (Reads—not simply decodes) Reads for a purpose—enjoyment or information	*Picture reads. Tries to decode. Tries to make sense using pictures and some words.*
Draws on prior knowledge What is already known is used to read new material	*Very limited prior knowledge. Limited vocabulary—unable to name many common ideas, concepts.*
Makes reasonable predictions (Samples, confirms, disconfirms words and/or passages)	*Predicts but cannot confirm.*
Reads on or skips Fluency/rate	*Choppy, due to limited decoding skills.*
Uses pictures for cues	*Yes.*
Self-corrects	*Not able to at this time.*
Reads in "chunks" Rapidly reads phrases, such as "Once upon a time . . ."	*N/A.*
Uses knowledge of letter–sound relationships	*Consonants—but not aware of vowels in reading or writing.*
Recognizes root words and endings	*No*
Observes punctuation (periods, question marks, exclamation points)	*Observes periods and capital letters.*
Finger points	*Yes.*
Expression	*No.*

FIGURE 8–3 A teacher's observations about a beginning reader.

ates, and gives feedback. The teacher provides students with an opportunity to read aloud, discuss books, talk about their writing, or discuss reactions, problems, successes, or disappointments. Portfolio conferences are focused conversations centered on demonstrated literacy behaviors.

Individual Conferences. The one-to-one teacher-student conference or individual conference offers a rare classroom opportunity; it provides an intimate and private time for teacher and student to listen and interact without interference from others. An informal conference can be as short as 3 minutes, whereas a scheduled conference is often about 20 minutes. The goal is to obtain personalized attention and feedback from the teacher.

As much as school is a sociocultural environment, it is also a psychosocial environment that profoundly impacts children's emotional, as well as educational, needs. The individual conference allows some needed private time for teacher and student. The student doesn't have to share time with anyone but the teacher, and the focus is on the

PARENT–TEACHER CONFERENCE REPORTS: K–2

Student: _Jennifer_   Grade: _1_   Teacher: _Mrs. U._   School: _Longfellow_

FIRST CONFERENCE SUMMARY—DATE: _Dec. 2_

Attending: Student _____

Reading Level: _pre-primer_   Publisher: _Ginn_   Mother ✔

Math Level: _1_   Publisher: _Heath_   Father _____

Other _____

Jennifer is a gentle, sensitive child. She has a quiet and reserved manner. Jennifer has made a fine adjustment to the first grade. She has many friends. She is helpful and kind to others.

Jennifer is making fine progress in reading. She is developing a good sight vocabulary and is able to sound out many words. She is proud of her progress.

Jennifer is also progressing in writing. She enjoys keeping a journal and writing stories in writer's workshop. She uses invented and conventional spelling in her pieces.

Jennifer is able to add through 10, graph, pattern, subtract through 10. She enjoys using the math manipulatives.

Jennifer is exhibiting confidence in herself. She participates in small and large group discussions. Mrs. S is excited about her reading, and is pleased with her progress.

FIGURE 8–4A Parent–teacher conference report for Jennifer in first grade.

PARENT–TEACHER CONFERENCE REPORTS: K–2

Student: _Jennifer_   Grade: _2_   Teacher: _Mrs. D._   School: _Longfellow_

FIRST CONFERENCE SUMMARY—DATE: _Nov. 17_

Attending: Student _____

Reading Level: _2_   Publisher: _Ginn_   Mother ✔

Math Level: _2_   Publisher: _Addison/Wesley_   Father _____

Other _____

Mrs. S. has been in close touch with me about Jenny's adjustment in second grade. Mrs. U., Jen's first-grade teacher, said Jen relaxes gradually to new situations.

Jenny is on grade level in all areas. Her standardized reading tests reflect good beginning second-grade comprehension and vocabulary skills, and her recent test results were excellent.

Jen enjoys reading, writing, and illustrating her work. She uses mostly inventive spelling with good phonics application. Memorizing word spellings for tests poses a challenge for her.

Jenny generally understands math concepts after working with the materials. Her lack of confidence, however, increases the difficulty. Working with counters more carefully will be helpful. She needs to memorize basic addition and subtraction math facts without using fingers.

I am encouraging Jenny to focus more on class instruction and discussion. Developing greater focus and self-confidence are important goals for this year.

FIGURE 8–4B Parent-teacher conference report for Jennifer in second grade.

Student Name: _____   **FICTION**

Date: _____

Title of the book: _____

Author: _____

Directions:

Put a check if the student can answer the following questions:

_____ 1. How did you choose the book?

_____ 2. Was this book **easy, just right,** or **challenging** for you to read?

_____ 3. Describe the setting in the story.

_____ 4. Describe the main character, and give at least three telling details.

_____ 5. What do you think was the main problem in the story?

_____ 6. How was the problem solved?

_____ 7. What was your favorite part of this book?

_____ 8. Did anything surprise you in the story?

_____ 9. How would you rate the book?

_____10. Would you like to do a Book Talk for the class?

_____11. What book will you choose to read next? Title:_____

_____

Evaluation Comments:

_____

_____

_____

FIGURE 8–5A Individual reading conferences for fiction book. *Source:* Developed by Lindy Vizyak.

youngster and school-related issues and reactions. In addition to being part of a community of learners, the student also feels distinctive and unique. Additionally, the natural egocentricity among young children and the need for attention and recognition among older students are well-met in this one-to-one setting, which can be informal and unplanned or scheduled in advance.

Group Conferences. When several students participate in a conference, the agenda and focus need to be clear. In group situations, some children can be overwhelmed by their more active peers, and the group dynamics need careful monitoring to ensure that all

Student Name: _____   **NON-FICTION**

Date: _____

Title of the book: _____

Author: _____

Directions:

Put a check if the student can answer the following questions:

_____1. How did you choose this book to read?

_____2. What did you like best about this book?

_____3. Tell about four new things you learned.

_____4. What did you notice about the illustrations?

_____5. Would you like to write a special report on this topic in Writer's Workshop?

_____6. What book will you choose to read next?

Book Title: _____

_____7. Would you like to give a Book Talk to the class?

Evaluation Comments: _____

_____

_____

_____

_____

FIGURE 8–5B Individual reading conference form for non-fiction book. *Source:* Developed by Lindy Vizyak.

are profiting. Group conferences are useful in gathering information for future instruction, monitoring the dynamics of groups that are working together, and observing each youngster's performance in a group. This is especially important in project-oriented classrooms with a great deal of collaborative work. How does each individual child function in these small group settings? The teacher should be aware of the dynamics inherent in group settings such as shyness or a tendency to dominate, as well as whether a group can stay focused. Assigning different roles to various group members (including a recorder to take notes during conferences) is another way of keeping group conferences productive.

Scheduling. The conference is a precious time that many children look forward to and treasure. Therefore, it must be carefully respected and planned for. Scheduled conference times should never be flippantly canceled or rushed. A timetable should be carefully scheduled, displayed, and rigidly adhered to so that conference time is not disrupted or

Reading Conference Record

(Responses were dictated by the child to the teacher.)

Date: _____ *April 25* _____

Name: _____ *Chris* _____

Title of the book discussed: _____ *Curious George* _____

Author of book _____ *H. A. Rey* _____

Reason for picking this book _____ *Because I like monkeys. They are really silly.* _____

Tell me something interesting about this story. _____ *He gets in really big trouble. He made a really big mess with ink.* _____

How do you plan to report on this book? _____ *I will draw a picture.* _____

Have you read any other books by this author? _____ *No.* _____

Would you like to? _____ *Yes, because he makes good books.* _____

Teacher's notes: _____ *Chris enjoys Curious George books very much. Share other books in the series with him. Provide other easy reading books that may be about animals and are humorous. Parents can follow up on this at home. Chris can also be encouraged to describe the picture he draws for his report, and an aide or another student can transcribe this. A language experience approach strategy should be continued.* _____

FIGURE 8–6 Student–teacher conference form for a bilingual first-grade student.

delayed. Those students who are not involved in a conference need to be busy and should be aware of collaboratively established guidelines so that conferences are not frequently interrupted or intruded on for inappropriate reasons.

Promote Success With Student Conferences. Growth must be monitored so that appropriate instructional changes can be made (Rhodes & Shanklin, 1993). As the literacy portfolio is discussed during a conference, the teacher notes how to change teaching strategies to meet the students' unique needs "so that students can take control of their own learning and teachers can improve their instruction" (Winograd, 1994, p. 421). Teachers learn to carefully listen to the children as they explain their thinking and learning processes.

In addition to focused listening, the following factors may be helpful in gaining a total picture of the student and are an integral part of the conference process: self-selection of material, rubrics, and criteria setting, record keeping, self-assessment, analysis of trends and patterns, noting strengths, and attending to weaknesses.

Self-selection Students learn to select materials that go into the literacy portfolio from mini-lessons and class discussions. Some materials are easier than others to assemble. For example, youngsters go through their folders, make specific decisions and selections using certain guidelines, and then are prepared to discuss their work during the conference.

Rubrics and other stated criteria Rubrics, as previously described in other chapters, are a set of scoring guidelines that indicate traits and dimensions of effectiveness on which the student will be assessed. They can provide structure for the conference and pinpoint standards useful for collaborative evaluation of actual work. They also provide a guide to assist the student in developing a strategy for meeting appropriate levels of performance. Figure 8–7 is a sample rubric that was developed by a group of third graders and their teacher in Garden City, New York, to help assess a piece of writing.

Record keeping Records must be maintained of verbal, informal, and formal assessments of the students' learning. Teachers must avoid becoming too entangled with record keeping so that they become overwhelmed or disheartened with the process. A loose-leaf notebook with tabs for each student is uncomplicated and functional. It is also convenient to keep a clipboard and small self-stick note pads handy to jot down notes as individual students are observed while reading with peers in small literacy groups or in reader's and writer's workshops. These notes are later transferred to the appropriate loose-leaf page and discussed during the conference.

Stice, Bertrand, and Bertrand (1995) suggest maintaining three types of records that both document and reflect on children's growth: (1) records of children's work, dated and retained to show changes and progress over time; (2) the teacher's informal observation records, including informal notes, observation summaries, and checklists, which are later incorporated into more formal records; and (3) the teacher's formal observations, such as miscue analysis, running records, conference notes, records of literature logs and response journals, and published works.

Students are also responsible for assisting with record keeping. For example, to make conferencing easier, they should include a table of contents that lists everything in the portfolio. Of course, journals, logs, and book facts are also a form of record keeping that reveal reading summaries, reactions, and reflections. During the conference, the teacher can record a summary of topics discussed as well as any related activities or strategies that should be undertaken. A copy of this should be provided to the student and a copy should be kept in the teacher's records and shared during teacher-parent conferences.

Teaching to needs During the conference, the teacher does more listening than talking. De Fina (1992) emphasizes that this is not a time to criticize or point out failure but is instead an ideal time to identify areas to be improved on, to give suggestions, and to plan strategies. A portfolio conference is not the time to overwhelm students with their deficiencies. As Jenkins (1996) states, "I am ever mindful . . . that is more important for [the student] to leave the conference with a sense of his accomplishments, and with two or three new learnings (across content and mechanics) which have been prioritized than with a head full of 'What I didn't do right'" (p. 231).

The conference also provides an ideal opportunity for on-the-spot teaching. As the student reads aloud or explains his or her work, the teacher notes not only what the student knows and has accomplished but what the student doesn't know. Allington (1994) indicates that in spite of all the rhetoric about curricula reform, children still do too little reading and teachers still do too much asking and assigning without enough actual instruction. "Children need fewer brief, shallow literary activities and many more extended opportunities to read and write" (Allington, 1994, p. 21).

Analyzing trends and patterns Some of the conference outcomes will be the ability to assess what each student can do, to analyze progress made, to determine together what the student has not incorporated into his or her schema that must be addressed, and to establish short-range learning goals. Without analyzing children's reading and writing patterns, without looking at trends in their literacy behaviors, the literacy portfolio conference would become merely an empty exercise. Instead, the conference allows for the verbalization of a reflective process: The students reflect on why they included specific materials and they self-assess their past performance.

Writing Rubric—Grade 3

	4	3	2	1
Mechanics	You extensively use correct punctuation, spelling, and capitalization.	You usually use correct punctuation, spelling, and capitalization.	You sometimes have errors in punctuation, spelling, and capitalization. Your writing is hard to understand.	You rarely use proper punctuation, capitalization, and spelling. Your writing is difficult to comprehend.
Imaginative language	You extensively use specific, vivid language appropriately.	You often use impressive vocabulary words appropriately.	You sometimes use new vocabulary words. You depend on many of the same familiar words (e.g., good, nice).	You rarely use interesting vocabulary.
Organization	Your writing is well-organized; you develop a clear plan. Your ideas are sequentially developed.	Your organization of ideas is usually clear. You develop your topic in an acceptable manner.	Your organization of ideas is not always clear. You have not really developed your topic.	Your organization is extremely weak. Your writing lacks a plan of organization. You rarely develop your topic.
Purpose	You take responsibility and ownership for your writing. You demonstrate a sense of audience and task.	You usually demonstrate a sense of audience and task. You are aware of your responsibility.	You sometimes do not demonstrate a sense of audience and task. You depend on others too much.	You don't establish a sense of audience.
Focus	Your ideas are clear and focused.	Your ideas and focus are usually clear.	Your writing is sometimes unfocused.	Your ideas are unclear and unfocused.
Craft	You clearly show skillful application of the writing process through attention to the use of engaging leads, interesting endings, relevant and appropriate supportive details, and varied sentence structure.	You usually show application of the writing process. You sometimes need teacher prompting.	You sometimes show application of the writing process. You often need teacher prompting.	You do not demonstrate knowledge and application of the steps of the writing process. You always need teacher prompting.

FIGURE 8–7 Sample rubric developed by third-grade students and their teacher.

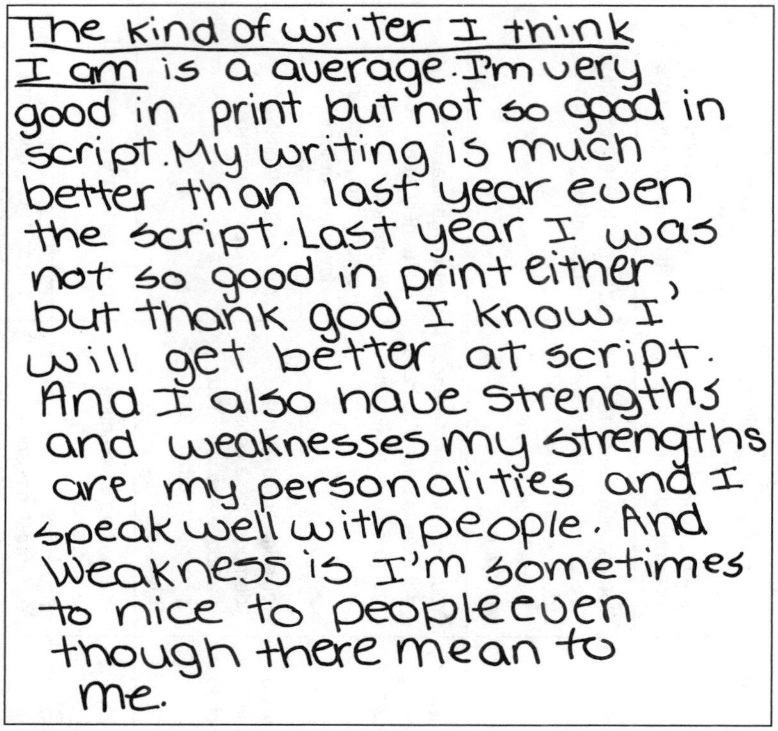

The kind of writer I think I am is a average. I'm very good in print but not so good in script. My writing is much better than last year even the script. Last year I was not so good in print either, but thank god I know I will get better at script. And I also have strengths and weaknesses my strengths are my personalities and I speak well with people. And weakness is I'm sometimes to nice to people even though there mean to me.

FIGURE 8–8 A fifth-grader's writing self-assessment.

In Figure 8–8 a fifth grader assesses herself as a writer. A teacher would obviously see many errors in this selection, such as word choice (there/they're, too/to). But again, a conference should focus on positives, and although intervention is needed in some areas, mechanical problems should not receive overriding attention and overwhelm a student; an overcorrected, red-penciled essay serves little constructive help. It is noteworthy that this student takes pride in printing legibly, in her personality, and in her effective speaking ability. She's optimistic about the likelihood of self-improvement, and the number of technical errors should not diminish her accomplishments, undermine an excellent sense of self, nor overpower her with too many areas for correction.

Teachers reflect on the effectiveness of their own instructional strategies and note trends from previous conferences. The analysis of patterns indicates the student's strengths, needs, and areas that are developing slowly. Some can be addressed with demonstrations and modeling during the conference or with a focused minilesson later, or they can be the topic for a group or whole-class lesson.

Teaching students how to have a conference For student-teacher conferences to be productive, students must learn how to engage in a conference. Jenkins (1996, pp. 227–228) suggests an approach for teaching children about writing conferences that is useful for all student conferences. She tells her third-grade students that the purpose of a conference is to learn from one another and that students will be expected to lead the conference. The tone of the interaction is most important so that the students feel respected. A dry-run conference is conducted for all students to observe, and the teacher role-plays a student who is going to share her portfolio with the teacher. The teacher, acting as the student, thinks aloud during the conference, describes the portfolio contents and explains her entries. After the role play, the class discusses what was observed and what was learned.

The format and topics of conferences will vary based on the purpose of the conference and the age and ability of the students. Even if students have had other experiences with conferences in previous grades, it is a good idea early in the school year to discuss how conferences will be conducted. Some teachers have a student sit in on another student's conference (after obtaining the permission of the conferee), and this can be done in tandem. However, if sensitive matters will be discussed, a conference should be confidential. Once students have learned how to have a conference with the teacher, this will, of course, assist them in conferring with each other as well as during parent conferences.

Teacher-Teacher Conferences

In every classroom it is not merely the students who are learning; the teacher is learning as well. Calkins (1983), Graves (1983), Stice, Bertrand, and Bertrand (1995), and Templeton (1991), among others, discuss the important concept of teacher as learner. As teachers learn new concepts and ideas for portfolios and journals, they should share this knowledge with their colleagues informally (e.g., over a cup of coffee in the teachers' lounge), or more formally (e.g., in planned faculty meetings and staff development seminars). An ideal method of sharing knowledge is a teacher-teacher mentoring program: A teacher who is comfortable and familiar with student-centered learning, employing extensive use of literature, is paired with a teacher who is unfamiliar with these approaches. Portfolio practices, pedagogical strategies, and conference guidelines can thus be shared, and even an experienced teacher benefits from support through dialogue with colleagues.

Teachers also need to share information about students who are enrolled in special programs or students who are instructed by a team. In teacher-teacher conferences, an instructional team can learn about a child in the regular classroom setting, and the classroom teacher learns about the child in other school settings, resulting in a collaborative, reflective, and holistic perspective. Too seldom do team members meet to collaborate on effective instructional methods and to share evidence of a student's progress as well as their concerns. For students receiving special education and ESL services, it is imperative that teachers have regular conference time. At mandated Committee on Special Education meetings, a student's portfolio provides concrete evidence of actual performance, which is helpful in supplementing information from standardized testing. A literacy portfolio provides evidence of a student's achievement because it is filled with representative samples of work, logs and records, and selected projects, so it should be shared with all of a child's teachers. As mentioned in earlier chapters, the final portfolio—edited, modified, and supplemented each year—should move on with the child as part of the permanent record.

Thus, teacher-teacher conferences have at least three purposes: (1) to receive additional information, (2) to understand the whole child, and (3) to adapt instructional strategies to meet student needs. The ability to make informed decisions requires conferencing with other teachers to effectively determine the child's progress and performance, socialization, and personal interactions in all school-related areas.

Conferences with future teachers provide authentic material, not merely a grade or test score, so that an appropriate and meaningful instructional program can be designed based on review, assessment, and evaluation of actual performance and progress. By reviewing the literacy portfolio, future teachers gain insight into students' writing abilities, reading accomplishments, and developmental achievements. This allows for appropriate instructional plans and modification of curricula and pedagogical directions. Paris (1991) indicates that the goals of portfolios and the new approaches to literacy assessment not only increase students' engagement in thoughtful reading and writing activities and provide detailed records of literacy development but also empower teachers by providing many instructional opportunities.

CONCLUSION

The primary purpose of assessment is to provide helpful, reliable, and authentic information about how children are learning, growing, and improving. Conferencing with data-filled children's work collected in portfolios is an excellent means to this end. Clay (1993), Goodman (1986), and Graves (1983), among others, strongly advocate evaluation, not through a nonproductive grading system but through self-assessment, cooperative learning, peer collaboration, and oral and written self-reflections. Educational reform, increased use of assessment measures, and rigorous standards are no longer buzz words but are the directions now being taken by schools across the country. We must use the strategies that we know are constructive to implement effective educational change. The benefits of conferencing with children, parents, and other teachers must be recognized as an integral part of the assessment process, indicating personal interactions, effective communication, growth over time, and thoughtful reflection in the pursuit of successful literacy accomplishments.

REFERENCES

Allington, R. (1994, September). The schools we have. The schools we need. *The Reading Teacher, 48,* 14–27.

Biemiller, A., & Meichenbaum, D. (1992, October). The nature and nurture of the self-directed learner. *Educational Leadership, 50*(2), 75–80.

Calkins, L. (1983). *Lessons from a child: On the teaching and learning of writing.* Portsmouth, NH: Heinemann.

Clay, M. (1993). *An observation survey of early literacy achievement.* Portsmouth, NH: Heinemann.

Collins, C. (1994). The teacher conference: A team effort. *The New York Times* (November 24), C9.

Courtney, A., & Abodeeb, T. (1999). Diagnostic-reflective portfolios. *The Reading Teacher, 52*(7), 708–714.

De Fina, A. (1992). *Portfolio assessment: Getting started.* New York: Scholastic.

Edmondson, J. (2001). Taking a broader look: Reading literacy education. *The Reading Teacher, 54*(6), 620–628.

Finders, M., & Lewis, C. (1994, May). Why some parents don't come to school. *Educational Leadership, 51,* 8.

Gill, S. R. (2000). Reading with Amy: Teaching and learning through conferences. *The Reading Teacher, 53*(6), 500–508.

Goodman, K. (1986). *What's whole in whole language?* Portsmouth, NH: Heinemann.

Graves, D. (1983). *Writing: Teachers and children at work.* Portsmouth, NH: Heinemann.

Hornsby, D., Sukarna, D., & Parry, J. (1986). *Read on: A conference approach to reading.* Portsmouth, NH: Heinemann.

Jenkins, C. B. (1996). *Inside the writing portfolio.* Portsmouth, NH: Heinemann.

Morrow, L. M., & Paratore, J. (1993). Family literacy: Perspective and practices. *The Reading Teacher, 47*(3), 194–200.

Olson, L. (1990, 24 April). Parents as partners: Redefining the social contract between families and schools. *Education Week, 9*(28), 17–24.

Paris, S. G. (1991, May). Portfolio assessment for young readers. *The Reading Teacher, 44,* 9.

Rhodes, L. K., & Shanklin, N. (1993). *Windows into literacy: Assessing learners K–8.* Portsmouth, NH: Heinemann.

Stice, C. F., Bertrand, J., & Bertrand, N. (1995). *Integrating reading and the other language arts: Foundations of a whole language curriculum.* Belmont, CA: Wadsworth.

Templeton, S. (1991). *Teaching the integrated language arts.* Dallas: Houghton Mifflin.

Tierney, R. J., Readance, J., & Dishner, E. (1995). *Reading strategies and practices.* Needham Heights, MA: Allyn & Bacon.

Wiener, R., & Cohen, J. (1997). *Literacy assessment portfolios: Using assessment to guide instruction.* Upper Saddle River, NJ: Merrill/Prentice Hall.

Winograd, P. (1994, February). Developing alternative assessments: Six problems worth solving. *The Reading Teacher, 47,* 420–423.

Literacy Portfolios for Diverse Learners

by

Leslie C. Soodak, Ph.D.
Associate Professor, Pace University,
New York

and

Beverly Parke, Ph.D.
Assistant Professor, Indiana Purdue University,
Ft. Wayne, Indiana

KEY WORDS AND CONCEPTS

IDEA/PL 94-142	diagnostic-prescriptive mode
deficit model	direct instruction
ability model	constructivist model
inclusion	integrated literacy instruction
reductionist model	

Assessing students with diverse abilities has been one of the greatest challenges educators have faced in the past 25 years. With the advent of PL 101-476, the reauthorization of the Individuals with Disabilities Education Act (1990) and its historic predecessor, PL 94-142, the Education for All Handicapped Children Act (1975), guidelines for assessing students with disabilities and concomitant procedural safeguards have been defined. The result has been an ongoing struggle to determine the most effective and least invasive manner to assess students with disabilities.

Assessment in special education is for one purpose—decision making. Berdine and Meyer (1987) list five decision points essential to special education: screening and identification; eligibility and diagnosis; placement and individual education plan (IEP) development; instructional planning and programming; and instructional program evaluation. The responsibility for conducting assessments lies with school psychologists, classroom teachers, special educators, and others who are part of the system that schools use to coordinate the delivery of services to this population. The process of ensuring that fair and accurate information is obtained and considered in decision making is labor-intensive and time-consuming. Ask school psychologists how they spend the preponderance of their time and they are sure to cite the assessment activities required under the special education statutes.

NEW DIRECTIONS IN SPECIAL EDUCATION ASSESSMENT PRACTICES

Historically, special education assessment teams have relied almost exclusively on the use of standardized tests. At a time when the field was characterized as one of *deficit*, these tests were used to determine the extent and type of deficiencies present in students who were referred to special education. However, an *ability* model is currently replacing this deficit approach as political and pragmatic forces have intervened. Taylor (2000) expresses the opinion of many when he points out that standardized tests rely heavily on recall and rote learning, which are only a fragment of the skills that students develop. The movement to provide more meaningful assessment information has led to a greater reliance on performance-based assessment "to more accurately depict what students can do" (Langerfield, Thurlow, & Scott, 1997, p. 93). Students with diverse abilities are benefiting from this change because it gives them a platform from which to display the many skills they possess. Focusing on ability rather than disability has created the need for methods and materials that display skills rather than document deficiency. Authentic assessment measures are filling the void.

There are three factors that account for the rapid move toward more authentic assessment procedures in special education. The first involves state and federal laws that regulate special education services. Educators and legislators wrestle with the best way to assure a *free and appropriate* education for students with disabilities. As new regulations are enacted, practices are changed to be in compliance with the laws. Initially, PL 94-142 established six principles that shaped special education service delivery. All of these principles impact on assessment procedures in some way. The principles include: zero reject, nondiscriminatory assessment, individualized education programs (IEPs), least restrictive environment, due process, and parental participation. Although PL 94-142 provides guidelines for conducting fair and unbiased student evaluations, it does not mandate the types of assessment measures that should be used in determining eligibility, developing instructional plans, or monitoring student progress. Thus, districts are constantly seeking tools and procedures that will serve their assessment needs.

The second factor that has influenced assessment practices in special education is inclusion. Although there is no single definition of *inclusion*, it is seen as the right of all students with disabilities to remain in mainstream classrooms and to be provided with the support necessary for full participation and individual growth. Effective inclusive schooling results in a dynamic partnership between special and general educators that benefits all students.

Because of greater diversity among students in classrooms and teacher accountability at an all time high, teachers are motivated to adopt instructional methods that help all students learn. "What do I do?" is a question voiced regularly to special educators as classroom teachers focus on the development and delivery of instructional activities that are appropriate for all students. In order to do so, they must determine what their students know, what they need to know, and through which instructional strategies they best learn. These pragmatic concerns drive decision making and result in the content and processes used in instruction. Assessment is used to define the universe of "what and how." Only the most comprehensive skills-based assessments yield this information. Intelligence (IQ) tests take a backseat when determining if a student can decode words. Scoring in the 35th percentile in reading is not helpful when determining if a student can write a friendly letter. Having to be accountable for demonstrating that students have made progress in constructing paragraphs is difficult if the only tool a teacher has to gauge progress is a norm-referenced measure. Thus, teachers are moving to pragmatic, authentic assessment measures that register small increments of growth in meaningful activities. The need for instructionally relevant information has resulted in the use of new of data-gathering procedures (e.g., skills inventories, writing samples, journals).

Inclusion will work only if all those involved strive to make it happen (Soodak & Erwin, 1995). Portfolio assessment facilitates inclusion by providing flexibility and encouraging teachers to look at the development of students as indicated by the students' body of work and to reflect on whether their goals and methods are effective in meeting the needs of all students, including those with disabilities.

The last factor leading to change in assessment practices is the growing acceptance of holistic measures (Keefe, 1992) in education. As with diagnostic measures, holistic measures have found their place. Areas not typically measured through standardized tests are now targeted for assessment. Finding ways to give "holistic views of student strengths and weaknesses" (Overton, 1996, p. 250) has found a niche in the overall assessment plan for students with special needs.

Skills needed for communication, literacy, and personal independence are essential for students with disabilities and are often listed among their IEP objectives. Measuring growth in these areas is difficult if the assessment team relies solely on standardized, norm-referenced tests. The limitations of standardized tests are readily apparent in literacy assessment. Because objectivity is central to standardized testing, standardized tests focus on skills that can be scored for accuracy, such as word recognition and comprehension skills. Standardized tests do not reveal how students use written and spoken language to communicate, including their ability to convey meaning, take the perspective of the listener/reader, and comprehend implicit as well as explicit meaning. Thus, these tests cannot provide a complete picture of students' abilities.

In contrast, Meltzer & Reed (1994) affirm that other assessment strategies are available. They find new assessment trends to be more:

- holistic and dynamic;
- multidimensional;
- reflective of students' metacognitive processes and strategic learning;
- accountable for the ongoing interactions among development and curricular effects; and
- related to instruction than in the past.

Authentic assessment procedures such as teacher-made tests, student self-evaluations, parent checklists, portfolios, videotapes, sociograms, and interviews make it easier to demonstrate skill development and program effectiveness as required by state and federal mandates. Most important, authentic measures provide information that is useful to classroom teachers working with diverse learners.

RETHINKING THE ROLE OF ASSESSMENT AND INSTRUCTION IN SPECIAL EDUCATION

In recent years, the number of students identified as having disabilities has grown at an alarming rate (Heward, 2000). This has caused concern because of the high expenditures needed for special education, including costs to the individual, in terms of the psychological effects of labeling (Ysseldyke, Algozzine, & Thurlow, 1992), and to society, in terms of the allocation of limited resources (Lipsky & Gartner, 1989). Concern also stems from the overrepresentation of students from minority and low-income backgrounds who are classified and placed in special education (Cummins, 1984). As educators grapple with cutoff scores and debate new categories, students continue to be labeled and served in various settings. The ease with which students are identified, which Ysseldyke and Algozzine (1982) characterized as an "overidentification phenomenon" (p. 122), coupled with the unlikely event of decertification (Gottlieb, 1985), has led to concern over current assessment and instructional practices.

The use of standardized tests is further complicated by the potential sources of error that are introduced by the "one-shot" approach to testing, which is typically used in administering this type of test. Students are usually tested once, outside their classrooms, by specialists they may or may not know. Clearly, students' performance is likely to be negatively affected by such factors as limitations in students' attention, the artificiality of the testing environment, and unfamiliarity with the tester. Bartoli and Botel (1988) argue that the use of tests that focus on isolated skills and evaluate performance at an arbitrary and static point in time underestimate student ability and may result in the diagnosis of a disability stemming from the evaluation procedures, rather than an actual problem in need of correction. It is particularly troubling that standardized tests are used to confirm the existence of a disability, given that students are often referred for evaluation because of poor performance on these same tests.

Additional questions have arisen as to whether it is wise to conduct assessments that result in exposing children to labels that do not reflect distinguishable categories. Also being discussed is whether the educational services provided to these students are effective (Lipsky & Gartner, 1989; Ysseldyke et al., 1992), particularly in the area of literacy instruction (Thomas & Barksdale-Ladd, 1994). Underlying these questions is concern about the very assumptions upon which current assessment and instructional practices have developed. Specifically being challenged is the reductionist approach to special education, which has prevailed for the past 25 years.

The Reductionist Model: Effects on Assessment and Instruction

Reductionist theory maintains that phenomena—people, ideas, concepts, etc.—are best understood when their component parts are identified and analyzed. Thus, a person is known when discrete skills and behaviors are evaluated; ideas are best understood when each component has been examined. In special education, reductionist theory has helped promote a deficit model of service by implying that the source of a student's problem is within the student, that is, disabilities are something that individuals have and identification of the deficit is needed in order to provide appropriate intervention. This assumption has had a profound effect on policies and practices in special education. The identification of disabilities takes place through an assessment process that focuses almost exclusively on revealing and analyzing the individual's deficits. Standardized, norm-referenced measures of intelligence and achievement are used to identify disabilities because, theoretically, they enable the evaluator to identify areas in which the individual is atypical. The student's identified deficits are then used as the basis for determining the disability category and to develop an appropriate educational plan for remediating the identified deficits.

Linking assessment and instructional practices based on an individual's weaknesses is commonly known as the *diagnostic-prescriptive model* of teaching. In special education, identified deficits are formally linked to educational goals in the student's IEP. Thus, skills in which the student is deficient become the basis for the student's curriculum. The teaching method that follows from this deficit model typically involves breaking down, or task analyzing, the targeted skill into its component parts and teaching each discrete unit using drill and practice. This method of teaching, often referred to as *direct instruction*, has been the most popular method of teaching in special education.

Practices based on reductionist theory have an appealing simplicity, but learning is not so simple. It is a complex process through which individuals attempt to make sense of their environment. It involves not only the use of specific skills but the individual's background knowledge, experiences, and emotions, as well as the interaction of these factors within the learning environment. According to Vygotsky (1978), development does not necessarily precede cognitive readiness for instruction; rather, a child's instruction interacts with the child's development. For students with learning and emotional problems, the importance of considering environmental factors in assessing performance is critical in that both intrinsic and extrinsic factors have been implicated in learning disabilities, emotional disorders, and mental retardation. Therefore, understanding a student's learning and emotional problems requires more than identifying isolated deficits; intrinsic and extrinsic factors must be assessed before determination of disabilities is made.

A second problem with applying reductionist theory to students with disabilities lies in its effects on curriculum and instruction. Basing instruction on an individual's deficit results in a splintered curriculum with no coherent framework for determining what is taught. Teaching isolated skills through drill and practice decontextualizes learning and hinders students from connecting and integrating new knowledge to that which was previously learned. Because higher-order thinking requires students to make connections among learned facts and principles, instruction that focuses on the mere acquisition of discrete parts does not promote this level of learning.

An Alternative Approach for Students With Disabilities: A Constructivist Model

An alternative theoretical framework that has gained interest posits that we learn through a *constructivist model*. Rather than viewing the learner as a passive recipient of discrete skills, this model holds that the learner actively constructs meaning and, therefore, is an integral part of the learning process. Learning occurs because it has meaning in light of the learner's background knowledge. Instruction based on holistic principles meets the needs of students with learning and emotional disabilities because it accommodates diverse learning styles without sacrificing the richness associated with higher-level learning. Most important, educational practices based on constructivist thinking encourage consideration of a multiplicity of factors that contribute to learning before arriving at diagnostic or instructional decisions. The overriding question therefore changes from "What is wrong with the student?" to "Why is the student not learning?"

CONSTRUCTING KNOWLEDGE THROUGH INTEGRATED LITERACY INSTRUCTION

In teaching literacy to students with disabilities, the importance of employing a holistic orientation becomes salient. Traditional approaches to learning language often view reading, writing, and speaking as discrete areas of functioning. On the assumption that smaller is better, component skills within each of these areas are taught to students in an effort to build competency and simplify learning. In *integrated literacy instruction*, language learning is viewed as a natural process that incorporates all modes of communication. Providing a real purpose for reading, writing, and speaking motivates students. Teachers who use an integrated language arts approach to learning focus on understandings and interpretations.

In holistic instruction, obtaining the right answer is de-emphasized as comprehension gains importance, thereby reducing stress on learners who are accustomed to failure. Thomas and Barksdale-Ladd (1994) point out that whole language literacy instruction provides a psychologically safe environment that encourages risk taking and reduces students' fear of failure. In fact, students are expected to assume responsibility for their own learning; they are given choices regarding the methods and materials they will use to acquire information and share their knowledge. Teachers who use holistic instruction can accommodate greater diversity than teachers who promote discrete skill instruction, because the emphasis is on forming a community of learners—a must in the inclusive classroom; both the goals and the methods encourage interaction and acceptance.

Heterogeneous instruction, where students are not labeled or separated by disability or achievement, is often used in holistic classrooms because cooperative learning is valued as a way of discovering how others think and learn. Attention to individual needs is provided for during individual conferences and by instruction in small groups that are flexibly formed and often are of short duration. This type of instruction accommodates diversity and is particularly important as we move away from segregated instruction of students with disabilities to mainstream instruction.

The potential benefits of using integrated literacy instruction have only recently been realized as special education teachers begin to abandon drill-and-practice methods in favor of more holistic approaches to language instruction. Teachers consistently point out that the benefits exceed academic gains because this approach enhances students' self-esteem and motivation to learn (Brazee & Haynes, 1989; Scala, 1993). Teachers indicate that the structured flexibility inherent in holistic teaching allows them to accommodate a wide range of student abilities and learning styles.

CONSTRUCTIVISM AND ASSESSMENT: COMPLETING THE CIRCLE OF CHANGE

Constructivist thinking has the potential to change the way students with disabilities are taught, as teachers focus on student strengths and provide greater meaning, function, and context to what is being taught. Integrated, thematic literacy instruction provides an opportunity for students with special needs to assume active and interactive roles during learning. However, unless the assumptions underlying these instructional modifications are extended to the assessment of students' learning, real and important change will not occur.

For example, if the diagnosis of learning disabilities continues to be based on deficits identified through standardized testing and if a student's curriculum is derived exclusively from these deficits, it is unlikely that the student's instructional plan will reflect the coherence associated with holistic instruction. Most important, the growth that students experience within an integrated literacy program may not be evident on traditional measures of student achievement. For curricular innovation to be complete, assessment of learning must capture the richness of new instructional processes. Too often, curricular innovations are not reflected in teachers' assessment practices, even when the apparent incompatibilities between the two are recognized (Soodak & Martin-Kniep, 1994). It is critical that curricular reform be extended to the assessment of student learning in a deliberate and rational manner.

The changes needed to align assessment practices with the goals of integrated literacy instruction are not radical, because special education teachers already assess students in valid, informal ways whenever they observe, teach, conference, and question their students. Effective special educators engage in ongoing assessment and base clinical judgments and educational decisions on a body of information they gather about their students. Many of the essential elements of authentic assessment are reflected in what is already being done on an informal basis by teachers who have long recognized the limitations of the formal evaluation process used to assess students in special education.

AUTHENTIC ASSESSMENT: EVALUATING STUDENTS IN SPECIAL EDUCATION

Changes in the assessment of students in special education are being called for by professional organizations (Executive Committee of the Council for Children with Behavior Disorders, 1989), researchers (Gahagan, 1994; Salvia & Ysseldyke, 1995), and classroom teachers (Crowley, 1989; Hobbs, 1993). Attention is being drawn to the use of authentic assessment and several models of authentic assessment (Bartoli & Botel, 1988; Glazer & Searfoss, 1988; Rhodes & Dudley-Marling, 1988) have been proposed as alternatives to standardized testing. Although each of these models differs to some degree in definition and emphasis, a number of important factors are common to each. Consistent with authentic assessment, each proposal recognizes the need for assessment to be (1) curriculum-embedded, (2) continuous, (3) varied in method, (4) varied in context, and (5) appropriate and sensitive to the student's developmental and cultural background. Perhaps most important, authentic tasks and contexts are used to sample both process- and product-oriented dimensions of learning (Valencia, 1990) often omitted in the assessment of students with disabilities. Additionally, the principles underlying alternative assessment are consistent with broader definitions of literacy by viewing reading, writing, and speaking as interrelated processes.

Several differences between authentic assessment and traditional approaches relate to the assessment of students with learning difficulties. Authentic assessment focuses on students' ability to construct and use knowledge, whereas traditional assessment focuses on isolating and identifying deficits. Figure 9–1 outlines important differences between authentic and traditional assessment methods in special education.

Perspectives on Portfolios

Portfolios are one form of authentic assessment that has particular relevance in special education. Choate, Enright, Miller, Poteet, and Rakes (1995) noted that portfolios establish a system that leads to organized collections of student work, which can include many forms of authentic assessment, such as work samples, observation records, and interview data. As in general education applications, the collection must include student involvement in selecting contents, the criteria for selection of entries, the criteria for judging merit, and documentation of student self-reflection (Paulson, Paulson, & Meyer, 1991). Many educators have made convincing arguments for the use of portfolios in the literacy assessment of students in general education (Graves & Sunstein, 1992). The needs of students with learning difficulties coupled with the unique role of assessment in special education provide the basis for an equally compelling argument for the use of portfolios in special education. This argument can be made from three perspectives: the student, the parents, and the teacher.

Portfolio assessment, characterized by Stiggins (1997) as a "collection of contributing assessments" (p. 453), has the potential to facilitate affective and cognitive development in a population of learners characterized as having deficits in both these areas. Reversing the negative effects of experiences with repeated failure involves restoring the students' sense of control over their own learning, which is achieved through experiencing earned success (Deshler, Schumaker, Lenz, & Ellis, 1984). Portfolios can assist in reversing feelings of learned helplessness by providing an opportunity for students to showcase work representing their accomplishments, thus focusing on strengths rather than on deficits. Furthermore, involving students in the selection of work to be included, as well as in the development and use of criteria for evaluating the work, may empower otherwise passive learners by actively engaging them in the evaluation process. Crowley (1989) described how self-evaluation in portfolio assessment increased the self-esteem, motivation, and risk-taking behaviors of seventh-grade students who had been labeled learning disabled for most of their school careers. According to Crowley (1989), "each, in his own way and in his own time, learned to value himself as an able learner" (p. 244). It has also been noted that when engaging in the portfolio process, students receive

Authentic Assessment	Traditional Assessment
1. The primary goal of assessment is to inform instruction.	1. The primary goal of assessment is the diagnosis of deficits.
2. The focus of assessment is on the processes underlying students' natural learning (e.g., the use of prior knowledge, learning strategies, self-monitoring skills).	2. The focus of assessment is on the products of learning, that is, the recall of information assumed to have been taught.
3. Assessment is ongoing and continuous; conclusions are tentative.	3. Testing occurs once; results are assumed to be conclusive.
4. Assessment documents changes over time, allowing the individual's growth to be evaluated.	4. Assessment involves comparisons to a "norm" group, which may or may not be representative of the test taker.
5. Assessment is curriculum-embedded; performance is evaluated in light of teacher expectations and instructional methods.	5. Assessment employs artificial tasks; setting and task demands are excluded from the assessment.
6. Students' cultural and linguistic backgrounds are considered in the evaluation.	6. Homogeneity of students' cultural and linguistic background is assumed.
7. The assessment process recognizes the interrelationships among literacy, academics, social skills, and classroom behavior.	7. The assessment considers each domain and skill to be discrete.
8. Multiple sources of information are used to confirm tentative conclusions regarding the students' performance.	8. Each source of information is used to provide a unique perspective on student functioning.
9. The classroom teacher plays a critical role in assessment; clinical judgment is valued.	9. The classroom teacher plays little or no role in assessment; objectivity is valued.
10. Students actively participate in the assessment; self-evaluation is an integral part of the assessment.	10. Students' participation in the assessment is minimal; students are rarely informed of test results.

FIGURE 9–1 Comparison between authentic and traditional assessment methods in special education. *Source:* Copyright 1993 From "A holistic/wellness model of reading assessment: An alternative to the medical model" in *Reading and Writing Quarterly, 10,* p. 109 by L. W. Searfoss. Adapted by permission of Taylor & Francis, Inc., http://www.routledge-ny.com

more attention (Montgomery, 2001). The benefits of greater interaction cannot be discounted.

Portfolio assessment encourages students to reflect on their own growth, to learn how to use metacognitive strategies, and to evaluate areas in which additional learning is needed. In other words, portfolios motivate students to think about their own learning. Because student work is evaluated over time and growth is valued, students are given a reason to review and question the quality of their performance and are credited for revising and improving their own work. By providing a "mirror (of) real-life circumstances" (Montgomery, 2001, p. 77), purpose is given to the items chosen as well as the students' educational experience.

Students are not the only members of the instructional team that profit from use of portfolio assessment strategies. Parents benefit as well. Although the need for parent involvement in the assessment process is widely recognized in special education, such involvement is usually limited to formal discussions at IEP meetings and parent-teacher conferences. Portfolios not only facilitate communication with parents (Tombari & Borich, 1999), they involve parents in instruction. Parents, in reviewing portfolios, are given an opportunity to analyze achievement on real tasks and interpret performance within the context of what is expected. Because portfolios include work samples collected throughout the year (and often longer), parents see progress that is often hidden in grade reporting. By providing parents with examples of student work that are selected and evaluated by both the teacher and child, parents are given the unique opportunity to interpret progress from each perspective.

Portfolios provide parents with the information needed to help their children be more successful. They can observe what is being taught and gain understanding about the criteria for evaluating performance. Portfolio conferences give parents the opportunity to provide information about their child's literacy involvement and other behaviors at home—information that can be used to plan and evaluate instruction. Parents can assist their children in generating artifacts for the portfolio and selecting the pieces for inclusion. Hobbs (1993), a resource room teacher, noted the power of portfolios in enhancing communication with parents:

> When I sent the portfolios home for the parents to review, most of them responded in writing to many of the items included. This opened a whole new avenue of two-way communication. Some of the comments were directed at me and some were notes of encouragement and praise for their child. Through the portfolios the parents became more involved in their child's education. (pp. 250–251)

Teachers also benefit from the use of portfolios. In every classroom, teachers expect to see individual differences among students. Some students assimilate new information effortlessly, whereas others need repeated practice or modified instruction; some students can sit for long periods of time, whereas others cannot attend for the duration of a class. Most relevant to literacy instruction is that some students can acquire reading and writing skills even when such skills are presented in a decontextualized manner, whereas other students are unable to use this information to communicate effectively in actual situations. Differences among students pose a significant challenge to the teacher, who must address the learning needs of all students in the class. Portfolios provide teachers with a framework from which to differentiate their teaching and assessment strategies. Perhaps most important, individual differences in learning can be assessed and addressed without drawing attention to the student who is struggling to keep up or fit in.

The portfolio assessment process facilitates teacher reflection. Evaluating students through teacher-made assignments allows teachers to consider the appropriateness of students' goals and the effectiveness of their own instructional methods and to truly individualize instruction based on student needs. Portfolios aid communication among the team of teachers who work with the child (e.g., the special education teacher, speech and language therapist, general education teachers). Additionally, portfolio assessment provides a unique opportunity for special educators to develop standards of performance that challenge students and prepare them for participation in the mainstream classroom.

Ten Steps to Portfolio Development

Special educators have found the portfolio format to be a "more flexible individualized approach to capture the learning outcomes" (Kleinert, Haig, Kearnes, & Kennedy, 2000, p. 57) of their students. Portfolios provide a "richer array of what students know and can do than paper-and-pencil tests and other 'snap shot' assessments" (Tombari & Borich, 1999, p. 189). Perhaps most important, portfolios structure a "flexible format for students to offer an ongoing contribution to their own learning" (Choate, et al., 1995, p. 336). By following the 10 steps described below, portfolios can become a reality for students with and without disabilities (see Figure 9–2).

Step 1: Determine the Purpose of the Portfolio. Friend & Bursuck (1999) remind us that portfolios are a *purposeful* collection of materials that emphasize student products. It is the chosen purpose of the document that defines the type of artifacts that will be included. Is this portfolio to be used in transition or career planning (Sarkees-

1. Determine the purpose of the portfolio.
2. Identify who will be part of the portfolio process.
3. Convene a meeting at which the portfolio process and contents can be discussed.
4. Review the types of artifacts that can be included in the portfolio with those contributing to the effort.
5. Construct an initial Table of Contents.
6. Determine responsibilities.
7. Determine the format that will be used to display the artifacts.
8. Create a system for monitoring, completing, and evaluating the portfolio.
9. Select the final artifacts to be included in the portfolio.
10. Evaluate and distribute findings to appropriate parties.

FIGURE 9–2 Ten steps in developing portfolios.

Wircenski & Wircenski, 1994)? Will it be part of the IEP re-evaluation process? Will it showcase functional skill levels across a given time period? Or, will it "tell the story" of a student's experiences in a particular program—a "celebration" portfolio (Stiggens, 1997)?

The designated purpose leads teachers, parents, and students to reflect on each measure as artifacts are chosen. For example, a portfolio used in the career planning or transition process should include documents that show the student's mastery levels in skills needed for this goal. Reading inventories, behavior checklists, videotapes of the student in work settings, and documents showing communication skills might all be a part of this portfolio as the purpose is to show what the student can do in the workplace. Compare this to a portfolio prepared for the purpose of celebrating the student's achievement across a span of time. Such a portfolio should have input from the student and parents as well as the teacher. Photos, best pieces of writing, peer comments, and interviews may be just a few of the artifacts chosen to represent the best the student has to offer. This document is likely to be kept forever in a special place and reviewed often by its creator.

The purpose of each of these portfolios is quite different; thus, the content is different. It may very well be the case that a student will have many portfolios, each representing a different purpose. For students with learning difficulties, the portfolio can be the primary record of even minimal change and, thus, the key to the assessment process.

When considering the purpose of the portfolio, it is also essential to keep in mind the role of portfolios in the overall assessment process. Cole, Struyk, Kinder, Sheehan, and Kish (1997) write, "If you are using portfolios to evaluate the progress of students with special needs, use them as supplemental not as an alternative to such assessment and evaluation procedures such as testing, grading, and curriculum-based assessment" (p. 412). Portfolios, then, are part of a multifactored assessment, not its substitute. They are but one means to document growth.

Step 2: Identify Who Will Be Part of the Portfolio Process. One of the most satisfying aspects of using portfolio assessment with diverse learners is that literally every student and parent can be part of the process. Typically, some students with disabilities are excluded from participating in "high stakes" (Langerfeld et al., 1997) assessment activities, because they are seen as too impaired for valid skills assessment. State-wide and norm-referenced achievement testing programs may exclude them altogether because the chosen assessments are seen as being ineffective in measuring student skills and may lower the overall achievement level that is so highly prized. Kleinert et al. (2000) counter by pointing out that it is the portfolio format that, in fact, allows students with more significant disabilities to be included in the state-wide assessment process. The

Kentucky Alternative Portfolio Project (Kleinert, Kennedy, & Kearns, 1999) is doing just that by including portfolios of students with severe disabilities in the state-wide assessment program.

Students certainly can be part of the assessment team. Preparing and selecting artifacts for inclusion are just two of the ways in which students can participate. The impact on students' self-determination is one of the ancillary effects of portfolio use (Tombari & Borich, 1999). Self-esteem, which is vital to all students, particularly those with learning difficulties, is immeasurably enhanced as students observe their own learning, master the ability to reflect on what they have learned, engage in literacy interactions, and share the products of their efforts with others.

Parents can also contribute to portfolio development. Depending on the purpose of the document, parents may hold critical perspectives that often are not observable in a school setting and can contribute such artifacts as anecdotes, observations of behaviors, and outside-of-school activity logs. Their participation in crafting the portfolio may also be valuable if they assist their child in selecting and evaluating artifacts for inclusion.

Educators with different specializations are also members of the portfolio assessment team. It is important that educators who have worked with the student in the past join in the assessment process with the current teacher or teachers. Because portfolio development is an ongoing process, teachers from previous years may lend needed perspective. Physical and occupational therapists, school psychologists, reading enrichment teachers, classroom aides, audiologists, special subject teachers, and administrators are but a few of the people who may have had contact with the student and, therefore, may have information pertinent to the portfolio process.

Step 3: Convene a Meeting at Which the Portfolio Process and Contents Can Be Discussed. It is wise to hold an organizational meeting with potential contributors to a student's portfolio prior to its compilation. This allows for clear definition of the purpose of the measure, clearly defined, discussion of potential artifacts, and identification of who might have information to include. Such a meeting can be held as part of an IEP review meeting, parent-teacher conference, or at another convenient time. More than one meeting may be necessary because the day-to-day activities needed to deliver services to students with disabilities keep team members very busy.

Step 4: Review the Types of Artifacts That Can Be Included in a Portfolio With Those Contributing to the Effort. At or prior to the organizational meeting, a list of potential artifacts can be distributed to give participants a sense of the products that can be used in portfolio development. Although norm-referenced testing can be a valuable part of the assessment, a more comprehensive list may encourage contributors to go beyond the measurements typically used in assessing students with disabilities.

Artifacts included in the portfolio should reflect the goals of the curriculum and the content covered, as well as the methods used to teach and the process by which the students acquire and use new knowledge. The types of information that may comprise a special education literacy portfolio are similar to other portfolios. Figure 9–3 lists various tasks and informal assessment tools that may be used for a literacy portfolio for students with disabilities. Although this list is lengthy, it is not exhaustive. As long as the purpose of the portfolio is served by including a work, it is an appropriate part of the portfolio contents.

Step 5: Construct an Initial Table of Contents. By developing an initial Table of Contents that lists the portfolio artifacts, critical pieces of assessment data can be identified and included. Responsible parties can be listed and contacted so that the portfolio contains all the vital information needed to serve its assessment purpose. Because this is only as an initial organizer, the Table of Contents may need to be revised at a later time in order to give an accurate representation of the work included in the portfolio.

FIGURE 9–3 Possible artifacts in a literacy portfolio for students with disabilities.

Informal reading inventories	Interviews
Writing samples	Certificates
Multiple drafts of writing	Letters to portfolio readers
Photographs of projects	Anecdotal records
Audio/videotapes of performances	Reflective journals
Self-regulation checklists	Art work
Edited writing samples	Transcriptions of confer-
ences	
Learning or dialogue logs	Criterion-referenced tests
Peer ratings	Curriculum-based tests
Computer screen prints	Story maps
IEPs	Observations of behavior

Abruscato (1993) makes a recommendation for the contents of a literacy portfolio drawn from the Vermont Portfolio Project, which focuses on writing (see Figure 9–4). Overton (1996) provides a list of potential organizers for a portfolio in the area of reading (see Figure 9–5). Including such organizers in the portfolio helps to clarify the purpose of the document for the evaluator or interested reader.

Step 6: Determine Responsibilities. For the most part, the students and their teachers will be responsible for contributing most of the artifacts that will be part of the portfolios. If the students are part of an inclusive classroom, both their general education teachers and their special education teacher-consultants will provide the bulk of the needed pieces. However, other members of the education team may hold valuable pieces of student work. For example, the unit's physical therapist or art teacher may be able to contribute information about development in fine motor skills. The reading teacher may have access to inventories or rubrics that show growth in word identification. Parents may offer data on feeding skills that are reflective of coordination.

Writing and disseminating a list of who is responsible for what activities is a good strategy for ensuring that all parties meet their oral commitments. Requesting updates can assist in timely delivery of the products for the portfolio process and also can be an impetus for highlighting any problems that the student may have during the course of the year.

Step 7: Determine the Format That Will Be Used to Display the Artifacts. Members of the assessment team should agree upon a tentative format for displaying the artifacts created by the student. The final format can be determined as the assessment deadline nears. The type and function of the information to be included may very well lead to a determination of format. It is becoming common for the format to go beyond the typi-

FIGURE 9–4 Table of contents for a literacy portfolio for students with disabilities (drawn from the Vermont Portfolio Project).
Source: From "Early results and tentative implications from the Vermont Portfolio Project," by J. Abruscato, 1993, *Phi Delta Kappan, 74*, p. 475. Copyright 1993 by Phi Delta Kappan. Adapted with permission.

Table of Contents

I. Best Piece

II. Letter to reader

III. Poem, short story, play, etc.

IV. Response to a prompt.

V. Prose piece for curricular area

VI. Piece using a uniform writing assessment.

FIGURE 9–5 Potential organizing sections for a reading portfolio.
*Source: Assessment in special
education: An applied
approach* by Overton, ©.
Adapted by permission of
Pearson Education, Inc., Upper
Saddle River, NJ.

Potential Organizing Sections
Curriculum-Based Assessments
Work Samples
Teacher-made Tests
Homework
Error Analysis
Informal Reading Inventory

cal file folder or binder. Increasingly, technology-based formats are being used because
they allow easy inclusion of video- and audiotapes, computer-assisted instruction summaries, and other products aided by assistive technology (Gardner & Edyburn, 2000;
Lindsey, 2000). Online presentations are also more frequently discussed because they
provide access to students' work beyond the confines of school. If this format is chosen,
the assessment team must be certain to obtain permission for its use from the student
and parents, because access to the evaluation information is more difficult to control and
rights to privacy must be respected.

The artifacts included in a portfolio must be organized so that a comprehensive picture of the student emerges. Because of the wealth of information produced during an
assessment period, it is useful to create subdivisions within the portfolio. However,
Bartoli and Botel (1988) cautioned that artificial subdivisions may fragment the learning
process, as happens with traditional assessments. Portfolio subdivisions, such as a working folder, a teacher folio, and a student's showcase portfolio (Gahagan, 1994), have
been proposed based on the purposes of assessment. Dividing content by skill area is
another popular format. For example, a student might have a reading portfolio and a
writing portfolio (Bartoli & Botel, 1988). Swicegood (1994) proposed a structure for portfolio development that has particular relevance to the assessment of students in special
education. He proposed four categories for organizing information: (1) measures of
behavior and adaptive functioning, (2) measures of academic and literacy growth, (3)
measures of strategic learning and self-regulation, and (4) measures of language and cultural aspects. He suggested that multiple indices be used within each subdivision and
that new subdivisions will emerge as the portfolio is developed and evaluated.

Step 8: Create a System for Monitoring, Completing, and Evaluating the Portfolio. To
maximize the potential for favorable outcomes with the use of portfolios, it is crucial that
implementation be well-planned and carefully monitored. It is next to impossible to go
back in time and capture a significant milestone or surprising event. Therefore, planning
for anticipated outcomes is essential to developing portfolios that accurately illuminate
the gains made by students with disabilities. Creating a system through which artifacts
can be coordinated, stored, and evaluated is essential to the portfolio development
process, and should be discussed at the initial organizational meeting.

Such a system may be basic to the assessment process used with all students with
disabilities, or it may be tailored to individual students as needed. A basic information
sheet should be placed in each portfolio. On this sheet, team members can record status information as it arises. Included are a student's name, date of first meeting, activities, dates that activities commence and end, supervisor, and any known evaluation
criteria (e.g., rubrics, checklists). Indicating a section for "notes" will entice participants
to record other pieces of information not registered on evaluation sheets but which have
an impact on the interpretation of artifacts (see Figure 9–6).

Portfolio Planning Sheet

Student Name: _Jennifer Simmons_   **Date:** _9/5/01_

Assessment Activity	Start Date	Supervisor	Evaluation Method	Completion Date
Original poem using haiku	10/12/01	Mrs. Johnston	Haiku rubric	10/25/01
Recitation video (content student chosen)	3/8/02	Mr. Freeman	Recitation checklist	3/28/02
Poem interpretation project	4/19/02	Mrs. Johnson	To be determined	

FIGURE 9–6 A sample portfolio planning sheet.

Regular meetings of the team can serve as convenient opportunities to review progress on students' portfolio development. If problems arise, the contents of the planned portfolio, or its system for artifact development, can be altered while time is still available for coordinating alternative assessment activities. Working from a timeline can keep team members on target to meet deadlines and keeping a written time line in the students' portfolio files can make meeting deadlines an easier task.

It is also important to agree on how artifacts will be evaluated prior to an actual event. Rubrics, checklists, inventories, and profiles may be found from previous assessment activities or from commercial publishers. If it appears that an anticipated artifact does not have a companion evaluation, time is available to design or locate a viable evaluation tool. Completing this process early in the portfolio development gives evaluators the time needed to become proficient at using the evaluation tools. This is particularly important if students or parents are participating in the assessment activities.

Step 9: Select the Final Artifacts to Be Included in the Portfolio. The selection of artifacts that will become part of the final portfolio depends on the student, the curriculum, and the purposes for the portfolio. For example, if the student is working toward developing learning strategies, it may be appropriate to include entries that demonstrate the student's organizational abilities, such as story maps and multiple writing drafts. If the portfolio is being used to document a student's affective development, it may be appropriate to include reflective journal entries, interviews, and self-regulation checklists. Video- and audiotapes may be useful if instruction is designed to enhance adaptive behavior or social skills or if oral expression is to be examined.

It is important that samples of student performance in the portfolio be accompanied by the date of completion and a description of the conditions under which the student completed the work. Particularly in special education, where many students require assistance before gaining independence, it is extremely helpful for the teacher or aide to add notations that specify the instructional context in which the work was created. The assistance provided to the learner and modifications in the instructional setting, methods, or materials should be specified; for example, "this piece was written with a teacher's aide, who recorded the student's oral story," or "the student produced this piece in a one-on-one setting in a resource room." Providing information about the accommodations made to facilitate performance allows for more accurate assessment of the student's abilities, facilitates replication in other settings, and suggests ways to develop independence in subsequent lessons.

Step 10: Evaluate and Distribute Findings to Appropriate Parties. If at all possible, students with special needs should be members of the teams that evaluate their portfolios. They may need special guidance when participating in the assessment. However, using checklists, interviews, or simple selection procedures may be all the direction that is needed. The reasons students provide for selecting their best work reveal the factors they consider to be important and should be noted. Being responsible for developing, and ultimately internalizing, criteria for evaluating their own work helps build the independent reasoning skills that are necessary for the development of self-determination.

Parents, too, may join in the final evaluative process. In doing so, parents can supply useful context to the evaluation process and be kept informed about how their children's skills have advanced during an evaluation period. When given evaluation formats, such as rubrics, parents are in the position to review the portfolio contents from a unique and informed perspective.

Other evaluators may include administrators, current and previous teachers, ancillary staff, and resource people used by the students outside of the school. Each person has a unique perspective that will contribute to an assessment that represents a true reflection of the students' progress and abilities.

Students may wish to display their portfolios or share them with significant supporters. Portfolios may go with the students as a summative evaluation piece or may be seen as formative and stay as part of students' files. Whichever the case, these portfolios will likely be tremendous points of pride and treasure troves of best work and memories.

Portfolios for Georgia and Nicholas

There is perhaps no better way to consider the potential benefits of using portfolios in special education than to examine representative samples. Although portfolios differ in how they are developed, the essential features invariably include extensive teacher planning and input, ongoing student reflection, and active parent participation. The number of self-evaluations included in the portfolios of students with special needs demonstrates that these students' work is highly valued. In fact, students' growth in skills and understanding can be noted in the evaluations of their own work over time.

Georgia's Portfolio. When Georgia was first referred for screening, it was apparent that her skills were not as advanced as those of her 6-year-old peers. Although she was a delightful child, her quietness was often mistaken for shyness rather than uncertainty. Her parents had asked that she be tested, because they were aware that her skills lagged behind those of her siblings, some of whom were younger, yet more advanced in readiness skills.

It was agreed that she would be tested and basic readiness evaluations were completed. Tests indicated that Georgia was working at a level more often seen in children aged 3.5 years. Although this wasn't a surprise to her parents, they were shaken when they were given a referral to the special education department.

After meeting with the staff and talking with Georgia's prospective teacher, Mrs. Turner, Georgia's parents were reassured when they were informed that she would be staying with her age peers in first grade. She would also be assigned to a special education teacher, Mr. Janis, who would work with Georgia and be a consultant to Mrs. Turner. It was clear from Georgia's work (see Figure 9–7) that she was having difficulty with fine motor skills as well as word comprehension. When given a task such as "Please draw the dog below the tree," she was unable to organize her thoughts and could not make the representation on paper or when given picture cards.

Georgia's case manager decided it would be wise to gather artifacts that could be kept in a portfolio, which would be used for classroom-based planning and at Georgia's IEP meetings. The document would be ongoing because it was to be used for placement decisions and instructional planning. Georgia enjoyed selecting items to be included and insisted that her picture of *Clifford, The Big Red Dog* be in the portfolio (see Figure 9–8).

FIGURE 9–7 Georgia's picture of Grandpa completed at age 6 years.

When Georgia's picture of Clifford was compared to the picture of her grandfather that she had completed a year earlier, it was clear that she had gained much more control of her fine motor skills. She also seemed to be improving in the proficiency needed to follow directions and illustrate through words the pictures she saw in her mind. Figure 9–9 shows even greater growth, because she is able to follow a prompt asking her to draw her family. It was encouraging to see that she depicted herself with a smile. She also showed higher-order thinking skills in her effort to embellish the family pictures with attributes not previously seen in her work. Complexity was also apparent in the more detailed stories she now told. Even a casual review of the items contained in Georgia's portfolio reveals her continued developmental immaturity (few 8-year-olds would draw their family in this way). It is through the combined artifacts included in her folder that her growth becomes apparent.

Nicholas' Portfolio. Nicholas was brought to the attention of the special education department when he was registered for school after moving from another state. At his previous school, he had been classified as a student with a disability. It was obvious from the first interview that he had been quite upset about the move and his uneasiness was apparent in his work. He had had a close bond with his former teacher and had made great strides through that partnership. Nicholas was sure there would never be another "Miss B."

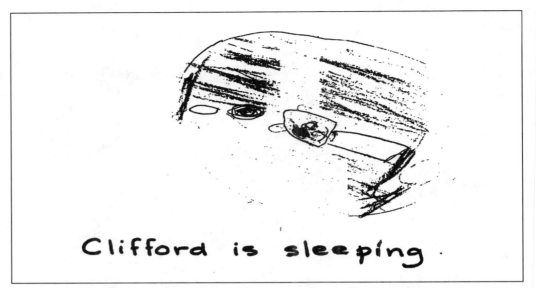

FIGURE 9–8 Georgia's picture (with teacher notation) completed at age 7 years.

The portfolio sent with Nicholas included a representative set of papers showing the skill levels he had attained. It was clear that he had regressed somewhat since the move and would need to be encouraged to meet his previous level of proficiency. When Nicholas was shown copies of his work that had been sent, he was very excited to talk about each paper. He proudly pointed out that he no longer reversed his letters (see Figure 9–10) and laughed at how he used to write his eights and nines. A spelling list

FIGURE 9–9 Georgia's picture completed at age 8 years.

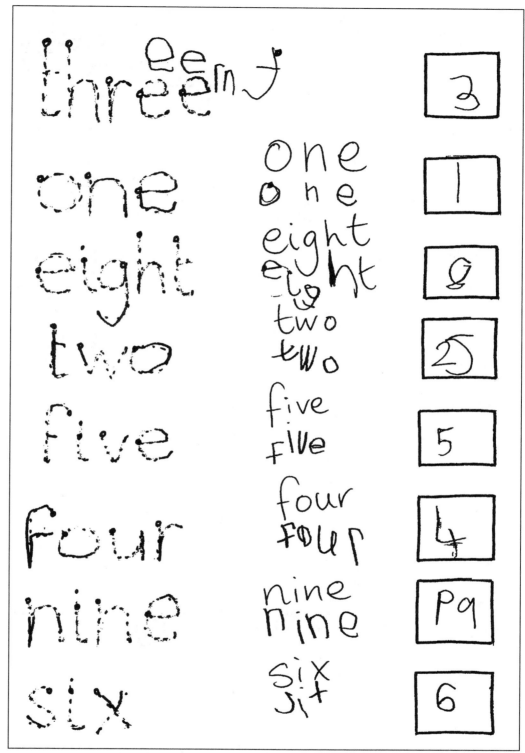

FIGURE 9–10 Nicholas' number tracing and writing at age 8 years.

(see Figure 9–11) gave him the opportunity to read the words and tell all about the Holiday Festival where he recited a poem and sang "Jingle Bells." When he came to the paper where he had answered questions based on a story he had read about a boy named "Gino," he paused (see Figure 9–12). He seemed confused as he tried to read his

FIGURE 9–11 Nicholas' spelling list completed at age 9 years.

responses and could not understand how he had been able to complete the lesson that he now had trouble comprehending. His excitement turned to sadness as he thought about the character in the story, who had moved and was waiting for mail from his old neighbors and friends, just as Nicholas was.

Nicholas did not know it, but he was using his work to reveal a great deal about his previous skills and growth. He had not only prepared the contents of the portfolio but was now using the artifacts to demonstrate his current ability level. At one time, his writing had been developed to the point that he was using upper- and lower-case letters. He was also using multiple word answers in his written work. The vocabulary he used included compound and plural forms of words. His comprehension levels had been sufficient to answer simple questions. These skills were not evident in the new school. Nicholas' new teachers were sure that he could quickly regain the lost skills and they were happy to have the portfolio that showed he had once been much more advanced. It was impressive that he was still able to recall the story of Gino even though he had read it some time ago. All were encouraged that Nicholas would soon be back to his previous skill levels and on his way to even greater achievements.

Based on Nicholas' success at his former school, it was decided that he would be part of the Reading Recovery program and visit the school's resource room each morn-

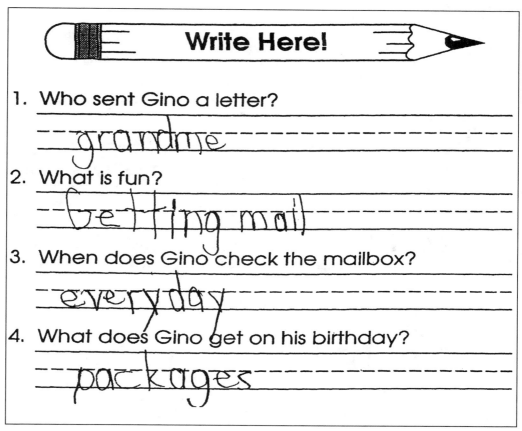

FIGURE 9–12 Nicholas' fixed response completed at age 10 years.

ing for his language arts block. This would require Nicholas to leave his classroom, but it was agreed that it would provide him the needed assistance to foster his literacy skills. At a follow-up meeting later in the year, no one could remember when Nicholas wasn't part of the school community. His determination and sunny outlook made him a favorite with the teachers and other students. They all cheered his progress and were a team of coaches that he gladly accepted. Everyone was heartened, but not surprised, when they saw the portfolio that now included the artifacts Nicholas had selected as his "best work." On top was a report he had researched, written, and read to his class (see Figure 9–13) about mammals. Although it was not nearly as detailed as those of his classmates, he had completed it on his own and was proud to tell anyone who would listen! He had obviously grown in his ability to express himself through writing. His word choice, punctuation, handwriting skills, sentence formation, and research abilities had matured a great deal since the initial meeting. He saw the change, as did his parents, and had trouble containing his surprise when he compared his current work with that of work completed just 6 months before.

Nicholas' mother reported during the meeting how he had convinced the local librarian to assist him in his research. She also recounted how the entire family had gotten so swept up in the world of mammals that it had become the topic of choice at the evening dinner table for weeks. Both she and her husband were thrilled that Nicholas had found a topic of such great interest that he would extend himself to gather as much information as he could. She recommended that his teachers use his budding interest in animals as a way to motivate him to develop more complex skills.

The experience of students and parents attest to how portfolios can facilitate learning within an environment that fosters independence and collaboration. Although good teachers might effect change in their students whether or not portfolios are used, port-

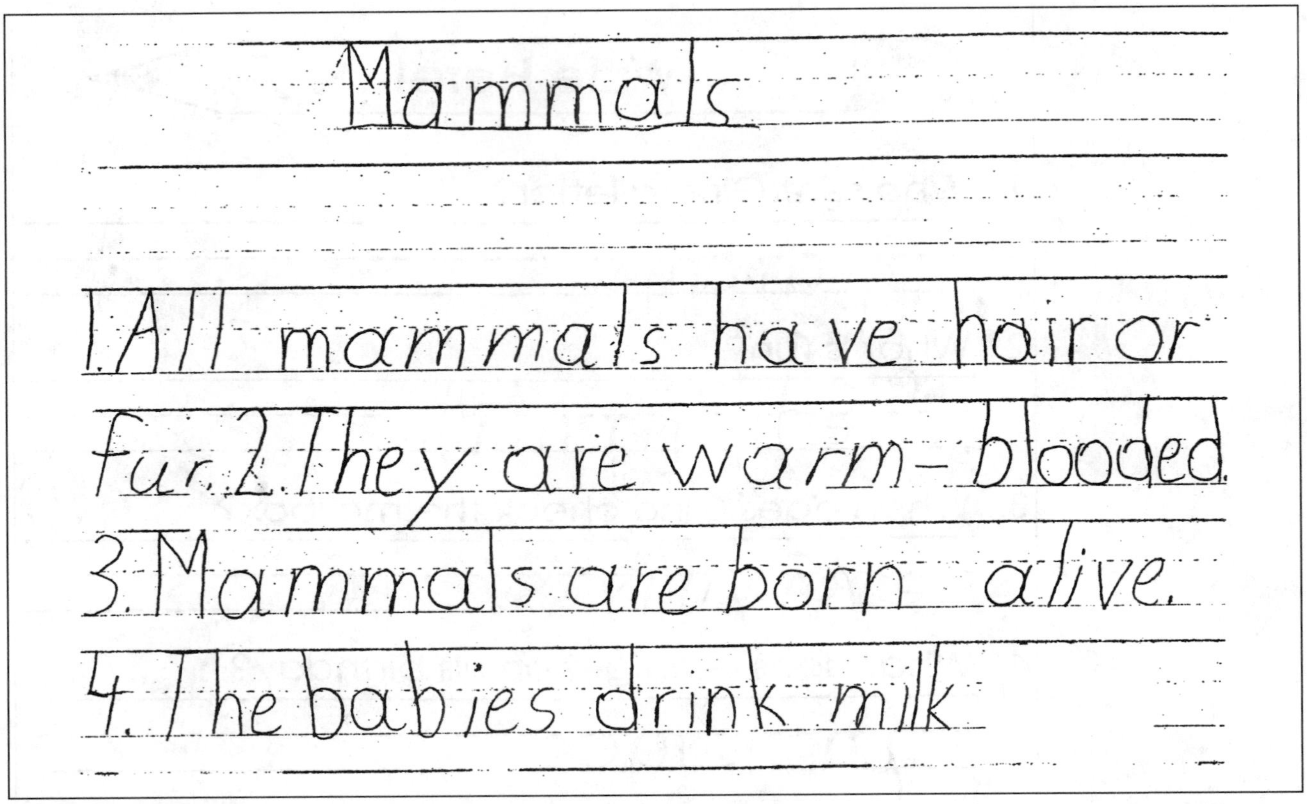

> ### Mammals
>
> 1. All mammals have hair or fur. 2. They are warm-blooded. 3. Mammals are born alive. 4. The babies drink milk

FIGURE 9–13 Nicholas' sentence response completed at age 10 years.

folios ensure that students, parents, and teachers recognize and learn from the students' efforts and accomplishments and clearly document change.

THE ROLE OF PORTFOLIOS IN COMPLIANCE ISSUES

Portfolios and IEPs

In special education, the IEP is an essential and mandatory document specifying what, where, how, and why instruction will be provided to a student with a disability. Each student's IEP is developed and reviewed annually, with the input of professionals and parents. Portfolios facilitate the development and implementation of a student's IEP by providing authentic, jargon-free information about student performance. Portfolios can be used throughout the IEP process, beginning with the initial referral to special education. At this point, the information included in the portfolio characterizes the student's abilities within the context of the teacher's expectations so that prereferral interventions can be made. Once a student is deemed eligible for special education, the portfolio is instrumental in the selection of instructional goals. Clearly, it is more appropriate to base instructional goals on samples of student work that are evaluated by both the teacher and the student than it is to select goals from deficits identified on standardized tests interpreted by clinicians who do not know the child well, if at all. The use of real work samples ensures that the student's individualized goals are relevant and functional.

As an ongoing record of student progress, the portfolio facilitates the mandated review of IEP goals. First, the portfolio provides an opportunity to reflect on the appropriateness, frequency, and effectiveness of instructional opportunities directed at meeting the identified goals. Second, the evaluation of progress toward goal attainment occurs naturally within the instructional framework and involves both the teacher and students. In fact, the portfolio encourages students to monitor and evaluate their own progress and to set their own goals. Last, as part of the mandated annual review of the IEP, the portfolio provides the information needed to revise goals and strategies as well as to select new goals and methods. As a representative body of student work collected over an extended period of time, portfolios provide a rich foundation from which to revise and plan instruction. What better way to decide what a student needs to learn or how a student might learn best than to look at how the student currently performs and what the student has done in the past? Students do not begin learning with each new IEP—portfolios allow past and present efforts and accomplishments to be considered in subsequent educational decisions.

Portfolios and Standards

Rigor, achievement, and standards are matters that are taking up increasing amounts of time for educators and those engaged in educational policy development. The goal is to develop schools that produce students who are competitive in the global marketplace as well as achieve at their highest levels. Legislated state standards are found throughout the country, and educators continue to work to address their requirements. An inordinate amount of time, money, and effort is being expended to this end. However, this expenditure is nothing new to those working with programs for students with special needs. They have been dealing with the issues brought forth in a compliance environment for decades.

The new challenge for this group is determining the role that standards and state-mandated assessments should have for students with learning differences. Should such students be exempt from taking proficiency tests? Do their grades count when determining accountability? Does it compromise the reliability of a measure when it is given orally, written in braille, or when other accommodations specified under an IEP are provided? How can assistive technology be harnessed to give more accurate results for those who cannot use typical paper-and-pencil means of recording answers? Questions like these are making implementation of the initiative difficult and are requiring school boards and state education departments to find satisfactory answers to the many unanswered questions.

The federal government is encouraging the states to identify assessment practices that enable students to show what they know. It is acknowledged that not all students are able to demonstrate their abilities through the use of typical proficiency exams. Therefore, states have been put on notice, through the 1997 revisions to the IDEA, that by the year 2000 they are to have developed and employed alternative assessment measures for students who cannot be reasonably included in the usual state assessment procedures.

As mentioned previously, Kentucky and Vermont are experimenting with the use of portfolios to bridge the assessment gap between general and special education. Both states have proposed plans that include students with special needs in the proficiency equation by using formats and evaluation procedures that are innovative and seemingly effective. Kleinert et al. (1999) reported that the scoring method used in the Kentucky project has been successful. Students with special needs are graded on a four-factor scale using the terms *novice*, *apprentice*, *proficient*, and *distinguished*. These terms are then converted into a parallel scoring system used for the other students taking the proficiency exams. Even students with the most severe disabilities can earn the rank of "distinguished," and their scores can be included in the testing activities and resulting scores.

With most states now engaged in some type of proficiency testing and the federal government exploring the viability of nation-wide tests, it seems likely that more states will take on the task of finding ways to fairly involve students with special needs in their high-stakes assessment programs. There is no reason not to do so when assessment procedures can be identified that take into account such factors as students' primary mode of communication and targeted learner outcomes.

LOOKING TO THE FUTURE

As classrooms become more heterogeneous and requirements for evaluating student progress become more prevalent, it is likely that the trend toward authentic assessment will continue in both general and special education. Keeping the purpose of evaluation activities in mind, the challenge of finding effective and efficient measures with which to make decisions will remain vital to the assessment and instructional processes. The instruction-evaluation bond will strengthen as the curriculum becomes more challenging and learner outcomes improve.

The emerging constructivistic approach in special education reflects a growing appreciation of students' strengths, abilities, and interests. Even the language used to describe students has changed from "handicapped" to "disabled" to "having special needs" as *capability* has surpassed *disability* as the critical attribute in the eyes of our society. Given that traditional assessment tools do not provide a comprehensive picture of performance that is consistent with changes in thinking about individuals with disabilities, the use of authentic assessment measures is likely to expand. The need to display what students can do appears to have found its place in the assessment process.

As portfolio assessment grows in use and importance, its role in a multifaceted evaluation may become the fundamental approach through which all students are assessed. Using authentic measures in conjunction with objective, norm-referenced tests yields a balanced presentation of what these students can do and how they compare to others. It would not be surprising to see broader acceptance of the use of multiple test formats throughout the educational system.

If the portfolio assessment process can inspire even a portion of what is possible, the benefits to learners with special needs could be truly overwhelming. We may enter an age where all students are seen as having "special needs" and instruction is engineered to maximize learning. Possibilities may soon turn to reality as we move toward an ability model of learning and authentic assessment becomes standard practice.

REFERENCES

Abruscato, J. (1993). Early results and tentative implications from the Vermont Portfolio Project. *Phi Delta Kappan, 74,* 474–477.

Bartoli, J., & Botel, M. (1988). *Reading/learning disability: An ecological approach.* New York: Teachers College Press.

Berdine, W. H., & Meyer, S. A. (1987). *Assessment in special education.* Boston: Little, Brown.

Brazee, P., & Haynes, S. W. (1989). Special education and whole language: From an evaluator's viewpoint. In K. S. Goodman, Y. M. Goodman, & W. J. Hood, *The whole language evaluation book* (pp. 249–260). Portsmouth, NH: Heinemann.

Choate, J. S., Enright, B. E., Miller, L. J., Poteet, J. A., & Rakes, T. A. (1995). *Curriculum-based assessment and programming* (3rd ed.). Boston: Allyn & Bacon.

Cole, K. B., Struyk, L. R., Kinder, D., Sheehan, J. K., & Kish, C. K. (1997). Portfolio assessment: Challenges in secondary education. *The High School Journal, 80*(4), 261–272.

Crowley, P. (1989). 'They'll grow into 'em': Evaluation, self-evaluation, and self-esteem in special education. In K. S. Goodman, Y. M. Goodman, & W. J. Hood (Eds.), *The whole language evaluation book* (pp. 237–247). Portsmouth, NH: Heinemann.

Cummins, J. (1984). *Bilingualism and special education: Issues in assessment and pedagogy.* Cleveland; Avon, England: Multilingual Matters.

Deshler, D., Schumaker, J., Lenz, K., & Ellis, E. (1984). Academic and cognitive interventions for LD adolescents: Part I. *Journal of Learning Disabilities, 15,* 108–117.

Executive Committee of the Council for Children with Behavior Disorders. (1989). White paper on best assessment practices for students with behavioral disorders: Accommodation to cultural diversity and individual differences. *Behavioral Disorders, 13,* 127–139.

Friend, M. P., & Bursuck, W. D. (1999). *Including students with special needs: A practical guide for classroom teachers* (2nd ed.). Boston: Allyn & Bacon.

Gahagan, H. S. (1994). Whole language assessment and evaluation: A special education perspective. In B. Harp (Ed.), *Assessment and evaluation student centered learning* (2nd ed.). (pp. 181–211). Norwood, MA: Christopher-Gordon.

Gardner, J. E., & Edyburn, D. L. (2000). Integrating technology to support effective instruction. In J. D. Lindsey, (Ed.), *Technology & exceptional individuals* (3rd ed.). Austin, TX: Pro-Ed.

Glazer, S. M., & Searfoss, L. W. (1988). *Reading diagnosis and instruction: A-C-A-L-M approach.* Upper Saddle River, NJ: Prentice Hall.

Gottlieb, J. (1985). Report to the Mayor's Commission on special education on COH practices in NYC. In *N. Y. C. Commission on Education, Special education, a call for quality*. New York: Mayor's Commission on Special Education.

Graves, D. H., & Sunstein, B. S. (Eds.). (1992). *Portfolio portraits*. Portsmouth, NH: Heinemann.

Heward, W. (2001). *Exceptional children* (6th ed.). Upper Saddle River, NJ: Merrill/Prentice Hall.

Hobbs, R. (1993). Portfolio in use in a learning disabilities resource room. *Reading and Writing Quarterly: Overcoming Learning Disabilities, 9*, 249–261.

Keefe, C. H. (1992). Developing responsive IEPs through holistic assessment. *Intervention in School and Clinic, 28*, 34–40.

Kleinert, H., Kennedy, S., & Kearns, J. (1999). The impact of alternate assessments: A statewide teacher survey. *Journal of Special Education, 33*(2), 93–102.

Kleinert, H., Haig, J., Kearns, J., & Kennedy, S. (2000). Alternate assessments: Lessons learned and roads to be taken. *Exceptional Children, 67*(1), 51–66.

Langerfeld, K., Thurlow, M., & Scott, D. (1997). High stakes testing for students: Unanswered questions and implications for students with disabilities (Synthesis Report #26). Minneapolis: University of Minnesota, National Center on Educational Outcomes. (ERIC Document Service No. ED 415 627).

Lindsey, J. D. (Ed.). (2000). *Technology and exceptional learners*. Austin, TX: Pro-Ed.

Lipsky, D. K., & Gartner, A. (Eds.). (1989). *Beyond separate education: Quality education for all*. Baltimore: Brookes.

Meltzer, L., & Reid, D. K. (1984). New directions in the assessment of students with special needs: The shift toward a constructivist perspective. *Journal of Special Education, 28*, 338–355.

Montgomery, K. (2001). *Authentic assessment: A guide for elementary teachers*. New York: Longman.

Overton, T. (1996). *Assessment in special education: An applied approach* (2nd ed.). Upper Saddle River, NJ: Merrill/Prentice Hall.

Paulson, L., Paulson, P., & Meyer, C. (1991). What makes a portfolio a portfolio? *Educational Leadership, 48*, 60–63.

Rhodes, L. K., & Dudley-Marling, C. (1988). *Readers and writers with a difference: A holistic approach to teaching learning disabled and remedial students*. Portsmouth, NH: Heinemann.

Salvia, J., & Ysseldyke, J. E. (1995). *Assessment* (6th ed.). Boston: Houghton Mifflin.

Scala, M. A. (1993). What whole language in the mainstream means for children with learning disabilities. *The reading Teacher, 47*, 222–229.

Searfoss, L. W. (1994). A holistic/wellness model of reading assessment: An alternative to the medical model. *Reading and Writing Quarterly: Overcoming Learning Difficulties, 10*, 105–117.

Soodak, L. C., & Erwin, E. J. (1995). Parents, professionals and inclusive education: A call for collaboration. *Journal of Educational and Psychological Consultation, 6*, 257–276.

Soodak, L. C., & Martin-Kniep, G. O. (1994). Authentic assessment and curriculum integration: Natural partners in need of thoughtful policy. *Educational Policy, 8*, 183–201.

Stiggens, R. J. (1997). *Student-centered classroom assessment*. Upper Saddle River, NJ: Merrill/Prentice Hall.

Swicegood, P. (1994). Portfolio-based assessment practices: The uses of portfolio assessment for students with behavioral disorders or learning disabilities. *Intervention in School and Clinic, 30*, 6–15.

Taylor, R. L. (2000). *Assessment of exceptional students: Educational and psychological procedures* (5th ed.). Boston: Allyn & Bacon.

Thomas, K. F., & Barksdale-Ladd, M. A. (1994). Using whole language with children whom we have failed to teach to read. *Reading and Writing Quarterly: Overcoming Learning Difficulties, 10*, 125–142.

Tombari, M. L., & Borich, G. D. (1999). *Authentic assessment in the classroom: Applications and practice*. Upper Saddle River, NJ: Merrill/Prentice Hall.

Valencia, S. (1990). A portfolio approach to classroom reading assessment: The ways, whats, and hows. *The Reading Teacher, 43*, 338–340.

Vygotsky, L. (1978). *Mind in society: The development of higher psychological processes*. Cambridge, MA: Harvard University Press.

Ysseldyke, J. E., & Algozzine, B. (1982). *Critical issues in special and remedial education*. Boston: Houghton Mifflin.

Ysseldyke, J. E., Algozzine, B., & Thurlow, M. L. (1992). *Critical issues in special education* (2nd ed.). Boston: Houghton Mifflin.

Using Portfolios With English Language Learners

by
Brett Elizabeth Blake, Ph.D.
Associate Professor, St. John's University,
Queens, New York

KEY WORDS AND CONCEPTS

English language learner (ELL)

bilingual

English as a second language (ESL)

second language acquisition

monolingual

innatist theory

behaviorist theory

social interactionist theory

TESOL (teaching English to speakers of other languages)

LEP (limited English proficiency)

ENL (English as a New Language)

*E*nglish language learners (ELLs) are the fastest growing population in America's public schools. In California, for example, ELLs represent the majority of school-aged children in public schools, and in New York City, more than 50 different languages can be heard in the schools, including Bengali, Greek, Vietnamese, Polish, French Creole, Spanish, Chinese, Russian, and Urdu. Soon, demographers predict, ELLs will become the majority population of school-aged children in public schools in places like Chicago, Hartford, and Houston. To help meet the demand, The U.S. Department of Education awarded more than $399 million for bilingual and ESL programs in 2000 (Turner, 2000). In many other cities, there is a remarkable change in the demographics of school-aged children, with non-English speakers creating instructional challenges these districts have never faced before. Many Hispanic immigrants, who are mostly monolingual, or limited English proficiency (LEP), are moving into urban areas (Malgady & Zayas, 2001). Even in midwestern cities such as Fort Wayne, Indiana, there are more than 62 languages and dialects spoken in the schools. The top language groups in the Fort Wayne community schools are English, Spanish, Bosnia Serbo-Croatian, Vietnamese, Burmese, and Laotian. In fact, Fort Wayne has the largest Burmese population outside of Burma! (Ramsey, 2002).

ELLs can be defined as those students whose primary language is not English and who are, therefore, learning English as a second language (ESL). It is necessary to define our terms and provide some background in bilingual education and ESL. In 1992, the U.S. Department of Education indicated that one out of four ELLs received no specialized instruction to help smooth their way to learning English. Children who speak little or no English can be placed in bilingual programs or in ESL programs, and the following sections describe the essentials of these two different programs.

Bilingual programs provide instruction using two languages, one of which is English. Each class can require two teachers, a native speaker of the minority language and an English-speaking teacher as well. Part of the curriculum is taught in the children's native language and part of the curriculum is taught in English. ESL instruction is also provided. Included in the curriculum are history, culture, and ethnic heritage from the children's country of origin so that they feel a sense of self-worth, community, and cultural identity. Most bilingual programs are transitional, which means that as soon as students are proficient enough to work in all-English classes they are moved into a class of English-only instruction. This can occur after 2 years of bilingual education, but many children remain in such programs for many years.

In a maintenance bilingual program, children are given instruction in both languages. Dual-language programs may have between 50% to 90% of instruction in the children's native language, which is why many people believe that English skills are not sufficiently emphasized and that the children are not truly prepared to enter mainstream classrooms. Many educators also feel that these children never become proficient in English, and therefore students in bilingual programs are at a disadvantage when they enter the job market and consequently have limited potential for upward mobility. Other critics feel that these programs emphasize the children's native culture and heritage to the exclusion of learning about American life.

Some ESL programs, which are also referred to as TESOL (teaching English to speakers of other languages) or teaching English to second language learners, are taught in conjunction with a bilingual class; some are "pull out classes," where children are given 45 to 90 minutes of instruction in English (several times per week) and then returned to their regular classroom. Other children are "immersed" in a regular classroom with primarily English dominant children and "sink or swim" until they become proficient enough to learn in English. ESL instruction is supplemental to regular instruction and ESL teachers instruct only in English. An ESL class can contain children from many different countries and every attempt is made to prepare the students for entry into mainstream culture. ESL instruction is based on building all aspects of children's English language skills in an integrated fashion.

The research and discussions about which program, bilingual or ESL, is more effective for children is fraught with controversy and has many political overtones. For example, research on children learning to read in a second language indicates the following contradictory information:

> Children should learn to read a language they already speak. However, it is clear that many children first learn to read in a second language without serious negative consequences. (August & Hakuta, 1997)
>
> Students don't lose academically when they spend time learning through the minority language (non-English). (Cummins & Corson, 1997)
>
> Research data show that bilingual and biliteracy programs have better outcomes than English-only or quick exit transitional bilingual programs that do not aspire to develop bilingualism and biliteracy. (Cummins, 1999)

Recent trends seem to indicate that ESL programs are more prevalent than bilingual programs because of language proficiency outcomes and the political climate. However, because many challenges face today's English language learners, it is imperative to understand the sociocultural and sociopolitical influences on learning. Too often ELLs are discriminated against and are wrongly perceived to be "less intelligent" based on their classroom behavior as they struggle to learn a second language. In reality, the students' behavior may be cultural in origin. For example, avoiding direct eye contact may be viewed by American teachers as a lack of respect, defiance, or simply not trying hard enough, yet for some children it is a behavior that reflects a cultural norm. A student's reluctance to ask questions or volunteer may also be perceived as indicators of low ability. Many ELLs continue to use their first language in peer and family interaction and this too may be interpreted as lack of motivation to learn English. All of this occurs in a climate where teachers are being held accountable for students' performance, and as a result, more students who do not meet grade level standards are being identified as "deficient."

There is also a disproportionate and adverse impact that high-stakes testing programs have on children with limited English proficiency (Pompa, 2001). Often students who truly have not attained proficiency in English may no longer qualify for ESL instruction after 1 or 2 years. Gaining proficiency in English can take as many as 3 years for the development of good interpersonal language facility, and much longer for attaining academic language proficiency needed to succeed in school subjects. Making the adjustment problem even more difficult for children who are ELLs is the large number of children who come from fragmented homes, who may have lived in countries with political unrest, who did not attend school consistently, who are in this country illegally, and who live in substandard housing, and thus may exhibit all of the psychosocial and sociopolitical problems associated with poverty and dislocation.

Controversy also exists about assessing second language learners for special education services, when it may be difficult to determine if poor achievement is the result of language factors or underlying cognitive processes. Consequently, some deserving ELLs may not receive the kinds of interventional services that their peers obtain. Conversely, there is particular sensitivity to the historical perspective that too many minority children (and certainly second language learners) have languished in special education settings because of inappropriate assumptions about their behavior, culture, and language facility.

Another significant problem is that in many classrooms, uncertified teachers are teaching ELLs without any experience in ESL methodologies and techniques, making it much more difficult for these students to learn English. Add to this unfortunate mix the requirement that ELLs must attain language skills quickly to reach the new standards set by state and city education boards. The educational crisis of urban America is exacerbated by the many second language learners, who often settle initially in inner cities where they have relatives and anticipated job opportunities. In these places, the large number of ELL persons adds to the competition for resources where there are already limited budgets, over-crowded classes, scanty materials, and a shortage of qualified teachers. In particular, some states such as in Texas, New York, California, and Illinois have recently required doubling classroom time for ELLs so that these students can pass new exams. Unfortunately, the mandate for all children to achieve often does not come with adequate resources. In summary, the picture for second language learners poses many significant concerns and unmet challenges.

USING PORTFOLIOS WITH ELLs: THE ROLE OF STANDARDS AND STANDARDIZED TESTING

As the 21st century unfolds, so does the debate on assessment, accountability, and standards for both teachers and students in public education in America. In fact, passing high-stakes tests has become synonymous with school success. These state-wide and national exams have critical implications for ELLs, when poor test performance often leads to "failure" or dropping out of school in anticipation of lack of success (Blake, 1997). The major challenge to using high-stakes assessment tools as a way to gauge language development of ELLs is that large-scale assessments, *unlike portfolio assessment*, cannot capture these students' diverse abilities, learning styles and, thus, developing knowledge in English. Simply put, standardized tests, which are already acknowledged to have significant limitations, are "based on the norms of native English speakers and therefore may certainly be culturally biased" (Fraser, 2000, p. 28). According to Fraser, "expected prior knowledge" on cultural life in America *alone* is enough to become a "deadly pitfall" for all but the most acculturated ELL (p. 28). When such individuals do not succeed on these tests, their educational outcomes and opportunities are limited.

What is the role of portfolio assessment in the face of increasing pressures and directives toward assessing all students through standardized tests? What is the role of portfolio assessment among ELLs in settings where being able to demonstrate their language development is crucial in showing language learning and growth? Portfolio assessment among ELLs remains the most powerful way in which we can document and highlight students' development in language and learning over time. Large-scale, standardized tests lack the breadth and depth required to make the knowledge and experience that these students bring with them truly visible. The use of portfolio assessment, particularly among ELLs, needs to continue in our classrooms as a balance to the imposition of new standards and high-stakes tests.

This chapter has several purposes. First it describes today's ELLs by providing vivid scenes of the lives of two such individuals. Second, the theories of second language acquisition will be discussed. Third, specific guidelines and information will be provided to promote the use of portfolios with ELLs. Finally, the major challenges faced by ELLs in the 21st century will be reviewed and ideas for the future direction of assessment and ELLs will be discussed. Overall, this chapter will highlight how using literacy portfolios can help teachers assess language growth for ELLs, facilitate understanding and appreciation of the complexities of these learners, and capture their intelligence, creativity, and desire to be successful in English in powerful and positive ways. Ultimately, this knowledge will help teachers provide better instruction for these students and enhance opportunities for their success in school and society.

WHO ARE TODAY'S ELLs?

The following sections describe the scenarios of two very different ELLs living in diverse settings.

A Migrant Camp

Colleen's friend diligently stops the van at the stop sign. I turn my head both ways and for a moment I wonder why she bothers to stop, we are so far out in the country all I can see is fields; no houses, no cars, no people. Colleen Lonigan, an ESL teacher, continues to talk to me, describing in quick sentences the conditions of the migrant camp I am about to visit for the first time. "It's better that we have [my] children with us, that way we're less of a threat and no one will run. Yesterday," she continues, "the border patrol raided the camp with their sirens roaring and guns pulled." Colleen has helped create a frightening image in my mind: young children barefooted and staring, mothers and fathers confused and exhausted, being "ticketed" and told, in English, that they must leave the country by a certain date.

The camp, indeed, is a frightening place to a first-time visitor like myself; comingled with the smell of garbage that has carefully been placed in black bags in an overflowing bin that has not been emptied in weeks is the acid-chemical smell of the porta-potties, perhaps also overflowing and not emptied for the same amount of time. And yet, the camp also seems like a place of warmth; a place that also smells of food cooking; a place that, today, abounds with sounds of laughter and music and of children playing as mothers and fathers return from 14-hour long days in the fields to their "homes"—cinder block barracks with a communal kitchen area—ready to share the evening meal. Colleen finds the child she has come to see and, speaking in Spanish, asks him to please come back to summer school. He smiles, they talk some more, she gives him a bag of clothes, pats him on the shoulder, and we leave. We begin the long drive back in silence. I don't even notice the stop sign this time, my head remains low and bowed; somehow the ritual of glancing side-to-side has become far less important.

An Urban ELL Classroom

Cynthia, a 10-year-old Mexican-American girl, was, like many of the other girls in the class, the eldest female child in the family. Because of this, Cynthia was often in charge of her younger siblings while her mother worked or visited friends. (Her father died a number of years ago.) This was no small task for a Spanish-speaking 10-year-old, left alone to care for younger siblings, living in poverty in a large city. Yet, Cynthia expresses pride as she writes about her dual role as cook and caretaker of her siblings:

> One day I was cooking Rice for my little sister and my brother. that time my mother was weith her friend to help her fix the car. And tack care of her baby. So my brothers and sister was hongri so I cook for them. I cook rice with meat and beans.

As you can see from the scenarios above, the lives of these children compound the academic issues that teachers must deal with. ELLs differ in many ways and are found in a variety of classrooms or classroom-like settings throughout the United States. There are many more scenarios not described here: Bosnian students from war-torn villages learning in rural America; Russian children sponsored by a local synagogue learning in suburban America; Hmong children adapting to the Midwest; Haitian teenagers working and learning in urban community outreach programs, and Iranian students, in Great Neck, New York, and Los Angeles, California.

Not all ELLs are children of poverty. Some are children of professionals and business people transferred to this country, and others led middle-class lives in their former countries. However, because of better family resources and a better education background in their prior schooling, many of these children fare better and present fewer demands on school resources than their less fortunate counterparts. Given the huge increase in the number of immigrant students, as well as their diversity and mobility, most teachers will teach one or more ELLs in their classrooms and will have to evaluate their progress. Unfortunately, many teachers report that they are ill-equipped for the challenge, are unfamiliar with appropriate methodology, and lack resources and time, and consequently they rely on practices, both instructional and evaluative, that are not geared for ELL students.

ADDRESSING THE NEEDS OF ELLs

Many teachers express frustration at the idea of having to teach and evaluate ELLs because, in their words, "We simply don't know where to begin!" and "We're not ESL teachers." When teaching diverse learners, it is important to be aware of certain questions and issues that may arise on a daily basis. These questions can serve as a starting point and they do not necessarily demand answers. They do require teachers to be especially thoughtful, careful, and understanding in their interactions with ELLs.

- How do I develop an understanding of who these students are (e.g., where they came from, the circumstances of leaving their home countries, their educational level)?
- How do students learn their first and second (or third) language?
- How do I integrate these students' learning experiences into the learning experiences of the entire classroom?
- How can cultural diversity be integrated into classroom learning?
- How do I assess development and growth of ELLs, especially in light of new standards, standardized testing, and national reform?
- How do I know when my ELL students are growing and developing as learners?
- Do I value the ways in which these students demonstrate their knowledge?
- What role do portfolios play in assessing and teaching ELLs?

To begin to answer these questions, and others, requires a review of some of the major theories of second-language acquisition.

Second Language Acquisition

"Need guys ice." Cassie, age $2\frac{1}{2}$, was an extremely competent and engaged speaker of English. (She still is as she celebrates her sixth birthday!) Because she heard both Spanish and English at home, and tried to keep up with two older brothers, Cassie had always had an "edge" in learning language: Motivation and desire were always present and opportunity was never lacking. One day when we were all gathered around in the kitchen of her grandparents' summer cottage, Cassie declared to me, "Need guys ice!" Without missing a beat, I reached into the freezer and placed into Cassie's small, outstretched hands, two ice cubes. Joyfully, she grabbed the ice cubes and skipped away as her mother, Shelly, could be heard saying, "What do you say, Cassie?"

Why is it that I understood perfectly what Cassie had asked me even though "need guys ice" is not a sentence I had heard before in English? How was it that a toddler was able to put together that particular string of words (if she had never heard nor imitated it before) to get the ice cubes she needed? And why didn't anyone "correct" her, telling her she was "wrong" and that she would never learn English by making such horrible mistakes? What Cassie had done was right on target in language learning. In fact, all "normally" developing children experiment with language and have the ability to learn one, or many, languages simultaneously, naturally, and relatively easily. This includes children who are learning both a first and second language.

Second Language Acquisition Theories

There are three major theories to explain how a child learns a second language (these theories need to be modified slightly when talking about adults, but here the focus is on children from birth to age 12): behavioralist, innatist, and social interactionist. Behavioralists believe that language is learned by imitation and rote memorization. In other words, children are "empty vessels" into which language is poured. Although behavioralist theory can account for some of a child's early acquisition, it cannot, for example, account for Cassie's request, "need guys ice." Cassie had never heard that phrase before (we can be absolutely sure that neither her parents nor her brothers had uttered that phrase), and yet that was the unique sentence that she created.

The "creation" of language is the central focus of the second major theory of second language acquisition: *innatist*. Innatist theory, which is attributed to the seminal work by Chomsky (1957), posits that all human beings are capable of creating an infinite number of phrases in an infinite number of languages. Chomsky hypothesizes that the human brain is "hard wired," resulting in a "natural" ability to create and use language. Innatists believe that around puberty, however, the brain literally hardens or "lateralizes," so that learning a language becomes less natural and fraught with many more challenges in later years.

The third major theory can be called social interactionist. A social interactionist views the "communicative give and take of natural conversations between native and non-native speakers as the crucial element of the language acquisition process" (Long & Porter, 1985). The focus here is on the social interaction and the subsequent ways in which second language learners adjust their language in order to be better understood the ways in which native English speakers modify their speech to try to make themselves better understood. According to this theory, meaning is constantly negotiated and refined; language cannot be learned in isolation without this dialogic interplay of words, phrases and, certainly, of meaning.

It is also important to note that language not only is inherently social but is also cultural and political. Language is never neutral. The language that a student speaks and how that language (as well as the student's ethnicity) is viewed politically, culturally, and economically may affect the way a student wants to, and is expected to, engage in language learning. Language is expressed through a wide range of contexts and experiences; contexts are always present and always changing. And it is important to recognize that these contexts may differ from our perceptions that Standard English is the only acceptable form of English in which to communicate and become participants in American schools and in American society. We must take care to remember that Standard English is only one form of expression in a global society.

USING LITERACY PORTFOLIOS WITH ELLs

Using literacy portfolios with ELLs not only helps teachers to assess their language and literacy growth in powerful and positive ways, but the use of portfolios also helps teachers to customize their instruction for ELLs, thereby maximizing ELLs' chances for success. For example, whereas teachers might not accept drawings (instead of words) or stories that are not written in Standard English from older English-speaking students, tailoring an ELL's portfolio to include this kind of work would be very important to such a student's success. Further, it would be absolutely critical for ELLs to begin collecting their work for their literacy portfolios at the very beginning of the school year, so that even if the portfolio process is limited to collecting drawings, one-word essays, or stories in another language, these students realize that there is a process to their development in English, as well as a process for evaluation. Such developmental portfolios provide feedback about the student's growth in very concrete and observable forms.

Encouraging ELLs to choose work to include in portfolios early on in the school year helps students to realize that they are active in their own learning and in their own evaluation. In addition, because using literacy portfolios as an evaluation tool doesn't always "feel" like assessment, ELLs will be less inhibited, and therefore more willing, to "allow" their work to be compiled and reviewed. Portfolio use can offset, in many ways, the challenges and fears that new language learners may feel in having to be judged and evaluated in a new school and in a new language.

The contents of a literacy portfolio for ELLs will look quite similar to those used with native English speakers, with a few exceptions. First, an ELL's portfolio may, at least initially, include simple drawings or work in the child's native language or a combination of both native language and English, because production in English may still be limited. It is especially important to retain this early work because it becomes a powerful way to highlight to parents, administrators, and the students themselves just how much language growth develops over time. (An important note: Second language acquisition theory and practice also tells us that developing and retaining literacy in one's native language will directly transfer into the development of literacy in one's second language, so that encouraging this work directly affects language growth in both languages!)

The portfolio may also include the following:

1. *Student's cover page and introduction.* This is very important for ELLs because it gives them a space to express who they are, where they come from, and in what language or languages they may have had literacy experiences. A student's cover page helps the teacher know the "whole" child better. Here are some questions for the student to answer for the cover page:
   a) Who am I? (e.g., where I come from, what language(s) I speak/write). Include a narrative about the student's education and other important background experiences before coming to the United States.
   b) Why did I choose these particular samples for my portfolio? How did I organize them?
   c) What do I like about these samples?
   d) What do these samples show I can do?
   e) What more do I want to be able to do?

2. *Parents' statement.* It is helpful to include a statement from the parents in the student's portfolio. Try to send home a very short, open-ended, questionnaire, in the parent's native language (if possible), asking the parents or guardian about their child. Parents of ELLs, as with most parents, want to be involved in their child's education and need to be asked and welcomed to participate. It is important to acknowledge that some ELL students may be living with extended family or family members (parents or others) who may be reluctant to communicate with the school, either because of their immigration status or the simple fact that they don't speak English. Here are some open-ended questions that will help elicit the information you want:
   a) My child enjoys school because . . .
   b) In school my child is concerned about . . .
   c) At home, my child is concerned about . . .
   d) My child's favorite stories include . . .
   e) In his or her free time my child . . .
   f) My child's favorite TV programs and characters include . . .
   g) I can best describe my child by saying that he or she is . . .

3. *Child as a learner.* This is an informal teacher assessment that provides information about whether an ELL has the background for the particular literacy experiences the student may encounter in an American school. Because many ELLs come to school with different (but not necessarily inferior) literacy and education experiences than native English speakers, it is important for teachers to try to trace and understand that development and exposure. Here are some statements that can provide more information for teachers of ELLs:
   a) The child reads and writes in _____ (list the languages).
   b) The child's home language is _____.
   c) The child spent _____ (no. of years) in school in his or her native country. What information is available about this school experience?
   d) The child's parents read and write in _____ (list the languages).
   e) The child's parents completed _____ years of formal schooling.
   f) The parents' former occupation is _____ and present occupation is _____.
   g) The child has literacy experiences at home. _____ (e.g., reading time with parents)

4. *Student work.* This is the heart of the ELL's literacy portfolio and the contents should be chosen collaboratively, that is, both the teacher and the student should have some say as to what they wish to include. Remember, what teachers con-

sider a student's "best" work, may not be what the student thinks he/she worked the hardest on or likes the most.

Let's now look at some of that work, including samples from Stephanie, Ana, and Joel, all of whom are ELLs in American public schools whose teachers believe in the use of literacy portfolios for assessment and instruction for all of their students, but most particularly for these beginning ELLs.

Stephanie is a second grader who speaks Spanish at home with her family and proclaims that she likes to play and eat ice cream (Figure 10–1). Notice that while her English is not yet "standard," it is developing. Stephanie included this paper in her portfolio to highlight information about herself.

Figures 10–2 and 10–3 illustrate a sixth-grade girl's literacy development. Ana, a Portuguese speaker from Brazil, began the 2000 school year in an American middle school in upstate New York after having just finished a 2-month summer immersion program in English. Her parents knew some English, and were able to help her make the transition more easily. Figure 10–2 represents Ana's attempts, during the first month of school, to gather information from a variety of sources, including the Internet, so as to present and synthesize facts and information to prepare a travel brochure. This project, one that meets New York State Learning Standard 1 for the English language arts ("students will read, write, listen, and speak for information and understanding"), was a favorite of Ana's, who chose to include information about the process she used to create a travel brochure. Her teacher, Mrs. Kuhn, was very proud of Ana's work, and saw her attempts at English language literacy to be worthy of documenting. Figure 10–3 shows Ana's work two months later, after a prompt from the teacher asking her students to retell the story, *The Greedy Triangle*, by Marilyn Burns.

Mrs. Kuhn's assessment of Ana's piece was that Ana was, indeed, "sequencing main ideas without including too many details," which is part of the learning standards in New York State. This piece eventually was typed and displayed in Mrs. Kuhn's classroom for all to see.

Figure 10–4 shows the work of Joel, a second-grader in Ivia Negron-Francais' dual-language classroom. Joel, a second language student from El Salvador whose parents speak only Spanish at home, had been in the United States since kindergarten when he began his participation in this dual-language program. Joel's story about his friend Anthony was saved as an example of a wonderful first piece in second grade. One month later, Mrs. Negron-Francais asked her students to write a fairy tale about what they would do if they spent a day with Don Juan. Notice how Mrs. Negron-Francais included Hispanic culture in her assignment and encouraged Joel to include this story in his portfolio.

Finally, it is important for teachers to include their own notes, anecdotal records, observations of ELLs at work as well as more formal evaluations in the students' literacy portfolios. Examples from both Mrs. Kuhn and Mrs. Negron-Francais' records follow. Mrs. Kuhn writes about Ana:

> Ana is using resources to collect information, the use of the Internet with support to locate specific facts. Natural prompting to collect data—no more than any other student. Note-taking skills are competent. Grammar and syntax deteriorate with nonfiction as background knowledge is weaker vs. personal narrative or response writing. Ideas are sophisticated.

Mrs. Negron-Francais writes about Joel:

> Joel is doing very well. In reading, he has some decoding strategies, and he is learning sounds/letters in English. He is very well-behaved.

What Teachers Can Learn From Portfolios of ELLs

The samples of work from these children show that literacy portfolios are crucial tools for assessment. Because of the information gained from the portfolios of ELLs, teachers can tailor their instruction to better meet these students' needs. For example, Mrs. Kuhn

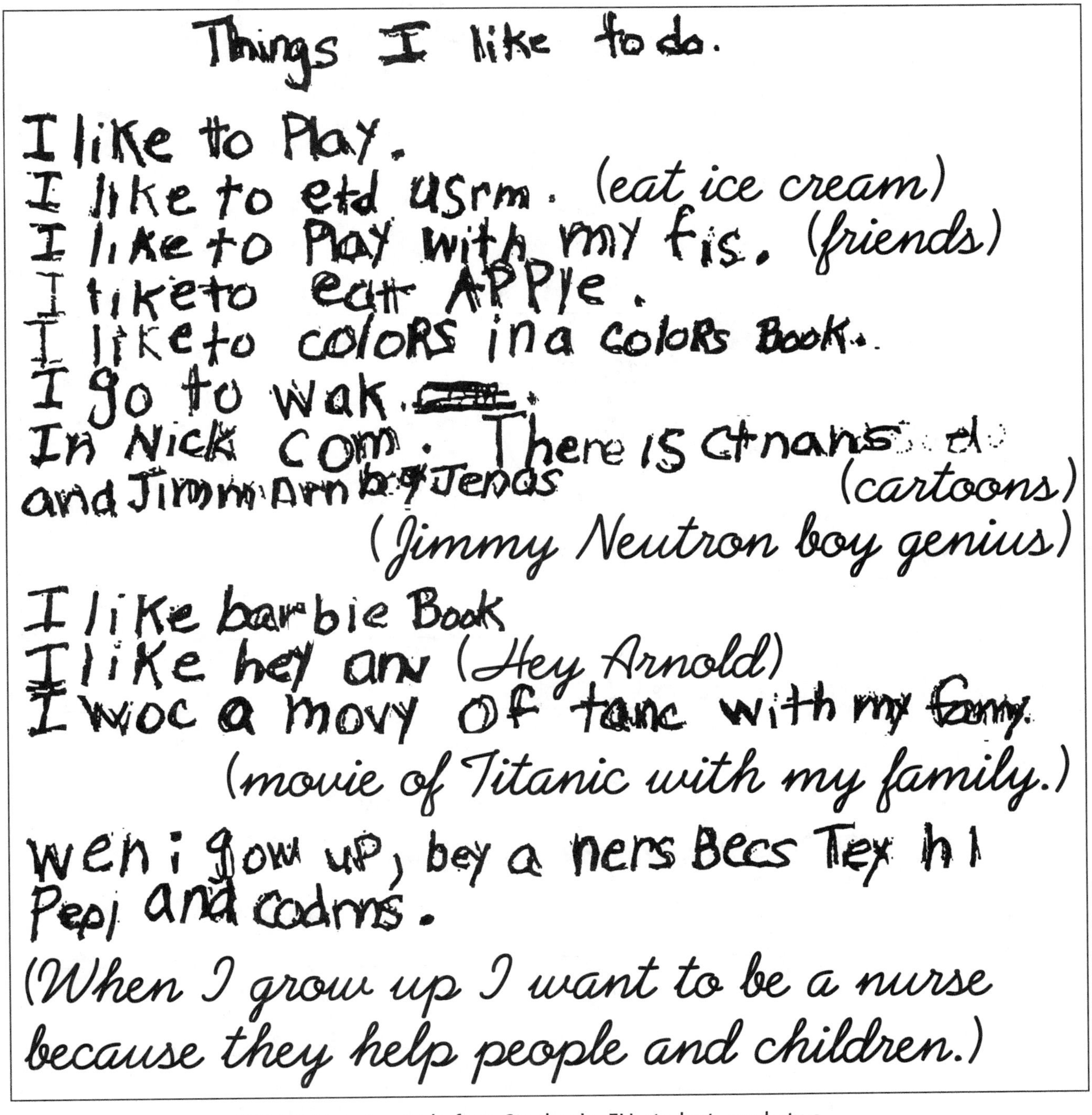

Things I like to do.

I like to Play.
I like to etd usrm. (eat ice cream)
I like to Play with my fis. (friends)
I liketo eat APPle.
I liketo coloRs in a coloRs Book.
I go to wak.
In Nick com. There is ctnans: el (cartoons)
and Jimm Arn bg Jenos
          (Jimmy Neutron boy genius)

I like barbie Book
I like hey arn (Hey Arnold)
I woc a movy of tanc with my famy.
          (movie of Titanic with my family.)

wen i gow up, bey a ners Becs Tex h I
Pepi and codrns.
(When I grow up I want to be a nurse
because they help people and children.)

FIGURE 10-1 A sample from Stephanie, ELL student, grade two.

Name _____ AnA _____   Date _____

The Region for my Travel Brochure is   CATSKILL MOUTAINS
                                         HUDSIN RIVER

• Tell some of the cities in this region:

- POUGH KEEPSiE
- TACONIC MOUTINS
- KINGSTON
- TERRY TOWN
- SLEEPY HOLLOW

• Describe the climate in this region:

- CLEAR
- DRY
- WINDY
- ALWAYS CHANGING
- AVERAGE JAN. TEm. $20° - 30°$
- YEARLY PRE. 40-48

• Tell some of the resources in this region:

- WILD LIFE
- PLANT LIFE
- FOREST - AND SOME OF OLD TREES
- CAMPING
- HIKING ⟩ - THEY PROVIDE
- WALTER WAYS

FIGURE 10–2 Travel Brochure Project by a sixth-grade ELL student.

found it wise to spend more time helping Ana gather and record necessary information rather than (initially) correct her grammar and syntax, although she noted Ana's struggles with English usage in her notes. Similarly Mrs. Negron-Francais modified her assignment to write a story by allowing Joel to number his sentences, thereby helping him to sequence his ideas in a logical fashion. Notice, too, Mrs. Negron-Francais made corrections on the work, but not so many as to discourage Joel from writing more in English.

Using literacy portfolios with ELLs allows them to share their strengths, backgrounds, and experiences, and provides space in which they can express themselves and display

- State some of the important waterways in this region:

> - HUDSON RIVER
> - GENESEE RIVER
> - ASHOKAN RIVER
> ~~KAATERSKILL FALL~~

- List mountains, landforms, or other interesting features of your region:

> - FOLLOW THE HUDSIN RIVER SOUTH YOU ENTER THE THE HUDSIN RIVER VALLEY AND CATSKILL MOUTAINS REGION.
> - CATSKILLS MOUTAINS RASE ON THE WEST SIDE OF VALLEY.
> - INFACT THESE MOUTAINS USED TO BE CALLED BLUE.

- List places of interest, activities, or anything else you think you should include in your brochure:

> - SUNNY SIDE (WASHINGTON IRVING FAMOUSE HOME)
> - PHILIPSBURG MANOR (OLD FARM SITE)
> - ALEXANDER JACKSON DAVIS HOME
> - GOTHIC REVIVAL CASTLE (TARRYTOWN)
> - CRAFTS FESTIVAL
> - KYKUIT, THE ROCKFELLER ESTATE
> - Montgomery Place
> - VAN CORTLANDT MANOR

FIGURE 10–2 continued.

their work. Parents and administrators are particularly pleased when, on parent-teacher conference day, they too can see the actual growth of their child in language and literacy. The smiles and "thank-you's" are especially satisfying!

> Once a triangle was trying to change his shape because he wasn't really happy with his shape. Then he went to shape shifther and he changed his shape for a square then a pentagon and his life now is really nice and more important. But he still was not so happy with it so he went again in shape shifcher and he maare the pentagon transform into the hexagon and hexagon was really happy now he doest have any friends anymore but he still not really happy then he went againg in shificher and change for lots and lots of shapes with lots of sides and points but he still not happy then he went again in shificher he said:
> - I want to be a triangle.
> And the shape shificher said:
> - Okay then.
> And he transform in a triangle and now he is so happy!!

FIGURE 10–3 A retelling of The Greedy Triangle by a sixth-grade ELL student.

CONTINUING CHALLENGES AND FUTURE DIRECTIONS

The teaching, assessment, and the education of the diverse population of English language learners in this country is, and will continue to be, one of the largest challenges educators face in the next few decades. Teachers must answer these challenges by understanding the needs and abilities of all diverse learners, regardless of their country of origin or language background. Literacy portfolios will continue to play an enormous role in assessing this nation's children if we are to embark upon a future that insists we educate *all* students so that they can be productive, successful citizens in a *global* world.

To summarize, let us review the questions posed earlier and answer them with the knowledge learned throughout this chapter and the recognition of the critical role of literacy portfolios for America's ELLs.

My Friend

My friend name is
Antoni .

I like Antoni
because We play with togther.
We share things with each other.

He is Big

FIGURE 10–4 "My Friend Antoni" by a second-grade ELL student.

1. *Question*: How do I develop an understanding of who ELL students are? How do these students learn language? How do they learn a second language, or a third? How do I maximize their educational experience in my classroom?

    Answer: I get to know my students as soon as possible. I ask them for writing and drawing samples to put in their literacy portfolios. I focus their initial writing on talking about themselves. I understand that it can be difficult to learn a new language and a new culture but that, in most cases, children learn language naturally and easily, and English language skills will develop with encouragement. I develop empathy and I think of a time when I myself felt like an "outsider."

2. *Question*: How do I assess ELLs' development and growth, especially in light of new standards, standardized testing, and national education reform? How do I know when my ELLs are growing and developing as learners? Do I value the ways in which ELLs demonstrate their knowledge?

BY Joel and Don Juan.

1 we ate Mexican food.

2 And we ate tacos

3 and dem we drek soda.

4 and den we played Loteria

5 and den we played musical chairs

6 an den we win in stichia'

7

8

FIGURE 10–5 "Don Juan" by a second-grade ELL student.

Answer: I can use literacy portfolios as a critical tool in helping my ELLs to demonstrate their knowledge. As did Mrs. Kuhn and Mrs. Negron-Francais, I will develop lessons and units that will not only incorporate state standards but will also allow for my students to grow as English language and literacy learners. I welcome the opportunity to show how literacy portfolios can complement standardized testing and reform. I will also identify the kinds of resource services my students need to succeed and make sure that these services are available to my students.

3. *Question*: What role do portfolios play in assessing ELLs?

Answer: Among ELLs, literacy portfolios are probably my best tool in assessing where my students are, not only as English learners but as writers, readers, subject area (e.g., math, science) learners as well. I also know that my ELLs will see portfolios as less threatening than standardized paper-and-pencil tests, and therefore will feel more comfortable creating work for the portfolios. I'm thrilled that at parent-teacher conferences, my literacy portfolios will show the growth and the development of my ELLs' language and literacy abilities. I also know that these portfolios can document for others how my students are progressing in my classroom.

FINAL THOUGHTS

Teachers of the 21st century are embarking on an adventure in education, one where they will be asked to teach and evaluate many different kinds of students from different backgrounds, many who have special needs, speak different languages, and display many abilities. This occurs in an educational climate of increasing pressure for teachers to document all that they do within the framework of teaching to the higher standards and expecting better outcomes from their students. Teachers are now held more responsible and accountable for student performance, which creates tremendous pressure to help students succeed in ways that are demonstrable to all. The use of literacy portfolios with diverse students, however, will help teachers keep assessment and instruction in perspective as they hold to the belief that all students can do many things well and succeed. No doubt this will require both time and patience, but teachers have to provide the opportunity for students to showcase their diverse abilities, as teachers highlight student growth and creativity. Literacy portfolios can certainly help do this! *Bonne chance!*

REFERENCES

August, D., & Hakuta, K. (1997). *Improving schooling for language minority children: A research agenda*. Washington, DC: National Academy Press.

Blake, B. E. (1997). *She say, he say: Urban girls write their lives*. Albany, NY: SUNY.

Burns, M. (1994). *The greedy triangle*. New York: Scholastic.

Chomsky, N. (1957). *Syntactic structures*. Gravenhage, The Hague: Mouton.

Cummins, J. (1999). Alternative paradigms in bilingual education research: Does theory have a place? *Educational Researcher, 28*,(7), 26–32.

Cummins, J., & Corson, D. (1997). *Bilingual education*. Dordrecht, The Netherlands: Kluwer Academic.

Fraser, K. (2000, Spring). The assessment of students with disabilities and students with limited English proficiency: A reflection on what people want out of testing. *The State Education Standard*, 27–30.

Long, M. & Porter, P. (1985). Groupwork, interlanguage talk and second language acquisition. *TESOL Quarterly, 19*(2), 207–228.

Malgady, R., & Zayas, L. (2001). Cultural and linguistics considerations in psychodiagnosis with Hispanics: The need for an empircally informed process model. *Journal of the National Association of Social Workers, 46*,(1), 39–49.

Pompa, D. (2001). Conferences probe second language research needs. *Reading Today, 19*(1), 1–3.

Ramsey, R. (2002). Proposal for graduate certificate in teaching English as a second language. Indiana Purdue University. Internal Senate Document. Fort Wayne, IN.

Turner, Tracy. (2000). Schools experience greater demand for ESL teachers. *The News Sentinel*. Fort Wayne, IN (Dec 5, p. 1A).

Index

Dr. Judith H. Cohen, Ph.D., J.D. (right)   is a Full Professor of Education at Adelphi University, Garden City, New York, where she has been the Coordinator of the combined undergraduate and graduate five-year teacher education program, called the Scholars Teacher Education Program (STEP). Dr. Cohen teaches both graduate and undergraduate courses in literacy. She began her teaching career as a junior high school English/Reading teacher for the Board of Education, New York City. After completing a Master's degree at Syracuse University in Reading Education, she returned to New York and worked as a reading intervention specialist on Long Island. Her doctoral studies were completed in Reading Education with a specialization in Special Education at Hofstra University and she has been a teacher educator for over 30 years.

Dr. Cohen has authored curriculum projects (many with Dr. Wiener), a textbook on resource room teaching, many articles, textbook chapters, and law review articles and is an active inservice educator working with school district personnel. As a reflection of her longstanding concern for children's welfare, she completed legal studies at Hofstra University and was admitted to the New York State Bar as an Attorney in 1989. She works as a child advocate in school districts and the courts of New York. For the past 36 years her professional career has been devoted to advocating for children both in the context of schools as a teacher, as a university professor devoted to teacher education, as a university program coordinator, and as an attorney promoting child welfare both in terms of literacy improvement and legal rights. Dr. Cohen is currently researching and writing the case history of a high functioning autistic individual for a forthcoming book.

Dr. Roberta Behr Wiener, Ed.D., MSW (left)   is Dean of the School of Education at Indiana University—Purdue University, Fort Wayne. She is a Full Professor of Literacy and Reading and has been an academic for more than 30 years. Prior to coming to Fort Wayne, Dr. Wiener was on the faculty at Adlephi University, on Long Island, New York, where she was the Chair of Education Studies, Director of Adult Learning and Development and former Associate Dean of the School of Education.

Dr. Wiener is the author of many articles, book chapters, books of high interest-low readability for adult literacy and the reading disabled, computer based literacy programs, and the text, *Literacy Assessment: Using Assessment to Guide Instruction.* She is a frequent speaker at national and international professional conferences, discussing various literacy topics and teacher education reform issues.

Additionally, Dr. Wiener is a certified psychotherapist who has worked with children, adolescents, and adults. She is researching the area of violence in children and adolescence for a future textbook. She is an active member of the Board of Directors of SCAN (Stop Child Abuse and Neglect) and the Three Rivers Literacy Alliances and is a member of dozens of professional and literacy organizations.